Africans into Creoles

Diálogos Series

KRIS LANE, SERIES EDITOR

Understanding Latin America demands dialogue, deep exploration, and frank discussion of key topics. Founded by Lyman L. Johnson in 1992 and edited since 2013 by Kris Lane, the Diálogos Series focuses on innovative scholarship in Latin American history and related fields. The series, the most successful of its type, includes specialist works accessible to a wide readership and a variety of thematic titles, all ideally suited for classroom adoption by university and college teachers.

Also available in the Diálogos Series:

Searching for Madre Matiana: Prophecy and Popular Culture in Modern Mexico by
Edward Wright-Rios

Women Drug Traffickers: Mules, Bosses, and Organized Crime by Elaine Carey

Emotions and Daily Life in Colonial Mexico edited by Javier Villa-Flores and
Sonya Lipsett-Rivera

Native Brazil: Beyond the Convert and the Cannibal, 1500-1900 edited by Hal Langfur

The Course of Andean History by Peter V. N. Henderson

Masculinity and Sexuality in Modern Mexico edited by Anne Rubenstein and
Víctor M. Macías-González

Modernizing Minds in El Salvador: Education Reform and the Cold War, 1960-1980 by
Héctor Lindo-Fuentes and Erik Ching

A History of Mining in Latin America: From the Colonial Era to the Present by
Kendall Brown

Slavery, Freedom, and Abolition in Latin America and the Atlantic World by
Christopher Schmidt-Nowara

Cuauhtémoc's Bones: Forging National Identity in Modern Mexico by
Paul Gillingham

For additional titles in the Diálogos Series, please visit unmpress.com.

Africans into Creoles

Slavery, Ethnicity, and Identity
in Colonial Costa Rica

RUSSELL LOHSE

University of New Mexico Press ⚜ Albuquerque

LIBRARY OF CONGRESS CATALOGING-IN-PUBLICATION DATA

Lohse, Russell, 1968–
Africans into Creoles : slavery, ethnicity, and identity in colonial Costa Rica /
Russell Lohse.
pages cm — (Diálogos series)
Includes bibliographical references and index.
ISBN 978-0-8263-5497-6 (paper : alkaline paper) — ISBN 978-0-8263-5498-3
(electronic)
1. Slavery—Costa Rica—History. 2. Plantation life—Costa Rica—History. 3. Slaves—
Costa Rica—History. 4. Slaves—Costa Rica—Social conditions. 5. Blacks—Costa
Rica—History. 6. Africans—Costa Rica—History. 7. Creoles—Costa Rica—History.
8. Ethnicity—Costa Rica—History. 9. Costa Rica—Race relations—History.
10. Costa Rica—History—To 1821. I. Title.
HT1056.C67L65 2014
306.3'62097286—dc23
2014001281

Cover design by Catherine Leonardo
Text composition by Felicia Cedillos
Composed in Minion Pro 10.25/13.5
Display Type is Minion Pro

To Shaun, Louie, and all descendants of Africans

brought to Costa Rica

Contents

～ℓ

Illustrations

~⦆

Acknowledgments

❧ OVER MANY YEARS I HAVE BEEN PRIVILEGED TO WORK WITH SOME OF the best scholars in Latin American history. Sandra Lauderdale Graham has helped me more than anyone else to think and write about the past. The subtle analyses and suggestions of Susan Deans-Smith profited me enormously when I was astute enough to recognize them. Aline Helg provided often trenchant and always valuable criticism as well as her unfailing encouragement. Jim Sidbury has always taken an interest in my work and been eager to help, although he agrees with my conclusions less frequently. Toyin Falola has also shown me extraordinary generosity.

In Costa Rica, I must thank Hernán Henry Maxwell and Siany Gordon Spence, who first opened their home to me and offered me their friendship more than twenty years ago. Dr. Rina Cáceres has also supported my research from the beginning. Without her help, I might never have been able to research this book. I have benefited from dozens of hours of sometimes heated discussions about colonial Afro–Costa Ricans with Mauricio Meléndez Obando in San José, Guatemala, Mexico City, and Austin. Paul E. Lovejoy has long taken an interest in my work and has read several chapters of this current work. His insights are invaluable. Anthony E. Kaye read the entire manuscript and made many thoughtful suggestions, which I have incorporated with profit. I also wish to thank Lyman Johnson, former editor of the Diálogos series, who provided a masterful line-by-line critique.

I wish to acknowledge the generous assistance of the Tinker Foundation, the International Institute of Education/J. William Fulbright Foundation, the William S. Livingston Graduate Fellowship at the University of Texas at Austin, and the Department of History at The Pennsylvania State University. I am also grateful for the courteous and professional assistance of the staff at the Archivo Nacional de Costa Rica and the Archivo de la Curia Metropolitana in San José, the Archivo General de Indias in Seville, the Archivo General de

Centro América in Guatemala City, the Archivo General de la Nación in Mexico City, and the Rare Books and Manuscripts Collection at the Nettie Lee Benson Library, University of Texas at Austin.

Joel A. Barker, Susan Whitney Barker, and Lawrence F. Sharp have helped and counseled me at every stage of my academic career. Frances Lourdes Ramos patiently listened to me puzzle over the fates of the survivors of the *Christianus Quintus* and *Fredericus Quartus* for years. Matt Childs, Robert Smale, and Solsiree del Moral have been unfailing comrades and incisive critics. And Linda Whitney has supported me in everything I have ever tried to do. I am grateful to all of them for their essential help.

Abbreviations

ACMSJ	Archivo de la Curia Metropolitana de San José, Costa Rica
AGCA	Archivo General de Centro América, Guatemala City
AG	Audiencia de Guatemala (AGI)
AGI	Archivo General de Indias, Seville
AGN	Archivo General de la Nación, Mexico City
Alf.	Alférez (second lieutenant, royal standard bearer)
ANCR	Archivo Nacional de Costa Rica, San José
Ayu.	Ayudante (adjutant, assistant)
C.	Sección Colonial Cartago (ANCR)
Cap.	Capitán
CC	Sección Complementario Colonial (ANCR)
dec.	*Década* (decade)
Esc.	Escribanía (AGI)
exp.	Expediente
FHL	Family History Library, Salt Lake City, Utah
fol.	Folio
Fr.	Fray (friar, brother)
G.	Sección Colonial Guatemala (ANCR)
Illmo. Sr.	Ilustrísimo Señor (His Grace)
LBC	Libros de Bautizos de Cartago (ACMSJ/FHL)
LMC	Libros de Matrimonios de Cartago (ACMSJ/FHL)
leg.	Legajo
Lic.	Licenciado (licentiate)
MCC	Mortuales Coloniales de Cartago (ANCR)

MRP	Muy Reverendo Padre (Most Reverend Father)
Mtre.	Maestre
Nic.	Nicaragua
part.	Partida
Pbo.	Presbítero (presbyter, priest)
PC	Protocolos Coloniales de Cartago (ANCR)
PH	Protocolos Coloniales de Heredia (ANCR)
PSJ	Protocolos Coloniales de San José (ANCR)
Sarg.	Sargento
Sarg. Mayor	Sargento Mayor
SFASDE	Sección Fondos Antiguos, Sección Documentación Encuadernada (ACMSJ)
SM	Su Majestad (His Majesty)
Sr.	Señor
tit.	Título (title)
vol.	Volúmen (volume number)

Introduction

✝ THIS BOOK IS A SOCIAL HISTORY OF AFRICANS AND THEIR ENSLAVED descendants in colonial Costa Rica, a small and peripheral colony of the Spanish Empire. Its argument is this: diverse ethnic origins, the small and sporadic nature of the slave trade to Costa Rica, the geographical dispersal of slaves in the province, and the close and constant contacts between Africans and people of other ethnic and racial origins led to rapid and profound creolization in two senses. First, within the contexts of colonialism and enslavement, Africans helped create a culture deriving from many sources—Iberian, indigenous, and African. Second, the Costa Rican slave population had become predominantly American born by the mid-seventeenth century and perhaps earlier. These conditions precluded the formation and reproduction of a slave identity or culture based in common African ethnic origins, shared place of residence, working conditions, or the refuge of the family. Although the realities of slave life in Costa Rica were surely unique, I do suggest that similar conditions obtained in other areas of Latin America not dominated by plantation agriculture, and these conditions worked against the forging of distinct identities based in either the African past or the American present.

In 1973, anthropologists Sidney Mintz and Richard Price revolutionized the study of slave cultures when they presented a paper (later published as a book) entitled "An Anthropological Approach to the Afro-American Past." Drawing on linguistics for its central metaphor, the essay suggested that "creolization" best described the processes by which Africans culturally adapted to New World slavery. Mintz and Price denied that Africans brought to the New World as slaves shared a "generalized West African cultural 'heritage'" or that most Africans in a given colony came from the same "'tribe' or cultural

1

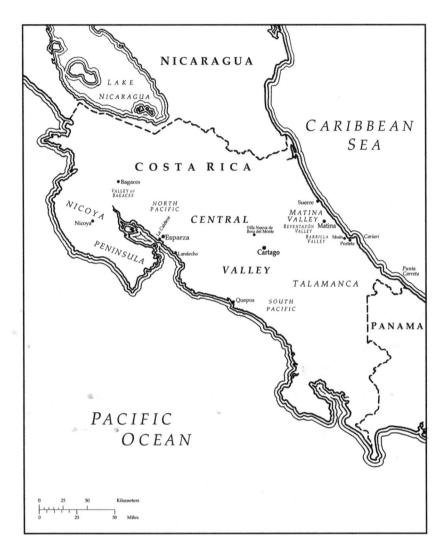

Map 1. Costa Rica (modern borders). Map by Mark Van Stone.

group."[1] On the contrary, they argued, a generalized West African culture "probably did not exist," and Africans arrived in the Americas not as "groups" but as "*crowds*, and very heterogeneous crowds at that."[2] Mintz and Price flatly denied that Africans shared a common culture when they arrived in the Americas: "The Africans in any New World colony in fact became a *community* and began to share a *culture* only insofar as, and as fast as, they themselves created them."[3]

Mintz and Price's essay became the classic exposition of creolization theory and an obligatory point of reference for subsequent students of American slave cultures. As suggested by the word "creole" itself, many readers concluded that the most relevant factors in slaves' experiences were to be found in the Americas, not in Africa. Unfortunately, this assumption led many historians of slavery to ignore Africa almost completely or to include only vague references to an ill-defined "African background" when they wrote about enslaved people in the Americas. Eventually, such attitudes provoked a heated response from revisionist scholars, most of them trained as Africanists. Paul Lovejoy criticized creolization theory as representative of "Eurocentrism and American-centrism." By contrast, he wrote, Afrocentric revisionists stress "agency and continuity" and "shift the emphasis from the birth of a new culture and society to the maintenance of ties with the homeland."[4] In his influential *Africa and Africans in the Making of the Atlantic World*, John K. Thornton argued explicitly against Mintz and Price, contending that European slavers drew "extremely homogeneous" human cargoes, usually from a single African port, and that the slave trade "did little to break up cultural groupings." Once on New World estates, "slaves tended to cluster around members of their own nation," further reinforcing cultural similarities.[5] In another widely read work, Michael A. Gomez argued for the cultural influence of specific West and West Central African regions on specific regions of North America.[6] The revisionist approach stresses the "slave route," tracing the experiences of Africans from their homelands through the Middle Passage into the Americas; its proponents insist it is counterposed to creolization theory.

For some observers, such as Africanist Kristin Mann, the "Africanist-creolist impasse" has "reached the limits of its usefulness. Surely," she writes, "the goal is not to prove that Old World or New World influences were more important in shaping the experiences of slaves, but rather to understand the relationship between them in specific historical contexts."[7] By now, it seems clear that the relative importance of Africa or America in the lives of enslaved people will not be decided by more theoretical pronouncements. And as Mann suggests, surely this is not the most important question—what is needed are more case studies grounded in specific historical contexts.

I seek to extend and deepen the study of the African Diaspora and the creolization debate by identifying the specific ships that carried an identifiable group of Africans from specific West African ports to a specific destination in the Americas. By tracing the experiences of Africans who arrived on two Danish slave ships that arrived in Costa Rica in 1710, I investigate conditions on the ground in a particular context and reveal pivotal moments when individuals who were forced to adapt to the institution of slavery began to act and think of themselves in new ways. Beginning with the examples of the *Christianus Quintus* and *Fredericus Quartus*, I examine slavery in Costa Rica as a whole from 1600 to 1750. Following the experiences of the girls and boys, women and men who arrived on the *Christianus Quintus* and *Fredericus Quartus* shows how the conditions of slavery in a unique local setting determined the constraints that slaves faced and how they responded to their condition.

I intend for this work to enrich the literature of comparative slavery through its focus on slavery in an area of the Americas that was not dominated by plantation slavery. Although early Costa Rica faced problems familiar to other regions of Latin America and the Caribbean, such as the destruction of the native population, the search for export crops, and the need for an adequate labor force, it never developed into a plantation society, and it remained on the margins of Atlantic markets. Slavery and race relations in Costa Rica developed in patterns strikingly different from those recorded in better-known plantation areas, such as Brazil, the Caribbean, and the United States South. The survivors of the *Christianus Quintus* and *Fredericus Quartus* underwent experiences common to all enslaved Africans, but to be a slave in Costa Rica implied a dramatically different experience from that of a slave in Brazil or Jamaica or South Carolina, Mexico City or Lima or New Orleans. Economic, social, and political circumstances in a multiethnic frontier colony that was linked only intermittently to Atlantic export markets uniquely conditioned the experiences of Africans and their descendants.

The chronological scope of the book spans the early to midcolonial period. This focus allows a close examination of the development of slavery in the colony, from its beginnings to its development as a mature institution. In addition, this period encapsulates the rise and fall of the cacao cycle, which linked Costa Rica to the wider world and brought the largest numbers of Africans to the colony. Many fine studies of slavery in Latin America have concentrated on the eighteenth and nineteenth centuries. I purposely end the study before any prospects of abolition appeared on the horizon. In my view, works that culminate with abolition tend to look for cracks appearing in the edifice of slavery that were most likely invisible to enslaved people of the time. I prefer to focus on those slaves—the great majority—who lived and died in bondage without hope of general emancipation.

This book adds to the growing literature on Africans and their descendants in colonial Latin America. As historians of other regions have shown, although slaves comprised a small part of the population, their importance in the economy, society, and even politics far exceeded their numbers. Slaves worked in every nook and cranny of Costa Rica's colonial economy. Slave ownership was by no means confined to the colonial elite. Africans and other slaves interacted constantly and intimately with members of all racial and social groups. Through an examination of Costa Rica, I seek to challenge historians to reconsider the impact of slavery in areas of Latin America where it has received little attention.

My work draws on the revisionist historiography that has challenged some of Costa Rica's most widely and deeply held myths. The myth of "rural democracy," in particular, continues to loom large in the popular consciousness. Many writers have traced Costa Rica's democratic tradition to the colonial period. Carlos Monge Alfaro advanced the classic articulation of the myth of rural democracy in the mid-twentieth century.[8] Monge Alfaro argued that colonial Costa Rica developed as an egalitarian society of small landholders, unique in Latin America. According to this version of national history, Costa Rica remained an impoverished backwater for centuries, neglected by the Spanish Empire. Deep class divisions never emerged because all members of society toiled equally for their meager subsistence. The province's isolation and chronic poverty forced all of its residents to work with their own hands, so each made of the situation what he would.[9]

Monge Alfaro and others further contended that colonial Costa Rica was a racially homogeneous society. The racial component of the myth is based on the notion that the few Indians living in Costa Rica at the time of the conquest were peacefully absorbed into Hispanic society, obviating the bloody racial conflicts that plagued other Central American regions. Similarly, the marginalizing character of the subsistence economy precluded the entrenchment of African slavery and the *sistema de castas* (caste system).[10] Spanish peasant immigration accounted for the overwhelming preponderance of the country's racial stock. Racially homogeneous, Costa Rica was therefore free of racial prejudice and discrimination. The lighter complexion of the population and the absence of racial tension made Costa Rica resemble a tranquil European country more than its Central American neighbors. Racial homogeneity predisposed the region to the harmonious coexistence (*convivencia*) accepted as a national characteristic.

Later scholars showed decisively that colonial Costa Rica was by no means an egalitarian society. Costa Rica might have been relatively impoverished, but poverty was relative. In an influential book, political scientist Samuel Z. Stone showed how a colonial elite had monopolized power early on and handed it down to its heirs over four centuries.[11] Nor was colonial Costa Rica racially homogeneous; some of Monge Alfaro's more extreme statements—that the encomienda and African slavery never existed in Costa Rica, for example—were easily disproved. Claudia Quirós demonstrated the extraordinary cruelty of the encomienda system and showed that the indigenous population had been destroyed, not peacefully absorbed into Hispanic society.[12] In a pioneering work, Lowell Gudmundson identified the ways in which Costa Rica's slaves had "disappeared" into the larger mestizo population.[13] And in a new series of works, historians and genealogists began to uncover and explore the dimensions of slavery in Costa Rica.

The earliest works noting the existence of slavery in Costa Rica emphasized its peripheral importance to the colonial society and economy.[14] Many years later, Oscar Aguilar Bulgarelli and Irene Alfaro Aguilar would argue that slavery provided the initial accumulation of wealth for Costa Rica's political and economic elites.[15] Genealogist Mauricio Meléndez Obando showed how African roots extended into dozens of Costa Rican families.[16] Rina Cáceres demonstrated the central importance of Africans and their enslaved and free descendants throughout the seventeenth-century economy and society.[17] *Africans into Creoles* expands on this scholarship, bringing a trans-Atlantic methodology, new sources, and new interpretative frameworks to illuminate the experiences of enslaved Africans in Costa Rica.

The *Christianus Quintus* and the *Fredericus Quartus*, two ships of the Danish West India and Guinea Company, left Copenhagen for the West African coast in late 1708. In April 1709, they arrived at the Danish trading factory of Christiansborg, near Accra, Ghana. Over a period of several months, the ships loaded hundreds of captives there and at other ports in Ghana, Togo, and Benin to the east. In September of that year, captives on the *Fredericus Quartus* attempted a shipboard rebellion, which the crew savagely repressed. The following month, the ships sailed for St. Thomas, Denmark's sugar colony in the Virgin Islands. Because of a series of navigational errors—or perhaps because the ships' captains never intended to go there—the *Christianus Quintus* and the *Fredericus Quartus* never reached the West Indies. Instead, after months of wandering the Caribbean, they arrived at a place called "Punta Carreto," Costa Rica, on March 2, 1710. When the ships' captains insisted on prolonging the trip further by sailing for Portobello, Panama, where they could sell the captives, the exhausted crew mutinied and released more than 650 African women, men, and children on the beach. It is the story of those women, men, and children and thousands like them that I want to tell.

Traces of their stories survive in archives in Denmark, Spain, Guatemala, and Costa Rica. The extensive documentation surrounding the voyages of the *Christianus Quintus* and the *Fredericus Quartus* from Africa to Costa Rica and the fates of their survivors offers exceptional opportunities to investigate, from a variety of perspectives, the processes by which one group of enslaved Africans became creole slaves. Johannes Rask, a Lutheran chaplain, sailed on the *Fredericus Quartus* to his assignment at Christiansborg Castle. He kept a journal of his impressions, which he used as the basis of a book he published many years later.[18] Commander Erich Lygaard, ranking officer at Christiansborg, recorded the arrival of the ships and described the conditions on the Gold and Slave Coasts at the time they arrived there, allowing the embarkation of the captives to be placed in the concrete perspective of African history.[19] Later, in Portobello and eventually back in Denmark, captains and crew members of the ships gave testimony on the events of the Middle Passage and on their eventual arrival in Costa Rica.[20]

Within a few weeks of their arrival, more than one hundred of the Africans who had been discharged on the beach were captured by Costa Rican colonists. Dozens of participants and witnesses, including Africans, Danes, Spaniards,[21] and Miskitu Indians, recounted the circumstances of their disembarkation and recapture. The human cargoes of the *Christianus Quintus* and *Fredericus Quartus* immediately became the subjects of jurisdictional disputes among Spanish officials in Costa Rica, Panama, and Guatemala, all of whom asserted a right to the Africans and argued their cases at length in documents now found in archives in Costa Rica, Guatemala, and Spain. By October 1710, fifty-eight of those Africans had embarked for Panama to be resold. A few went north to Nicaragua or Guatemala, but nearly half were sold at auction in Costa Rica.[22] From that point, many of the captives surface periodically in Costa Rican notarial, sacramental, and criminal records at pivotal moments in their lives—when they were bought and sold, when they married, when they baptized a child, gave evidence in a criminal trial, or even gained their freedom. In 1718, after charges of smuggling surfaced against Costa Rican settlers, the Royal Audiencia of Guatemala initiated another lengthy investigation of the origins of these and other African-born slaves in the province, generating thousands of pages of proceedings.[23] In this second inquiry, more than one hundred African slaves were interrogated about their ethnic origins, the circumstances of their arrival in Costa Rica, their previous masters, and the other Africans who had arrived with them.[24] These unusual inquiries recorded the slaves' own words—or as close to their own words as we are ever likely to get—and help inform the fragmentary glimpses provided by the serial documents.

Taken together, these sources allow us to follow identifiable groups of men, women, and children from their home societies in Africa through the circumstances that resulted in their enslavement, through the horrors of the Middle Passage to their arrival, escape, and recapture in Costa Rica, where they were reduced to slavery and where, decades later, a few became free men and women again. In many ways, the experiences of the survivors of the *Christianus Quintus* and *Fredericus Quartus* were exceptional, but in just as many, their experiences were typical of those of thousands of Africans who came to be enslaved in Costa Rica in the sixteenth, seventeenth, and eighteenth centuries. Through the exceptionality of their story, we gain insight into the experiences common to all.

The African men and women transported to Costa Rica on the *Christianus Quintus* and *Fredericus Quartus*, like all Africans forced into the Atlantic slave trade, underwent a series of wrenching changes that necessarily affected the ways in which they conceived of the world and their places within it. At home, their individual identities were tied to highly localized communities defined by such elements as kinship, a belief in descent from common ancestors, and veneration of spirits tied to the lands on which they lived.[25] Most, however, did not understand these complexes of cultural traits as comprising ethnicities—they came to understand their differences from other peoples through war, enslavement, and diaspora.

Although conditions in Africa changed radically from 1600 to 1750, wars always produced the overwhelming majority of the captives exported to the Americas. These conflicts resulted from highly specific, local circumstances, but they occurred within the context of the violent changes provoked by the increasing orientation of West and West Central African rulers toward the Atlantic trade with Europeans. The African captives who were captured and deported to the Americas understood their fates in terms of the specific conflicts that resulted in their enslavement but also grew to understand the larger forces that affected all other captives with them.

The abstraction of the Atlantic slave trade became real to African women and men through the brutal experience of the Middle Passage. The Atlantic crossing represented an irreparable rupture with the past, but not a "social death" or the reduction of African human beings to "things."[26] It marked the blending—under violent and dehumanizing conditions—of "old" identities based in the home societies of Africa with new ones born in the diaspora, manifested in the birth of relationships among shipmates. The relative importance of "new African-derived ethnic identities outside the continent," the Middle Passage, and experiences of New World slavery differed according to the infinite variations of the local circumstances in which they unfolded.[27]

When African women and men arrived in Costa Rica, they entered, against their will, into a determined set of social relations. "The Negro," as Karl Marx wrote, "is a Negro. Only under certain conditions does he become a slave."[28] Marx neglected to note that Africans were also not "Negroes" (blacks) before they became slaves. Dark skin was a phenotypical trait so universally shared that in Africa, it was worthless in identifying individuals or groups. It assumed ideological significance only when it became a mark of degradation in slavery.[29] In Costa Rica, the newly enslaved experienced their new status through individual relationships with their Spanish masters, who tried to control their lives as they did those of all members of subordinated groups in the province. Through a series of actions designed to assimilate Africans to their new status as slaves during the process British planters called "seasoning," masters tried to convert Africans into mere extensions of their own wills. These same processes, however, allowed Africans to form new relationships among themselves and with creole slaves and servants that went beyond their masters' control and even their understanding. Like the men and women they tried to dominate, masters confronted limitations on what they could accomplish.

Colonial Costa Rica can be divided into three major geographic and ecological zones: the North Pacific, Central Valley, and Caribbean lowlands. Before the conquest, these were inhabited by culturally distinct groups of indigenous peoples, including the Chorotega and Bagaces peoples of

Mesoamerican origin, in the North Pacific; the Huetar-speaking people of the Central Valley; and the Suerre, Pococí, Talamanca, and Tariaca peoples of the Caribbean side. For a variety of reasons, including divisions among the Spaniards and fierce Indian resistance, the conquest of Costa Rica came late. Not until the 1560s could the Spanish invaders subdue the Central Valley and divide the Indians in encomiendas. A handful of African and creole slaves accompanied the early conquerors. The encomenderos supported themselves by demanding Indian produce, marketing the surplus, and concurrently establishing haciendas and estancias, where they raised produce and livestock, including mules, for sale in the Isthmus of Panama. By 1600, the indigenous population had plummeted disastrously, and in this context, the Spaniards began to import more African slaves. Facing the twin problems of the diminution of the Indian population and a decline in commerce in Panama, by the mid-1600s, some Spaniards began to shift their economic operations to the nascent cacao industry in the Caribbean region. The relatively short cacao boom, over by 1750, provided the conditions for an increased importation of Africans.[30]

Estimates of the slave population of Costa Rica are nearly impossible. There is a severe lack of reliable data for the colonial period in general, and the problem is much worse for the slave population. Although many secondary studies continue to cite the nineteenth-century demographic estimates by Bishop Bernardo Augusto Thiel, Thiel's methodology cannot be reconstructed and his figures have been convincingly debunked.[31] Whatever the value of Thiel's figures for the general population, they do not account for the slave population at all. The first systematic censuses of Costa Rica were not conducted until the late eighteenth century, beyond the chronological scope of this work.[32] Nor did they include slaves. Earlier documentation is fragmentary and, again, generally excludes the enslaved population entirely.

Although most contemporary estimates of Costa Rica's population include data on the indigenous population, few contain information on members of other racial groups. Those that do neglect to mention the enslaved population. For example, a 1681 survey undertaken by Governor don Miguel Gómez de Lara categorizes the population of free residents of Costa Rica by race but completely omits mention of slaves.[33] A small regional census from the North Pacific Valley of Bagaces in 1688 lists seventeen slaves in the valley's total population of 297 (about 5.7 percent). The slave population of the Central Valley would have been much higher.[34] A major source for seventeenth-century demography, often cited by historians, is a 1691 "census" of Cartago, also generated by Governor Gómez de Lara. This document lists nominally 496 male Spaniards (probably including mestizos), along with the odd female property owner, and just sixty-three male "mulatos, free blacks, and low mestizos" (about 11 percent of the total). As the document tells us nothing about household or family size, it is an extremely crude measure of the free population and, again, contains no information whatsoever on the slave population.[35] Similarly, although it includes counts of people of various racial groups, the 1741 census of Costa Rica by Governor don Juan Gemmir y Lleonart contains no data on the slave population.[36] One noteworthy characteristic of the governors' estimates is the strong growth of the free black and mulatto population—from 8 percent in 1681 to 11 percent in 1691 to 22 percent in 1741.

For good reason, then, very few historians have ventured to estimate the size or proportion of the slave population in colonial Costa Rica. Leading scholars of the subject, including Rina Cáceres, Oscar Aguilar Bulgarelli, and Mauricio Meléndez Obando, do not take up the issue, although Cáceres points out the methodological problems involved.[37] Although he does not refer specifically to the slave population, according to historical anthropologist Michael D. Olien, "at no time throughout the

TABLE I.1. Estimates of Population of Costa Rica Based on Contemporary Sources, 1492–1751 (Percentage of total in parentheses)

YEAR	INDIANS	SPANIARDS	FREE BLACKS AND MULATTOS	MESTIZOS	TOTAL
1492	400,000 (100)	0 (0)	0 (0)	0 (0)	400,000
1569	69,875				
1611	8,248				
1681	1,077 (62)	520 (30)	129 (8)	16 (0.9)	1,742
1691		496 (89)	63 (11)		
1741	804* (8)	1,707* (17)	2,142* (22)	5,300* (53)	9,953*
1751	2,811 (20)				14,337

*Includes only people eligible to receive communion.

Sources: Denevan, Native Population of the Americas, 291; Quirós Vargas, La era de la encomienda, 129; AGI, Indiferente General 2978; AGI, Contaduría 815; ANCR, C. 83; Fernández, Colección de documentos, 9:255–64; AGCA, A1.17, exp. 5016, leg. 210; University of Texas at Austin, Nettie Lee Benson Latin American Collection, Joaquín García Icazbalceta Collection, vol. 20, no. 7.

colonial period did the Black population number more than 200 individuals."[38] Olien provides no documentation for this assertion, but it probably
derives from Bishop Bernardo Augusto Thiel's "Monografía de la población
de Costa Rica" (mentioned above).[39] Recognizing weaknesses in the data,
Olien also suggests that "the number of Blacks remained small and stable,
and the number of part-Blacks grew rapidly through the entire colonial
period."[40] Several problems can be seen in Olien's statements. First is the
lack of documentation for his estimate of two hundred individuals, discussed below. Second, although the number of African slaves in the colony
may have remained relatively small, it did not remain stable. As reflected
in the number of notarial transactions involving slaves, the importation of
Africans spiked in the late seventeenth and especially the early decades of
the eighteenth century.

María C. Alvarez Solar has offered another estimate of the enslaved popu-
lation of Costa Rica. Drawing on the *Indices de los protocolos de Cartago*,
Alvarez Solar determined that eighty-eight slave owners composed testaments
disposing of 457 slaves between 1680 and 1725. Based on these figures, she cal-
culates that the average Cartago slave master owned 5.2 slaves. Accepting
Governor Gómez de Lara's estimate of 530 (although there were actually 520)
Spaniards in Costa Rica in 1681 and assuming that *all* Spaniards owned slaves,
Alvarez Solar multiplies that figure by 5.2 and concludes that there were "2,500
to 3,000" slaves in late seventeenth-century Costa Rica.[41] Alvarez Solar's estimate, however, is at variance with the governor's own. Gómez de Lara reported
Costa Rica's total population in 1681 at 1,742 persons.[42]

One firm source for the black slave population—probably Bishop
Thiel's—is the 1751 *visita* of Bishop Pedro Agustín Morel de Santa Cruz.
Morel de Santa Cruz estimated the number of people in the Caribbean
Matina Valley at 201, making clear that most of Matina's residents were black
slaves.[43] Virtually all of the slaves living in Matina were adult males. Given
the nearly equal sex ratio among Costa Rican slaves (see table 2.2 in chapter 2),
theoretically, two hundred enslaved women might have lived in the Central
Valley. This minimum does not include any adult males or children. In light
of the bishop's estimate of the population of the Central Valley (Jurisdiction
of Cartago) at 4,289 persons, female slaves alone might have constituted a
minimum of 5 percent of the total population of the Central Valley in 1751.[44]
If we assume that the slave population of Costa Rica was between 5 and
7 percent of the total population in 1751, then, there might have been seven
hundred to one thousand slaves in Costa Rica in that year.

The most remote province of the Kingdom of Guatemala, Costa Rica was a hierarchical colonial society yet bore little resemblance to those founded on mining or plantation agriculture. Endemic internal and external conditions, especially a chronic labor shortage and weak trade relations, severely constrained the aspirations of Costa Rica's self-styled Spanish elite throughout the colonial period. Their straitened financial resources sharply limited the ability of Spanish colonists to purchase African slaves. Along with Spanish mercantilist policies, the relative poverty of Costa Rican elites decisively conditioned the extent and nature of the slave trade in the province. Without a large indigenous population, the resources with which to purchase large numbers of African slaves, or stable connections to the Atlantic slave trade, Spaniards relied from the beginning on a mixed labor force of Indians, free mulattos, mestizos, and African and creole slaves. The absence of large groups of ethnic Africans and slaves' constant, intimate contact with members of other racial and ethnic groups encouraged creolization. A new and unique African American culture among the enslaved, deriving from several African cultures, did not develop in Costa Rica. Instead, from the earliest decades of Spanish settlement, Africans contributed to and absorbed elements of a local culture that derived from Iberian, indigenous, and African roots. They immediately conveyed this local culture to new arrivals from Africa, as well as to the new generations of American-born children who soon made up the majority of Costa Rica's population of African descent.

The nature of the work to which masters put their slaves sustained this contact between different groups in colonial society. Work required that slaves be allowed varying degrees of physical mobility and responsibility that sometimes offered them opportunities to pursue their own interests. Despite their apparently organic relationship to the nature of labor itself, however, such opportunities ultimately derived from the masters, who delegated authority according to their own perceived needs and cultural dictates. The importance masters attributed to slaves' gender, and to a lesser extent, their color and place of birth, conditioned their ideas about what labor was appropriate to each group and, thus, decisively influenced the choices available to enslaved women and men.[45] Slaves did not choose the work they did, nor did they establish relationships or form communities just as they pleased. But although they always lived within the limits imposed by the master-slave relationship, their status as slaves formed only one of several overlapping identities.[46]

Enslaved Africans came from specific homelands. They became ship-mates on particular vessels and veterans of "seasoning" on particular prop-erties. They came to answer to individual masters and mistresses and to identify with their other slaves and servants. They recognized similar cul-tural characteristics and came to associate on the basis of those character-istics, with Africans of similar origins, although these might live on other properties. They learned new ways of work. African men and women learned new rules of behavior particular to each gender. The vast majority learned to speak a foreign language and to pay their respects, sincerely or otherwise, to a foreign god. They lived among Spaniards, Indians, free mu-lattos, mestizos, and other slaves and observed where each group fit in the local hierarchy, noting that there were always individual exceptions, people who temporarily stepped out of or permanently lived out of their "place." They found that although they did the same work as people of these other groups, they were treated differently. They came to understand that they occupied a legally sanctioned class position at the lowest level of a society that cared nothing for their African past and allowed them few opportuni-ties to remember it with those who shared it. They nevertheless assumed and remade roles as friends and family members in new communities that transcended ethnicity, race, and even slavery. Aided by unique conditions in Costa Rica, a highly visible minority of enslaved Africans proved able to exploit their new roles and relationships for social and material advantage in pursuit of the ultimate goal: freedom. Their conspicuous success encour-aged other slaves to imitate the strategies and cultivate the relationships that seemed to lead to it. An inescapable lesson seemed to be that the path to success and freedom lay outside the slave community, extended by free relatives and sympathetic masters and patrons. All of these processes con-spired to make assimilation to the creole culture of Costa Rica exception-ally rapid and profound.

Chapter 1 traces the route of the *Christianus Quintus* and *Fredericus Quartus* from West Africa to Costa Rica. The Africans sold as captives to the Danes came from the Gold Coast and the Slave Coast and shared much in common culturally. Most had been enslaved as the result of wars such as that between Akwamu and Kwawu (1708–1709) or the civil war in Ouidah during the same years. Although the average length of the Middle Passage in the first decade of the eighteenth century was about 74 days, some of the captives on the Danish ships languished on board for eleven months from the time they were first loaded onto the "floating tombs" at the fort of Christiansborg to their final disembarkation in Costa Rica.[47]

Chapter 2 identifies the origins of the Africans who came to Costa Rica in chains between the sixteenth and eighteenth centuries. African slaves in Costa Rica came from dozens of societies in all major regions of West and West Central Africa. Although patterns in the importation of captives to Costa Rica corresponded to those in the Atlantic slave trade generally, the Africans who arrived in Costa Rica were immediately immersed in an ethnically diverse slave population. Their varied origins ensured that no single ethnicity predominated among Africans in Costa Rica.

Chapter 3 looks at the slave trade to Costa Rica and its implications for slave identity. With few exceptions, captives did not arrive in Costa Rica directly from Africa. Instead, they made numerous stopovers in places such as Jamaica, Barbados, Curaçao, Cartagena, Portobello, and Panama City before continuing to Costa Rica's ports of La Caldera or Matina. At each stop, ties between captives were severed and new ones created. If they began their long journey surrounded by countrymen, chances were that they would be separated from their companions again and again. Those repeated divisions meant that those captives who shared the experience of these Middle Passages especially valued their relationships as shipmates.

Chapter 4 discusses the introduction of Africans to their status as slaves in Costa Rica. From the moment of capture, Africans were enslaved and kept slaves through violence. When they were purchased in Costa Rica, Africans suffered further, ideological domination as their masters attempted to remake them into compliant, Hispanicized slaves. They received new names as symbols of the new identities forced upon them by the masters. They learned a new language and a new religion meant to reconcile them to their new status as enslaved workers bound to a particular master in a determined set of social relations.

Chapter 5 examines the diverse types of work slaves did and how these affected their social lives. The gendered division of slave labor in Costa Rica had all-important effects on the social lives of enslaved people. Female slaves lived exclusively in the Central Valley and North Pacific regions. Masters confined them largely to domestic service. Although that term should be interpreted broadly in the context of Costa Rica, most enslaved females lived in close proximity to their masters and were subject to heightened vigilance and control. Only male slaves, many of them African, lived and worked in

Matina in the Caribbean zone. By contrast, they lived largely unsupervised by whites and, to a great extent, enjoyed independent lives.

Chapter 6 looks at slave resistance. Flight was the most common type, especially among Africans, but slaves were often recaptured. Group *cimarronaje* was almost unheard of. Many slaves opted to flee to new masters whom, they hoped, would be less oppressive than the old. Although this tactic could alleviate individual sufferings, by its nature it could do little to lessen the plight of slaves as a class. Violent resistance, too, remained individual; rebellions seldom materialized. In their daily lives, though, slaves found many, less dramatic means of resistance.

Chapter 7 discusses the families that slaves created and how they associated these with freedom. Although most slaves never experienced Catholic marriage—the only form recognized by Spaniards in colonial society—they formed other kinds of families. In some cases, female slaves formed networks to care for their children. In others, documents obscured the presence of slave fathers in their children's lives. A few slaves succeeded in marrying in the Church. The few male slaves who married, most of them Africans, usually chose free women of other racial origins as wives, which ensured freedom for their children and sometimes for themselves. This choice, however, further undermined the possibility of transmitting African values and traditions.

The epilogue documents the eighteenth-century beginnings of an English-speaking black community in Costa Rica. A plethora of factors conspired to prevent the formation of a distinctive culture among Costa Rican slaves, but these men and women, fugitives from other slave societies, had brought their own culture of resistance with them. Settled on the site of the future capital of Costa Rica, these self-liberated former slaves, ancestors of today's Afro–Costa Rican population, began the long process of overturning racial oppression.

CHAPTER ONE

A "Guinea Voyage" Gone Wrong

From Africa to Costa Rica, 1708–1710

✝ ON MARCH 10, 1710, SENTINEL ALFONSO RAMÍREZ SCANNED THE HO-rizon from his post in the watchtower overlooking the Caribbean near Matina, Costa Rica. Suddenly he made out "two shapes" running on the beach below, which just as suddenly disappeared from view. Afraid they might be enemy Miskitu Zambos—a hostile people indigenous to Nicaragua and Honduras, who regularly raided the area—Ramírez immediately sent soldier Miguel Gómez to notify Captain Gaspar de Acosta Arévalo, the lieu-tenant in charge of the Matina Valley. The next day, Ramírez sent several soldiers to search the beach for the "shapes." Juan Bautista Retana, José Ortega, Isidro de Acosta, and several others returned with two excited black women, from whom "not a word could be understood."[1]

The first of those young women came to be called Nicolasa Mina. Years later, she recalled that "she came in a ship that was accompanied by another, and that it was of the English, and that it went to pieces on the beaches of Matina." Nicolasa had "gone out swimming, and went to a watchtower, and from there they took her to the Lieutenant of the Valley, Gaspar de Acosta." She was about fifteen years old when Acosta brought her, with twenty-one other African men and women, to Costa Rica's capital, Cartago.[2]

The ship that brought Nicolasa and hundreds of others to Costa Rica was called the *Christianus Quintus*. It was not English, as she believed, but Danish, and as she noted, sailed in convoy with another ship, the *Fredericus*

Quartus. Both ships had already made slaving voyages to the Americas, beginning in 1698. The Danes were relative newcomers and junior partners in the "Guinea trade." Although Danish slave ships began sailing occasionally to West Africa in the 1670s, only after the reorganization of the Danish West India and Guinea Company in 1697 and the expansion of Denmark's Caribbean colonies did the Danish share of the African commerce rise in importance.[3] During the War of Spanish Succession (1701–1714), when hostilities among major European nations caused disruptions in the supply of captives to the Americas, neutral Denmark expanded its involvement in human trafficking, selling captives at greater profits as planter demand outstripped the supply of Africans.[4] Even then, Danish involvement in the slave trade remained small. The Danish West India and Guinea Company rarely if ever sent more than two ships at a time from Copenhagen to Africa and then to the Caribbean. Denmark never filled the demand for captives, even in its own sugar colonies. Without large-scale manufacturing, the Danes had to purchase the overwhelming majority of the goods they sold in West Africa from other European nations who were their direct competitors, such as the Netherlands. As a result, they had to sell their merchandise at higher prices than their Dutch, English, French, and even Portuguese rivals.[5] Nevertheless, in the long term, even the Danes made handsome profits from trade in West Africa. Between 1709 and 1746, the Danish West India and Guinea Company sent goods to Africa worth approximately six hundred thousand rixdollars (roughly £118,000 in the currency of the time) and sold the return cargoes for more than two million rixdollars (roughly £394,000).[6]

In October 1708, the crews of the *Fredericus Quartus* and *Christianus Quintus* began preparing for a voyage to West Africa.[7] The *Christianus Quintus* left Copenhagen at the end of that month or in early November, the *Fredericus Quartus* about five weeks later on December 5.[8] Both ships carried an assortment of goods. Like other European nations, Denmark tried to keep up with changing African tastes in an attempt to profit from the latest preferences, but its traders often arrived with goods of poor or outdated quality that were difficult to exchange for slaves. For example, the *Fredericus Quartus* carried thirty crates of old bedsheets (*slaplagerne*), eight crates of firearms, 522 iron bars produced in Norway and 648 from Sweden, and nineteen barrels of cowries, among other sundry articles.[9] These goods served a variety of uses in West Africa. Old bedsheets were cut into strips and used as raw material by weavers, as well as for feminine hygiene. Iron bars were refashioned into tools and weapons by smiths and sometimes used as currency, but they had decreased sharply in value since the late seventeenth century.[10] As the main form of currency on the Slave Coast and in the Yoruba kingdom of Oyo, cowry shells formed the single most important article imported to those areas for re-export to the interior. Yet cowries comprised a relatively small portion of the goods brought by the Danes, who favored cheap textiles, as reflected in the cargo of the *Fredericus Quartus*.[11] The voyage out passed without incident for both ships, which rounded the Canary Islands in January 1709. After several stops, including Gorée Island (Senegal), Cape Mesurado (Liberia), and Tabou (Côte d'Ivoire), the *Fredericus Quartus* joined the *Christianus Quintus* at Kutru (Côte d'Ivoire) on March 13, 1709.[12]

On March 17, the *Fredericus Quartus* called at the Dutch fort at Cape Apollonia on the Gold Coast. The next day, the crew purchased some gold and the first four captives of the voyage. Over the next few days in port, they purchased five more. On March 22, 1709, both ships put in at the Brandenburger Fort Friedrichsberg at Cape Three Points (Cabo Três Pontas), where Captain Diedrich Pfeiff of the *Christianus Quintus* exchanged nine barrels of brass bangles (known as "manillas," another form of African currency) for 650 pounds (295 kilograms) of ivory, a small quantity of gold, some firewood, and eleven captives.[13] Johannes Rask, a newly appointed Lutheran chaplain sailing on the *Fredericus Quartus* to his future post on the Gold Coast, commented:

> I noted not the least resentment on [the captives'] part, not even any physical opposition, at their being handed over to us, from which I concluded that the slaves must truly be treated very badly by their own people, since so few show discontent at being sold. But the revolts which they instigate, at times, when they are still near land (since they would never do so at sea, because if they did gain control they would never find their way to land again), these revolts happen purely because they are afraid of the sea and the journey. In this respect I have heard of an unpleasant conception the slaves have—. . . they believe that the *Blanke*, as they usually call the Christians [*sic*: Europeans], buy them for one purpose, which is that when they are out to sea they will sink them to the bottom and use them to gather *bossies* [cowries].

Rask's observations are curiously contradictory. It is hard to reconcile the alleged indifference of the captives to boarding the slave ships with their admitted propensity for revolt and dread of whites. The apathy Rask perceived most likely reflected the exhaustion and demoralization of people on the brink who contemplated revolt as a last, desperate chance to save themselves. At a time when most scholars agree that racism did not exist, Rask strained to explain why these Africans would rebel against enslavement.

The captives' belief that they were destined to be thrown into the sea, their lives exchanged for cowry shells, reflected their awareness that they had been converted into commodities. Tied, yoked, or chained together, they had arrived at hinterland markets after days, weeks, sometimes months of crossing forests, grasslands, rivers, or deserts littered with the bones of captives who had gone before. At these ancient trade centers, African merchants exchanged a dazzling variety of goods, such as food, textiles, salt, precious metals, beads, animals, and iron for the human commodities.[14] Typically, a number of routes converged at each large market, bringing captives from an ever-widening radius of the interior. At these hinterland markets, captives were again separated from their companions and thrown together with others. Although most had been captured in war, others were political dissidents, debtors and unredeemed hostages, common criminals, or simply unlucky peasants snared in the slavers' nets.[15] Local masters bought and sold men, women, and children according to their particular preferences in accordance with the social value attached to people of different ages and genders.[16] Most African slaveholders preferred female captives, who usually commanded higher prices than men. In most African societies (with the notable exception of those in the Bight of Biafra), women performed the bulk of agricultural labor. Equally as important, women served their masters sexually and bore them children. In much of Africa, control of people rather than of land formed the basis of political power.[17] Torn from their homelands, enslaved women were stripped of membership in their lineages of origin and thus had no maternal kin who could claim rights over their labor or their children. Masters therefore theoretically held unquestioned authority over their enslaved concubines and their children and, through them, increased their retinue of dependents and thus their political power.[18] Although enslaved women and their children became absorbed into the lineages of their new masters, they were often accepted only as inferior junior members and condemned to the status of permanent outsiders.[19] Being uprooted, forcibly incorporated into new societies as slaves, and losing control of their children to a master were familiar if heart-wrenching experiences for many African women by the time they were sold into the Atlantic slave trade.[20]

The captives reached the end of their trek at the disease- and vermin-ridden dungeons and barracoons of trading forts near the coast, where pale-skinned foreigners stood over them with guns and whips and slopped them with gruel once or twice a day. Some were sure these ghostly beings came from the land of the dead, and most assumed that they were witches and cannibals; everywhere in Africa, terrifying rumors circulated among the captives that the Europeans intended to eat them. Here, captives encountered men of a strikingly different skin color, most for the first time. They soon learned that the strangely dressed, pale-skinned captors attributed great significance to this difference in appearance and made little distinction in their treatment of African men and women, regardless of their different ethnic and linguistic backgrounds. Weakened by malnutrition, dehydration, and hunger, many captives fell victim to the diseases that raged through the filthy and overcrowded barracoons. One in ten—sometimes as many as 40 percent—of the captives never left Africa alive.[21] The length of their stay depended on the number of captives held at the forts and the number and capacity of ships that arrived there. It could last from days to months. Although the captives could not control the sickness, pain,

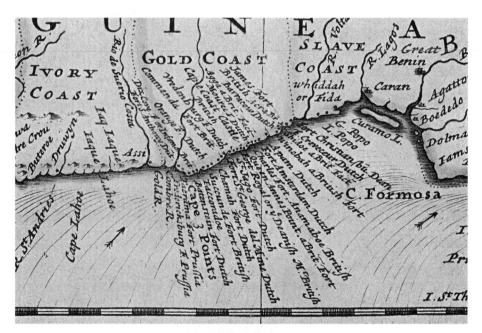

Map 2. Detail of Map of West Africa, by H. Moll, ca. 1730.
Courtesy of the Colonial Williamsburg Foundation.

and death that surrounded them, depending on the time they were imprisoned on the coast, they could begin to form new associations there as they shared their sufferings.[22] When several hundred captives had been assembled, they were put into canoes and ferried by local Africans to the towering vessels waiting offshore.[23]

Needing provisions, the two ships bought some grain at the English trading station at Dixcove in early April 1709 before stopping at the Dutch fort of Komenda on April 13, where the *Fredericus Quartus* purchased seven captives and some palm oil.[24] Slavers of the various European countries disagreed on the best diet for captives during the Middle Passage, often adjusting their shipboard diets according to the origins of the Africans they purchased. The Danes favored pork, beans, and barley gruel flavored with palm oil, varied with weekly rations of grain and perhaps a shot of brandy. This menu represented an ideal, rarely the reality. Ludewig Rømer, stationed on the Gold Coast in the 1740s, admitted that the Danes often provisioned the captives mostly with yellow peas, which constituted "an unhealthy diet at sea."[25] By late April, both ships had arrived at the Danish fort of Christiansborg, their last port of call on the Gold Coast.[26]

The Atlantic trade brought momentous changes to the societies of the Gold Coast, and the most far-reaching transformations yet had been occurring over the past half-century. During the seventeenth century, control of commerce replaced control of production as the decisive factor in politics; newly armed "lords of firepower" rose to supplant the traditional "nobles" as the regional ruling class; and loosely tied confederations of independent polities fell before more powerful, centralized territorial states backed by improved military organization and technology.[27] The coastal trade presented immediate military and political implications, especially because of the importation of European firearms. The technological advantage of superior weaponry combined with mass conscript armies enabled the states that controlled the trade with Europeans to conquer new territories, securing greater access to the commodities that became the new foundations of wealth and power.[28]

As a coastal people, the Ga-speakers of the polity of Accra in the area around Christiansborg had both benefited and suffered from the commercial and political changes of the past fifty years. At its peak in the mid-1670s, Great Accra thrived as a center of regional trade, boasting a population of between forty and fifty thousand.[29] Long a center of salt production, during the seventeenth century the small coastal state expanded its power by imposing stricter control over eastern trade routes to the coast. Rather than allowing the neighboring northern states free access to the coast, the kings of Accra established a market at Abonse, on the northern frontier, where they required African foreigners to trade. Merchants from Akan-speaking inland states, such as Akwamu, Akyem, Asante, and Kwawu, brought large quantities of gold, ivory, and slaves to trade for the prized Accra salt, as well as European goods, including arms and gunpowder. "Bag of salt" became a derisive term for slaves, emphasizing a person's reduction to a commodity.[30] To help confine the inland traders to the northern market, the Accra employed warriors from the neighboring state of Akwamu to the northwest.[31]

Although their operations remained limited in comparison to those of other European nations trading on the Gold Coast, the Danes acquired an important trading station there when they purchased land from King Okai Koi of Accra and built Christiansborg Castle in the 1660s. Christiansborg was one of three European trading stations in the immediate area, the others being the Dutch Fort Crevecoeur and the English James Fort.[32] "Here there is such plenty of Gold and Slaves, the path being free and safe for the Merchants, that no one is in danger of wanting its share," gushed Dutch slave trader Willem Bosman around 1701.[33] Advantageously positioned at the easternmost port of call on the Gold Coast, the Danes at Christiansborg often procured European goods at bargain prices from ships in need of fresh water and supplies before they continued on to the Slave Coast.[34]

With the growth of their plantation colonies in the New World, European traders increasingly sought slaves over other commodities, which were surpassing gold exports in value by the time the *Christianus Quintus* and *Fredericus Quartus* arrived at Christiansborg.[35] According to Carl Christian Reindorf, author of the Gold Coast's first history based on local oral traditions, it was by "that nefarious traffic" in captives that the rulers of Accra grew rich. Their increased wealth ignited the jealousy of the kings of Akwamu, who gradually tired of their auxiliary role in the commerce and decided to "crush" the Accra and seize control of the lucrative Atlantic trade for themselves.[36] Beginning in the late 1660s, intent on monopolizing the gold and slave resources of the hinterland, Akwamu's King Ansa Sasraku began a series of expansionist wars.[37] Akwamu eventually extended its overlordship over the neighboring states of Kwawu and Krepi, routinely raiding their residents for slaves to sell to the Europeans on the coast.[38]

In 1679, Akwamu conquered Accra and reduced it to tributary status, forcing a large number of Ga- and Adangme-speaking people into exile in Anlo, just east of the Volta River on the upper Slave Coast. These refugees profoundly altered the demographic, cultural, and economic environment of the societies where they settled.[39] By 1710, Akwamu controlled crucial trading areas of the Gold Coast from Winneba to the Volta and beyond, dominating the trade routes into the interior as far north as the frontier with Asante.[40]

The European trade not only transformed relations between the states of the Gold Coast, it radically changed social relations within them. As war and slave raiding ravaged their villages, dispossessed peasants flocked to densely populated towns such as Accra. There, gangs of young men known to the Danes as *siccadinger*, typically men who were unemployed and unmarried, began to organize. Lacking kinship ties or rights to land or subsistence, these destitute youths readily hired their services to wealthy political leaders and merchants, who deployed them to seize captives from their rivals in nearby areas. Gangs of *siccadinger* roved the countryside, where they abducted peasants and transported them, bound and gagged, to the coast for sale to European factors. The activities of the *siccadinger* created widespread disorder among the small states near the coast, and by the late seventeenth century, the old social structure proved clearly that it was incapable of controlling them.[41]

The predatory activities of the *siccadinger* fatally undermined a system of independent polities, but when coordinated, these activities became a powerful weapon in the rise of a new empire. The rising state of Akwamu shrewdly incorporated the *siccadinger* into its military forces, institutionalizing their pillaging and kidnapping as a key tool in wealth accumulation. All prisoners captured in war legally belonged to the king and the elders, and many prisoners were redistributed as booty among the *siccadinger* to secure their continued loyalty. Peaceful citizens of Akwamu, as well as those of neighboring states, became vulnerable to arbitrary enslavement simply to finance the lavish lifestyle of the king and his retainers. As Akwamu's kings enriched themselves, their political advisors, and their armies of *siccadinger*, their subjects came to regard them as tyrannical and abusive. The king of Akwamu's "Arbitrary Despotick Power," wrote Willem Bosman, "occasions the Proverbial saying, That there are only two sorts of Men in *Aquamboe*, of which the King and his Friends are one, and their Slaves the other."[42] In addition to his regular army, for example, King Akwonno (1705–1725) was reputed to have one thousand "crafty young men" in his service. He was said to spend the value of a thousand slaves each year just on rum to entertain his troops.[43]

In 1707, Akwonno launched a full-scale war of conquest against Kwawu, another Akan state to the north and a major supplier of gold, ivory, and slaves to the coastal trade. By April of that year, European traders on the coast complained that the war had disrupted the flow of commodities to their stations. The Kwawu withdrew across the northern hinterland to the Asante frontier, where they mustered the strength (perhaps afraid of provoking Asante by entering its territory) to rout the Akwamu in February 1708. This "crushing defeat" forced the Akwamu to retreat to their capital to re-equip and reinforce their army. The Danes at Christiansborg replenished Akwonno's supplies of arms and gunpowder in exchange for slaves. In late summer 1708, the Akwamu attempted another invasion of Kwawu but were again repulsed.[44]

Temporarily thwarted in his northern campaign, Akwonno turned his attention to the kingdom of Accra to the southeast. Akwonno suspected that Accra's rulers, technically his tributary dependents, had been conspiring against him, and in late November 1708, he punished them with an assault. The Accra king Ni Ayi escaped to safety with his household and most of his armed retainers, but chief Ama Kuna and his personal guard were slaughtered by the Akwamu as they attempted to flee. Emboldened by his success, Akwonno and his army set up camp in the area and, during the following months, repeatedly assaulted the coastal towns of Osu, Labadi, and Teshi. The Akwamu annihilated Labadi in a single night, killing or enslaving some one thousand people.[45]

Although he claimed that "the war is no concern of ours" and would have welcomed any solution to it that reopened trade, Lygaard effectively aided an Akwamu victory by continuing to supply Akwonno with arms during his attacks on the Accra.[46] When the Accra sought Danish assistance in defending themselves against a second Akwamu attack, Lygaard refused to provide them with gunpowder or grant them asylum in the castle. Instead, the Danes barricaded themselves inside their fort and watched as Akwonno and his army slaughtered and enslaved the Accra on the beaches below. In the aftermath of the Akwamu victory, Lygaard lavished gifts on Akwonno, who withdrew to his capital in victory on April 1, 1709.[47]

The Akwamu wars against Kwawu and Accra and the prolonged blockade of the castle itself formed the immediate background to the arrival of the ships *Christianus Quintus* and *Fredericus Quartus* at Christiansborg on April 16 and 25, 1709, respectively. The Akwamu had brought trade with the interior to a virtual standstill. When the Dutch refused to pay him tribute,

Akwonno blockaded the roads to Accra. The renewal of the war with the Kwawu, "from whom the slaves come" as Lygaard wrote, threatened to halt supplies and inflate the prices of the few captives who did arrive at the coast. By the end of April, the Danes at the fort had only twenty-seven captives on hand.[48] These certainly included Kwawu, as Lygaard specified, as well as some of the Accra captured in the towns of Osu, Teshi, and Labadi in the preceding months.

Due to the political instability that frequently disrupted trade to the coast, European slavers often failed to obtain a full slave cargo at Accra. In these cases, they sailed east to fill their ships at ports along the Slave Coast. Caught in these common circumstances, the *Christianus Quintus* proceeded to Ouidah on the Slave Coast for its cargo, while the *Fredericus Quartus* stayed behind at Christiansborg. To prepare for the voyage east, the *Christianus Quintus* was fitted with slave benches, part of its cargo was unloaded, and its stores were completed with goods transferred from the *Fredericus Quartus*.[49] This work was surely accomplished by Africans living in the towns near the fort and by the Danish West India and Guinea Company's "castle slaves."

Like the other ports on the Gold Coast and, indeed, in much of West Africa, Christiansborg had no natural harbor and was exposed to extremely powerful surf. Ships could anchor safely only at a distance east of the fort.[50] Upon the arrival of a ship, African "beachboys" swarmed the strand, carrying merchandise to and from the castle on their heads, while canoemen relayed goods between ships and shore.[51] Renowned for their skill, the canoemen of Elmina on the western Gold Coast worked at ports throughout the Gold and Slave Coasts. The crucial process of loading and unloading cargo depended entirely on these workers, as Europeans realized: "Those canoes laden with goods and men, are conveyed by the *Mina* Blacks over the worst and most dreadful beating seas, all along the coast . . . where no manner of trade could be carried on between the shore and the road, without that help."[52]

In May 1709, the *Christianus Quintus* left the Danish fort for the Slave Coast to fill out its cargo. Around the second week of June 1709, the *Christianus Quintus* stopped at Little Popo seeking slaves.[53] The *Fredericus Quartus* remained in port at Christiansborg during most of this time,[54] attempting to make up its cargo from the slaves who arrived at the castle. Traders from the interior Akan-speaking state of Akyem arrived at the Danish station frequently but brought few captives. By August 19, 1709, the

Fredericus Quartus had purchased 357 slaves. About 34 percent were adult females, and another 5 percent were described as "girls"; with about 61 percent males, the cargo of captives obtained at Christiansborg came close to the Europeans' ideal cargo: two-thirds males. Twenty-two captives had already died on board when Captain Diedrich Pfeiff decided to sail to Keta on the upper Slave Coast to fill the rest of the cargo.[55] The *Fredericus Quartus* arrived there on September 1, 1709, and by September 12 had purchased thirty-five slaves. Captain Pfeiff felt optimistic that he would acquire the rest of the cargo he sought there.[56]

The upper Slave Coast, just east of the Volta River, had long been the scene of intense commercial and cultural exchange between the Gold and Slave Coasts. Several groups of Gold Coast immigrants and their descendants contributed to the rich ethnic diversity of the region. By the mid-seventeenth century, a group of mina canoemen of Gold Coast origin established a commercial outpost at Aneho (Anécho) in Little Popo among the Gbe-speaking Hula (Xwla).[57] In 1679, the Akwamu conquest drove large numbers of Ga- and Adangme-speaking refugees just across the Volta to Anlo, where they introduced new techniques in fishing and salt production to the area, as well as new religious and kinship practices.[58] By the 1690s, Anlo was already trading in slaves, "of which they are able sometimes to deliver a good number, but yet not so many as to lade a Ship."[59] A decade later, increasing productivity in fishing and salt production at Keta meant larger surpluses to exchange in the interior for slaves and ivory. These changes attracted greater numbers of European ships to stop there.[60]

Seeking captives, the *Christianus Quintus* arrived on the upper Slave Coast on June 14, 1709. Captains Hans Hansen Maas and Jost von den Vogel, Factor Peder Pedersen Tøjberg, and the chaplain, Anders Winther, all of the *Christianus Quintus*, drowned in the breakers at Little Popo when their canoe capsized. Having purchased sixty slaves to date, the surviving crew members, now commanded by Anders Pedersen Wærøe, sailed about thirty miles east to the great port city of Ouidah, arriving on June 21, 1709.[61]

Ouidah served as the port of the powerful kingdom of the same name. Between 1700 and 1710, more slaves were exported from Africa than in any previous decade. The Bight of Benin exported more slaves than did any other region in Africa during those years, and Ouidah exported more slaves than did any other port in that part of the gulf known as the "Slave Coast." In the ten years before the *Christianus Quintus* arrived, nearly forty-six thousand African slaves were exported through the port of Ouidah.[62]

Ouidah exported more slaves than did the Gold Coast in large part because its centralized political structure was more effectively mobilized for the traffic. Ouidah's powerful king maintained strict control over the slave trade, designating a corps of administrators for its specialized functions.[63] Writing of Ouidah in the 1690s, Dutch slave trader Willem Bosman asserted that "most of the Slaves that are offered to us are Prisoners of War, which are sold by the Victors as their Booty."[64] Although subjects of Ouidah were also enslaved as punishment for crimes or nonpayment of debts, these cases reportedly formed a small minority. A French observer around 1715 estimated that less than 5 percent of the slaves sold at the port of Ouidah originated within the kingdom.[65] The neighboring kingdom of Allada supplied the majority of the captives sold there, but Allada itself functioned largely as a re-exporter of slaves from states further in the interior, especially Dahomey and Oyo. According to leading specialist Robin Law, a majority of the slaves sold at Allada probably came "from or at least through Dahomey."[66] This powerful expansionist state geared its military organization toward a "slave-raiding mode of production" that formed the basis of the domination of the ruling elite. The Dahomeans raided neighboring interior peoples for slaves, whom they then traded to less bellicose "middleman" coastal states such as Allada and Ouidah.[67] Large numbers of slaves originating in the Yoruba empire of Oyo also arrived at the ports of Jaquin, Offra, and Ouidah by way of Allada. Prisoners taken in Oyo's wars constituted the major source of these slaves, with some people from the neighboring states of Nupe and Borgu as well.[68]

When the *Christianus Quintus* arrived, trade at Ouidah was still recovering from the political instability occasioned by the death of King Amar the previous year. "This country is always in great disorder and confusion when Kings die, which brings great disadvantages to the trade," a Dutch trader at Ouidah complained in February 1709.[69] Although Ouidah's monarchy was ideally transferred by primogeniture, in practice, rival claimants usually resorted to violence to contest succession. At the time of Amar's death, the oldest of his sons, Huffon, was just twelve years old and had not been formally designated as his father's heir. As a result, Amar's senior chief, the Gogan, attempted to claim the throne.[70] According to custom, the new king received a sword from Lukumi, the legendary home of the royal dynasty in Yorubaland, to legitimate his accession by symbolizing his authority to impose capital punishment. After Amar's death, "for some reason" the sword never arrived. Consequently, many of Ouidah's chiefs refused to recognize Huffon's authority.[71]

In the political culture of the Slave Coast, the administration of justice formed the most important duty of the king, and in the absence of a recognized monarch, the rule of law could not be imposed. This was far more than mere rhetoric. Until a new king was proclaimed, no executive or judicial authority existed. Crimes were committed with impunity, as Robin Law explains: "accounts, based on observation of the accession of King Huffon in 1708, claim in fact that on these occasions murders as well as thefts were committed, so that 'it seems that justice has died with the king'; wise people stayed at home, or went around in armed bands for self-protection, until the interregnum was over."[72] The suspension of royal justice meant that people ordinarily protected from enslavement became vulnerable to abduction and sale. As a result, a greater proportion than usual of the slaves exported from Ouidah at this time probably originated within the kingdom itself, a circumstance made yet more likely by a further disruption of the supply of slaves.

While Huffon's authority remained sharply contested, the kingdom's provincial chiefs struggled openly against each other and the central monarchy. Some looked to Allada in their challenge to the young king.[73] Just as the kings of Ouidah received the ceremonial sword from Lukumi, they customarily rendered tribute to the neighboring kingdom of Allada to solemnize the transfer of power. When Huffon withheld tribute from the king of Allada upon assuming the throne, the latter in turn refused to perform necessary funeral rites for the late king Amar.[74] This ritual dispute occurred in the long-term context of economic warfare between the two largest slave exporters on the Slave Coast: Allada had repeatedly interdicted trade to the port of Ouidah for several prolonged periods since at least the 1690s. In 1709, the Allada king reimposed the blockade on Ouidah, slowing the supply of slaves to a trickle. "The passages through this country are being kept closed by the King of Ardra [Allada] to such an extent, that hardly a single slave comes through," Dutch trader Jan De Paauw complained from Ouidah in September 1709.[75]

On August 11, 1709, Anders Pedersen Wærøe, captain of the *Christianus Quintus*, wrote from Ouidah that he had managed to purchase 211 slaves there so far. He complained of his inability to secure a full cargo because many ships of different nations were trading at the port, and the Scandinavian iron bars he carried were "far too small and short" to compete with those offered by other Europeans.[76] Before leaving Ouidah on September 28, 1709, the *Christianus Quintus* had purchased 323 slaves—159 men, 151 women, eleven boys, and two girls. The near gender parity among the captives reflected conditions in Africa rather than the desires of the Danes; throughout the period of the slave trade, Europeans strove for ideal cargoes composed of two-thirds males and one-third females. As a rule, at Bight of Benin ports, they very nearly achieved their goal. Females made up an average 35 percent of slave cargoes exported between 1663 and 1713. The higher percentage of females among the captives purchased by the *Christianus Quintus* in 1709 reflected political conditions in Ouidah at the time of the ship's arrival. Fewer captives than usual were captured soldiers, more were women seized in civil disturbances. Added to the captives purchased along the upper Slave Coast already on board, those bought at Ouidah brought the total to 383 slaves. Prolonged coasting and waiting at various ports meant an increasingly unhealthy atmosphere for the captives on the ship. Illness circulated and food and water supplies became contaminated and ran short. Ten captives had already died. On September 28, 1709, the *Christianus Quintus* sailed from Ouidah for the Caribbean.[77]

Just two nights after the *Fredericus Quartus* arrived at Keta, a slave rebellion broke out on board while the ship was anchored off the coast. On the night of 14–15 September 1709, some of the slaves in the hold succeeded in breaking free of their shackles. When they tumbled out onto the deck, they awakened some of the crew members. The rebels succeeded in badly injuring two of the whites before the crew subdued them in a fierce struggle. The following morning, a meeting of the ship's council determined the fate of the rebels. As an example to the other captives, the boatswain severed the right hand of the man identified as the rebel leader and passed it before the faces of "all the other slaves" on board. According to slave trader Thomas Phillips, this grisly warning held special significance for natives of the Slave Coast, "for they believe that if they lose a member, they cannot return home again." The Danes then cut off the leader's left hand, and finally his head. To terrorize the captives further, they hoisted the headless corpse onto the mainyard sail, where it hung suspended for two days. The crew also tortured other captives implicated in the rebellion by whipping them and rubbing them down with a painful mixture of malaguetta pepper, salt, and ashes.[78]

The available evidence provides no direct indications of the ethnic origins of the slave rebels on this ship. The great majority of the captives on board the *Fredericus Quartus* had embarked at Christiansborg: a total of 323, including 173 adult males, 109 adult females, twenty-four boys, and seventeen girls.[79] This group certainly included Akan-speaking soldiers captured by the Akwamu in the war against Kwawu, as well as Ga-speakers seized in the raids of the towns surrounding Accra. Some may have been loaded on the ship in mid-April, as long as seven months before.

Along the upper Slave Coast, factor Peder Pedersen of the *Christianus Quintus* had purchased thirty-two men, seventeen women, and five boys. At Keta, Captain Pfeiff bought another fifty men, forty-five women, nine boys, and a single girl. Of a total 482 slaves purchased, forty-nine had already died. Even before setting sail, the ship's supplies were severely depleted. Perhaps fearing another slave uprising, Pfeiff decided not to return to Christiansborg for another twenty slaves who had arrived there, and left Keta bound for St. Thomas in the Danish West Indies on October 2, 1709, carrying a cargo of 433 slaves.[80] Perhaps its captives shared the dreadful sense of West Central Africans, who saw in the open sea a fulfillment of the traditions that told of an immense expanse of water separating the land of the living from the land of the dead—an impression that was only confirmed in the months ahead.[81]

After the *Fredericus Quartus* rejoined the *Christianus Quintus* off the Slave Coast in October 1709, the ships sailed together. Trade winds made it easy for European sailors to get to the "Guinea Coast" but hard to sail west again into the Atlantic. Strong currents pulled ships east along the West African coast toward the Bight of Biafra and Cameroon. For the voyage to the Americas, slavers turned south in the Bight toward the Portuguese island of São Tomé, where they usually stopped and hoped to catch a westward current to America. The turn was crucial, however, and although most slavers stopped at the Portuguese islands for provisions, they found this part of the journey notoriously difficult. Countervailing currents could halt ships at sea for weeks just miles from the islands. Sailing toward São Tomé to take on supplies, the crews of the *Fredericus Quartus* and the *Christianus Quintus* found the winds against them and were unable to make land. Aiming for Príncipe, there too the ships found the winds hard and failed to reach port.[82] The ships' captains then attempted to reach Cape Lopes de Gonçalves (in modern Gabon), where they hoped finally to take on some water, firewood, and fruit, and tried to find a favorable course for the West Indies. On the way, the *Fredericus Quartus* met three Portuguese ships and learned that Denmark had gone to war with France. After hearing that two French ships had anchored off Cape Lopes, the ships' captains dared not sail into port. By November 20, 1709, the ships had run so low on supplies that they reduced the slaves' rations. For twelve days, they waited off Cape Lopes while their provisions continued to dwindle. By December 30, 1709, fearing another slave rebellion, they sailed for the Americas without adequate food or water.[83]

After a month at sea, the ships were nearing the islands of the eastern
Caribbean, and the ships' captains decided to stop at Barbados for news of
the war between Denmark and France. Sailors on the *Christianus Quintus*
sighted land on January 21, 1710, but Captain Pfeiff ordered that they continue on to Barbados. By February 8, 1710, they still had not reached the
British island. The ships had steered badly off course, and food supplies were
now dangerously low. Captain Wærøe and the officers of the *Fredericus
Quartus* decided to sail south to latitude 10° north, but a few days later, they
turned northward to 13° north, the latitude of Barbados. On February 10,
Captain Pfeiff asked Wærøe to share some of his ship's provisions with the
Christianus Quintus, but Wærøe claimed to have only enough supplies remaining to last fourteen days. Conflicts began to sharpen between the crews
and the ships' officers over which course to take.[84]

Finally, on February 14, 1710, the two ships reached an island. Captain
Wærøe and First Officer Ide Quant went ashore, but the island seemed to be
uninhabited. The next morning, a small English bark on its way to Jamaica
stopped, looking for sea turtles for provisions. The Danes learned that they
were on Santa Catalina (Providence Island) in the western Caribbean. Their
supplies had run critically low because they had sailed past their destination
by some twelve hundred nautical miles. The Danish officers now amended
their plans. Instead of sailing back toward St. Thomas, they decided to sail to
Portobello, the Caribbean port of the Spanish province of Panama, to sell the

Map 3. Detail of the
Map "Mexicque, ou
Nouvelle Espagne"
(1656), by Nicolas
Sanson (1675),
Showing Costa Rica
and Santa Catalina
(Providence Island).
Courtesy of the
Birmingham
(Alabama) Public
Library.

slaves there.[85] At least, this was the account they later presented in a Danish court—an enslaved Jamaican crew member and another witness contended that the two captains always planned to sail for Panama, where slaves would undoubtedly fetch a higher price than in the West Indies.[86]

By this point, morale among the ships' crews was completely exhausted. Captives on both ships continued to die from lack of provisions and disease. By February 18, 1710, fifty-five more slaves aboard the *Christianus Quintus* had died—thirty-five men, seventeen women, and three boys—318 survived. On the *Fredericus Quartus*, disease had killed another eighty slaves. Only 353 now remained alive.[87] Mortality on the Danish slavers exceeded the already horrific 18 percent average death rate on the Middle Passage in the first decade of the eighteenth century.[88]

On February 19, 1710, the *Fredericus Quartus* and *Christianus Quintus* left Santa Catalina. Again the ships veered off course and were blown five hundred nautical miles away from their destination of Portobello, landing at "Punta Carreto" on Costa Rica's Caribbean coast on March 2, 1710.[89] The ships' provisions were now completely exhausted, and the Danish crews rejoiced to see two English fishing boats nearby. Pfeiff urged the sailors of the *Fredericus Quartus* to have patience. Astonishingly, he insisted they continue on to Portobello. His crew absolutely refused, afraid they would starve if they found the sea calm. Instead, they demanded their pay on the spot and also demanded that the Africans be put ashore to spare what scant provisions remained. Pfeiff protested that he had no money to pay them, nor did he have authority to break open the Danish West India and Guinea Company's gold chest. At this, seaman Peder Laursen Møn announced that the sailors would help themselves to the gold and board the English fishing boats. Disregarding Pfeiff's warnings, on March 4, the crew disembarked the captives, who immediately ran into the bush. The sailors then broke open the company chest, divided the gold among themselves, hurled the empty chest into the sea, and boarded the English barks, whose sailors had volunteered to carry them to Portobello. A Danish boy who survived later testified that during the night of March 7, he saw a fire start on the quarterdeck in a pile of tar, pitch, and refuse. By midnight, the *Fredericus Quartus* was completely ablaze.[90]

The crew of the *Christianus Quintus* also abandoned ship. According to the later testimony of the crew members, Captain Anders Wærøe himself distributed thirty-two rixdollars of gold among the crew. After putting the captives ashore, the boatswain cut the ship's anchor cable. The *Christianus Quintus* ran aground and was splintered in the surf.[91]

When they reached the shores of Caribbean Costa Rica, the women and men brought on the *Christianus Quintus* and *Fredericus Quartus* entered a violently contested area. Although Columbus had claimed the Caribbean coast for Spain in 1502, the Spaniards never attained complete control of the Caribbean region at any time during the colonial period. In 1710, people of diverse origins—Talamanca Indians, African and creole blacks, mulattos, mestizos, European- and American-born Spaniards, Miskitu Indians and Zambos, Englishmen—interacted frequently in the Caribbean zone, often on violent terms. (In fact, at the time the *Christianus Quintus* and *Fredericus Quartus* arrived, the Talamanca Indians were in the midst of a rebellion against Spanish rule.)[92] All but the indigenous Talamanca, some of whom preserved their independence until the twentieth century, were allied with one of two major world powers. All held ideas about the meanings of dark skin combined with "African" features, meanings they attributed to all the women and men of diverse origins who arrived on the Danish slavers.

Soon after they escaped their Danish captors on the coast of Costa Rica, the just-arrived Africans fell prey to others. North of Matina, the Miskitu Indians and Zambos, some of whom descended from Africans shipwrecked on Central America's Caribbean coast in the early seventeenth century, lived in several dozen villages dispersed along the coast of Nicaragua and Honduras.[93] In the seventeenth century, British colonists entered into a long-lasting alliance with the Miskitus and began to establish scattered settlements in Belize and further south along the part of the Central American coast they called the "Mosquito Shore."[94] Scholars disagree on the extent to which that relationship altered Miskitu society, but by the end of the seventeenth century, the Miskitus had combined their traditional annual hunt of the sea turtle along the shores of Costa Rica and Panama with the new activity of raiding the region's native peoples for slaves to sell to their British allies on the Mosquito Shore and in Jamaica.[95] By 1705, if not earlier, the Miskitus began capturing Spanish-owned black and mulatto slaves from Matina.[96] It is less well known that British "Shoremen" and Jamaican privateers also made occasional forays into Costa Rica to hunt turtles and seize slaves themselves.

Like the Danes and the English, the Miskitus lumped Africans together as "blacks." Taken prisoner and brought to Cartago, two Miskitu Indians later related how they and their British allies had recaptured hundreds of the Africans on the Matina coast. On May 2, 1710, "Suyntin" (Quentin?), age twenty-one, and Antonio, eighteen, both of whom described their trade as to "sail the seas as a corsair," recalled that they had been at home in the Miskitu country when two English sloops arrived, seeking provisions and men. The Englishmen explained to them that they had left many blacks at the mouth of the Estrella (now Changuinola) River, after having "fought with two other [ships] going to Portobello." They needed men to guard the blacks while they sailed to Jamaica for another ship.[97] Although they supplied additional details, Suyntin and Antonio essentially corroborated the account offered by the Danes. Suyntin, Antonio, and twenty-three other young "Mosquitomen" agreed to help their English allies and went with them in the ship to Costa Rica, planning to raid for Talamanca Indian slaves while they awaited the Englishmen's return.[98] After "four months" (probably a mistranslation by the interpreter), the Englishmen had not returned with the ship as they had promised. Having had no more luck in hunting Talamanca Indians than to kidnap "one head" (una chupa), a little Indian girl (indiezuela chiquita), the Miskitus decided to march the captured blacks by land back to their country. Because many of the Africans were weak from hunger and in no condition to hike, the Miskitus decided to leave about thirty of them at Moín, bringing seventy-five to Mosquitia, where they would "hold them in their service" until the Englishmen returned.[99] Asked how many blacks there had been, Antonio "signalled the hairs of his head."[100]

According to information later supplied by the Danes to Spanish authorities in Portobello, 671 Africans remained alive when the two ships reached the shores of Costa Rica. Spanish officials at Portobello later seized twenty men and a young boy with the rest of the Danes' property. Of the remaining 650 Africans, nothing is known with certainty of the vast majority.[101] Historical linguist John Holm has speculated that many of them were assimilated by the Miskitu Indians of Nicaragua's Caribbean coast.[102] Many certainly met with the Miskitus, but if they were taken to Mosquitia they were probably sold to the British or enslaved in Miskitu villages, not granted freedom and a warm welcome.

More than one hundred of the Africans put ashore from the Danish ships can be accounted for. On March 10, 1710, six days after the Africans were disembarked at "Punta Carreto," Alfonso Ramírez at the watchtower at Matina spied two women running on the beach below. The next day, a group of soldiers captured two young African women.[103] Matina's lieutenant governor Captain Gaspar de Acosta Arévalo dispatched additional soldiers to search the beach for ships. From the captured black women, the Spaniards learned that there were other Africans further south on the coast. Upon reaching the beach at Portete three days later, Acosta and his men found eight African women who threw themselves at the feet of the Spaniards, signaling their great hunger and gesturing that there were more survivors along the beach and reefs. Acosta sent one of the black women with three soldiers to search. They returned four days later with a group of twenty-four black men and women whom they had found between Portete and nearby Punta Blanca. Through an African slave interpreter, these captives reported that there were still more blacks at Portete. A second search produced two additional men and six women. One man died shortly after arriving at Matina, and eleven of the Africans were left there, too sick to travel. Twenty-two captives made the journey to Cartago, Costa Rica's capital.[104]

Upon their arrival in Cartago on April 14, 1710, the surviving Africans from the Danish ships were counted, inspected, and their value assessed. All of the seven men and fifteen women were described as "sick and maltreated." One man was not expected to live and was not evaluated with the others.[105] Five men and thirteen women were classified as of *casta arará*, of Slave Coast origin; two women of *casta mina*, from the Gold Coast or perhaps the upper Slave Coast; and two men of *casta carabalí*.[106] The last identification, referring to the Bight of Biafra, was clearly an error, as neither of the ships had obtained captives east of Ouidah. The Africans were placed in the temporary custody of Cartago resident Juan López de la Rea y Soto, who assumed responsibility for their care and security.[107] On May 2, 1710, Gaspar de Acosta Arévalo returned to Cartago, bringing another group of ten slaves who had stayed behind to recover in Matina. One remained there, too ill to travel. This second group of Africans had been captured near Portete shortly after the first and consisted of three men and seven women, all described as of casta arará. Along with the first group of twenty-two, they were also "deposited" with Juan López de la Rea y Soto.[108]

On April 23, a party of Spanish officers in Matina captured another group of forty-five Africans, seizing them from the Miskitu Zambos on the beach near the mouth of the Moín River. Juan Bautista de Retana received forty of the Africans at his cacao hacienda in Matina to "care for" them. The next day, at Andrés Chacón's hacienda at Matina, interpreters took statements from both the Miskitus and the Africans, who told the Spaniards that there were yet more blacks hiding near Moín. Captains don Juan Francisco de Ibarra and José de Bonilla returned to Moín to search. Then Captain Antonio de Soto y Barahona and a group of eight men set out for Cartago with their Miskitu prisoners and five of the Africans, leaving the others to recuperate at his hacienda in Matina. Barahona arrived in Cartago on May 1, 1710, with the Miskitus Suyntin and Antonio, as well as five Africans—three men and two women of casta mina.[109] Ten days later, Juan Bautista de Retana arrived in Cartago with a second group of thirty-eight Africans—thirteen males and twenty-one females, again, all described as of casta mina. In the remainder of the group of forty-five captured by Retana and Captain Antonio de Soto y Barahona, the males of the group ranged in age from twenty-six at the oldest to eight or nine at the youngest; the females were from about forty to eight years old. One African had drowned, and another, ill, had stayed behind in Matina, Retana explained.[110]

Yet another group of Spaniards apprehended a third group of Africans on April 24, 1710. Having received word the previous day about the Africans at Moín, Captain don Juan Francisco de Ibarra y Calvo assembled a group of twenty-four male residents in the Valley of Matina and went down to the beach to search for the Africans. They arrived at the beach of Moín that night and began to search by candlelight. The next morning, Ibarra and his men found a group of twenty-six Africans "walking together"—nine black men and seventeen black women. Ibarra returned with the Africans to his hacienda in Matina, where he left them to recover, as some were "very maltreated." Ibarra pointed out to the officials that there were no provisions in Matina to feed the Africans, who were in danger of starving to death.[111]

In the event, Ibarra did not bring the blacks to Cartago for more than five weeks, arriving with four African men and twelve women on June 11, 1710, all described as of *casta nangu*. One black man had died in Matina, Ibarra explained, and nine others had drowned while crossing the Reventazón River in a canoe.[112] As the canoe reached the middle of the raging river, Ibarra testified, one of the blacks stood up. He shouted at him to sit down, but "being *bozales*, others stood up," and the canoe capsized. All the blacks drowned in the raging water; Salvador Picado and the canoeman barely escaped with their lives.[113]

In fact, no such accident occurred, as authorities suspected at the time, and the nine young Africans remained very much alive in Costa Rica. Despite persistent inquiries backed by threats of torture, no incriminating evidence could be amassed against Ibarra for almost a decade.[114] But in 1719, these Africans themselves testified how Ibarra had kept some of them as his own slaves and sold others to interested parties.

On April 16, 1710, about a month after they were put ashore at Punta Carreto, several of the Africans recaptured near Moín were interviewed in Cartago by Francisco, a Slave Coast native of casta arará, who served as

interpreter.[115] Among the questions Francisco posed was an unusual request
for an African account of the Middle Passage. He spoke first to an African
man called Juan, who explained that he had been given that name on the
beaches of Matina.[116] Juan's narrative suggests contemporary Slave Coast attitudes about the morality of the trans-Atlantic slave trade and constitutes a
rare account of the Middle Passage from the perspective of the Africans
enslaved.

"Juan," described as a black man of casta arará, explained that he was
more than forty years old, a native of "Guinea," and that "they stole him from
his country and put him with many others of his *casta* in one of three ships
that were anchored" offshore.[117] One of the ships, he said, burned at sea, killing all on board; the other two ships wandered at sea for a long time, when
one of them was lost. The remaining ship, Juan related, was taken by "the
people," and having sighted land, was making for it when they met with "a
great storm, [and] many bolts of lightning struck the ship, killing the captain
and many people."[118] The ship was badly damaged and lacking provisions.
Those commanding the ship ordered that the blacks be put ashore in two
canoes they had brought. Juan was brought ashore with "thirty companions,
twelve men and twenty-two women" [sic], who immediately set about searching the beach for something to eat, as they were starving and had been given
nothing. After putting the Africans ashore, the crew had sailed off in two
canoes. The Africans saw no one else until seven men captured them and
took them to a place Juan learned was called Matina, where one of the survivors died.[119] With a few slight differences, two more African men called
Nicolás and Miguel repeated Juan's testimony almost verbatim.[120]

Despite some points in common, the narratives of Juan, Nicolás, and
Miguel differed strikingly from the accounts offered by the Danish sailors.
Juan, Nicolás, and Miguel spoke of three ships "that had anchored, and from
there they went to sea."[121] Their claim that a third ship was burned at sea and
that all on board perished finds no echo in the Danish account—the Danes
mentioned neither a third ship nor such a holocaust. At some point in the
crossing, the Africans said, a second ship was "lost." Again, the Danes recalled
no such mishap, and according to their account, the two ships remained together.[122] The most dramatic divergence in the African and Danish accounts
emerged in the Africans' description of the fate of the last remaining ship. Juan
alleged that it had been struck by "many bolts of lightning, . . . killing the captain and many people." The Danes also testified about a severe storm, which
had blown them off their intended course to Punta Carreto. But according to

the Danes, the ships had been destroyed by mutineers, not by a storm. They mentioned no lightning strikes; those Danish crew members who perished died from starvation and disease; and neither Captain Diedrich Pfeiff of the *Fredericus Quartus* nor Captain Anders Wærøe of the *Christianus Quintus* had been killed or even injured—indeed, both eventually returned to Denmark.[123]

Some of these discrepancies may be plausibly explained. The sources make no mention of the specific language in which Francisco conducted his interviews; it is possible that he misunderstood, and very likely that he embellished, some of what was told him. The translated testimony as it was preserved can only faintly echo what the Africans said and what they intended by what they said. For example, "Juan" almost certainly never said that he was from "Guinea," and it is unlikely he claimed to be of "casta arará"—Francisco offered these glosses as a translator seeking to distill and convey the sense of what he heard in terms comprehensible to his Spanish-speaking audience.

In the brief accounts they narrated to Francisco, Juan, Nicolás, and Miguel summarized, edited, and recast the horrific events of the past several months. They conspicuously omitted the shipboard slave rebellion, which the crew had punished with execution and torture. They made no mention of the hundreds of Africans who died of disease and starvation or to the many stops the ships made on their wayward journey to Punta Carreto. But the Africans not only failed to relate all they had seen: they related things they had not seen. The captives almost certainly could not have witnessed the destruction of the ships, as they were put ashore on March 4, and the ships were not destroyed until three days later. It seems unlikely that they witnessed the burning of a first ship or the "loss" of a second ship at sea, even the existence of which cannot be verified. In the accounts they offered to Francisco, these Africans meant to tell another story based in their own cultural values and understandings.

By 1710, when testimonies were collected, Francisco had been a slave in Costa Rica for at least eight years, serving two masters in the dangerous work of pearl diving.[124] As a "*ladino* in our Castilian language," he was beyond doubt conversant in Spanish and understood the connotations of the words he chose in translation.[125] Slaves in Costa Rica, even Africans, almost never used words such as "stolen" (*hurtado*) or "taken" (*cogido*) to describe their enslavement. When they did, it was in specific reference to seizure by force. For example, *congo* slave Felipe Cubero, a West Central African, claimed to have been brought to Costa Rica by Spaniards who seized him (*lo cogieron*) on the beach near Cartagena, Colombia, after he ventured outside the city to hunt iguanas.[126] Antonio Civitola, also a congo, said he had been captured (lo cogieron) in Matina by Miskitu Indians who later sold him to his Costa Rican master.[127] Micaela, a Yoruba of *casta aná*, recalled that don Juan Francisco de Ibarra had captured her with many of her shipmates (los cogieron) on the Matina coast.[128] These descriptions all referred to unusual situations in which the Africans had been seized through overpowering force.[129]

The word "stolen" (hurtado) was used yet more rarely; in fact, apart from its usage by Juan, Nicolás, and Miguel, I have found only one other case in which an African used the word to refer to his enslavement. In 1720, Miguel Largo, probably from the upper Slave Coast, testified that he had been "stolen [when he was] little in the mina country" (*lo hurtaron chiquito en la tierra de mina*).[130] Without implying that enslaved Africans were content with their condition in either Africa or America, they came overwhelmingly from societies which recognized the legitimacy and legality of slaveholding in prescribed circumstances.[131] Africans in Costa Rica may have emphasized that they were "stolen" when referring to circumstances in which their enslavement occurred outside the usual mechanisms, such as sale or pawn by kin members, judicial enslavement, or even capture in war, which would have been better translated as "being seized" (*ser cogido*). When Africans claimed to have been "stolen," I suspect that they meant to say something especially pointed by the word: They were free people who had been "stolen" by "thieves" who had no right to hold them as slaves—in this case, the Danes.[132]

Around 1715, an anonymous French observer described the worship of a thunder god, who was said to punish thieves by hurling lightning bolts, by natives of the Slave Coast kingdom of Ouidah.[133] This figures among the first documentary references to So, the Slave Coast god (*vodun*) of thunder and lightning, who is also frequently known as Hevieso due to his original association with the town Hevié.[134] Among the most powerful and feared of all *vodun*, Hevieso visited his vengeance on wrongdoers by hurling his double-edged axes in the form of lightning bolts. When lightning flashed, it was Hevieso striking down a victim with his unerring axe. Trees felled by lightning were believed to be the gathering places of witches, which Hevieso destroyed in order to deny them cover for their evil workings. Hevieso never missed his target. If lightning was sighted but no victim or damage could be found, he had simply struck down a guilty party somewhere else.[135]

Hevieso, the thunder vodun of the Ewe, Aja, and Fon pantheons, is explicitly linked to Shango, the thunder god (*orisha*) of the Yoruba.[136] Indeed, the two share many identical attributes, including the double-edged axe, the hurling of lightning bolts as stone fragments that must be retrieved by priests, and the special vengeance visited on thieves.[137] Although the origins of the relationship between the Slave Coast cults of Hevieso and the Yoruba cults of Shango have not yet been established, by the early eighteenth century, cultural exchange, which included religious elements, between the Slave Coast peoples and the Yoruba was well cemented and perhaps many centuries old.[138] The same anonymous Frenchman who described the worship of the thunder god noted the prominence of Yoruba priests in Ouidah around 1715.[139] Although ultimately the most widely celebrated, Shango was only one of the thunder gods revered by Yoruba-speaking peoples. Jakuta, identified with both Shango and Hevieso by the twentieth century, may once have presided over an older, independent cult. Among western Yoruba in what is now Benin, Ara reigned as the local thunder god before later becoming associated with Shango. Both shared a complex of mythic qualities with Shango and Hevieso, including their punishment of thieves by lightning.[140]

By 1710, thunder gods such as Hevieso, Shango, Jakuta, and Ara were widely venerated and similarly conceived throughout the Slave Coast and western Yorubaland. The thunder god controlled a fearful natural force which he unleashed, not at random but directed at his enemies who violated earthly laws. When Africans in Costa Rica claimed they were "stolen," they sought to emphasize that they had been wrongfully enslaved by "thieves" who had no right to their persons. Without any traditionally sanctioned authority, the Danes had torn kinfolk from the lineages to which they belonged. Like witches, for their own selfish and greedy motives, they fomented chaos in society, disordering sacred bonds of kinship and community. The Danes' malicious ability to twist supernatural forces to their own ends became evident in their navigation of the open sea, another world to Slave Coast and Yoruba peoples, who had no seafaring traditions. But other awesome powers existed to meet them. The thunder god avenged such crimes by hurling lightning bolts at the thieves and witches who violated the moral order.

In the religious worldview of the Slave Coast and Yorubaland, the Danes who stole the Africans from their country had incurred the predictable result of a violent thunderstorm. Because they knew the lightning of the thunder god never missed its target, the Africans assured their interviewer that the captain and his crew of manstealers had been struck down in a great storm that restored a measure of justice to the earth.[141] Lightning also destroyed their slave ships, as it felled the trees that sheltered witches, and for the same reason: they harbored evil. The narrative offered by the ararás Juan, Nicolás, and Miguel would have made perfect sense to the aná Agustina and other Yoruba on board. Hidden in its confusing details were traces of the cultural understandings that gave meaning to the shared and particular experiences of enslavement and the Middle Passage that had brought them to Costa Rica.

CHAPTER TWO

Stolen from Their Countries

The Origins of Africans in Costa Rica

✝ ON SEPTEMBER 7, 1719, DON DIEGO DE LA HAYA FERNÁNDEZ, GOVER-nor and captain general of the Province of Costa Rica, summoned an enslaved African man to his presence for interrogation. The governor soon became frustrated, because although the man had come to Costa Rica nine years before on one of the Danish slave ships *Christianus Quintus* or *Fredericus Quartus*, he "does not know the Castilian language." De la Haya found the man called Miguel Largo, of the *mina* nation, to be "unacculturated and very set in his ways" (*bozal y muy cerrado*). De la Haya decided to postpone the interview until such time as an interpreter could be found.[1] Eight months later, an official reported back that after questioning several slaves in the vicinity, he found that even "those of [Miguel's] own nation do not understand him."[2] Unlike many African slaves in the Americas, Miguel apparently had no countrymen nearby—perhaps anywhere in the province—with whom he could share memories. At the end of June 1720, the governor tried again to question Miguel. "Having questioned and re-questioned him," de la Haya wrote, "as far as could be understood, everything boiled down to that they had stolen him when he was little from the *mina* country."[3]

Miguel, probably born on the upper Slave Coast around 1690, appears never to have adapted to his condition as a slave in Costa Rica. He remained what Brazilian historian Katia Mattoso called, apparently without irony, a "maladjusted slave."[4] Miguel might have had many reasons for his taciturnity

Map 4. Major Regions of West and West Central Africa. Map by Mark Van Stone.

in answering the governor's queries in 1719, but in one sense, his answers re-called and resonated with the experience of all captives who came to Costa Rica over the centuries. West and West Central Africans of the seventeenth and eighteenth centuries could not conceive of personal identity apart from community identity. Membership in a family and lineage, descent from com-mon ancestors, veneration of local spirits, roots in ancient homelands—each formed an inseparable component of community life and of an individual's identity in community. Such elements, commemorated and reinforced in innumerable ways in daily life, defined the individual and established his or her place in the visible and unseen worlds.[5]

Miguel and others from what he called the "mina country" shared a complex of objective and subjective characteristics, such as similar language, customs, traditions, social values, belief in a common origin, and territory. All of these traits form components of what social scientists call *ethnicity*.[6] Outsiders, such as the governor, attributed an "external ethnicity" to peoples from a huge geographical area, calling them minas or other names according to perceived fundamental similarities.[7] In their home societies in Africa, however, most men and women like Miguel did not call or consider themselves members of a particular "ethnic group" but people tied to specific lineages, religious practices, customs, and homelands.[8] For millions of African women and men, self-identification and self-naming—the adoption of "internal ethnicities"—emerged from the specific historical processes that brought diverse African peoples together in the era of the slave trade.[9]

Enslavement marked the beginning of diaspora. In many societies, separation from home and family formed the very act that defined one as a slave.[10] A moment of irrecoverable loss, it was also one of new beginnings. From dozens of diverse polities and ethnicities in all the major regions of West and West Central Africa, enslaved men and women began to overcome their vast differences in language and culture from the moment they were torn from their ancestral homelands. When Africans forcibly entered the diaspora through the slave trade, they came to perceive commonalities with men and women they would never have encountered had they not been enslaved. Those elements of their identities most closely tied to lineage and locality could not survive being uprooted by enslavement, but captives soon found and forged new links that became just as important. The traumas of capture and transport to the coast began the processes by which African men and women came to see themselves as belonging to new groups that expanded, literally with almost every step. Separations and recombinations occurred at every stop along the way. Identities and identifications constantly emerged, shifted, dissolved, and became reconstituted. Disruptions, continuities, and reconfigurations of identity began for enslaved African men and women long before they arrived in Costa Rica.

In the Americas, the captives' new perceptions of common languages, beliefs, and practices became yet more inclusive, heralding the formation of what Douglas B. Chambers has called "diasporic ethnicities": "new African-derived

ethnic identities outside the continent."[11] Chambers's formulation acknowl-
edges broad cultural and linguistic commonalities among African peoples
from the same regions but emphasizes that most Africans understood, experienced, and strengthened such commonalities through the processes of enslavement.[12] In the context of slavery, ethnicity must be regarded as an
ever-changing rather than a fixed identity that underwent important shifts in
response to turning points in the captives' experience of enslavement, the slave
trade, and, later, American slavery.[13] The concept of diasporic ethnicity, an
identity drawing both on the African pasts and the American presents of the
captives, provides a useful point of entry to the consciousness of enslaved
Africans in the New World.

     Questions of identity and identification are paramount to understanding
slavery through the "ethnic lens," but establishing how Africans defined
themselves as opposed to how others defined them—distinguishing between
internal and external ethnicity—is an unavoidably difficult, sometimes impossible, task.[14] The relative absence of ethnic designations attributed to
"black" women and men in Costa Rican documents presents a grave problem
to the researcher of African ethnicity in the colony. In 505 notarial documents, such as testaments, dowry inventories, donation certificates, mortgage
notes, and others pertaining to "blacks" from 1607 to 1750, 56 percent contain
no reference to continent of birth, let alone ethnicity.[15] To some extent, conclusions about the relevance of ethnicity among the enslaved in Costa Rica
must therefore remain tentative.

     The names used by slave traders and masters to refer to regional and
ethnic origins provide clues to captives' self-ascribed identities but also pose
special problems.[16] Known as "national" or casta names in Spanish America,
they cannot be assumed uncritically to refer to specific African origins but
need to be interpreted in the context of the slave trade that produced them.[17]
Wherever possible, casta names should be compared with other evidence—
including specific information on contemporary political events in Africa,
knowledge of patterns in the Atlantic slave trade of the time, and in the best
case, with the ethnic identities claimed by the Africans themselves.[18]

     The impact of African ethnicities in the New World varied widely ac-
cording to specific local conditions. As leading Africanist historian Joseph
Miller writes, these determined whether "enough people of the right sort, at
the right moment, and in the right circumstances could make effective use
of experiences in their former lives." Whether slaves in the Americas could
draw meaningfully on their past experiences of Africa depended on events

within that continent, patterns in the Atlantic slave trade, and local conditions in the receiving societies.[19] Many of the transformations in identity that Africans in Costa Rica underwent were common to enslaved Africans everywhere in the diaspora. The nature of the slave trade to Costa Rica and the character of slavery within Costa Rica, however, held even more profound consequences for African women and men, who quickly came to identify with others of different origins, rapidly transforming their own identities in the process.

Reflecting changing patterns in the Atlantic slave trade, the ethnic composition of the African population of Costa Rica varied widely over time. The terms employed to describe the Africans reflected this dynamic. The first enslaved black people to enter Costa Rica came with the conquistadores. Most were not Africans at all but creoles from the Iberian Peninsula and elsewhere in Spanish America. A few came as personal attendants to the Spanish conquerors and remained strongly identified with their powerful masters, reproducing a pattern of patron-client relations prevalent in most African societies.[20] As elsewhere in Spanish America, black expeditionaries became embroiled in conflicts among conquistadores, sometimes influencing the outcome of political events and collecting rewards from grateful patrons—again, the continuation of a characteristic feature of slavery in Africa. At least one conquistador of African descent received an encomienda in Costa Rica, a rare distinction for men of color. This first generation—the "charter generation"—of enslaved and free blacks and mulattos formed an integral part of Costa Rica's rapidly developing creole culture.[21]

Other slaves, more likely to be African born, were soon brought to provide the backbreaking labor necessary to establish settlements. Virtually all of these earliest forced immigrants arrived by way of Panama or Nicaragua, imported in small groups under special licenses issued to Spanish immigrants to the New World. The scant documentation surviving from the sixteenth and early seventeenth centuries suggests that, as in the rest of Spanish America, men and women from Upper Guinea predominated among the earliest Africans in Costa Rica. Along with natives of the Bight of Biafra, they maintained a small but constant presence in early colonial Costa Rica. Like the early attempts to settle the region generally, several sixteenth-century plans to import large numbers of African slaves to Costa Rica came to nothing. Although present throughout the colony, enslaved black immigrants came to sixteenth-century Costa Rica individually or in small groups as involuntary companions of Spanish conquistadores and officials.

When the Portuguese shifted their slaving operations to West Central Africa in the late sixteenth and early seventeenth centuries, men and women called *angolas*, many of them Kimbundu-speakers from a relatively small area along the Kwanza River, emerged as the clear majority among Africans imported to Costa Rica, as in other parts of the Americas.[22] As other European nations entered the Atlantic slave trade in the mid-seventeenth century, the supply of African captives increased dramatically. West Central Africans continued to predominate but came from an ever-expanding area and reflected an increasing ethnic heterogeneity. As slave traders acquired captives from other areas of the continent, men and women from the Gold Coast and Slave Coast began to arrive in significant numbers.[23] By the early eighteenth century, Costa Rica's capital of Cartago and the Caribbean Matina Valley hosted sizeable concentrations of Africans. However, no single ethnic group or even region of origin predominated. Arriving in small numbers and coming from diverse ethnic backgrounds, Africans in Costa Rica could not maintain or recreate their home cultures and communities. Instead, they quickly began to form new kinds of relationships and identities based in the shared experience of enslavement.

Creoles: Slaves and Conquerors

The first black man who arrived in Costa Rica came not on a slave ship but with some of the first Europeans to explore the Americas, years before the "discoveries" of Mexico or Peru. "Diego el Negro" arrived at Cariari or Cariaí, now Puerto Limón, on September 17, 1502, as a "cabin boy" (*grumete*) aboard the caravel *Capitana*, one of four ships commanded by Admiral Christopher Columbus on the latter's fourth and final voyage to the New World.[24] Little is known of Diego except that he served on the *Capitana*'s crew, that he was the only man on any of the ships designated as a "negro," and that later, on November 2, 1505, a *cédula* issued in the name of King Fernando ordered that Diego be paid 15,133 *maravedíes* (about 445 "pieces of eight") for his labors on the voyage.[25] It is not known specifically what work he performed on board the ship, nor his activities on American shores—indeed, we cannot even be certain that he came ashore in Costa Rica. Ordered to be paid on his own account for his work on the voyage, Diego was probably not a slave. But as a "cabin boy," Diego may well have performed work that was also undertaken by slaves. It is possible that Diego was born in Africa;

the Portuguese referred to sailors from the seafaring peoples of Senegambia, Upper Guinea, or Cape Verde, whom they hired, as "grumetes."[26] More likely, he was one of the thousands of black creoles born in Iberia since the Portuguese had begun importing slaves directly from West Africa in the 1440s, one of the children and grandchildren of West Africans who had survived the Middle Passage to Europe.[27] By 1500, slaves of African descent made up roughly one tenth of Seville's population, and for decades after the discovery of the New World, Seville remained an obligatory stopping point for slaves bound for the Indies.[28] A 1501 decree by Their Catholic Majesties Fernando and Isabel permitted the introduction only of slaves "born in the power of Christians, our subjects and natives."[29]

Likely born in Iberia, Diego's name indicates that he had been baptized a Christian. Whatever his birthplace, he had lived in Spain and was able to communicate in the Spanish language. Although nothing is known about Diego's reasons for embarking on the *Capitana*, we do know that he completed the voyage and returned with the ship to Hispaniola on August 7, 1505.[30] Although he participated as a subordinate in the exploration and conquest, he remained clearly identified with the Spaniards with whom he came and was recognized by the king for his labors. The first of the black men who arrived in Costa Rica, Diego came as both servant and conqueror.[31]

From the beginning, black men such as Diego accompanied the conquistadores as armed and unarmed auxiliaries. Almost immediately following the first settlements, Spaniards imported larger numbers of enslaved Africans for essential work such as clearing paths through the forests and building roads and settlements. Throughout the sixteenth century, as parties of conquistadores set out to explore Costa Rica from Panama and Nicaragua, they continued to include small numbers of black slaves. The few black slaves who entered Costa Rica in the first decades of the sixteenth century had lived in Spain or other Spanish colonies. As a result, their cultural skills and knowledge were similar to those of Spaniards in the New World as well as in the Old.

These early black arrivals adapted rapidly to their new environment in Costa Rica. In July 1528, the celebrated chronicler Gonzalo Fernández de Oviedo y Valdés left Managua for the Nicoya Peninsula, accompanied by a Spanish servant, two male black slaves, an enslaved black woman, and a number of indigenous slaves.[32] Oviedo's *Historia general y natural* not only establishes the presence of black slaves in Nicoya by that date but indicates that some had already learned indigenous languages and customs. When he cut himself on some rocks, Oviedo suffered from a deep gash the length of his foot that made walking extremely painful. With no access to Spanish medical treatment, Oviedo feared he would become permanently lame even if he did not have to amputate the foot; he might even die from his injury. The enslaved black woman told Oviedo that "the Indians said" cocoa butter was good for dressing sores and offered to apply some to his wound. After a few weeks' rest in Nicoya, Oviedo found himself completely healed. Impressed with the curative powers of the cocoa butter, he made the black slave woman extract the unguent from two *fanegas* (3.1 bushels) of cacao pods, which "she knew well how to do."[33] Within a colonial context of conquest and slavery, this enslaved black woman, unnamed in the documents, had adapted to her local environment to become an agent of cultural exchange between peoples of Africa, Europe, and America.

From the beginning, enslaved people of African descent took part in the conquest of Costa Rica, but their numbers remained in the dozens, in contrast to, for example, the thousands of black slaves who accompanied the invading armies in Peru.[34] A few enslaved blacks, most of them creoles, accompanied the conquistadores as body servants. When more secular and ecclesiastical officials began to arrive after the conquest of the Central Valley in the 1560s, black and mulatto slaves formed part of their entourages, imported under individual licenses from the Crown.[35] In 1573, for example, Governor Diego de Artieda Chirinos received a *real cédula* authorizing him to import twenty black slaves to Costa Rica "for the service of [your] person and home and for whatever may be most convenient to do in the said province." The following year he received permission from the Council of the Indies to bring a mulatto slave, Gaspar, and an enslaved black man, Luis, to Costa Rica. Both had previously served Artieda in Mexico.[36] Under the individual licensing system, the Crown attempted to strictly regulate the number of captives imported to the Indies. Captain Gonzalo Pérez of the *Nuestra Señora de la Concepción*, for example, received permission to sail from Sanlúcar de Barrameda to Costa Rica in 1575 with his enslaved black page, Lázaro, only on the condition that the black man return to Spain on the first available ship.[37] A very few enslaved black women can be proved to have accompanied the early Spanish expeditions to Costa Rica. Black maids, cooks, and sometimes concubines must have come in greater numbers than the documents reflect.[38] Strongly identified with their masters, slave men inevitably became implicated in the conflicts between Spaniards and local Indians. In 1610, for example, Juan Gallardo, a mulatto slave of don Diego de Sojo, joined in sacking the Cabécar Indians' most sacred temple for gold. The desecration provoked the Cabécares to kill Gallardo and several others, igniting a general Indian rebellion that expelled the Spaniards from Talamanca for decades.[39]

Extraordinarily but not uniquely,[40] mulattos constituted a plurality and probably a majority of Costa Rica's slave population. Although data are extremely fragmentary before the 1650s, from that decade on, the proportion of mulattos in Costa Rican notarial documents either equaled or exceeded that of "blacks" among slaves for whom information on race was recorded. Of 1,620 testaments, dowry inventories, donation certificates, mortgage notes, and other documents recorded between 1607 and 1750, five hundred (31 percent) fail to note the race or color of the slave. Five hundred and five (31 percent) referred to blacks, 599 (about 37 percent) referred to mulattos,

TABLE 2.1. Race or Color of Slaves by Decade, 1607–1750 (Percentages in parentheses)

DECADE	RACE AND COLOR UNKNOWN	MULATTO*	BLACK	TOTAL
1600	0 (0)	0 (0)	1 (100)	1
1610	0 (0)	0 (0)	0 (0)	0
1620	0 (0)	7 (64)	4 (36)	11
1630	3 (33)	1 (11)	3 (56)	9
1640	6 (35)	3 (18)	8 (47)	17
1650	14 (36)	12 (32)	12 (32)	38
1660	18 (21)	39 (46)	28 (33)	85
1670	19 (24)	29 (37)	30 (39)	78
1680	15 (15)	55 (54)	32 (31)	102
1690	32 (20)	83 (51)	47 (29)	162
1700	26 (12)	113 (51)	81 (37)	220
1710	132 (34)	126 (33)	127 (33)	385
1720	88 (43)	61 (30)	56 (27)	205
1730	80 (47)	44 (26)	47 (27)	171
1740–1750	67 (49)	42 (31)	27 (20)	136
Total, 1600–1750	500 (31)	615* (38)	505 (31)	1,620

* Includes sixteen zambos.

TABLE 2.2. Gender of Slaves by Decade, 1607–1750 (Percentages in parentheses)

DECADE	UNKNOWN	FEMALE	MALE	TOTAL SLAVES
1600	0 (0)	0 (0)	1 (1)	1
1610	0 (0)	0 (0)	0 (0)	0
1620	0 (0)	2 (18)	9 (82)	11
1630	0 (0)	4 (44)	5 (56)	9
1640	0 (0)	10 (59)	7 (41)	17
1650	0 (0)	25 (66)	13 (34)	38
1660	0 (0)	53 (62)	32 (38)	85
1670	3 (4)	46 (59)	29 (37)	78
1680	0 (0)	51 (50)	51 (50)	102
1690	1 (1)	94 (58)	67 (41)	162
1700	0 (0)	103 (47)	117 (53)	220
1710	8 (2)	168 (44)	209 (54)	385
1720	0 (0)	93 (45)	112 (55)	205
1730	6 (3)	92 (54)	73 (43)	171
1740–1750	0 (0)	58 (43)	78 (57)	136
Total, 1600–1750	18 (1)	799 (49)	803 (50)	1,620

and sixteen (less than 1 percent) to zambos (people of mixed African and indigenous descent).[41] Of the "blacks," eighty-six (5 percent of all slaves) were specified as creole. The creole population, then, black and mulatto, comprised at least 42 percent of the total slave population; Africans made up a minimum of about 9 percent.

Another highly unusual characteristic of Costa Rica's slave population is the high proportion of females recorded between 1607 and 1750. In several decades, females made up a clear majority of slaves recorded in testaments, dowry inventories, and other documents. Only in the 1710s and 1720s—after the arrival of the *Fredericus Quartus* and *Christianus Quintus*, during a period of intensive smuggling, and among the decades that saw the highest cacao production—did records of males exceed those of females by as much as 10 percent. Over the long term, the numbers of female and male slaves recorded in the documents proved almost exactly equal (799 females versus 803 males).

These findings hold important implications for the study of creolization in Costa Rica, both in the sense of the creation of a colonial culture deriving from many sources and in the procreation of a predominantly American-born slave population. By the mid-seventeenth century and probably earlier, newly arrived Africans found themselves surrounded by a larger group of slaves of creole origin (mulattos and blacks), as well as free blacks and mulattos, ladino Indians, Spaniards, and mestizos, who shared a common culture. Of necessity, Africans rapidly adapted to the majority culture regardless of their ethnic origins. An equal or high ratio of males to females suggests at least the possibility of the natural reproduction of the slave population, which would also be consistent with a majority of creoles in the slave population. As there is very little evidence to suggest that African parents passed on elements of their native cultures to their children, slave children who were creoles were brought up with the "principles and ideals" of the dominant culture.[42] Both these factors favored the rapid and profound assimilation of Africans and their descendants to the Costa Rican creole culture that was forming by the seventeenth century.

The "charter generation" of enslaved men and women, blacks and mulattos, born in Europe, Africa, or America, immediately became a vital part of the Costa Rican creole society they helped to found. Like their masters, most of these men and women had already lived in Spain or other Spanish American colonies. They understood the language, logics, and rules of Spanish society, including those that governed slavery, even as they helped to shape them. Living and working closely with Spaniards, Indians, mestizos, mulattos, and creole slaves, the first Africans to reach Costa Rica learned the rules of their new surroundings quickly. Spanish-speaking, baptized Catholics, bound to a particular slaveholding household, working at tasks determined by the unique local environment, the rapidly creolizing charter generations were able to draw on their hard-won experiences to help those who followed them adapt to slavery in Costa Rica.[43]

The First Africans: Upper Guinea

Like the early creoles, some of the first Africans brought to the New World had previously lived in the Iberian Peninsula. To varying degrees, these earliest enslaved African immigrants had already learned something of Portuguese or Spanish culture. In the first half of the sixteenth century, a

majority of captives exported into the Atlantic slave trade came from Upper
Guinea, particularly Senegambia, the sub-Saharan region first contacted by
the Portuguese in the 1440s. Captives known as *jolofos* formed the largest
group of those black Africans imported to Spain who were identified by casta
or "nation," and with the so-called discovery of the New World, Africans
who had lived in Spain comprised a large proportion of those taken to the
Americas in the first decades of the conquest.[44] As demand for African slaves
increased with the establishment of Spanish colonies, growing numbers of
captives came to the Americas directly from West Africa.

Europeans employed the name "jolofo" (also *gelofe, gilofo, jalof, jolof,*
and other variations) to refer to subjects of the Jolof Empire founded by the
legendary Njaajaan Njaay in the thirteenth century. A loose confederation
of six densely populated states, each of which held from 50,000 to as many
as 75,000 people, Jolof united most of the territories between the Senegal
and Gambia Rivers at its height in the fifteenth century.[45] In early modern
Senegambia, the name "Jolof" referred to this political entity; in the present
day, "*Wolof*" refers to the ethnic group that dominated its territory demographically and politically. Minorities of other origins, principally the indigenous non-Muslim Sereer, as well as small groups of Manding traders,
Fulbe pastoralists, and Moorish scholars from the Sahara, also lived within
Jolof territories. Despite potential ethnic, linguistic, and cultural differences, Jolof's inhabitants shared a strong regional identity. "Nowhere" in
Senegambia, writes Senegalese historian Boubacar Barry, "did any Wolof,
Manding, Peul, Tukulor, Sereer, Joola or other ethnic group feel they were
strangers."[46] European slave traders also assumed an essential unity, applying the name jolofo to all groups living within the Jolof Empire.[47] Thousands
of captives entered the early Atlantic slave trade under the name jolofo.
Most were ethnic Wolof, but others were members of the other ethnic
groups living in Jolof, especially the Sereer.

Pedro Gilofo became the first recorded *cimarrón* (runaway slave) in
Costa Rican territory, absconding for more than twenty days to the "Indians
of war" in 1540.[48] At least one jolofo slave in Costa Rica continued to identify
with an Islamic past in the early seventeenth century. To their great amuse-
ment, Manuel *de tierra jolof* told a festive gathering of Spaniards in 1609 that
he refused to "deny Bujame" (Muhammad).[49] Despite Manuel's profession
of faith, there is no direct evidence that he continued to practice his religion
in Costa Rica, nor are there known records of other jolofos or Muslims in the
province at the time. Although the records of Pedro's and Manuel's actions

suggest a jolofo determination to resist slavery and maintain a cultural heritage, their extreme rarity also indicates the paucity of jolofos in the province and suggests their inability to unite with countrymen to preserve an ethnic- or religious-based identity and, consequently, an obligatory adaptation to creole society.

Larger numbers of Upper Guinea natives arrived in Costa Rica by the early seventeenth century, reflecting the steady growth of the Atlantic slave trade. Africans identified as *mandinga* appear in Costa Rican documents as early as 1619.[50] Like the name "jolofo," "mandinga" represented an apparently straightforward ethnic name that in fact was employed by European slave traders to refer to a broad geographical area encompassing many ethnic groups.[51] The Manding (also Mandingo, Mandinka, Malinke) were a Mande-speaking ethnic group originally native to a small area along the left bank of the Niger River. In the early thirteenth century, legendary king Sundiata founded the Mali Empire, which at its height in the fourteenth century extended over the entire Sahel-Sudan region of West Africa, from the Manding homeland in modern Mali to the Atlantic and from Mauritania in the north to Guinea-Bissau in the south. Subjects of provinces of the Mali Empire included Moorish Arabs, Berbers and Tuareg, Fulbe and Tukulor, Wolof, Bamana (Bambara), and Dogon, as well as the majority, ethnic Manding.[52]

The Portuguese used "mandinga" to refer to people from all areas of West Africa still under the waning influence of Mali, especially the states along the River Gambia. Along the Atlantic coast, captives called mandinga came from an area extending from the north bank of the Gambia to the Rio Cacheu in Guinea-Bissau, or even further south, to the Biafara territories along the Geba River.[53]

European slave traders persistently, if not always accurately, associated the mandinga with Islam, as they did the less Islamized jolofo. Some European slavers applied the name "mandinga" to all Muslims of Upper Guinea, transforming it from a marker of ethnicity to one of religion.[54] Like most African "ethnic" names used in the Americas, the term "mandinga" referred to different peoples over time and even at the same time, assuming different meanings according to the origins and knowledge of the slave traders and masters who used it. "Mandinga" could refer to the Manding themselves or to captives sold to European slave traders by Mande-speaking Muslim merchants from the Senegambia to Sierra Leone. As a result, Walter Rodney and others argued that many captives came to the Americas "incorrectly designated as Mandinga."[55] French factor André Brüe claimed in 1723

that the Manding *never* sold their own people; *all* of the captives brought by
Manding to the coast, he asserted, were Bambara (Bamana) from the far in-
terior of modern Mali, a people who for centuries violently resisted conver-
sion to Islam.[56] In fact, the term "mandinga" could refer to members of what
Michael Gomez has called "a plethora of ethnicities" from whom the
Manding drew captives.[57]

This diversity, however, can be overdrawn. Manding, Bamana, and
Dyula, spoken along a vast arc extending through the modern countries of
The Gambia, Senegal, Guinea-Bissau, Guinea (Conakry), Mali, Liberia,
Sierra Leone, and Côte d'Ivoire, are generally mutually intelligible and have
often been considered regional variants of a single Manding language.[58]
Muslims separated by great distances in Upper Guinea shared a faith that
transcended ethnicity and geography. Their beliefs and practices would to
some extent have been familiar to non-Muslims from those areas as well.
Muslim holy men earned the respect of non-Muslims throughout Upper
Guinea for their literacy, knowledge of pharmacology, and the efficacy of the
magical charms they commonly made and sold.[59] A handful of Africans
called mandingas continued to arrive in Costa Rica throughout the seventeenth and well into the eighteenth century.[60]

Non-Muslims from further south in Upper Guinea were known in Costa
Rica as blacks of the *nación de los ríos* or *casta de los ríos*, another geographic
name referring to a vast area between the Senegal and Geba rivers,
encompassing the modern states of Senegal, The Gambia, and Guinea-Bissau.[61]
Many ethnic and linguistic groups shared these territories, but centuries of
contact between peoples such as the Balanta, Biafada, Papel, Bijagó, and Brame
resulted in a shared regional culture that became especially strong in the
diaspora.[62] Many Papel (Bran), for example, could speak Banhum, Casanga,
Balanta, Mande, and Biafara. Balanta often spoke Papel and Mande, and Nalu
usually understood Biafara.[63] The Casanga ethnic group, who occupied a
"narrow strip of territory" between the Casamance and Cacheu rivers on both
sides of the modern Senegal-Guinea-Bissau border, likely gave their name to
the Casamance kingdom and river.[64] Juan Cacanga, the black father of a free
mulatta girl confirmed in Cartago in 1625, may have belonged to this ethnic
group.[65] Casanga were also sometimes "erroneously considered Mandinga."[66]
The related Banhum (Bagnoun) people, also from the Casamance River Delta
in southern Senegal, became known in Mexico and Ecuador as *bañol*, and in
Costa Rica as *bañón* and *buñón*.[67] Sixteenth- and seventeenth-century sources
described the Biafara (also Biafada and Beafara, not to be confused with Biafra

in eastern Nigeria) as living in an area south of the Geba River that extended eastward from the coast to the lower Corubal River (also in Guinea-Bissau). Both the frequent victims of Bijagó slave raids and prodigious slave traders themselves, *biafara* appeared frequently in sixteenth-century documents in most of Spanish America—including in Cuba, Mexico, Guatemala, Panama, Colombia, Venezuela, Ecuador, and Peru—but only rarely in Costa Rica.[68]

Slaves known in colonial Spanish America as *bran* came from several ethnic groups now known as Brame, Manjak, Papel, and Mankanya.[69] From a small area in western Guinea-Bissau and the extreme south of Senegal, the bran contributed "staggering numbers" of captives to the Atlantic slave trade and figured prominently among the few Africans of Upper Guinea origin in Costa Rica.[70] The name appears as the surname of slaves in Costa Rica as early as 1602, when Francisco Bran stood as godfather to thirteen individuals.[71] Almost uniquely among African names, Bran persisted as a surname among free descendants of African slaves in Costa Rica. Diego Bran served as a soldier

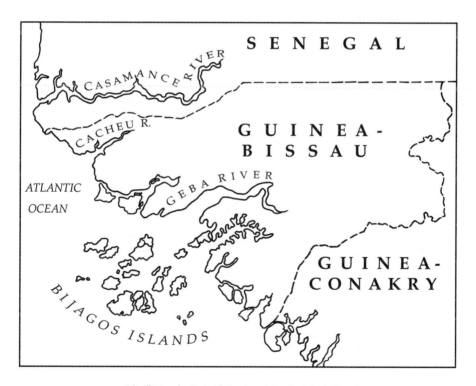

Map 5. The "Ríos de Guiné" Region. Map by Mark Van Stone.

in the free mulatto militia in Esparza from the 1720s through the 1740s; José Bran of Bagaces was a master shoemaker in 1747.[72]

The name *biojo*, also found in Costa Rican documents, derived originally from Bijagó, the name of an ethnic group indigenous to the Bijagós (Bissagos) Islands just off the coast of Guinea-Bissau at the mouth of the Geba River. Renowned boatbuilders and fishermen, by the seventeenth century, the Bijagó had redirected their traditional activities overwhelmingly to slave raiding on the mainland and re-exported large numbers of Upper Guinea Africans from several ports throughout the islands. Europeans applied the name "biojo" both to the Bijagó themselves and to their victims, including Biafaras, Balantas, and Nalus. Slave traders complained that like other Africans of Upper Guinea, biojos proved rebellious and prone to suicide.[73]

In the sixteenth and early seventeenth centuries, many of the captives exported from the Guinea River region into the Atlantic slave trade left by way of the Cape Verde Islands—overwhelmingly from the island of Santiago, a major transshipping point for slaves to the Americas. From the mid-fifteenth century, slave traders used the name *cabo verde* to refer to men and women exported from Cape Verde who had been kidnapped from the same Upper Guinea societies discussed above. In 1466, the Portuguese king authorized colonists in the islands to export captives from the *"rios de Guiné"* regions of the adjacent mainland.[74] Although slavers paid more for captives in the islands than when they travelled directly to the Upper Guinea coast, the cabo verdes presented several advantages from the Europeans' point of view. Historian T. Bentley Duncan wrote that captives purchased at Cape Verde "had already endured the trauma of their first sea passage; their bonds with the mainland were already loosened; their incentive for escape was weakened, and the opportunity to do so much diminished. The slave trader at Santiago found perhaps a more resigned, a more bewildered, and a more manageable slave cargo than he would have found on the Guiné coast."[75] Natives of Upper Guinea exported by way of Cape Verde had already undergone some of the dehumanizing "seasoning" that American masters found essential to reduce free African men and women to their status as slaves. As that process pushed them together in their suffering, however, they drew on strengths they already shared. Most people in the region known as *los ríos* lived in small polities or decentralized societies, but these were linked by central markets, and many people were bi- or multilingual. Facility in more than one language was of incalculable value in allowing people of different origins to help each other share the burdens of captivity during the weeks or months in Cape Verde and beyond.

Although most cabo verde captives were soon exported, some remained in the islands long enough to absorb and contribute to a new culture forged from elements originating in Upper Guinea, Portugal, and shared experiences of enslavement. Known locally as *crioulos*, these other men and women whom slave traders and masters called cabo verdes had spent years enslaved in the islands, learned creole Portuguese, and practiced Catholicism. Still others, often descended from local Portuguese men and mainland African women, had been born into the Luso-African creole culture of the islands and had never lived in an indigenous African society.[76] Cartago slave Ramón Durán no doubt came from one of the latter two groups; sometimes taken for a *criollo* (crioulo), he was elsewhere identified as a cabo verde.[77] An extremely imprecise, generic label, the name cabo verde concealed significant ethnic, cultural, linguistic, religious, and even racial differences.[78] Nevertheless, the Spanish Crown regarded the cabo verdes as sufficiently homogeneous, and sufficiently undesirable, to forbid their importation to Spanish America after 1702, a prohibition that remained in effect for six years.[79]

As demonstrated in the variety of casta names with which they designated them, Spanish slave masters recognized an impressive ethnic diversity among Africans from Upper Guinea—perhaps an indication that Upper Guinea natives themselves emphasized their locally based identities more than captives of other regional origins.[80] Some names, such as bañón, readily corresponded to identifiable ethnic groups. Others, such as jolofo and mandinga, although initially deriving from a specific ethnic group, came to apply more loosely to people of varied origins. Seemingly straightforward identifications, such as the casta name "jolofo" with the Wolof ethnic group or "mandinga" with the Manding, need to be assessed in the light of other contemporary evidence on the movements of Senegambian peoples, the nature and extent of warfare between societies, and their involvement in the Atlantic slave trade, to name a few considerations. Names such as "biojo" or "mandinga" might refer to the African peoples who sold slaves or to captives of other ethnic origins whom they enslaved and sold. Most general were names deriving from geographic locations, such as "de los ríos" and "cabo verde." These terms corresponded not to the ethnic origins of enslaved Africans but to centers of the slave trade and provide only indirect indications of the ethnic origins of the men and women to whom they were applied.

TABLE 2.3. Casta Names as Recorded in Costa Rican Documents, 1603–1748

CASTA NAME AS RECORDED IN COSTA RICA	NUMBER OF REFERENCES	YEARS OF FIRST AND LAST REFERENCE
Upper Guinea		
Bañón, Buñón	3	1613, 1705
Biafara	1	1603
Biojo	2	1688, 1696
Bran	8	1602, 1740
Cabo Verde	6	1688, 1725
Cacanga	1	1625
Cancán	2	1739
De los Ríos	2	1674, 1679
Fulupo	1	1711
Gilofo, Jolof	2	1540, 1610
Mandinga	7	1619, 1722
Sape	1	1656
Total	34	
West Central Africa		
Angola	35	1607, 1719
Congo	106	1648, 1744
Congo Braco	1	1701
Loango	3	1682, 1722
Matamba	1	1686, 1688
Yaga	2	1719
Total	148	
Gold Coast		
Mina	75*	1674, 1748
Slave Coast		
Aná, Saná	13	1711, 1720
Arará	33	1675, 1731
Barbá	1	1719
Lucumí	3	1613, 1720
Mina	75*	1674, 1747
Nangu	16	1710
Popo	12	1700, 1733
Total	77 (152*)	

Bight of Biafra		
Carabalí	12	1613, 1746
Ibo	2	1744
Monco	1	1744
Total	15	

*Mina may include people from the Slave Coast as well as the Gold Coast. All should be excluded from a conservative estimate of the Slave Coast.

Sources: Andrés Vega Bolaños, ed., *Colección Somoza*, vol. 6 (Madrid: 1540); Fernández, *Colección de documentos*, 8:484 (1688); ACMSJ, LBC, no. 1 (1594–1680); ACMSJ, Confirmaciones de Cartago (1625); ACMSJ, SFASDE, Caja 20 (1692, 1696, 1719); AGCA, A3 (6), exp. 124, leg. 10 (1604); AGN, Inq., vol. 474, exp. 6 (1610); ANCR, C. 11 (1638); C. 109 (1700), C. 113 (1702), C. 187 (1710), C. 211 (1713), C. 231 (1710), C. 233 (1710), C. 234 (1710), C. 224, 231, 232, 240, 243, 251, 259, 262, 265 (all 1719), C. 292 (1722), C. 455 (1744); ANCR, CC 243 (1711), CC 250 (1710); CC 3798 (1734), CC 3864 (1740), CC 4075 (1719); CC 3919 (1686), CC 243 (1711), CC 250 (1710), CC 3792 (1726), CC 3919 (1686), CC 4111 (1718); CC 4121 (1720); ANCR, G. 34 (1613), G. 55 (1624), G. 185 (1710), G. 187 (1716), G. 188 (1700, 1710); MCC 774 (1711), MCC 1052 (1738); ANCR, PC 801 (1607)–PC 915 (1736); ANCR, PH 573 (1721)–594 (1749); ANCR, PSJ 411 (1721)–415 (1738); *Indices de los protocolos de Cartago*, vols. 1–3.

Because of their small numbers and, in part, because of their ethnic diversity, most natives of Upper Guinea resident in Costa Rica quickly adapted to their local environments in Costa Rica—the earliest, in particular, joining the established creole slaves who took their place among Indian, free mulatto, and mestizo servants. A few Upper Guinea Africans resisted rather than adapted to slavery. In the mid-sixteenth century, Pedro Gilofo immediately perceived a common interest with the Indians resisting Spanish invaders in Talamanca. The natives, however, probably viewed him as an undesirable alien, and it was very likely their rejection of him that forced him to return to the Spanish camp, paying with his life for his unsuccessful escape.[81] More usually, it seems that slaves born in Upper Guinea found it relatively easy to blend in to their Spanish-dominated surroundings. By 1603, slave Juan Biafara fit into the mixed labor system on a hacienda near Nandayure on the Nicoya Peninsula, speaking Spanish and working alongside Indian laborers.[82] Manuel *de tierra jolof* showed an easy cultural conversance, joking with Spaniards as he served them at a fiesta in the pueblo of Pacaca in 1609.[83]

Natives of other regions of Upper Guinea also became culturally fluent, earning the trust of their masters. Jacobo, who declared himself a mandinga, came to Costa Rica from Martinique around 1706. He had lived among

Europeans long enough to train in their tradition of stonemasonry, and he became so thoroughly acculturated that his master took him for a creole.[84] The West African known at various times in his life as Raimundo, Ramón Durán, and Ramón Calvo was already a grown man when he was baptized in Cartago in 1687. In 1719, by then about fifty and known as Ramón, he took advantage of a trip to Panama to flee, remaining at large for more than a year. When his mistress authorized an agent to apprehend him, she described Ramón as a creole. Although Costa Rican masters commonly lied to conceal the origins of slaves imported illegally, in this case, Ramón's mistress had every reason to describe her fugitive property as accurately as possible. If she knew herself that Ramón had been born in Africa, she must have considered his foreign origins imperceptible to strangers. When he purchased his freedom at the age of fifty-five in 1725, however, Ramón called himself a cabo verde.[85] In general, Africans from Upper Guinea quickly joined their American-born fellow slaves and servants as permanent subordinates in Costa Rican society. Several became so integrated that observers could not distinguish them from their creole companions.

West Central Africans

Although all the regions of Western Africa were represented among the enslaved population of Costa Rica, West Central Africa contributed the largest proportion of captives by far. As in other parts of the Americas, West Central Africans arrived early and comprised a clear majority of the enslaved African population throughout the early and mid-colonial period.[86]

In the early seventeenth century, the majority of West Central Africans—indeed, of all Africans—imported to Costa Rica were known as angolas. In this period, most of these men and women were Kimbundu speakers of agricultural background from a relatively small, hilly area around the Kwanza River.[87] Angola was used to refer to captives exported from Luanda, who left Africa in increasingly large numbers after 1580.[88] They entered the Atlantic slave trade as victims of the "widespread community breakdown, refugee flight, and uncontrolled banditry and raiding" that dominated life in the region during the period coinciding with the Portuguese monopoly of the slave trade to Spanish America (1595–1640).[89]

Angolas appear often in records after 1600. The earliest surviving record of a slave sale in Cartago, in 1607, was of Juan, a native "of the angola country."[90] By 1612, María Angola had given birth to a creole daughter, Isabel, in Cartago.[91] Angolas were also found in the Pacific region. Four angola slaves—Pedro, Francisco, Juan, and María—lived in the household of their master near the bustling Nandayure shipyards on the Nicoya Peninsula at the time Juan Martín de Montalvo made his will in 1623.[92]

Although Panamanian officials registered the name "congo" as early as 1565, if not before, very few Africans known as congos arrived in Costa Rica before 1650.[93] According to specialist John K. Thornton, before the mid-seventeenth century, slaves exported into the Atlantic trade from Kongo were "almost always" drawn from beyond the kingdom's borders.[94] By the 1660s, however, increasing numbers of people—ultimately hundreds of

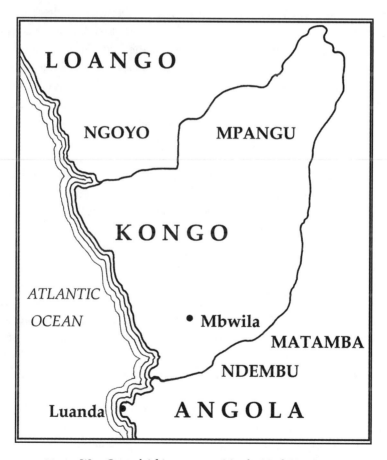

Map 6. West Central Africa, ca. 1650. Map by Mark Van Stone.

thousands—from within the Kingdom of Kongo were shipped across the Atlantic. The increasing enslavement of people within the kingdom's borders reflected the impending breakdown of the old order.[95] The defeat of Kongo forces by the Portuguese in the battle of Mbwila (Ambuíla) in 1665 marked the beginning of a half-century of destructive civil wars that resulted in the enslavement and export of hundreds of thousands of Kongo subjects. The new social and political order that eventually arose in Kongo based its power precisely on "mediating between the interior and the coast in the rapidly developing Atlantic slave trade."[96] From the 1670s, congos appeared regularly in all types of Costa Rican documents, surpassing angolas, and in all probability many of these men and women did come from the kingdom of Kongo.

Men and women from West Central Africa, overwhelmingly described as congos and angolas, far outnumbered natives of other African regions of origin in colonial Costa Rica. To a large extent, their predominance reflected the enormous scale of Portuguese slave trading in Angola and Kongo, as well as the expansion of slaving activities by the British, Dutch, and French in the region by the mid-seventeenth century. As well, Costa Rica's marginal involvement in the slave trade and the relative poverty of potential slave buyers in the colony favored imports of West Central Africans, whom wealthier buyers saw as undesirable and passed over for captives of other origins. Richer Peruvians and Panamanians could always outbid Costa Ricans for choice slaves. By the early seventeenth century and long after, slave masters almost universally accounted congos and angolas as sickly, lazy, and prone to flight.[97] "An Angolan Negro," wrote the British ship's surgeon John Atkins in the 1730s, "is a proverb for worthlessness."[98] When wealthy planters in the British Caribbean refused to buy West Central Africans, British slave traders re-exported them by the thousands to Spanish America. Given a choice, Panamanian masters refused to purchase them, but as an official of the Portobello Asiento wrote in 1725, "the greater the demand, the fewer the objections" to "the sorts of negroes least coveted." Although they often preferred Africans of other castas, Spanish American buyers purchased West Central Africans in massive numbers because of their availability and cheapness.[99]

Although many West Central Africans came from areas relatively near the Atlantic coast, especially in the early years of the Atlantic trade, commercial networks and slaving routes extended far into the interior, ultimately encompassing an area as large as Europe. In the Americas, Kimbundu- and

Kikongo-speaking people used to thinking of themselves as members of lineages and subjects of small, highly localized states developed a broader consciousness of the commonalities they shared with others from this vast region. Despite their differences, the cultures of the hundreds of peoples "from Cameroon to Angola and from Gabon to eastern Zaïre" can be considered "local variations of a single cultural system adapted to different environments and historical circumstances," as anthropologist Wyatt MacGaffey, a leading authority on Kongo, has argued.[100] The circle of people accepted as insiders expanded greatly as West Central Africans adopted a diasporic ethnicity as congos and angolas. Furthermore, colonial Costa Ricans may have recognized important differences between the peoples of West and West Central Africa, as well as those between Africans and creoles. In 1719, the creole slave José declared that "he was not from Guinea, nor from Angola, but a creole and born in the city of Cartago."[101]

The Gold Coast

Like other casta or "national" names, the significance of the designation "mina" cannot be taken for granted but requires careful contextual and temporal analysis.[102] The name initially referred to the Portuguese trading fort established at São Jorge da Mina in 1482, through which captives from many parts of Africa passed.[103] After this fort fell to the Dutch in 1637 and Portuguese and Brazilian slave traders began to purchase most of their captives further east, they continued to use the term "mina" to include natives of the Slave Coast, as slavers obtaining captives from ports east, such as Allada and Ouidah, first paid a tax at Mina (Elmina). In Brazil, mina was used to describe Africans embarked at Great Popo, Ouidah, Jaquin, and Apa on the leeward side of the Slave Coast, not slaves of Gold Coast origin.[104]

Other slave traders used "mina" to refer to natives of the Gold Coast. Increasing demand for African slaves in the Americas led to a fierce competition among European powers for a lucrative share of the growing Gold Coast slave trade, provoking momentous social, political, and economic changes. In the mid-seventeenth century, militaristic states such as Akwamu, Denkyira, Fante, and Asante gained strength and derived much of their wealth from the Atlantic trade. As a result of the complex cycle of local warfare and slave "production," captives of Gold Coast origin, exported mainly by the Dutch and British, comprised an increasing proportion of African slaves to the Americas after the mid-seventeenth century.[105] As the Dutch, Britons, and Danes dramatically expanded slave exports from the region, by the mid-seventeenth century, many slaves known in Spanish America as minas, such as those brought by the *Christianus Quintus* and *Fredericus Quartus*, indeed came from the Gold Coast.

Notwithstanding a reputation for ferocity and rebelliousness, Gold Coast slaves came to be preferred by British planters in the Caribbean by the 1690s, commanding substantially higher prices than captives of Slave Coast origin.[106] A few minas arrived in Costa Rica from Panama as early as the 1670s.[107] There, too, they seemed already to enjoy a reputation that translated into high prices. In 1680, Alférez Alonso Mateo Hurtado of Esparza paid four hundred pesos each for the young mina men Antonio and Andrés, despite the fact that their Panamanian seller acknowledged them to be "drunkards, thieves, and runaways."[108] By the turn of the eighteenth century, a small but growing mina presence in Costa Rica reflected the increased proportion of Gold Coast natives sold into the trans-Atlantic slave trade generally.[109] Other minas came from the upper Slave Coast, including women and men from a group that called themselves minas.[110] Several arrived during those years as part of an illegal shipment brought by a smuggler known as "the Greek," whose collection also included many West Central Africans.[111]

A small number of minas were already established in Costa Rica when in 1710 the *Fredericus Quartus* brought several hundred more Africans who had embarked on the Gold Coast. Most, if not all, of the captives loaded onto the *Fredericus Quartus* at Christiansborg between April and August 1709 would have been called mina. The bulk of the "minas" on these two ships were certainly Akan-speaking prisoners taken in the Akwamu war against Kwawu and Ga- and Adangme-speaking people from the coastal area around Accra, all sold by the Akwamu to the Danes at Christiansborg. Akyem traders, also Akan speakers, also brought a "very few" captives to the Danish fort while the *Fredericus Quartus* was anchored there; those captives would have been speakers of an Akan language as well.[112] The handful of slaves purchased at Cape Three Points and Kormantin, probably Fante and Akan speakers, would also have been included in the mina group. A number of the captives loaded on the upper Slave Coast might have been identified as mina as well; these might have included Fante speakers from Aneho and Ga-Adangme speakers from Glidji.[113]

The Akan-speaking peoples—including Akwamu, Kwawu, Akyem, and others—recognized their common origins and ancient, if often hostile, historic ties. They spoke different dialects of the same language (Twi), shared deeply ingrained notions of how the world worked at physical, spiritual, and abstract levels, and organized their societies on similar religious, kinship, political, and military lines.[114] Over time, the Ga-Adangme peoples adopted many Akan practices and beliefs. Both groups emigrated in substantial numbers to the upper Slave Coast, where they made a profound cultural impact on this area of complex, overlapping ethnic identities. Arriving in relatively large numbers in Costa Rica, men and women from the Gold Coast and upper Slave Coast drew on different but related ethnic, cultural, and linguistic legacies to create a diasporic ethnicity in the colony.

The Slave Coast

By the mid-seventeenth century, the Bight of Benin became a major supplier of slaves to the Americas, earning the name "Slave Coast" and eventually leading all African regions in the export of captives between 1700 and 1730.[115] Derived from the name of the kingdom of Allada, the name "*arará*" came to be used throughout Spanish America as a generic term for peoples originating from the Slave Coast.[116] A few captives called arará had arrived in Costa Rica by at least the 1670s. By the first decade of the eighteenth century, ararás formed a visible part of Costa Rica's African population.[117] Members of other Slave Coast ethnic groups left the continent through the ports of Little Popo (Aneho, Anécho) and Great Popo. The *Nuestra Señora de la Soledad y Santa Isabel*, confiscated at La Caldera in 1700, carried Africans of Slave Coast origin known as *popos* as well as ararás.[118] Popos, as well as some minas, shared a common language with the ararás (now called Gbe) and religious sensibilities forged over centuries of extensive contact. A few women and men of other ethnic origins, including Yoruba and Borgu, came from areas far in the interior that supplied the Atlantic trade with large numbers of captives only in the nineteenth century.

Although most captives exported from the Slave Coast in the early eighteenth century were natives of the region (broadly defined), Africans of other ethnic origins further inland were entering the trade in growing numbers. At least one Yoruba woman, known as "María of the *lucumí* country," arrived in Costa Rica by way of Panama as early as 1613.[119] Several Yoruba and at least one Borgu woman arrived in Costa Rica on the *Fredericus*

Quartus in 1710, almost certainly embarked at Ouidah the previous year. At
least sixteen persons, initially identified as of *casta nangu*, were captured on
the Matina coast in April 1710.[120] *Nangu* is an early variant of *nago*, the
name applied by speakers of Aja, Ewe, and Fon to western Yoruba-speaking
groups.[121] Some of these individuals identified themselves as being of *casta
aná*, a name that can be identified with the Ana, a western group of Yoruba-
speakers in modern Togo and Benin.[122] In 1716, Antonia, another survivor
of this voyage, identified herself as being of *casta barbá*.[123] *Bariba* was the
Yoruba-language name given by the Oyo to their neighbors in the kingdoms of Borgu, including a western group in the north of modern Benin
and Togo.[124]

The ethnic diversity of the upper Slave Coast confounded Costa Rican
officials and masters, who commonly recorded different casta names for
the same individuals over time or even at the same time. For example,
Captain Juan de Escobar purchased an adolescent girl at auction in the
Pacific coast town of Esparza in 1700. In two records of this same transac-
tion, she was described as a mina in one document and a popo in the
other.[125] Although Miguel Largo described himself as a mina, his popo
shipmates claimed he was one of them.[126] Antonia, described as a popo in
her bill of sale, gave her own casta as barbá.[127] Masters and officials repeatedly cited one woman as aná, although she was known to all as María Popo
and claimed that casta as her own.[128]

These ethnic names, however, were far from meaningless. There is
some evidence to suggest that the persistent classification of these men and
women as popo reflected the social reality of diasporic ethnicity at work in
Costa Rica. Although she had been born in Costa Rica, María Popo's
daughter Juana claimed her mother's ethnicity as her own, choosing to
describe herself as a popo.[129] The masters' and officials' inclusion of Yoruba
(aná), Borgu (barbá), and minas among the popos—as well as a creole girl
who identified herself as a popo—suggests that men and women of various
upper Slave Coast origins used the term not to refer to a specific African
ethnic group but to a larger and more culturally viable association that they
forged in Costa Rica. Their chosen popo identity also had a basis in their
African pasts. People from all over the upper Slave Coast and its hinterland—of Aja, Borgu, Ewe, Hula, Mina, and Yoruba origins—shared a heritage of centuries of cultural exchange. Strengthened in the crucible of
enslavement, it could provide a strong basis for a shared identity in the
diaspora.

An Isolated Minority: The Bight of Biafra

The tendency to subsume men and women of different ethnic origins under a single name reached an extreme in the case of Africans exported from the ports of the Bight of Biafra. A few natives from the region—broadly defined—had arrived in Costa Rica by the early seventeenth century. In virtually all cases, functionaries called them *carabalíes*—a name that, according to historian Femi Kolapo, had a "fantastically omnibus character."[130] The name carabalí originally referred to Elem Kalabari, the Ijo (Ijaw)-speaking community on the east side of the Niger Delta known as "New Calabar" (modern Kalabari, Nigeria). Ijo-speakers comprised the majority of captives exported from New Calabar, while a minority spoke Igbo and Efik.[131] María and Diego, both "of the *carabalí* country," were brought to Cartago by merchant Hernando de Luna from Panama and sold to Salvador de Torres in 1613.[132] Melchor Carabalí had established roots in Cartago by 1622, the year his daughter, Isabel, was baptized.[133]

Over time, the name carabalí came to be applied to a large number of ethnic groups in the Bight of Biafra hinterland; Africanist David Northrup affirms that contemporary Europeans applied the name or its equivalent,

Map 7. Major Ports and Ethno-Linguistic Groups of the Bight of Biafra Region, Seventeenth and Eighteenth Centuries. Map by Mark Van Stone.

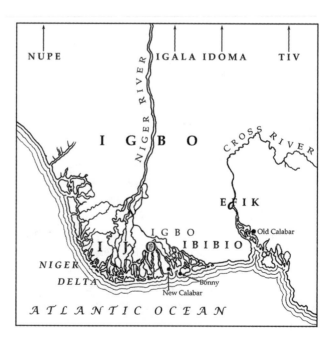

Calabar, to "everyone from the region."[134] By the mid-seventeenth century, slave exports from the Bight of Biafra rose substantially, as the Efik towns at the Cross River, called by Europeans "Old Calabar" (modern Calabar, Nigeria), entered the trans-Atlantic slave trade. European slave traders applied the name "carabalí" to captives exported from "Old Calabar" as well as "New Calabar," despite the fact that, according to Northrup, there was no "evidence of any historical or linguistic connection between Old Calabar and Elem Kalabari." In the late seventeenth century, Africans identified as carabalíes continued to appear occasionally in Costa Rican documents, but they now came from a greater range of Bight of Biafra peoples, possibly including Ijo, Efik, Ibibio, and Igbo speakers.[135] In 1659, Adjutant Juan Gómez Rico declared Florencia, a *negra de casta carabalí*, among his modest property consisting mainly of mules.[136] In 1686, Nicolás González of the Valley of Barva gave Marcela, a carabalí then about twenty, to his daughter Andrea as part of her dowry.[137]

Between the late seventeenth and the mid-eighteenth centuries, slave exports from the Bight of Biafra more than tripled. Beginning in the 1730s, Bonny emerged as the region's most important slaving port. Its rise was linked to the expansion of the Aro trade network that supplied Bonny with large numbers of Igbo captives, who comprised between 60 and 90 percent of the slaves embarked at that port.[138] The name *ibo*, recorded by Sandoval in 1627, occurs rarely in Costa Rican documents.[139] Presumably, however, most slaves of Igbo origin, who may have comprised as many as 65 to 80 percent of all captives exported from the Bight of Biafra between 1662 and 1750, became known in Costa Rica as carabalíes.[140] In an important methodological essay, however, Femi Kolapo cautions that over time, the name might have been expanded to refer to the Igala, Nupe, Idoma, and Tiv peoples with whom the Igbo traded far in the Nigerian hinterland.[141]

Like other Africans, carabalíes arrived in Costa Rica rarely and in small numbers, which restricted their opportunities to communicate with men and women of similar background. A process by which Bight of Biafra natives of different ethnicities came together in "cultural identities-in-formation" while still in Africa continued and deepened with their arrival in the Americas, where it extended to people of more disparate origins.[142] Although a few carabalíes arrived in Costa Rica with companions of the same casta, they immediately found themselves living and working with people of other African and American origins. Carabalíes María and

Diego arrived together in Cartago in 1613 with captives of Upper Guinea (bañón and mandinga), Bight of Benin (lucumí), and West Central African (angola) origin and were sold to a master who also kept Indian servants, a free mulatta, and another black man, presumably American born, in his Cartago home.[143] A young man and woman described as being of casta carabalí arrived at La Caldera on the *Nuestra Señora de la Soledad* in 1700 with people of all ages from the Slave Coast and West Central Africa. They were purchased by a master who also bought six young congo men and women.[144] Other carabalíes came alone and were sent to remote areas of the province, hundreds of miles from their countrymen. María Francisca had been purchased in Panama by her master, who took her to live on his hacienda in the Valley of Bagaces with a black creole slave woman, Agustina. She was about sixteen years old when listed in her mistress's testament in 1732.[145] José, born in the Bight of Biafra around 1720 and acquired from the Royal Asiento in Panama, and Francisco Cubero, a local mulatto, were both purchased by a Cartago official on the same day in 1746.[146]

The handful of women and men in Costa Rica from the Bight of Biafra region arrived intermittently, usually alone, over a period of a century and a half. They almost certainly came from a number of small polities and linguistic groups in the Niger and Cross River Deltas. In the early seventeenth century, most Africans known as carabalíes were probably Ijo speakers, with a minority of Igbos. By midcentury, European slavers stopped at more Biafran ports, and the captives they purchased came from a larger area, which included speakers of Ibibio and Efik, as well as what was by then an Igbo-speaking majority. By the early eighteenth century, the captives included not only Igbo, Ijo, Ibibio, and Efik but perhaps also Igala, Nupe, Idoma, and Tiv from far in the Nigerian interior. Some of the tiny minority of Bight of Biafra natives who arrived in Costa Rica might have been able to preserve relationships with people of similar cultural and linguistic backgrounds, especially in the early seventeenth century, but this is not certain. From the beginning, most carabalíes came to Costa Rica with Africans of other origins, with whom they had already begun to establish relationships. Already handicapped by their small numbers, their ability to form and maintain ties with people of similar background diminished further over time as carabalíes came from increasingly diverse groups and became increasingly scattered throughout Costa Rica.

Conclusion

From dozens of societies, each with its own history, customs, and religious beliefs and practices, the African men and women who became slaves in Costa Rica comprised a far more heterogeneous group than the natives or Europeans in the province. But as the slave trade threw together these strangers from diverse areas, they began to perceive similarities in the fellow captives around them, especially in language, which provided one of the major elements of a new diasporic identity. Most men and women who came to Costa Rica from West Central Africa, by far the largest group of Africans in Costa Rica, spoke dialects of two or three related "Bantu" languages—Kimbundu, Kikongo, and perhaps Mbundu (Ovimbundu)—that to varying degrees were mutually intelligible. Although many of the captives may not have understood each other perfectly or have been able to express advanced concepts to one another—at least initially—the differences between these languages roughly corresponded to those in the Romance family, and very likely the captives soon developed their own "patois based on one or more of the Bantu languages."[147] The peoples of the Slave Coast represented in Costa Rica, including natives of Anlo, Popo, Allada, Ouidah, and Dahomey, shared even more cultural elements. All spoke variants of what linguists now consider a single language (Gbe) and shared nearly identical religious and cosmological beliefs.[148] The Yoruba, including the Ana subgroup, occupied some of the same territories as the peoples of the Slave Coast, shared many basic beliefs about how the world worked, and practiced a religion that in many particulars corresponded exactly to that of the Slave Coast. Shango, for example, one of the most venerated divinities (*orishas*) of Yorubaland, shared identical traits with Hevieso, the thunder deity (*vodun*) of the Slave Coast.[149] Enslaved Yoruba and Slave Coast natives likely understood the experiences of enslavement and the Middle Passage in much the same way. The Yoruba, in turn, had deep historical connections to the peoples of Borgu.[150] The Akan-speaking peoples throughout the Gold Coast likewise shared a common cosmology and language (Twi), which had in turn deeply influenced the culture and religion of the nearby Ga- and Adangme-speaking peoples.[151] The Wolof- and many of the Mande-speaking peoples of the Senegambia and Upper Guinea shared a common history of subjection to the Jolof and Mali Empires. Most adhered to a deeply entrenched caste system and lived under Muslim rulers.

Such deep historical, linguistic, and religious ties favored the formation of diasporic ethnicities in Costa Rica. People from groups who arrived in the province in smaller numbers, sometimes their lone representatives, became associated and came to identify with those of more numerous "nations," such as the popo and mina from the same broadly defined regions of Africa. Antonio de la Riva, of *casta dalá*, and Miguel Largo, a popo whom even "those of his own nation do not understand," came to call themselves minas. Antonia of casta barbá, perhaps the only native of Borgu in the colony, was eventually regarded as a popo. In Costa Rica, people of similar linguistic and cultural backgrounds were able effectively to choose membership in one or more "nations." Popos were identified with the aná and vice versa. These inclusive diasporic ethnicities, grounded in an African past, became stronger through the experiences of enslavement, the Middle Passage, and slavery in Costa Rica. They soon came to overlap with identities formed exclusively in the New World.

CHAPTER THREE

Middle Passages

The Slave Trade to Costa Rica

Why was Slavery illegal in some cases?

pg 76

AFRICANS ENTERED COSTA RICA IN ONE OF THREE WAYS: (1) THEY
were imported legally, most often singly or in small groups, from other provinces, mainly Panama; (2) they were brought illegally, usually to the Caribbean
Matina coast, by Spanish or foreign smugglers; or (3) occasionally, slavers
bound elsewhere ended up in Costa Rica due to storms or navigational errors.[1]
Ironically, such unforeseeable accidents provided some of the largest documented infusions of Africans into the colony. The largest group of Africans
ever to arrive in Costa Rica came unexpectedly with the *Christianus Quintus*
and *Fredericus Quartus* in 1710.

The small numbers of Africans who arrived in Costa Rica for most of the
sixteenth century arrived with Spanish immigrants under individual licenses
issued by the Council of the Indies.[2] From 1595, the adoption of the Asiento
system produced an explosion in the numbers of Africans brought to Spanish
America in the trans-Atlantic slave trade.[3] Their ambitions always
constrained by their relative poverty, Costa Rican colonists could not acquire
Africans in large numbers despite their proximity to major centers of the
slave trade directly to the south in Portobello and Panama City. With a few
exceptions, legally imported slaves continued to arrive in the province
intermittently and in very small numbers. Faced with high taxes on these
human cargoes, in the seventeenth century, Costa Rican colonists turned to

smuggling Africans, just as they smuggled almost everything else. An unknown number of Africans arrived illegally throughout the seventeenth century, as reflected in edicts issued against the contraband trade. But if, as Matthew Restall estimates, about 1 percent of the approximately three hundred thousand Africans sold to Spanish America by 1650 went to Yucatan, probably no more than half as many went to Costa Rica.[4] The rise of Costa Rica's cacao economy in the late seventeenth century created the conditions for an expansion of the slave trade to Costa Rica. By the early eighteenth century, ships carrying dozens of Africans arrived on the Caribbean coast of Matina, greatly contributing to the growth of the African-born slave population. Two unplanned arrivals, fortuitous for Costa Rican slave buyers, brought several hundred Africans to La Caldera in 1700 and Matina in 1710, further augmenting the African population.

The small-scale, intermittent nature of the slave trade to Costa Rica held profound implications both for the development of Costa Rican slavery as an institution and for slave cultures and communities. Sixteenth- and early seventeenth-century black and mulatto creoles, many born in Spain, elsewhere in Spanish America, and increasingly in Costa Rica itself, set the tone early for the slave community. Although clearly on unequal terms, these early creoles helped to forge and became fully integrated into a local culture shared by members of all racial and social groups. Although they made up a substantial proportion of the total slave population, the small numbers of Africans who arrived in the early decades soon became accustomed to the local environment. By the late seventeenth century, African new arrivals comprised an increasing proportion of the slave population. Although recent research has conclusively established that the human cargoes of Atlantic slave ships were less ethnically diverse than traditionally believed, further "Middle Passages" between their first ports of disembarkation and their final destinations in the Americas separated and recombined Africans of diverse ethnicities at various points.[5] Only the survivors of the *Christianus Quintus* and *Fredericus Quartus* sailed (more or less) directly from Africa to Costa Rica. The thousands of other Africans who came to the province between the sixteenth and eighteenth centuries endured numerous stopovers. A man or woman brought to Costa Rica might easily have disembarked at Jamaica or Curaçao, Cartagena, Portobello, and/or Panama City before completing the final leg of his or her hellish journey to Costa Rica's ports of La Caldera or Matina.

Costa Rica and the Asiento Slave Trade

By the early seventeenth century, considerable numbers of African-born slaves began arriving in Costa Rica, coinciding with the expansion of the trans-Atlantic slave trade under the Asiento system.[6] Under the terms of the Asiento, individuals or corporations contracted with the Spanish Crown for the exclusive right to bring a predetermined number of Africans to authorized ports during a specified period. Between 1595 and 1640, hundreds of thousands of enslaved Africans arrived in colonies such as Mexico and Peru, where demand was great and, more importantly to slave traders, colonists often paid in coveted silver.[7] Despite enormous growth in the availability of African slaves, Costa Rica remained at the margins of the Atlantic slave trade. No slave ship ever intentionally sailed directly from Africa to Costa Rica, nor did a continuous or substantial trade in slaves develop between Costa Rica and other American colonies. With rare exceptions, slaves in the seventeenth and eighteenth centuries continued to arrive much as they had in the sixteenth: brought in small numbers from other colonies, they were bought and sold by private arrangement between individuals. In the vast majority of cases, slaves were sold singly or in small groups. This held true even in the common circumstance that a prospective buyer contracted an agent to buy a slave outside the province. Large slave auctions were memorable events that were recalled by both colonists and captives for many years afterward.

Directly to the south of Costa Rica, the Isthmus of Panama was a center of the Spanish American slave trade (first in indigenous, then in African captives) almost from the beginning of the conquest.[8] In the seventeenth and eighteenth centuries, both Portobello, on Panama's Caribbean coast, and Panama City, on the Pacific, became authorized ports of the Asiento. Under the terms of several seventeenth-century Asiento contracts, Portobello was one of just three authorized ports in Spanish America, and because of higher prices, slave traders consistently preferred to sell their captives in Portobello rather than in Cartagena or Veracruz.[9] In addition to the legal slave trade, Portobello became a favorite market for contraband slaves.[10]

During the period of Portuguese dominance of the trans-Atlantic slave trade (1595–1640), most Africans sold in Spanish America arrived in Cartagena and Portobello directly from West Central and West Africa.[11] After 1640, however, as more European nations entered the slave trade on a large scale, Asiento contractors who had difficulty procuring captives in Africa often secured permission to fill their quotas with slaves purchased

Map 8. Detail of the Map "Le Golfe de Mexique" (1717), by Nicolas de Fer, Showing Costa Rica and the Isthmus of Panama. Courtesy of the Birmingham (Alabama) Public Library.

from the Caribbean colonies of the Dutch and British. Before being shipped to Cartagena and Portobello, a large share of the Africans bound for Spanish America had already disembarked on Caribbean islands such as Curaçao, Jamaica, or Barbados.[12] Seven *congo* slaves purchased in Portobello by don Lorenzo de Arburola y Ribarén in 1690, for example, had arrived on the Isthmus by way of Curaçao on the *San Pedro y San Pablo.*[13] Most remained only briefly at such island entrepôts and thus underwent no significant "seasoning" or acculturation to any American society there.

Although the numbers and origins of Africans who arrived at the Isthmus of Panama varied widely over time, the procedures of Spanish officials for disembarking them remained similar. In Portobello, Asiento officials inspected and inventoried the captives just arrived from Africa or the

Caribbean. First, inspectors boarded the slave ships to inspect their papers, verify the count of captives, and ensure that they carried no unauthorized goods. Corruption was inherent to human commerce, and slavers spent liberally on bribes and "gifts" to persuade royal officials to ignore discrepancies throughout the slave trade period.[14]

After these preliminaries, captives were disembarked and held in pens for closer inspection while awaiting auction or transportation to Panama City. First, officials noted the sex, approximate age, and sometimes the origin of each. Men, women, and children from all parts of Western Africa shared the continued misery of the holding pens. One group imported by the *asentistas* Domingo Grillo and Ambrosio Lomelín in 1666, for example, included ninety-one men, women, and children from the Bight of Biafra (sixty-one *carabalíes* and thirty *ibos*), fifty-one from the Slave Coast (*aradás*), thirty-seven from the Gold Coast and/or upper Slave Coast (*minas*), one man from West Central Africa (congo), and five girls of unidentified origin. The inspectors also verified that the captives had already been scarred with the brands of the Royal Asiento. Some of the group had suffered additional tortures and were missing eyes, ears, and limbs. Next, a surgeon examined them and separated the sick and dying from the healthier captives.[15]

Slave traders kept their human cargoes in Portobello from a few days to several months, where they "refreshed" the Africans with food, fresh water, and clothing. Healthier—or at least healthier-looking—Africans would command higher prices. To allow them to recover so they would be more presentable for sale, in March 1716, the 349 captives brought from the Slave Coast by the *Dunwich Merchant* received rations of plantains, corn, fresh and salted beef, and tobacco (probably to be chewed, not smoked), and were provided with suits of canvas (*cañamazo*) or "old sheets." Local men guarded the Africans, lighting candles and lamps to watch them by night. A surgeon attended the sick, and a midwife was hired to help with the birth of a child. Despite attempts at medical care for those within, the pens of Portobello, like the barracoons in Africa, could prove as deadly as the Middle Passage itself. At least thirteen women, men, and children brought to the Isthmus on the *Dunwich Merchant* died within five weeks of arrival (about 4 percent of the Africans who had arrived), succumbing to such illnesses as "malignant fevers," smallpox, and "side pains." Priests collected sixty-six pesos for burying the dead and another twelve for providing the death certificates of Africans who passed on during the days at Portobello.[16]

Although thousands of Africans were purchased at auction in Portobello, many slave traders hoped for even higher profits in Panama City. There the inspections, inventories, and frenzied buying and selling resumed. After sale, many were again loaded onto ships at the port of Perico. A majority of these went to Peru, where some, in turn, would be resold to Ecuador, Bolivia, or Chile. Very few of the Africans sold in Panama City were purchased by Costa Rican buyers and sailed north to La Caldera, from where they might go on to Esparza, Nicoya, Nicaragua, or even Guatemala in addition to Costa Rica's Central and Matina Valleys.

Costa Rica enjoyed relatively easy sea access to both Portobello and Panama City, and for the entire colonial period, most legally imported slaves entered Costa Rica by way of Panama. But the overwhelming mass of Africans transshipped from Panama went to South, not Central, America. Costa Ricans seeking slaves found themselves at an insuperable disadvantage vis-à-vis other Spanish American buyers, especially Peruvians, who were able to afford higher prices.[17] At Panama City, professional slave traders bought large lots of Africans at prices far beyond the reach of Costa Ricans, often paying with silver in quantities that few if any Costa Ricans could lay their hands on. In June 1666, don Juan de Cevallos bought a lot of "sixty *piezas,* two-thirds of them males and one-third females." Despite the physical condition of several of the Africans—some afflicted with hernias, others missing eyes or limbs—Cevallos paid 470 pesos each, for a total of 28,200 pesos. *Alférez* Francisco de Acosta purchased a lot of fifty captives, thirty-four of them men, who likewise suffered from various illnesses and injuries, at 450 pesos each, for a total of 22,500 pesos. Such sums exceeded the total fortunes of some of Cartago's wealthiest residents.[18] Cevallos and Acosta may well have been speculators who quickly broke up their large lots of slaves into smaller groups for resale. In small numbers, Africans sold for much more.[19] By contrast, the mean price of the five adult black men and women sold in Costa Rica, none of whom were described as suffering poor health, was just 316 pesos in the 1660s.[20]

Few if any slave traders were persuaded to forsake silver-rich Peru to sail north to Costa Rica. The prices of slaves in Cartago always paled before those paid in Peru. Drawing on a large sample of slave sales recorded in notarial records, Frederick Bowser calculated that a *ladino* (Spanish-speaking, African-born) black man between the ages of 16 and 25 sold in Lima for an average price of 454 pesos in 1630. By contrast, Jerónimo, a 20-year-old black creole, brought just 300 pesos in Cartago in 1632.[21] In 1648, Diego, a mulatto, was sold in Cartago for 250 pesos. In Lima, 2 years later, black male ladinos sold for more than twice as much, at an average price of 522 pesos.[22] Between 1607 and 1700, black male slaves between the prime ages of 16 and 25 sold in Cartago at a mean price of 350 pesos (n = 20), with a maximum price of 540 pesos paid for Juan, a black creole, in 1660. During the same period, in Lima, the average price of black male slaves of the same ages never fell below 480 pesos and rose to a high of 588 pesos in 1620.[23] In the Peruvian highlands, African slaves cost much more. Twenty-seven black males between 16 and 25 years of age sold in one Cuzco parish between 1655 and 1682 brought an average price of 640 pesos.[24] Furthermore, in Costa Rica, a province chronically short of silver currency, sellers often had to settle for payment in local produce (*géneros de la tierra*). For example, in 1632, a passenger on an incoming ship exchanged an African man from the Bight of Biafra (carabalí) for 250 pesos' worth of tallow, tobacco, and indigo, which he loaded at La Caldera.[25] By the eighteenth century, Costa Ricans usually paid for slaves, as they paid for everything else, in 97-kilogram (214-pound) sacks of cacao valued at 25 pesos. Although Costa Rican whites coveted African slaves no less than their wealthier counterparts in Peru, they never developed a trade commodity that could compete successfully with Peruvian silver.

Nevertheless, a small proportion of the Africans sold in Panama City were taken north, and La Caldera, Costa Rica's Pacific coast port near Esparza, came to function as a center of the small regional slave trade. For slaves, as well as for other imported commodities, La Caldera sometimes served as a stopover between Panama and Nicaragua. In 1716, for example, Captain don José Antonio de Espinoza disembarked at La Caldera with two slaves—Agustín, a ten-year-old mina boy, and María, an eighteen-year-old *mandinga*—whom he had purchased from the Royal Asiento in Panama City and had arranged to bring overland to a buyer in Granada (Nicaragua). Agustín died before he could complete the trip north.[26]

On rare occasions, slave merchants from other provinces traveled to Costa Rica specifically to sell captives, usually in small numbers—a circumstance that increased the likelihood of ethnic diversity among the captives and accentuated the importance of shared experiences of bondage in the relationships between them. For example, Fernando de Luna, a resident of Los Remedios (Panama), arrived in Cartago in 1613 to sell five Africans for a total of two thousand pesos. From four widely separated regions of Africa—Upper Guinea (*bañón*), the Bight of Biafra (two carabalíes), the Bight of Benin (*lucumí*), and West Central Africa (*angola*)—these two women and three men had already experienced the horrors of the Atlantic crossing and the holding pens of

Portobello and had shared the trek to Costa Rica.[27] Between 1639 and 1643, Cartago's royal treasurer noted that slaves arrived regularly at La Caldera on the Pacific and Punta Blanca, on the Caribbean coast, from Panama City, Portobello, and Cartagena.[28] Very rarely, slave traders brought sizeable shipments of slaves to Costa Rica. Guatemalan merchant Pedro Ortiz de Mendoza, for example, brought forty-seven African men and women from Panama City to the Pacific region's Valley of Landecho in July 1673.[29] Again, they came from widely separated parts of Africa, including West Africans of Gold Coast or upper Slave Coast origin (minas), as well as West Central Africans (congos). Ortiz remained in Cartago selling slaves well into the following year.[30]

Much more commonly, merchants and travelers sold a slave or two while in Cartago on other business or empowered an agent to sell slaves on their behalf. Cartago also served as a center of the small-scale regional slave trade, uniting buyers and sellers from various parts of Central America. In 1688, Pedro, a black man belonging to a resident of Chame (Panama), was sent by his mistress to be sold in Cartago. There, he was purchased on behalf of Captain don Melchor de la Cerda of Granada and remitted to Nicaragua.[31] In 1706, Captain Juan Agustín Ruiz de Meza, a resident of Natá (Panama), bought a twenty-year-old congo man named Domingo in Panama City. Ruiz then traveled to Cartago, where he sold Domingo to Captain Diego Miguel González de Algarín, a resident of León (Nicaragua).[32]

Local buyers who wanted slaves more urgently than the haphazard supply of captives to Costa Rica could provide often contracted travelers to Panama City and Portobello to purchase slaves on their behalf. For example, in 1638, Diego de Ocampo Figueroa undertook to buy one male and one female slave for Alonso Gómez Macotela when he sailed from La Caldera to Panama City.[33] In 1665, Alférez Sebastián de Aguirre, about to leave on a trip to Panama City, accepted two hundred pesos from Domingo Jiménez Maldonado and his wife doña Juana de Sojo to purchase an enslaved black girl for the couple. Aguirre stipulated that if the girl died on the return trip, Maldonado and Sojo would not attempt to hold him responsible for the loss.[34] Don Lorenzo de Arburola y Ribarén purchased slaves on several occasions for Cartago residents while in Portobello, qualifying him as a local slave trader. In October 1689, Arburola purchased seven congo slaves for Cartago buyers from the Asiento in Portobello.[35] In addition, Arburola returned to Costa Rica on that occasion with Juan de Acevedo, a black creole, whom he sold in Matina, remitting the proceeds to Juan's former owner in Portobello.[36]

As these sales make clear, most slaves acquired legally entered Costa Rica alone, in pairs, or in small groups. On the way, they passed through several points at which the fragile bonds they had formed with other captives were severed. Separated from their homelands upon enslavement, the relationships they formed in the coffles, barracoons, and slave ships proved transitory. Costa Rican colonists often traveled personally to Panama to procure slaves and brought them back to the province by boat or overland, beginning unusually close relationships with their slaves as they navigated the ocean in small craft or drove their captives through dense forests. Although the experience did not necessarily reduce slaves to a "childlike dependence," their masters did come to occupy a central place in their lives.[37] In contrast to plantation slave societies, on the small properties in Costa Rica, many slaves—especially females—lived in intimate contact with their masters and enjoyed only limited opportunities to interact with countrymen and shipmates. The fact of birth in Africa and the shared experience of the Middle Passage could not be entirely erased, however, and for a time provided bases on which slaves could form new identities in Costa Rica.

The Illegal Slave Trade

With the decline of legal commerce between Costa Rica and other Spanish colonies, smuggling linked the province to the wider world, including the Atlantic slave trade.[38] Unlike the legal slave trade, which virtually guaranteed that Africans arrived in Costa Rica only in small numbers, at least on occasion, Africans smuggled into the province arrived by the boatload in the late seventeenth and early eighteenth centuries. The illegal slave trade to Costa Rica accounted for a substantial number of the Africans imported to the province. Although the extent of the contraband trade will never be known with certainty, some historians have suggested that as many Africans entered Costa Rica illegally as legally.[39] In a small society such as Costa Rica, however, the illegal arrival of a large shipment of Africans was unlikely to pass unnoticed. As one slave mistress accused of smuggling pointed out, "a slave is not an ornament that can be carried in the pocket."[40] For the smuggling of Africans and other contraband merchandise to succeed, government officials had to collude in the trade.

The Crown cared little for the conditions in which Africans made the Middle Passage. Its interest began only with the arrival of the captives and their eligibility for taxation as merchandise or its claim to confiscate the captives outright if purchased from "enemies of the Crown." Functionaries at the ports readily accepted bribes to overlook the egregious discrepancies between the declared and actual numbers of Africans imported and waive the various duties owed to the Crown.[41] This practice occurred at Costa Rica's ports as well on a much more limited scale. For a few years in the mid-seventeenth century, the slave trade at La Caldera, as well as at Costa Rica's Caribbean port of the time, Punta Blanca, became brisk enough to attract the attention of royal officials. Costa Rica's treasurer, Juan de Morales, charged that between 1639 and 1643, none of the buyers of Africans from Panama City, Portobello, or Cartagena had paid the obligatory sales taxes (*alcabalas*) they owed.[42] Unfortunately, Morales gave no indication of the volume of the trade, but illegal slave importations continued intermittently throughout the century. Later in the seventeenth century, there is some suggestion that Asiento slave ships made unauthorized stops in Costa Rica. In 1673, Queen Regent Mariana issued a *cédula* referring to the illegal importation of Africans to Costa Rica, warning the governor to prosecute any further incidents.[43]

By the first decade of the eighteenth century, the smuggling of Africans and other contraband items to Costa Rica's Caribbean Matina coast was an open secret in which the highest provincial officials commonly colluded. The best-documented period of smuggling occurred under Governor don Francisco Serrano de Reyna, who assumed his post in 1695 and held it until he was removed from office in 1704. Trading with smugglers in Matina was so common during his tenure that some claimed not to know it was illegal. Muleteer Severino de Aguilar said in 1703 that he "did not know for certain" whether trading with foreign smugglers was prohibited, because he was "a creole of this country." Aguilar declared that he had bought goods from contrabandists only because "His Honor the governor of this province has given permission."[44] Mulatto soldier Adjutant Luis de Salazar asserted that three ships had arrived in Matina in 1700, all manned by "pirate corsairs," including one captained by a man known as "the Greek." The smugglers set up booths on the beach for weeks at a time, openly selling their wares "as in public shops." On one occasion that year, Salazar had seen more than thirty Africans at the port of Matina. According to Salazar, Governor Serrano de Reyna allowed the illegal trade to continue in exchange for a 20 percent cut of the value of the items purchased.[45] Others said that Serrano de Reyna imposed a flat rate of twenty-five pesos on each African smuggled in. Not always content with kickbacks, the governor had sometimes extorted the twenty-five pesos and then seized the Africans anyway.[46] Furthermore, the governor appropriated smuggled Africans himself. Years later, Pedro Arburola, a congo who had arrived with "the Greek" in 1700, recalled that when he had arrived in Costa Rica, he was first held in the governor's home in Cartago.[47]

In 1702, another illegal shipment of slaves arrived in Costa Rica in a bizarre episode. Fray Francisco de San José, a Franciscan friar, had determined to build a mission to the Indians of Talamanca. As a means of raising funds, he decided to enter the slave trading business on a one-time basis. In March 1702, the friar sailed to Portobello, where he arranged with ship's captain Andrés de Verroterán for the delivery of about two dozen Africans to Moín on Costa Rica's Matina coast later that year. The friar reasoned that just as the governors of Cartagena and Portobello had purchased African slaves to repair military fortifications, so he was justified in buying slaves, even from foreigners, for so holy an enterprise as building a mission.[48] Verroterán arrived with two sloops (*balandras*) at Moín in June 1702, reportedly from Jamaica, and turned over the Africans to Fray Francisco. Claiming to have royal authorization for the importation and sale of the Africans, the friar issued a proclamation warning secular officials not to obstruct his plans.[49] Fray Francisco took the Africans to the cacao hacienda "Madre de Dios," then set about soliciting contributions from the neighbors to pay for the captives.[50] It took nearly a month for the friar to assemble the cacao to pay for the slaves, during which time Verroterán remained unmolested in port at Moín, waiting for payment.[51] With each *zurrón* (a 97 kilogram/214 pound leather bag) of cacao worth twenty-five pesos, Severino de Aguilar and his nephew, Hipólito de Trejos, worked for eight days straight to haul the cacao to the sloops with their seven mules.[52]

Governor don Francisco Serrano de Reyna had other plans for the Africans. He rejected Fray Francisco's claim that superior authorities had authorized the slave purchase, reasoning that "His Majesty (may God save him) never gives such orders to religious missionaries."[53] The governor ordered his protégé Adjutant Lázaro de Robles to go with four other mulatto soldiers to establish a checkpoint at the Indian pueblo of Turrialba. Serrano de Reyna stationed other soldiers at the pueblo of Tucurrique, thus covering both approaches to Cartago. Robles's written commission specified that he was to search all travelers, seize all contraband goods, arrest the offenders, and send them to Cartago for prosecution.[54] Verbally, however, Serrano de Reyna told Robles to target certain individuals for arrest and let others pass.[55] Domingo Guerrero and three other mulatto soldiers manned the station, where they seized one African boy from Blas Suárez and another from

"Francisco the Carpenter." Captain Antonio de Soto y Barahona, on the other hand, was allowed to continue unmolested to Cartago, carrying a little black girl in his mule train.[56] Mestizo soldier Juan Ramón de la Cruz went to Cartago, where he turned over one of the African boys and the bulk of the confiscated textiles to the waiting governor.[57]

False documents formed the stock-in-trade of corrupt officials like Serrano de Reyna. In 1702, the governor composed records of investigations he supposedly conducted into the illegal commerce. Serrano de Reyna claimed to have searched various homes in Cartago, sending his lieutenants to the haciendas of Matina to do the same. According to the record of the investigation, the officials "found nothing involving the smuggling of any black."[58] A string of witnesses declared that they "did not know nor had news that such blacks are bought in the Matina Valley."[59] Marcos Hernández, a soldier stationed in Matina, said that while stationed in a watchtower on the coast he had never seen "any resident of Matina buy any black or other article of clothing [sic]."[60] As Lázaro de Robles later explained, Serrano de Reyna fabricated the proceedings to "hide [the fact] that the said governor had known everything that had happened." The governor "allowed the commerce, and [only] pretended to proceed against those who" participated in it, Robles said.[61] Father don Manuel José González Coronel confirmed that the smuggling "could not have occurred" without the complicity of Serrano de Reyna.[62]

Subsequent governors jumped enthusiastically into the illegal slave trade, adopting the local customs established by their predecessors. In 1713, the Audiencia of Guatemala appointed Sergeant Major don José Antonio de Lacayo Briones of Granada (Nicaragua) as governor of Costa Rica.[63] Contraband also thrived during his tenure; Captain Juan Gómez de Ocón y Trillo alleged that "there has not been a year in which there was not" illegal commerce in Matina since Lacayo Briones assumed the governorship.[64] Francisco Alejandro Bonilla said that "a number of times" (*repetidas veces*), Englishmen from Jamaica had come in ships "loaded with clothing and blacks" to conduct a trade "fair" on the beaches of Matina.[65]

While the illegal arrivals of ships such as "the Greek's" in 1700 and Verroterán's in 1702 were exposed by the Audiencia of Guatemala and, consequently, were well documented, other ships and boats carrying African slaves came and went, leaving only traces in the documentary record. Much like those imported legally, many such Africans arrived in small numbers. Catalina, a West Central African of *casta loango*, had been purchased in Portobello by Fray Agustín Valerino, who brought her by boat to Matina and then sold her to his sister in Cartago.[66] In 1706, Captain Antonio de Soto y Barahona gave don Lorenzo de Arburola y Ribarén money to go to Portobello and buy an enslaved man trained as a stonemason for him. Arburola returned with Jacobo, a middle-aged mandinga artisan who had previously lived in Martinique.[67] Isabel, an enslaved African woman about fifty years old in 1719, had arrived in Costa Rica many years before. "Her master, José de Aguilar, brought her," she recalled, "but she did not know from where, because it was night when he was walking with her" secretly on the road to the Central Valley.[68] Although the best-documented cases of illegal slave imports derive from the late seventeenth and early eighteenth centuries, the contraband trade continued to bring a few Africans to Costa Rica well into the eighteenth century. In 1739, for example, Captain Pedro Ricardo de Andrade captured a foreign sloop on the Matina coast and confiscated a single African man from the ship.[69]

Unforeseen Occasions

In addition to those imported by the Asiento or by smugglers in the early eighteenth century, hundreds of Africans arrived in Costa Rica by accident. On at least two occasions, ships carrying Africans elsewhere were forced by storm or other mishap to Costa Rican shores. In a province where Africans usually trickled in by ones, twos, and threes, both whites and blacks recalled these memorable occasions for decades afterward. More importantly, these incidents contributed to a "re-Africanization" of Costa Rica's enslaved population.[70] In addition, these forced immigrants became the objects of controversies that impacted all levels of Costa Rican society. As the newly arrived Africans changed the face of the slave community, their masters concealed and falsified their origins to avoid paying import taxes. Willingly or unwillingly, people from all social and racial groups of Costa Rican society joined in the cover-up.

In October 1700, a ship arrived unexpectedly at Costa Rica's Pacific port of La Caldera, near Esparza.[71] According to its captain, the *Nuestra Señora de la Soledad y Santa Isabel* had been bound from Panama City's port of Perico to Paita, Peru, when a storm forced it north to Costa Rica. Inspecting the ship's papers, Esparza's lieutenant governor don Gregorio Caamaño found that the captain had no license to transport merchandise.[72] In the middle of the night, an anonymous member of the ship's crew came to

Caamaño's home and notified him that the ship had arrived with an illegal cargo. Although the *Nuestra Señora* carried a bill of lading for some of the merchandise it was taking to Peru, the informant had seen a number of African captives secretly loaded aboard at a small island off the coast of Panama City. The ship's captain had now disembarked them at a hiding place near La Caldera and was planning to sell the blacks illegally in Costa Rica.[73] Following up on the tip, Caamaño and Juan Antonio Bogarín, Lieutenant of Royal Officials in Esparza, went down to the coast and found forty-one Africans hidden in the bush near the port. In addition to the Africans, the *Nuestra Señora* carried a wide array of imported goods, including several varieties of luxurious cloth, leather, shotguns, a copper kettle, and ship's anchors. Caamaño and Bogarín confiscated the Africans and the merchandise in the name of His Majesty and, over the next five months, sold the blacks at public auctions in Esparza.[74] In March 1701, Caamaño and Bogarín divided the proceeds of the sales to date into thirds according to their understanding of imperial law, designating a total of 2,809 pesos for the Crown and equal amounts for themselves, as the presiding judges in the case, and for the anonymous informant. They remitted the Crown's share to Governor don Francisco Serrano de Reyna in Cartago.[75]

That was the story Caamaño and Bogarín recorded in the official proceedings relating to the confiscation of the cargo of the *Nuestra Señora*, compiled more than two months after the events described. A few years later, Bogarín confessed that the account had been fabricated to cover his own misconduct, that of Lieutenant Governor Caamaño, and that of Governor Serrano de Reyna. Bogarín claimed that he had been persuaded to sign the false documents when Caamaño began "threatening him that he would have to cut off his head if he did not do it."[76] As Bogarín later related, the frigate arrived at La Caldera during a storm, taking in water and badly damaged. Although smugglers often claimed necessity as a pretext to enter Spanish ports for illegal trade, in this case the ship faced real danger.[77] Upon hearing of the *Nuestra Señora*'s arrival, Caamaño went to the port to investigate. Looking over the cargo, Caamaño immediately perceived the potential for profit afforded by the emergency. Inspecting the ship's license, Caamaño found some irregularities and confiscated the blacks, removing them from the port to Esparza. The owners of the ship and merchandise pleaded with Caamaño to return the Africans, offering him a bribe of 1,500 pesos to reconsider. A lengthy round of negotiations ensued. Caamaño finally accepted three thousand pesos' worth of clothing and returned the Africans to the ship.[78]

Most of them, anyway. Although the official records Caamaño and Bogarín wrote referred to forty-one blacks, in reality, the *Nuestra Señora* had brought fifty-four. According to one of the Peruvian owners of the Africans, the human cargo was worth more than thirteen thousand pesos.[79] Around midnight, Caamaño sent "twelve [*sic*] blacks, the best of the lot" to don José de la Haya Bolívar's estancia in the Valley of Landecho, about six to seven leagues (33 to 39 kilometers/21 to 24 miles) from Esparza.[80] Caamaño sent two more Africans to Governor don Francisco Serrano de Reyna in Cartago—the cost of doing illegal business. When Captain Francisco de los Reyes asked about the expensive payoff, Caamaño replied that he did not mind "giving a wing to someone who has given me a [whole] chicken."[81] And Caamaño had already decided to profit even more from the shipment. "That money has to stay among us and in the province," he confided to Reyes.[82]

Notwithstanding the bribe he had accepted, Caamaño confiscated the cargo of Africans and merchandise. He then proceeded to stage a series of auctions, at which he enlisted proxies to buy slaves on his own behalf and for his partner, Governor Serrano de Reyna. Bogus records of the auctions described the Africans as sickly children, but their purchasers later admitted that most were healthy young men and women. Caamaño and Serrano de Reyna exaggerated the illnesses of the Africans in the proceedings to justify the rock-bottom prices for which they sold. Africans worth up to four hundred pesos were sold for a quarter of their value; Serrano de Reyna protested to his superiors that the captives were "so broken-down [*estropeados*] and sick that not even in Panama could they have sold for more."[83] Alberto Pérez de Parga, for example, purchased six young black men and women for a total of 650 pesos. They were described in the documents as eight to nine years old, "very thin and full of sores, four of them with bursting ulcers [*bubas reventadas*] all over their bodies."[84] In reality, Bogarín later said, the Africans "were neither boys and girls [*muleques*], nor were they sick, but rather full-grown and well-built blacks [*negros hechos y buenos*]." Pérez's name was listed on the sale, but the end buyer was don Gregorio Caamaño.[85] Don José de Casasola y Córdoba later admitted that the congo boys and girls he had purchased in December 1700 had not been for himself but for Governor Serrano de Reyna. All had been healthy, not sick and maltreated, as the documents claimed.[86] Caamaño noted a payment to the anonymous informer who had alerted him to the smuggling in the official records, but in reality no such person existed, and he and Bogarín pocketed the nearly three thousand pesos themselves.[87]

Suspicions about how Costa Rica's governor and his lieutenant in Esparza had handled the seizure of the *Nuestra Señora* spread beyond the province within a few weeks of the ship's arrival. In January 1701, the governor of Nicaragua penned a letter to the Audiencia of Guatemala about the incident that piqued the judges' curiosity.[88] One of them, the Licentiate don Francisco de Carmona, went to Costa Rica to investigate. His findings ultimately put an end to Serrano de Reyna's career of profiteering. As Carmona uncovered more and more evidence of malfeasance, the president and *oidores* of the Audiencia ordered Caamaño to repay the 8,405 pesos and four reales earned from the auction of the Africans and other merchandise confiscated from the *Nuestra Señora* to the royal treasury in August 1701.[89] In response, Caamaño packed up his belongings and fled the province. Governor Serrano de Reyna countenanced Caamaño's hasty departure, citing what Carmona called "frivolous pretexts."[90] The president of the Audiencia agreed and, in January 1702, ordered Serrano de Reyna to repay the proceeds from the sales.[91]

Serrano de Reyna dodged responsibility for months, but in 1704, Carmona arrested the governor, confiscated his property, and put him in the Cartago jail. After making a statement, Serrano de Reyna was taken under guard to Guatemala City. Once there, however, he slipped away from his captors and took refuge in the city's Augustinian convent. Initially, the Audiencia meted out a stern punishment. In September 1705, the president and oidores of the Audiencia condemned Serrano de Reyna in absentia to be perpetually barred from political, military, and administrative office; to two terms of service at the military fortress in Ceuta, North Africa; to a fine of six thousand pesos; and to repay 1,217 pesos he had received for his role in prosecuting cases of smuggling.[92] But a year later they relented, removing Serrano de Reyna's disqualification from service and commuting his fine to three thousand pesos.[93] His career in colonial administration was finished, however, and the disgraced governor returned to Spain in 1709.[94]

Early in his investigation, Carmona had complained of the obstacles he faced in a letter to the president of the Audiencia. On learning of his presence in the province, "all" Cartago slaveholders had taken their slaves out of the city and "hidden" them. "Nobles and plebeians" alike participated in the illegal slave trade; Carmona believed in the Costa Ricans' "almost universal guilt." Witnesses were reluctant to speak with him because of "the fear they generally have of [Serrano de Reyna] in the province." Carmona was certain that the governor "has made threats."[95] Adjutant Lázaro de Robles, for example, who executed many of the governor's illegal directives, told Carmona that he was "so terrorized that he would have left the country and gone to another province had he not found himself with family obligations" in Costa Rica.[96] In light of the difficulties of prosecuting smugglers, Carmona proposed that the Audiencia issue a pardon (*indulto*) to offenders upon payment of a fine to the Crown. The president and oidores firmly rejected this suggestion.[97] Although he capably prosecuted Serrano de Reyna's corruption, Carmona soon turned around and indulged in it himself. Ignoring the Audiencia's decree, Carmona offered the pardons on his own initiative, pocketing more than four thousand pesos from Cartago slave owners. The ultimate fate of the money remained a mystery.[98] In the end, the profits deriving from the illegal slave trade proved too tempting for the otherwise diligent investigator from the Audiencia.

"*Carabelas*": Shipmates

In most documents pertaining to the trans-Atlantic slave trade, Africans appear as objects, not subjects—as just one more commodity on merchant ships. True, Africans were a peculiar sort of merchandise that caused slave traders constant anxiety, but except for the danger they could present to life or profit, their humanity mattered little to their captors. Everything about the slave trade to Costa Rica conspired to deny Africans their humanity by uprooting them from their communities and severing the roots of their African identities. But in the midst of the death and degradation of the Middle Passage, captives created meaningful relationships that, in the right circumstances, could survive and transcend that traumatic experience.

Patterns in the Atlantic slave trade as a whole, as well as the piecemeal nature of the trade to Central America, contributed to the ethnic heterogeneity of Costa Rica's African population. Africans were redivided and resold at each slaving port, and each time, the likelihood increased that they would be separated from people of similar origins. By the time they reached Costa Rica, most African men and women—especially those imported legally—had been sold and resold a number of times. Chances for contact with people of similar background diminished at every stage. Many African men and women who had been purchased through legal channels arrived in Costa Rica alone. In contrast to areas with more regular access to the slave trade, only exceptionally did Africans arrive in Costa Rica with countrymen, even in small groups. Initially, they understood their new experiences in their own cultural terms, but to communicate with their fellow captives, they immediately had to translate their needs, thoughts, and emotions into new meanings that could be shared by others.

Africans who arrived in larger, illegal shipments shared a different experience. Identification with specific African ethnicities might fade, but the fact of birth in Africa and relationships formed in the course of the Middle Passage remained important. In a classic essay, anthropologists Sidney Mintz and Richard Price argued that relationships between shipmates emerged as some of the earliest and most enduring institutions among enslaved Africans.[99] After years or even decades in slavery in Costa Rica, Africans typically knew the whereabouts of their shipmates, whom they called carabelas ("caravels"), despite separation by time and distance.[100] Ties between shipmates sometimes assumed the force of kinship.[101] About thirty years old in 1719, María, a slave of María Calvo, had arrived as a young girl and did "not know her *casta*," although her face bore the identifying ritual scars common to many West African ethnic groups. Nevertheless, she had a "sister," María Victoria, who had arrived on the same ship. María Victoria— also unable to name her casta—did not call María her sister but did state that they were shipmates.[102] María Popo, a native of the Slave Coast, referred to the Yoruba (*aná*) Micaela as "her sister." Although the women claimed different ethnic origins, they had been shipmates and companions during "seasoning" in don Juan Francisco de Ibarra's country house.[103] Ten years after arriving in Matina on the *Christianus Quintus* and *Fredericus Quartus*, the Yoruba women María and Petrona were reunited with Manuel, a shipmate originally from the Gold Coast or upper Slave Coast. They called him *papaligua*, possibly a corruption of a Yoruba word for "father."[104] In these cases, the new "fictive" family relationships based in the shipmate bond transcended ethnicity.

In the early eighteenth century, the *Nuestra Señora de la Soledad*, the *Fredericus Quartus*, and the *Christianus Quintus* brought hundreds of Africans to the province. In Costa Rica, a colony in which the arrival of a shipload of Africans constituted a memorable occasion and slaveholdings were limited, the shipmate bond transcended boundaries of estate and ethnicity. The number of captives arriving on either of the Danish ships probably rivaled the number of Africans of any single ethnic or linguistic origin already in the province and certainly exceeded the number of slaves living on any single property. Survivors of the *Fredericus Quartus* and *Christianus Quintus* shared the exceptionally difficult experience of the Middle Passage on those ships with more people than they did native language, similar ethnic background, indigenous or Muslim religion, or ownership by the same master. The shipmate bond permitted broader webs of relationships than any of these other potential bases of identity allowed.

This did not mean, however, that the shipmate relationship simply supplanted African identities. If the shipmate bond could help Africans constitute new identities, it could also help them to maintain old ones.[105] Pedro de Rosas, for example, said in 1720 that "he does not know which one might be" his casta, but that "who will able to say is Pedro Mina, . . . his shipmate [carabela]."[106] Fellow slaves on the same estate could also reinforce ethnic identity. Although, having arrived twenty years before as a young boy, Pedro could not himself recall, "from what his companions have told him, his mother was of *casta congo*."[107] Shipmates and slaves on the same estate could help reinforce ethnic identity in those who had arrived too young to remember Africa and could contribute to the formation of new diasporic ethnicities in Costa Rica. Ultimately, the shipmate relationship served to bridge Old World and New World identities.

CHAPTER FOUR

Becoming Slaves in Costa Rica

✦ ON FRIDAY, APRIL 25, 1710, AND AGAIN ON APRIL 28 AND MAY 1, THE *LADINO* Indian Baltasar Calvo, a crier (*pregonero*) employed by the town *cabildo*, filled Cartago's central plaza with his voice. "*A la almoneda y con moneda* [to the auction and with money]," he called. Calvo pointed to the Africans standing at the doors of the cabildo, inviting "gentlemen who wish to make a bid on the black men and women present." To guarantee maximum attendance, officials tried to hold public auctions on Sundays and feast days after Mass. The sight of the African captives in the public square attracted "a concourse of people" to observe the spectacle, including the merely curious as well as seriously interested potential buyers.[1] Before convening the sales, officials recorded the approximate ages and physical characteristics of the captives during an "inventory and evaluation" and selected experts (*peritos*) to estimate the captives' value. In the case of the survivors of the *Christianus Quintus* put on sale in April 1710, Royal Treasurer Blas González Coronel and his lieutenant selected Sergeant Major Juan de Zavaleta and don Lorenzo de Arburola y Ribarén.[2] Swearing to perform his duty objectively, Arburola had considerable qualifications for the task, having bought and sold at least nine slaves over the past three decades.

On these occasions, no buyers stepped forward.[3] For prospective Costa Rican slave buyers, purchasing a slave was no easy decision; many Africans cost more than the cacao haciendas where they would work. Slaves consequently formed the most valuable property of *vecinos'* estates. Prospective slave buyers meticulously examined the captives so they would choose the best investments, considered the uses to which they would put them, debated with themselves as to whether they really needed them and could afford them, and at last silently agreed with themselves on the bottom line of how much they were willing to spend. On the other hand, in several cases in the early eighteenth century, Costa Rican officials conspired to sell the captives to cronies at discounted prices much cheaper than could be had in Panama, sometimes incurring the wrath of their superiors in Nicaragua and Guatemala for cheating His Majesty's interests.[4] On Sunday, May 18, 1710, Captain Juan de Astúa purchased an eighteen-year-old woman of *casta arará* for 208 pesos.[5] A month later, Father don Juan Antonio de Moya bought a nine-year-old boy at the price of 130 pesos on June 22.[6] Large auctions, such as those held in early 1710, occurred rarely. Even in the case of the captives brought by the *Christianus Quintus* and *Fredericus Quartus*, one-on-one transactions were far more common means of acquiring slaves.

Captives understood that the moment of sale decided their futures for a long time to come. As Walter Johnson, an expert on the antebellum New Orleans slave market, has pointed out, slave traders had to convince prospective buyers that captives would prove good investments, and by departing from "carefully scripted roles," slaves could ruin the deals.[7] In most cases, the formulaic language of legal documents only hinted at the ways slaves influenced their futures at the moment of sale. For example, in 1706, Captain Diego Miguel González de Algarín bought Diego, a twenty-year-old *congo* man recently arrived from Africa, for 450 pesos. "For certain causes and motives," González soon repented of the purchase and returned Diego to the seller. He accepted Francisco, a creole black of the same age, as a substitute.[8] Although Diego had initially seemed satisfactory, within a few days, he managed to convince González that he would not suit him as a slave. His would-be master had failed to "break" him.

Violence

Violence lay at the heart of slavery, beginning with the moment of enslavement in Africa. Slave traders used violence to maintain control of captives on the march to the African coast; on the Middle Passage; in the holding pens of the British and Dutch Caribbean, Cartagena, Portobello, and Panama; and on the other Middle Passages of the sea voyage and forced marches overland to Cartago. When Africans arrived at the homes of their new masters in Costa Rica, initially there could be only rudimentary communication between them. Violence, therefore, formed a kind of substitute, shorthand language, the most direct means available to masters to "teach" African captives that they had become slaves. Obedience formed the indispensable first lesson; when masters secured it, they could convince themselves of their superiority to the captives.[9] Masters conveyed their most immediate, unmistakable instructions by inflicting pain. They continued to use violence after slaves became acculturated; it remained part of their permanent vocabulary and ultimately formed the only means by which masters could secure slave labor and the products of slave labor.[10] Perhaps twenty years after her slave Francisco Caracata arrived in Costa Rica, doña Josefa de Oses explained that she had had him chained to a barred window "because she could not subject him."[11] Masters saw violence as constituting a natural part of what they believed was their necessary and legitimate domination of their inferiors.

Unlike slaves in large plantation societies, some of whom might see their masters only once or twice in a lifetime, virtually all slaves in Costa Rica knew their masters personally, and most experienced direct, intimate, and often brutal contact at their hands. The survivors of the *Chistianus Quintus* and *Fredericus Quartus* immediately began especially close relationships with their new Costa Rican masters, as in some cases their masters had literally captured them. When Captain don Juan Francisco de Ibarra captured the Yoruba (*aná*) Micaela and Agustina, they were both about twenty years old. Ibarra kept a pair of shackles in his home. Having once served as the *alcalde* of the *Santa Hermandad* (sheriff of the rural constabulary), he would certainly have used them in a professional capacity and perhaps also on his slaves.[12]

Direct documentary evidence of the physical abuse of slaves, however, is rare, suggesting that authorities rarely intervened in masters' "punishment" of their slaves. Significantly, one of the only criminal cases brought against a Costa Rican master for violence against a slave was prosecuted not in Costa Rica, but in León, Nicaragua. In 1722, while on a trip to León, fourteen-year-old don Tomás del Corral ordered his slave Miguel, a *mina* man of about twenty-five, to stay and watch some mules while he attended to an errand. Miguel left the mules unsupervised when his other young master, don Manuel del Corral, summoned him to bring a horse. When Tomás returned and found the mules unattended he exploded in a violent tantrum, attacking Miguel with a sword and permanently disabling him.[13] Although such direct

evidence of master violence is scant, on the other hand, documents frequently mentioned slaves' wounds. It is often impossible, however, to know
whether these were caused by torture or by accidents. Lázaro, Juan, and
Isabel were all described as "one-eyed."[14] Josefa, a middle-aged arará woman,
was scarred with "an old burn from the top of her throat to below the navel."[15]

Sexual violence, too, was inherent to slavery—systemic if not always systematic. Adding a dimension to their domination of female captives, slavers
often raped girls and women from the first moments they captured them.[16]
For many African women, purchased for their reproductive as well as productive capacities, sexual exploitation formed a familiar aspect of slavery.
Crew members and male captives continued the rapes on the Middle Passage.
Slave trader Jean Barbot reminisced that on Atlantic crossings, African
women "often made us pastime . . . [and] afforded us abundance of recre-
ation."[17] In the Americas, masters regarded sexual domination of female
slaves as part of their property rights. As with cases of physical abuse, masters' sexual victimization of slave women rarely made it into official records.
In general, masters' sexual relationships with their slaves became "problems"
only when they reached the level of public scandal. Doña María Trejos of
Cartago, for example, tolerated the "illicit friendship" of her husband with a
mulatta slave for more than twelve years before demanding "the punishment
of these public sins" in 1771.[18]

Although she was not a slave, the experience of Felipa Arias, a twelve-
year-old servant (criada) of don Miguel de la Haya Bolívar in the Bagaces
Valley, was surely shared by enslaved girls and women. Early in 1724, Felipa
begged for help, pleading "for the love of God and of his mother Most Holy
Mary and by the honor of God, that her master had violated her."[19]
Recognizing his intentions, Felipa had previously told her mistress that "her
master was pursuing her, to which [her mistress] paid no attention and for
which reason her mistress punished her." As so often happened in other slave
and slaveholding societies, Felipa's mistress blamed the victim for her husband's unwanted attentions.[20] Finally, Haya Bolívar took Felipa from her bed
in the house to a nearby plantain field, where he stuffed a rag in her mouth
and raped her. Between her master's threats and promises, Felipa kept silent
the next day, but when she realized that he intended to continue raping her
every night, she determined to flee. Having no one else to turn to, she went
to her master's brother, don Gabriel de la Haya Bolívar.[21] Extraordinarily,
Gabriel de la Haya notified the authorities of his brother's crime, and they left
a record of the incident.

Contrary to the wishful thinking of some nationalist historians, there is little reason to believe that slaves in Costa Rica were "more gently treated" or experienced less physical abuse than did captives in other parts of the Americas.[22] First, the physical "punishment" of dependents, including slaves, formed an integral and accepted part of daily life in colonial Latin America. The patriarchal ideology that guided Spanish American (and other) colonial societies held that just as God sometimes chastised his creatures and the king disciplined his subjects, so the father's authority over his wife, children, servants, and slaves sometimes required physical punishment. According to this ideal, masters could beat, whip, or otherwise "punish" slaves as long as they did so in a corrective, dispassionate, and exemplary manner without giving way to emotion, malice, or caprice.[23] Girls and women, especially slaves who were never supposed to question their masters, were unlikely publicly to report sexual abuse in societies where law and convention blurred the lines between consensual sex and rape.[24] There was thus no reason that routine abuse of a slave should merit written comment.

Second, the absence of references to violence against slaves should also be accepted as evidence that in Costa Rica, the colonial state seldom intervened between master and slave. In a small city such as Cartago, where face-to-face interactions characterized most social intercourse, slaves personally knew the officials to whom they legally had the right to appeal for protection. In theory, Spanish "absolutism" tempered master-slave relations throughout Latin America.[25] But in practice, slaves knew that the interests of slave masters and Spanish absolutism (on this issue, at least) were often identical, because in Costa Rica, slave masters often *were* the colonial state: "a group of persons who ruled, who commanded, who dominated and who in order to maintain their power possessed an apparatus of physical coercion, an apparatus of violence, with . . . weapons."[26] Cabildo members, governors, civil and ecclesiastical judges, and other officials figured among the colony's slaveholders. In 1700, for example, the Cartago cabildo included *Alcalde Ordinario de Primer Voto y Teniente de Gobernador en lo Político* (chief magistrate and lieutenant governor in charge of public order) Nicolás de Céspedes, *Alcalde Ordinario* (magistrate) don Francisco Bruno Serrano de Reyna, *Alférez Mayor* (standard-bearer) don José de Casasola y Córdoba, *Alcalde de la Santa Hermandad* (chief constable) Blas González Coronel, and *Depositario* (trustee) don Cristóbal Martín Cubero. All were slave owners, and at least three were big cacao planters. At that time, slaves could not hope to exploit a conflict between the locally elected cabildo and the governor appointed by

the Crown: Governor don Francisco Serrano de Reyna was not only a slave-
holder but an enthusiastic participant in the contraband slave trade.[27] Slaves
had little hope of assistance from these men who inflicted violence on them
personally, as slave owners, and potentially, with the shackles, jails, whips,
garrotes, gallows, and armed troops available to them as representatives of
the state. Omitting from documents the violence they inflicted, masters and
the state that served them together conspired to condemn slaves to suffer
forever in silence.

"Seasoning"

After arrival in Costa Rica, enslaved Africans began what planters in British
America called "seasoning." This brutal process involved adaptation to a new
disease environment, exposure to new ethnic groups, sale, the beginnings of
a relationship with a new master, the imposition of a new name, learning
unfamiliar work, an introduction to a new religion, and more.[28] On the
Middle Passage, captains and crews made little if any attempt to instruct the
captives in the norms of European culture. Concerned only with delivering
their merchandise to port, they maintained discipline through naked violence; nobody had illusions otherwise. Slave traders made no pretense of and
had no interest in acculturating the Africans. Simply controlling the captives
formed their main objective during transport.[29]

Masters had more complicated concerns. Once the captive arrived on his
or her new master's property, the emphasis shifted from mere physical control
to adapting the captive to a new social relationship and to her or his place in a
new productive system. Control remained imperative but was no longer sufficient. It now became a prerequisite to the goal of appropriating the surplus
product created by the enslaved worker.[30] Masters expected slaves to be not just
fearful but obedient, not only in work but in a host of ways in daily life.
Obedience—which need have nothing to do with consent—required that
slaves understand what masters expected of them; it involved a whole complex
of cultural norms of which Africans initially knew little or nothing. To make
a slave of a free woman or man—that is, to make her or him into a productive,
enslaved worker in a particular relationship to a master—ultimately required
a more sophisticated blend of physical and ideological forms of domination.[31]

Inevitably, African captives arrived in the Americas malnourished and
sick. At least one man from the *Christianus Quintus* or *Fredericus Quartus*

died just a few days after reaching Matina.[32] At this early stage, the Spaniards attempted to provide the valuable captives with healthy food. Alférez Jacinto de Rivera traveled to the Barbilla Valley, where he purchased plantains and meat for the captives, hiring mules to carry the sickest to the capital.[33] The march from the humid lowlands of Matina to the cool mountains of Cartago also took a toll on the new arrivals.[34] Another African man drowned in one of the rushing rivers on the way to the Central Valley.[35] When thirty-two Africans finally arrived at the Cartago home of Captain Juan López de la Rea in April 1710, all were sick, some with little hope of survival. Four died in the following three months. Captain Antonio de la Vega Cabral held twenty-two Africans in his home in Cartago for almost two months between May and July 1710. Cabral invested in two blankets to warm the sickest, and his wife applied "unguents" to cure them. Even these rudimentary measures appear to have had some effect, as none of the Africans died during those first fifty-seven days in Cabral's home.[36] Compared to recent arrivals from Africa elsewhere in the Americas, these survivors of the *Christianus Quintus* and *Fredericus Quartus* fared remarkably well. In the French Caribbean during the same period, on average, at least one quarter of captives died soon after disembarkation.[37]

Although some masters preferred creoles because they had already adapted to the rules of American slavery, others believed that this familiarity made them potentially more rebellious and therefore preferred to purchase bozales because they were uncorrupted by experience with European culture.[38] This ignorance, some slaveholders believed, made the Africans pliable and docile. At this stage, masters began the process of indoctrinating the recent arrivals. Africans began to learn the dimensions of their servitude, a process that included the attempted replacement of their previous identities with new ones defined solely by their status as slaves.[39]

The Slave Name

As one of the first steps in reducing African men and women to American slaves, masters labeled them with new names. Within minutes of capturing them on the beach near Moín in 1710, Captain Gaspar de Acosta Arévalo and Lieutenant Juan Bautista de Retana named each of more than thirty Gold Coast and Slave Coast men and women, presumably so they could tell them apart. "The black men and women had no names at all" when he found them,

Acosta claimed ignorantly.[40] Acosta's view was not original but consonant with prevailing stereotypes held by even the best-educated Spaniards. The Crown attorney (*fiscal*) for the Council of the Indies, for example, believed in 1708 that the "barbarians" of the African interior "do not know each other by name because they have none, but only tell each other apart by the outward signs of their bodies."[41]

On the contrary, Africans believed that names held extraordinary power and never assigned them arbitrarily or whimsically. In all of the societies from which the men, women, and children of the *Christianus Quintus* and *Fredericus Quartus* came—including Ga, Akan, Mina, Ewe, Yoruba, and Bariba—names held strong significance. As in other cultures, some names immediately identified a person as a member of a particular family group, clan, or lineage, and naming ceremonies served to introduce a newborn to the community.[42] According to a modern Ga writer, a Ga from the Accra region of the Gold Coast could tell from the name of another "to which family he belongs as soon as he hears the name of that person." A family name was only one of several, however. Ga children also inherited their father's name and received a personal name.[43] Akan children, including the Kwawu, received names reflecting matrilineage, day of birth, another day-name dedicated to the child's "destiny-soul" (*kra*), and a name chosen by their father, typically for an admired person who would, it was hoped, bestow some of his or her good qualities on the child.[44] For the Mina of the upper Slave Coast, to be named after an ancestor meant to inherit all of his or her defects as well as virtues. Names connected their bearers to the visible and invisible worlds, and a secret name conferred through divination could not be spoken aloud without risking death.[45] Among the Fon of Dahomey, a mother gave her child a personal name at birth, always kept secret thereafter. Like the Mina, both the Fon and the Bariba of northern Togo and Benin believed it essential to keep a child's birth name secret in order to prevent ill-wishers from using it for occult purposes. The Fon bestowed an array of names on their children according to an exceedingly complex system. A host of considerations determined the choice of names, including whether one's older siblings were twins; whether one was born with his or her eyes facing the sky, at the market, or while his mother was traveling; the gods into whose cults the child's parents were initiated; and many others.[46] Names not only introduced West Africans as individuals but established them as family members, natives of homelands, devotees of gods, and heirs to a past.

Spanish slave masters knew nothing of these vital traditions. Most of the time, they were utterly unconcerned with recording any aspects of African cultures, which they viewed as barbarous when they bothered to consider them at all.[47] For masters, the African backgrounds of their captives assumed relevance only insofar as they hindered or facilitated assimilation to slave status. Spanish slave masters might not have given much thought to the implications of uprooting free Africans from their pasts, but they certainly intended to remake them as Hispanicized slaves. Spaniards almost invariably renamed Africans immediately; renaming marked a further removal from the home societies that the Africans had been forced to leave.

Who named the Africans? When newly arrived Africans were sold at auction, notaries recorded physical descriptions and sometimes ethnic origins, but not names.[48] With the possible exception of some West Central Africans who might already have borne Portuguese names, new arrivals were clearly named by their masters, often before they learned anything else of Spanish culture.[49] The Slave Coast men subsequently known as Juan, Miguel, and Nicolás memorized their new names moments after being captured by the Spaniards on the coast near Moín, surprising their interrogators with them when they told their stories in their native language just a few days after arrival.[50] Not uncommonly, masters named slaves after themselves. Soon after purchasing a congo boy who arrived at La Caldera in 1700, Father don Diego de Angulo Gascón named him Diego de Angulo Gascón.[51] In 1710, Alférez don Antonio de la Riva y Agüero purchased a young mina man who had been captured from the survivors of the *Christianus Quintus* and *Fredericus Quartus*, naming him Antonio de la Riva y Agüero.[52] Masters chose the names of their bozal slaves from a limited repertoire of names that were much the same as those of other Costa Ricans. María and compound variations thereof, such as María Josefa, María de la Candelaria, and similar combinations, were by far the most common female names, followed by Juana. Juan and its derivatives were most common for males, followed by José, just as in the population at large.[53] Unlike slave masters in the British and French Caribbean, Spaniards in Costa Rica associated no mocking or degrading names exclusively with slaves, at least on paper.[54]

The earliest documents from Costa Rica carefully identified men and women of African descent with their current or past masters, treating their status as property with at least as much importance as their individual identity. The first surviving record from the parish church of Cartago, dating from 1595, lists the mother of a baptized child as "Juana, slave of Peñaranda."[55]

Although most slaves were known simply by Christian names followed by the formula "slave of . . . ," a minority adopted or were assigned surnames. Unlike today, Spanish surnames followed no general rule in the colonial period. Siblings, for instance, often called themselves by different surnames, and people were often known by their second surnames rather than their first. Slaves' surnames frequently derived from their first master, the master to whom they had been enslaved the longest, or the master or mistress with whom, for whatever reason, they most closely identified.[56] For example, María, a mulatta, was born to Agustina, a slave of doña María de Ortega, around 1662. After passing to two more owners, she continued to be associated with her first mistress and was known in 1689 as "María de Ortega."[57] Blas González Coronel purchased Lorenza, a *loango*, from a smuggler around 1700. Although he owned her for only about one year, Lorenza was still known as Lorenza González in 1719.[58] Antonio Granda, a congo slave of Governor don Lorenzo Antonio de la Granda y Balvín until the latter's death in 1712, always kept the governor's surname, although he was owned by the family of Captain Juan Sancho de Castañeda for the next thirty-six years.[59]

Masters also regarded ethnic origins as important in distinguishing African slaves. In the first decades of the seventeenth century, for example, Francisco Angola's and Melchor Carabalí's surnames pointed to origins in West Central Africa and the Bight of Biafra region, respectively.[60] Common throughout the colonial Americas, this practice continued in Costa Rica as long as Africans continued to arrive there. Like many African names that identified people with particular lineages and places, these casta surnames recalled distinct origins. Slave masters, however, used the ethnic surnames to serve as further identifiers of slave status, employing nomenclature inherited from slave traders. In time, however, such names also came to reflect the slaves' own identification with Africans of similar background and a diasporic ethnicity recognized in Costa Rica. Africans continued to be called by these diasporic surnames even after they attained their freedom. A West Central African woman, free by the early eighteenth century, was known locally as "Juana la Conga." A Slave Coast–born freedman, Pedro Arará, kept his ethnonymic surname when he served in the free colored militia of Matina in 1718.[61] Presumably, these were the surnames by which Juana and Pedro were already best known. They may also have used them to maintain identification with their diasporic ethnicities. A few Africans passed ethnic names on to their free descendants, such as Diego Bran, a militiaman, and José Bran, both free mulattos who lived in the North Pacific region in the mid-eighteenth century, and José Matamba, a Cartago mulatto whose surname recalled a province of the kingdom of Kongo.[62]

African slaves probably continued to use African names among themselves, although there is scant evidence of this in Costa Rica or indeed in much of Spanish America. The lack of documentation of African names probably relates to the Spaniards' ostensible concern with baptizing slaves, as well as to their indifference to African cultures.[63] In 1710, Captain don Juan Francisco de Ibarra y Calvo brought a group of nine Africans to his country house soon after their arrival in Matina on the *Christianus Quintus* and *Fredericus Quartus*. Among them were two young women of Yoruba origin and a young man from the Gold Coast or upper Slave Coast. A decade later, renamed Petrona and María, the women met the young man, now called Manuel, again. Petrona revealed that "in her language, he was called Papaligua," perhaps a tin-eared notary's version of the Yoruba *Baba Elegba* ("father").[64] Papaligua was almost certainly not "Manuel's" original name; rather, it was a Yoruba name granted by his new companions. Like the European name imposed by his masters, "Manuel's" new African name signified his membership in a new community of captives.

An Alien Language

In Spanish America and Brazil, masters used the word "bozal" (*boçal*) to refer to unacculturated Africans with no knowledge of Spanish (or Portuguese), just as slave masters in colonial British America spoke of *outlandish* Africans, *new negroes*, and *salt-water negroes*.[65] Ladinos had acquired some fluency in Spanish. On the other hand, any African-born slave might be called a bozal regardless of his or her language skills. Slaves who became fluent in Spanish were referred to as ladinos, but becoming ladino did not necessarily mean that a slave was no longer bozal. For example, in 1723, the slave Miguel was described as a "*bozal* black of *casta mina*, *ladino* in the Castilian language, which he speaks and understands."[66]

In the early eighteenth century, African-born slaves continued to speak several of their native languages in Costa Rica, almost certainly including Gbe, Twi, Kikongo and/or Kimbundu. There is little evidence, however, that they passed their languages on to their children or to other young captives. Antonia de Aguilar had arrived from Africa at a young age. In 1720, she stated that she was African born but did "not know her *casta* because she [did] not understand any language" spoken by other Africans in the province.[67]

As a rule, Africans in Costa Rica must have had to learn Spanish quickly, as they soon had to learn to communicate with their masters and others. Many apparently spoke with strong accents all their lives; to contrast the point, Alférez José de Guevara insisted that his slave Juan José could not be African born because he was "so *ladino* that he seemed to be a creole."[68] A few never learned more than enough for rudimentary communication. Ten years after arriving in Matina on the *Christianus Quintus* or *Fredericus Quartus*, Miguel Largo had difficulty making himself understood in Spanish.[69] Twenty years after arriving on one of the same ships, a document described mina Miguel Maroto as "between *bozal* and *ladino*."[70]

Learning Slave Labor

Masters viewed acculturation as necessary because Africans needed to understand what was expected in their new roles as slaves. Above all, slaves had to work, and they had to work within a determined set of social relations. In the islands, "seasoning" sometimes lasted up to three years. Masters frequently introduced the captives to plantation work gradually, initially putting them to work at light tasks before sending them to the fields. Some masters, especially in the Caribbean, assigned slaves to diverse jobs depending on physical ability and age. In Costa Rica, masters tended to purchase slaves for specific needs and put them to work immediately. Apart from allowing a brief period of convalescence, most masters seem to have made no special effort to acclimatize recently arrived Africans or ease their transition to slavery. Don Juan Francisco de Ibarra put nine young Africans, young women as well as men, to work in a cornfield at his house in the countryside soon after their arrival in Matina in 1710—work that was no different from that which some of them continued to do years later.[71] Natives of the Gold Coast, Slave Coast, and western Yorubaland, they were probably all familiar with the crop, and some or all might have already had experience in agricultural work.[72] For these young women and men, now Ibarra's slaves, the rules of slavery and the strange words in which they were expressed—not the work itself—were new.

Others learned completely unfamiliar work. Soon after they arrived on the *Nuestra Señora de la Soledad* in 1700, don Gregorio Caamaño sent twelve

African men to the South Pacific in a boat with Captain Francisco Conejo to learn to dive for pearls and to dye thread. It is improbable that any had done this work before. Four of the men, for example, came from the Slave Coast (three *popos* and one arará), whose peoples had no tradition of sea travel.[73] Three more from West Central Africa (congos) might have known of the extensive shell-diving industry near Luanda, but that work was carried out exclusively by women.[74] To aid in the transition to slave labor, Caribbean masters often assigned acculturated Africans or creoles to train the new arrivals in the plantation régime.[75] Similarly, Caamaño sent his creole slave Lorenzo to the Pacific with the African men, where he must have instructed them in elementary Spanish as well as the dangerous work of diving. They were gone more than a year, their "seasoning" surely complete by then.[76]

A Spiritual Conquest?

No less than learning Spanish or learning new methods of work, entering the Catholic Christian community formed an essential part of reducing free men and women to slavery. Unfortunately, existing sources cannot provide a sufficient basis from which to assess the thoroughness or superficiality of Africans' indoctrination in Christianity, nor do they contain much information on Africans' practice of other religions.

There is nothing to suggest that either local priests or masters worried particularly about the religious practices of slaves. Unlike in other areas of the Americas, Costa Ricans rarely if ever singled out slaves as especially lax in their faith—a fact that can be interpreted as proof of ecclesiastical inattention or even as evidence of the successful evangelization of the slaves. But Africans were baptized in numbers far smaller than might be supposed, and there is no reason to believe that they did not preserve and recreate African-derived religions in Costa Rica as they did everywhere else in the New World. Travel to other provinces and, no doubt, the continued forced immigration of countrymen allowed some Africans to reconnect with the spirituality and rituals of their homelands. Limited evidence from Costa Rica shows that some Africans sincerely embraced Christianity, devoutly practicing their faith after winning their freedom. Not surprisingly, creoles and mulattos seem to have been more fully integrated into Costa Rica's spiritual life, demonstrating a conversance with both official and popular varieties of Christianity.

Because Iberian laws officially prohibited the importation of Muslim or "heathen" slaves, Africans with little exposure to Christianity legally had to be instructed in Catholic doctrine and baptized before embarking on the Middle Passage. Although some Catholic priests in Africa attempted to comply sincerely with these requirements, others showered water indifferently on crowds of captives. In Cape Verde, as many as three hundred or even seven hundred captives were baptized at once, sometimes just before departure while they were already in chains below deck. Some priests in the Americas, denying the adequacy of such instruction, baptized Africans a second time.[77] For example, in 1637, Cartago parish priest Father Baltasar de Grado baptized Dominga, his own slave, a second time, although she said she had already been baptized "in her country." Two years later, he baptized Agustín, a slave of Costa Rican Governor don Gregorio de Sandoval, although Agustín, too, reported having been baptized previously in "Guinea."[78] If death seemed imminent, priests or laymen in Costa Rica sometimes baptized newly arrived Africans just after arrival and before they had received any religious education. In mid-March 1710, while Captain Gaspar de Acosta Arévalo and his party of slave catchers were driving a group of survivors from the *Christianus Quintus* and *Fredericus Quartus* to Cartago, it became clear that one of the African men was mortally ill. Jerónimo Pacheco hastily baptized him before he expired.[79] After arriving at the home of Captain Juan López de la Rea on April 14, an unnamed African woman was buried in a shroud on May 6, her funeral officiated by a priest and sacristan. She could not have been buried in a Catholic ceremony had she not been baptized, but she almost certainly had received no instruction in Christianity before she died.[80]

Slaves' knowledge of Christianity and their ability to practice that religion if they so chose depended above all on the attitudes of their masters. The religion of their slaves probably caused little concern to most Costa Rican slaveholders. On the contrary, in 1711, Bishop Benito Garret y Arloví threatened Costa Rican landowners with excommunication if they prevented "Christian Indians, mulatos, and slaves" from hearing Mass on days of obligation. Three years later, his edict ignored, he made good on his warning.[81] It is clear from Cartago's surviving baptismal registers that only a small minority of masters complied with their duty to baptize their African-born slaves. Only about thirty-eight men and women identified as adult Africans were baptized in the parish church of Cartago between 1595 and 1750. In the 1690s and 1720s—among the decades when civil notaries recorded the largest numbers of transactions involving African-born slaves—none of the slaves baptized in the Cartago church were noted as Africans.[82]

Baptism marked another step in the African's immersion in Costa Rican society. Catholic masters held an obligation to see to the religious instruction of newly arrived African captives so that they might promptly be baptized. Some masters dominated the spiritual lives of their slaves as well as their persons. Two years and four months after they purchased María and Petrona, doña Cecilia Vázquez de Coronado and her husband Captain Salvador Suárez de Lugo became godparents to the young women.[83] There is no reason to believe that the African girls had any say in the choice of their sponsors. Vázquez de Coronado and Suárez de Lugo added another dimension to their domination of their new slaves by assuming responsibility for the young women's religious education—as the Church specified, "to exercise a constant vigilance over their spiritual children."[84] They further insisted on their centrality in their slaves' lives by becoming María's and Petrona's "fictive" parents, symbolically substituting themselves for the families the African women had lost.

TABLE 4.1. Baptisms of Adult Africans by Decade, 1630–1750

DECADE	NUMBER OF BAPTISMS*
1630	2 (5)
1640	2 (5)
1650	0 (0)
1660	0 (0)
1670	8 (21)
1680	8 (21)
1690	0 (0)
1700	13 (34)
1710	4 (11)
1720	0 (0)
1730	1 (3)
1740	0 (0)
Total	38 (100)

*Numbers in parentheses show the percentage of the total number of slave baptisms in 1630–1750.

Sources: ACMSJ, Libros de Bautizos de Cartago, nos. 1–6 (1595–1738)/FHL, VAULT INTL film 1219701, items 1–5, VAULT INTL film 1219702, item 1.

TABLE 4.2. Slave Baptisms by Decade, Cartago, 1595–1750

DECADE	BLACK SLAVES	MULATTO SLAVES	SLAVES UNIDENTIFIED BY COLOR	TOTAL SLAVES*
1595	0	0	3	3 (1)
1600	8	4	5	17 (4.7)
1610	2	1	4	7 (2)
1620	5	0	0	5 (1.4)
1630	7	3	1	11 (3.1)
1640	8	3	5	16 (4.5)
1660	1	1	1	3 (1)
1670	10	3	14	27 (7.5)
1680	11	11	16	38 (10.6)
1690	5	2	5	12 (3.4)
1700	24	14	9	47 (13.1)
1710	5	1	14	20 (5.6)
1720	5	1	15	21 (5.9)
1730	7	25	35	67 (18.7)
1740	10	11	43	64 (18.1)
Total	108	80	170	358 (100)

*Numbers in parentheses show the percentage of the total number of slaves baptized in 1595–1750.

Sources: ACMSJ, Libros de Bautizos de Cartago, nos. 1–6 (1595–1738)/ FHL, VAULT INTL film 1219701, items 1–5, VAULT INTL film 1219702, item 1.

For María and Petrona, Christianity was inseparable from their relationship to their masters. Their baptism implied not only a reordering of their spiritual worlds but another way in which they were bound to their masters; the religious relationship reflected and reinforced the secular relationship.[85]

Given the opacity of the sources, there is little firm evidence to indicate whether most Africans embraced or resisted conversion. For Africans, indoctrination in Christianity formed an essential component of their reduction to slavery in Costa Rica—and they recognized as much. When asked who had been his first master more than twenty years after he had arrived in Costa Rica, Pedro Mina, a native of the Gold Coast or upper Slave Coast, recalled "that he came to the Port of Matina in an English sloop, and that

Juan Fernández el Montañés bought him, and taught him to pray."[86] Colonial authorities envisioned prayer as an essential part of the daily regimen of slave life on the cacao haciendas, to be imposed by force if necessary. In the late 1730s, Governor don Francisco Carrandi y Menán charged his lieutenant in the Matina Valley with ensuring that "the slaves and overseers of the haciendas and the rest of the servants" attend Mass on feast days and "pray the rosary of Most Holy Mary every night before they lie down in their beds."[87]

Some Africans balked at conversion, and others were left to believe or not believe as they chose. When María, a congo slave, died suddenly around 1717, her master, Sergeant José Damián de Molina, attempted to have her buried in the Cartago church. Father don Diego de Angulo Gascón denied her body a Christian burial, however, because she had never been baptized. A previous owner, don Nicolás de Guevara, said that María was "too thickheaded (*ruda*) to learn the Christian doctrine."[88] The religious traditions in which Africans had been raised often militated against easy conversion. With few exceptions, by the early eighteenth century, Christianity had failed to make inroads in Africa outside Kongo and Angola. Most natives of the Gold Coast or Slave Coast, where Christianity was little known beyond slave-trading port cities, would initially have found the religion thoroughly alien.[89] Although to object overtly would be to invite the repression of the Inquisition, privately, Muslims from Upper Guinea might have found the "idolatrous" trappings of baroque Catholicism offensive and vehemently rejected its tenets, as several scholars have suggested they did in other areas of the Americas.[90]

On the other hand, some Africans who arrived in Costa Rica already professed Catholicism, and others had some knowledge of Christianity. West Central Africans not only comprised the largest ethnic contingent among enslaved Africans in Costa Rica, but women and men from Kongo and Angola had had the most sustained and thorough exposure to Christianity of any of the African peoples. Diego Angulo, a congo who arrived in Costa Rica at the age of nine in 1700, was probably enslaved as a result of the civil wars that shook Kongo between 1691 and 1709 and deported by way of Luanda. He might well have already known something of Christianity when he arrived in Cartago. By the seventeenth century, Catholicism had spread widely in West Central Africa. Even non-Christian Kongolese had their children baptized by the thousands, believing that the sacrament afforded effective protection against witchcraft. Diego was purchased by one of Cartago's parish priests, the Licentiate don Diego de Angulo Gascón, who renamed the slave boy after himself.[91] Diego might easily have recognized some of the Catholic images that adorned his new master's home. He surely knew the crucifix: Kongolese artists excelled at making crucifixes by the lost-wax method, and virtually all Kongolese respected the cross as a powerful *nkisi* (sacred object). By the early eighteenth century, its use was "ubiquitous" among Kongolese, who frequently wore it as a defense against witchcraft.[92] Diego must also have recognized engravings of Saint Anthony, whose cult enjoyed enormous popularity in Kongo, including among non-Christians.[93] Perhaps the second most-revered saint in Kongo was Saint Francis of Assisi, devotion to whom was unrivaled in Cartago. As in Europe and America, Kongo Catholicism emphasized the veneration of the Virgin Mary, and Cartago boasted its own sacred image, the Virgin of los Angeles.[94] Diego would have found much that was familiar to him in the Catholicism practiced in his new surroundings.

But even if he knew nothing of Christianity before his arrival, in his master's home, Diego had every opportunity to pursue a Catholic spiritual life. He now found himself in an environment dominated by religious practice. As a young boy, Diego probably served his master as a body servant, accompanying him on his priestly errands around Cartago. Father Angulo was likely the best-read man in Costa Rica at the time, with twenty-seven books in his private library—most on religious themes, including some titles in Latin and Portuguese. The priest would have frequently received parishioners in his home, dispensing spiritual advice as well as socializing.[95] Just by listening and observing, Diego must have learned more than his share of Church doctrine. Even if he had wanted to, he could not avoid doing so.

Some slaves of devout masters lived surrounded by the trappings of religion, attended church services, and received Christian instruction. Not surprisingly, priests tended their captive flocks with particular zeal. In 1625, the bishop of Nicaragua and Costa Rica confirmed Francisco, a black slave of Father Baltasar de Grado from "Guinea."[96] At his home and sugar mill in the Valley of Barva, Sergeant Major don Francisco de Ocampo Golfín maintained a full chapel with a gilded altarpiece and a statue of Our Lady of the Rosary, where his twelve slaves doubtless attended Mass. The devotion to the Virgin of the Rosary had been introduced to Kongo in the mid-sixteenth century, where Ocampo Golfín's congo slaves Miguel and Manuel might have known of it.[97] Don Bernardo García de Miranda and doña Josefa de Casasola y Córdoba owned three slaves. The couple maintained a chapel in their home, fully equipped for the saying of Mass and crammed with three statues of the Infant Jesus, one of Saint Anne and the Virgin Mary, and one each of Saint Joseph and Saint Agatha.[98]

Although their sincerity may be open to question, those Africans who were questioned directly seem always to have professed Christianity. After arriving in Costa Rica in 1710 on the *Fredericus Quartus* or *Christianus Quintus*, Petrona, a Yoruba of casta aná, was baptized three years later in the parish church of Esparza near the Pacific coast.[99] In September 1719, José de Ollo Echavarría asked her whether she was a baptized Christian. She replied that "yes, she was, by the grace of Jesus Christ Our Lord," a verbatim answer from Catholic catechisms, which Ollo Echavarría judged "capable."[100] After fleeing to Matina from the Miskitus in 1733, Manuel García declared that he was a Christian "by the grace of God and therefore he had come from among the Mosquitos to end his life among Christians."[101]

At least some Africans believed sincerely in Christianity, as demonstrated in their continued devotion to "Holy Mother Church" after they attained their freedom.[102] After his manumission in 1730, congo Diego Angulo remained a devout Catholic. Diego kept two religious statues in his home, including one of Saint Anthony.[103] With his family, he actively participated in the social life of Cartago's free colored neighborhood, which centered around the church of the Virgin of los Angeles. Diego might have believed that the Virgin Mary had appeared in Kongo, just as it was believed that she had appeared at the site of the church he attended in Cartago.[104] In 1742, his "brothers" elected him an officer (*mantenedor*) in the confraternity dedicated to the Virgin. As a black former slave, being elected a *diputado* (delegate) of the confraternity of the Virgin of los Angeles might have brought Diego a special satisfaction. In Kongo, mulattos and the nobility, not black ex-slaves, dominated the Catholic brotherhoods.[105]

Diego García, a freed West African known as a *cabo verde*, also demonstrated Catholic fervor at the end of his life. If García was a *crioulo* from the islands, he would have been a Catholic before deportation from his homeland.[106] In 1743, he commended his soul, as was customary, to "My Intercessor and Advocate, Queen of the Ages, Most Holy Mary, Mother of God and Our Lady." He instructed that his body be interred in the Cartago parish church with a solemn burial service, including a vigil and a sung Mass. Most significantly, he designated part of his legacy to establish a chaplaincy (*capellanía*) in his name, appointing don José Miguel de Guzmán y Echavarría to sing five Masses per year for his soul and the rest of those in purgatory at a cost of two pesos each.[107] The following year, García's executor presented receipts for the twenty-nine pesos in cacao and eight pesos in silver paid for his funeral, burial, shroud, wax candles, Masses, and mandatory donations—a sum equal to the cost of a burro, a small house, or even an elderly slave. To establish the chaplaincy her husband had willed, García's widow Manuela Gutiérrez guaranteed it with a cacao hacienda and designated the rents paid on it in the future to finance the endowment "perpetually and forever more."[108]

At least one enslaved woman participated in lengthy theological discussions and assumed the role of sometime defender of Catholic orthodoxy. In 1757, María Josefa de Chávez, a twenty-six-year-old mulatta slave of doña Josefa Liberata Chacón, denounced José Nicolás López, a free mulatto "foreigner," before Father don Manuel José González Coronel, commissary of the Inquisition in Cartago. López, María Josefa declared, had expressed heretical beliefs about the creation of the universe and its moral structure. While socializing at the home of the free colored militia officer Juan Solano in the plains near Ujarrás, the friends' conversation had turned to the controversial topic of religion. López began to argue that "God had been formed out of nothing, and for three days was a ball of fire within a cloud, and after three days fell to earth and became a sinner like us. Although it is true that there is a hell," López continued, "no one is damned nor are there any damned, and if there was no hell, everyone would want to be gods." Like other Costa Ricans, slaves learned much of their Catholicism from the sermons of Franciscan evangelists. María Josefa knew the teachings she had heard from the friars well, and could not let comments such as López's pass uncontested. "How [was it that] none were damned," she demanded, "if the missionary fathers preached it every day?" When López alleged that the friars lied, María Josefa went to the commissary to condemn him.[109]

The understandings that slaves formed of Christianity varied widely. Slaves' observance of Catholicism, or the lack of it, reflected the relative incorporation or exclusion of slaves from the broader society. In addition to their own spiritual inclinations, slaves' participation in religious life depended on factors such as their geographical distance from churches, which was closely related to their position in the colonial economy and their relationships with their masters.

African Indigenous Religions

The practice of African indigenous religions was closely tied to the question of ethnicity. Traditional African religions could be practiced in Costa Rica only when sufficient numbers of Africans of similar ethnic origins were present to practice them or when Africans of one ethnic origin initiated others into their belief systems. Such opportunities varied according to factors such as patterns in the ethnic composition of slaves exported from Africa and imported to Costa Rica, patterns in the residence of Africans in the colony, and the religious proclivities of individual slaves and their masters. Costa Rica lacked the institutions that sometimes allowed slaves to maintain, recreate, or draw upon African religious traditions in other American societies. There is little evidence, for example, that slaves in Costa Rica joined the Catholic confraternities that elsewhere were organized along African ethnic lines (although some ex-slaves did). They did not establish *cabildos de nación* or other associations that could provide cover for religious practices based in the Old World. It is plausible that groups of Africans met in Cartago, its forested environs, or in Matina for religious purposes, but no evidence proves that they did so, nor is there much to suggest that they passed on African-based traditions to their children or to other creoles.

One clear case of the practice of an African religion concerned captives of Slave Coast origin who called themselves ararás. Diego de Ibarra was a wealthy merchant, rancher, and planter of Panamanian origin, married to doña Ana de Retes, the creole daughter of a Cartago elite family of encomenderos.[110] Over time, the couple came to qualify as some of Costa Rica's largest slave owners. Retes received several slaves through donations and inheritance, and Ibarra brought others to Costa Rica whom he had purchased in Panama. Ana de Retes owned ten slaves by 1699.[111] Like many Costa Rican elites, Ibarra combined a number of economic activities. By 1691, he owned a cacao hacienda of 500 trees in Matina, a livestock ranch in the Valley of Santa Ana with 800 head of cattle, 200 mares, and four burros for breeding mules, as well as a sugar mill that produced about fifty *arrobas* (567 kilograms/1,250 pounds) of sugar annually.[112]

Perhaps on a business trip related to his role in the mule trade, when Ibarra visited Panama City around 1678 or 1679, he found himself suffering from a deterioration of his vision. María Arará, a slave of local resident doña Leonor García, told Ibarra that she believed that a curse was responsible for his poor eyesight, and offered her assistance in seeking a cure from a healer of her country who worked with herbs. The healer was unable to visit Ibarra but suggested that Ibarra send "a person of satisfaction" of the arará nation on his behalf. Ibarra sent María and Feliciano, another slave of casta arará belonging to doña Leonor, as well as his own slave brought from Costa Rica, Antonio Arará, begging them to consult the healer for a cure. The three slaves went to the healer, who took a carved wooden idol from a box and spoke to it in the "*arará* language," asking it about Ibarra's illness. All three slaves heard the idol respond in a muffled voice (*voz delgada*) that Ibarra's poor vision was due to a curse put on him by another of his slaves, Melchora, a "mulata zamba." As soon as he heard this story, Ibarra took Antonio to don Juan Melgarejo, comissary of the Inquisition in Panama City, to report the incident. When he returned to Cartago, Ibarra denounced Melchora to the secular authorities and had her imprisoned. She escaped from the Cartago jail and was later apprehended and sold to a new master in León, Nicaragua.[113]

The incident denounced by don Diego de Ibarra shows that religious, as well as economic and social, influences traveled along the extensive commercial circuits between Panama, Costa Rica, and Nicaragua. As a companion of his master, Antonio Arará traveled between Costa Rica and Panama, where he was able to renew social contacts with Africans of his own ethnic, linguistic, and religious background. Yet even his practice of an African ethnic religion reflected local preoccupations born of slavery in the Americas. As slaves of the same master, Antonio and the "mulata zamba" Melchora inhabited not only the same household but the same religious universe. The arará slaves asserted the efficacy not only of their own magical and religious traditions but of other traditions, such as those that Melchora allegedly practiced, presumably of European and/or American origin.[114] It is unclear why María Arará, a slave of the Panamanian doña Leonor García, offered to intercede to effect a cure for don Diego de Ibarra's failing eyesight. The answer may have rested in her relationship with her "countryman," Antonio Arará. Very likely, Antonio had discussed life in Costa Rica with his fellow ararás María and Feliciano. It is possible that his relationship with his fellow slave Melchora was strained and that Antonio sought to settle a score and at the same time wished to curry favor with his master by seeking a cure for Ibarra's affliction. Don Diego de Ibarra's reaction to the African religious practices suggests the limits of tolerance for popular religion by the Spanish elite. He was willing to consult an enslaved African healer, but when he heard the details of the ceremony, Ibarra became alarmed and reported the incident to the Inquisition.

Islam

Evidence of Islam among slaves in Costa Rica, as of any non-Christian religious practices among slaves, is exceedingly rare. An incident in Costa Rica brought to the attention of the Inquisition in 1610 hints that at least one enslaved West African man was recognized to come from a Muslim background. In August 1609, some prominent members of the Cartago elite assembled at the Franciscan convent in the Indian pueblo of Pacaca to celebrate the Assumption of the Virgin Mary. Serving them at table was Manuel, a slave of Luis Cascante de Rojas, known to be an African of *tierra jolof*.[115] One of the celebrants, Gaspar Pereira Cardoso, had acquired the habit of joking with Manuel in a pointed way. Pereira offered Manuel money if he would "forgive *Bujame*." Manuel replied good-naturedly that even if he were offered a lot of money, he would not do that.[116]

Pereira found humor in making a game of heresy. "Bujame" (elsewhere, *buxame*) undoubtedly represents a corruption of "Muhammad," and by enticing Manuel to "forgive" the Prophet of Islam, Pereira mockingly tempted him with committing sacrilege. It seems likely that the revelers found special humor (or Pereira thought that they would) in making this preposterous suggestion to an African known to be of Muslim background; the joke would have fallen flat had Manuel been, say, an *angola* or a *carabalí*.[117] Needling Manuel before his guests suggests that Pereira expected his companions to share in the joke—that they, too, were aware of Manuel's religious orientation. In another version of the incident, Pereira offered Manuel a *real* and a *maravedí* to *deny* "Bujame." Manuel, a "joker" (*burlón*), rejoined that he wouldn't do so for less than a peso.[118] In this account, Pereira implied that he suspected Manuel still considered himself a Muslim, unwilling to repudiate Islam's central tenet.

The incident in Pacaca tells us little about Manuel's religious sensibilities and almost nothing about the practice of Islam among enslaved Africans in Cartago; it reveals much more about the social limits of religious humor in colonial Costa Rica.[119] Did Manuel have coreligionists in Cartago, their Muslim origins hidden behind Spanish names and their practice of Islam unobserved or unrecorded by literate contemporaries?[120] The sparse and opaque sources cannot tell us. But the repartée at the convent in Pacaca at least shows that Costa Rican slave masters recognized that Africans were not the interchangeable "*piezas de Indias*" of slave trade terminology. Even if superficially, the elite revelers in the Convent of San Francisco recognized that Africans came from different peoples with different pasts. In Manuel's case, they apparently possessed the elementary knowledge that some Africans in the tierra jolof were Muslims, whom they in turn associated with stereotypes of "Bujame" that more likely derived from the *reconquista* heritage of the Iberian Peninsula than from an understanding of West Africa itself.

A growing body of scholarship addresses the practice of Islam by African slaves in the Americas.[121] Historian Sylviane Diouf concludes that due to factors such as their importation in small numbers, inability to form religious communities, and theological exclusivity, Muslim Africans in the Americas faced nearly insurmountable difficulties in transmitting or propagating their religion.[122] Her insight applies especially to Costa Rica, where not only Muslims but all Africans confronted extreme challenges in preserving or recreating links to their Old World origins. Whether or not scattered individual Muslims proved able to maintain their faith, their numbers could not sustain a Muslim community, nor did Islam provide a sufficient basis for a common identity among slaves in Costa Rica.

⁕ Conclusion

Immediately upon arrival in the Americas, masters began the process of forcibly adapting captive Africans to their new status as slaves. In the first and last instances, they used violence to force Africans and creoles into that role. Ideological as well as physical measures, however, soon came to form essential components of the ongoing process. The transformation of free women and men into slaves made them into both labor and capital. Slave masters' need to convert Africans into enslaved workers always provided the primary reason for "seasoning" and acculturation. They cared whether Africans learned the Castilian language only insofar as it was necessary to communicate work commands; some Africans never learned it. Of course, the common idiom also allowed Africans to communicate with each other, creole slaves, and free servants as well as masters; it was more, therefore, than the master's language. Some masters took their legal and social obligations to indoctrinate Africans in Catholicism seriously; others apparently cared little about the conversion or religious observance of their slaves. A few Africans maintained ties to the indigenous and Islamic religions of their homelands. Some West Central Africans were already Catholics when they arrived; Catholicism was not, therefore, only a weapon of their oppressors. Members of all racial groups and social classes, however, shared "official" Catholicism and popular magical and religious practices; new cosmologies and rituals permeated their new environment. When Africans came to terms with them, they necessarily changed as a result. The work slaves undertook continued to inform their experience and shape their evolving identities.

CHAPTER FIVE

Work and the Shaping of Slave Life

✝ IN THE ABSENCE OF KNOWN MINERAL WEALTH OR EXTENSIVE PLAN-
tation agriculture, Costa Rica never relied on African slavery as its dominant
mode of production.[1] Spaniards nevertheless imported black slaves to Costa
Rica from the earliest days of the conquest, as they did in all other parts of
the Americas. In Cartago, the colonial capital, the white elite prized enslaved
Africans and their descendants as "domestic servants." Pointing out the economic underdevelopment of the province, historians emphasized that slave
ownership in Costa Rica was limited to a few ruling families.[2] Comparing
the human property of Costa Rican slave owners with the vast numbers of
people enslaved in other colonies, they concluded that Costa Rican slavery
was "non-economic" or "domestic-patriarchal" in nature.[3] Undoubtedly, the
variable labor requirements of the small-scale Costa Rican economy created
a slaveholding system markedly different from those in other New World
colonies. Although most Spaniards did not possess the capital to procure
large numbers of African slaves, they employed slaves not only in domestic
service but in virtually all the economic activities they undertook in Costa
Rica. Slaves constituted an essential sector of the labor force in all regions of
the province.

Colonial Costa Rica never developed a monocultural economy in which
production of a lucrative staple dominated every aspect of life. Precisely for
this reason, few slave owners could afford to confine their slaves to domestic
service.[4] On the contrary, many wealthy Spaniards pursued numerous business interests and used both African slaves and free workers in all their

117

enterprises. Costa Rican slaves performed manual labor wherever their masters sent them, and most slaves worked at a variety of tasks. The occupations in which slaves worked dictated where they lived and, therefore, their opportunities for contact with other slaves, determining their ability to maintain African or to create new cultural forms.

The place of work and residence, inextricably related to gender, became one of the most important factors shaping slave life. In contrast to plantation societies, a more or less strictly gendered division of labor characterized slavery in midcolonial Costa Rica. Female slaves usually lived in or near their masters' homes in the Pacific region or, more commonly, the Central Valley. The proximity of the master subjected them to heightened vigilance and constrained their opportunities to pursue outside relationships. It also required adaptation to the masters' values and hindered the preservation or development of a distinct culture of the enslaved. Male slaves, on the other hand, exercised greater physical mobility and experienced a broader range of social contacts. In the Caribbean valley of Matina, male slaves, many of them African, lived remarkably independent lives. Female slaves, however, were excluded from the region and from the opportunity to raise families there.

A master's varied economic interests commonly led to wide physical movement and wide social contact for slaves, especially men. The slave of a wealthy master might divide his time between the master's home and farm in Cartago, a cattle or mule ranch in the Pacific area, and a cacao plantation in the Caribbean region of Matina. As the owner of twenty slaves in 1715, Miguel Calvo was among the largest slaveholders in the history of the province.[5] In the 1680s, Calvo employed his male and female slaves not only as domestic servants in his home in Cartago but as ranch hands and cacao workers on his rural properties in Bagaces and Matina.[6] Intense and sustained contact with people of other racial and cultural backgrounds meant that neither Africans nor creoles created a distinctive slave culture but rather participated in a broadly shared creole culture that crossed ethnic, racial, and class boundaries.

Slaves in Costa Rica lived and worked in one or more of three major regions: the North Pacific, the Central Valley, and the Atlantic lowlands. The North Pacific had the smallest slave population. Slaves formed just one part of a local labor force that also included Indians, free blacks and mulattos, and mestizos. Industries such as indigo processing, pearl diving, and the production of purple dyes sometimes used black slaves, but these remained minor enterprises compared to cattle and mule breeding, which became the major activities in the North Pacific and relied mainly on free workers. Free mulattos and blacks dominated the countryside, where they comprised a clear majority of the non-Indian population and played key roles in all industries.

In the Central Valley around Cartago, black and mulatto slaves joined Indians, free blacks and mulattos, and mestizos as servants in Spanish households. Although "domestic servants," their work was rarely if ever confined to such activities as cooking, cleaning, and waiting at table. Rather, they raised corn and wheat, cared for livestock, fished, hauled produce, and carried out dozens of other tasks, as well as attending their masters' homes. "Jacks of all trades," they might or might not work directly in production for the market.[7] If they did not, slaves, as well as free servants, were still economically vital in the simple and immediate sense that they directly contributed to the improved well-being of their owners by working longer and harder than necessary to pay the costs of their own upkeep.[8] In addition to the household economy, small farming, and the care of livestock, a number of Central Valley slaves worked in sugar production, which remained on a small scale and was mostly confined to the domestic market.

The cacao-producing region of Matina on the Caribbean coast most closely resembled the plantation model. Matina was overwhelmingly dedicated to the production of a single crop for export, grown with slave labor.[9] After exhausting other potential sources of labor, planters had turned to African slaves as the primary labor force by 1700. Enslaved men in Matina enjoyed a freedom of movement and, for some, a social mobility that contrasted starkly with the harsh restrictions confronting slaves in plantation societies. At the same time, a de facto gender segregation kept female Africans in the Pacific region and Central Valley, sharply limiting the opportunities for the reproduction of slave families and culture in the Caribbean zone.

In October 1710, the young women who would become known as María and Petrona, Yoruba of *casta aná*, survivors of the *Christianus Quintus* and *Fredericus Quartus*, were sold in Esparza, a few miles from Costa Rica's Pacific coast. They were soon taken to San Francisco de Tenorio, the hacienda of doña Cecilia Vázquez de Coronado, their new mistress, in the North Pacific Valley of Bagaces.[10] Separated from Costa Rica's Central Valley by a volcanic mountain range and several often impassable rivers, the region developed strong economic and cultural links to Nicaragua and Panama.[11] Dominated by large landholdings devoted to cattle and mule breeding, Bagaces hosted a highly mobile, ethnically and culturally diverse population. In 1688, the 110 blacks and mulattos made up about 37 percent of the valley's total population of 297. Seventeen were slaves (about 5.7 percent).[12] Because María and Petrona were likely the only Yoruba speakers in the region, no other members of their "nation" could help them in their adjustment.[13] Although they surely encountered blacks and mulattos in Bagaces, whether free or slave, they were nearly all creoles.

Of necessity, the closest relationships María and Petrona formed were with members of other ethnic and cultural groups. Although most Bagaces landowners preferred to live in the more comfortable cities of Cartago or Rivas, Nicaragua, doña Cecilia Vázquez de Coronado and her husband, Sergeant Major don Salvador Suárez de Lugo, resided at San Francisco de Tenorio year-round.[14] No doubt they played powerful roles in the lives of their slaves. When María and Petrona were baptized in the city of Esparza after sixteen months in Bagaces, doña Cecilia and don Salvador stood as their godparents.[15] Nothing is known of the fathers of María and Petrona's four children except, perhaps, that they were not Africans: all the children were described as mulattos.[16] Like virtually all slaves in Bagaces, the other slaves at San Francisco de Tenorio, including María Egipciaca and her two young children, Mónica de la Cruz and José Francisco, were creoles.[17] The geography and demographic structure of the Valley of Bagaces militated powerfully against the preservation of María and Petrona's Yoruba heritage. They lived in a creole world.

The Nicoya peninsula was the first region of the territory now in Costa Rica that the Spaniards brought under military and political control. The Indians of Nicoya immediately fell victim to an extensive trade in indigenous slaves tied to Panama, Peru, and the Caribbean. The first economic activities the Spaniards developed in Nicoya and Nicaragua were in no way productive but predatory and destructive: looting and slaving.[18] Depopulation was especially severe in the North Pacific. Historical geographer Linda Newson has estimated that the population of Nicoya declined by more than 97 percent between the 1520s and 1570s, from about 62,700 to just 1,800 people.[19] On the eastern coast of the Gulf of Nicoya, the devastation was, if anything, worse. Small pueblos were completely depopulated within a few decades.[20] Indian slave exports from Nicaragua and Nicoya to the Caribbean, Panama, and Peru then reached a peak of perhaps ten thousand persons per year between 1536 and 1540.[21] The famous New Laws issued in 1542 outlawed the Indian slave trade and Indian slavery, but Indians remained severely exploited under the encomienda. Officially, the New Laws forbade the exaction of Indian tribute in labor, commuting it to payment in manufactured goods or produce.

But in fact, "personal service" remained common and, despite its illegality, was even recorded among the 1548 tribute obligations of Indian pueblos such as Nicoya and Nandayure to their encomenderos.[22] The extraordinarily severe abuse of Nicoya's Indian population eventually moved the Crown to intervene: it placed the Indians under its own direct jurisdiction by declaring the region a *corregimiento* in 1554 and an *Alcaldía Mayor* in 1560.[23]

Spaniards employed other sources of manpower, including black and mulatto slaves, even in the era when Indians supplied the overwhelming majority of laborers. Most of the industries of the North Pacific did not require large numbers of workers. Surpassing all other activities, livestock breeding emerged as the most important industry in the North Pacific. In the seventeenth century, livestock breeding centered on mules for Panama. In the eighteenth, although the mule trade remained significant, breeders concentrated on cattle. According to historian Claudia Quirós, cattle production rose 394 percent between 1700 and 1750.[24] Variable labor demand resulted in a mixed slave and free work force.

Slaves formed a small minority of hacienda workers in the Pacific region, as they did in the population at large. In agriculture and animal husbandry, in some cases enslaved men of African descent supervised the labor of free workers. Slaves who held supervisory positions were often older men. For example, Juan, an enslaved man estimated to be fifty years old, served as administrator (*mandador*) of his master's ranch (*hato*) in 1683. Juan was responsible for 320 head of cattle, twenty-two mares, fifteen horses, fifteen mules, and five oxen, as well as for supervising the other hands (*mozos*) on the estate.[25] In 1719, another Juan, a mulatto slave also about fifty, oversaw a smaller property at his master's ranch in San Antonio.[26] Hacendados organized the labor forces on their properties hierarchically. Slaves were bound to their masters in a way freemen were not, but in return for their supervision of free mulatto, slave, and Indian workers, enslaved overseers customarily enjoyed special privileges, including access to land for subsistence plots and grazing. According to historian Lowell Gudmundson, the position of overseer on haciendas was "almost always" occupied by a slave, at least in the late colonial period, and these slaves acquired their own herds of livestock.[27]

In 1714, Miguel, a *congo*, was the only one of twelve slaves owned by his master serving at El Higuerón ranch in the Valley of Bagaces. The ranch consisted of five thousand head of cattle, four hundred mares, and twenty horses, as well as some buildings and corrals. Most likely, Miguel served as

overseer, and he probably also looked in on his master's other nearby properties in Bagaces and Chomes.[28] According to historian Claudia Quirós, the
mandador del campo was usually acknowledged to be the best horseman on
the property.[29] If that was true in Miguel's case, he probably learned to ride
"on the job" in Bagaces; horses and cattle were rare in many parts of equato-
rial Africa due to the tsetse fly.[30] The privileges and authority he likely enjoyed over free workers would have tended to undermine the legal distinctions
of freedom that separated them. In fact, compared to the poor free people of
color in the area who "maintain themselves from their own labor and the
milk of the few cows they have raised," Manuel exercised far greater responsibility and probably enjoyed a higher status.[31]

In general, however, overseers, slave or free, worked alongside the men
they supervised, as the work demanded relatively little manpower. For example, in 1738, the hacienda San Nicolás de las Piedras in the eastern
Tempisque Valley consisted of one thousand milk cows, 1,459 year-old heif-
ers, five hundred year-old mares, a herd of two thousand "wild" cattle, three
yoke of oxen, two riding mules, and thirty tamed horses. Reportedly, just ten
men cared for all this livestock. A typical hacienda might consist of a "big
house," the residence of the owner; another house for the workers and for
storage of tallow and grain; a shed for tools; a pen where calves were held and
the troughs (*canoas*) for making cheese were kept; and a stone corral where
cattle were held during roundups. Most of the work on haciendas revolved
around the cattle, which were exploited for dairy products as well as for beef
and by-products such as tallow and leather. Workers constructed enclosures,
protected the livestock from wild animals, milked the cows, and made cheese
daily.[32] Periodically, the men rounded up the herds for branding, transport,
or slaughter. On the largest estates, the roundup (*vaquiada*) could last all
summer, taking five months of hard work to brand and inventory the cattle.[33]
Workers met their subsistence needs by growing provisions such as corn,
beans, and plantains, as well as producing milk, cheese, and beef for their
own consumption and for market.[34] For other necessities, they relied on itinerant Cartago and Nicaraguan merchants who advanced them goods such
as cloth, agricultural implements, and horse bridles on consignment for
quantities of tallow.[35] Both enslaved and free workers developed a sense of
proprietorship over the ranches and their livestock, to the chagrin of their
masters. Second Lieutenant (*alférez*) Tomás de Chávez, owner of a hacienda
in the Jurisdiction of Esparza, foresaw that after his death, the workers on his
ranch would claim rights to the animals they had raised. He stipulated in his

will that "no slave nor free servant of mine is to be allowed use of the mules or cattle that they say I have given to them."[36]

A 1688 census from the Valley of Bagaces shows that on many Spanish-owned haciendas, free and enslaved people of different racial groups lived and worked side by side. For example, the wealthy Spanish captain Miguel Calvo maintained male and female Indian workers, a black slave woman, and three free mulattas among the thirteen people on his property.[37] Sergeant Andrés Clavijo likewise maintained a slave woman and a free mulatta, as well as an Indian man and his wife.[38] Captain Nicolás Gutiérrez headed a household of twenty-seven people, including four slaves, three mulattos un-identified by condition, one free person of unspecified race or gender, and at least nine Indians of both sexes.[39]

In the sparsely populated North Pacific, slaves were few in number and widely scattered geographically. By the eighteenth century, enslaved Africans, creoles, and mulattos comprised just a small minority in most parts of the North Pacific region. Of the total 668 persons who were baptized in the parish church of Esparza between 1712 and 1750, the years from which the earliest records survive, only fifteen were slaves (2.3 percent).[40] Only one or two en-slaved men or women, if any, lived on most properties in a region dominated by free mulattos. Enslaved men and women forged their strongest relationships with other residents on their own haciendas, regardless of legal condition, race, or ethnicity. In some minor industries, such as pearl diving, enslaved workers might be found in greater concentrations, allowing them to unite for their own objectives, including flight.[41] But in most cases, because they were a small mi-nority among Indian, free mulatto, and mestizo workers, slaves tended to iden-tify with other workers. When masters used male slaves as overseers, they undercut the unity of slaves with workers of other racial and ethnic origins. Enslaved overseers had good reasons to cultivate the confidence and goodwill of their masters, who often rewarded them with privileges and authority over other workers, including freemen. In the end, the privileges and status they earned derived from the master. By overseeing other workers, their loyalty extended and reinforced the masters' power.

In the Central Valley, slaves of African descent formed part of the labor force from the first years of Spanish settlement in Costa Rica.[42] In the late sixteenth and early seventeenth centuries, the wealth of Cartago's elite de-rived primarily from the encomiendas and land grants (*mercedes*) they had received in the 1560s. Already small compared to the encomiendas in other Spanish colonies, receipts from Indian tribute declined rapidly with the native population itself. By 1619, Juan de Fonseca's encomienda in the pueblo of Barva contained only ten tributaries and that of Catalina Gutiérrez, fifteen. Similarly, twenty-one Indians paid tribute to García de Quirós.[43] Accordingly, Costa Rican elites looked for other sources of labor and income. Many encomenderos also acquired slaves of African descent. An encomendera with grants in Ujarrás and Barva, doña Mayor de Benavides owned at least ten slaves in the years 1616–1625.[44] No doubt slave ownership implied prestige for Cartago's wealthiest residents, but few, if any, Costa Rican slave masters could afford to employ their slaves exclusively in domestic service.[45] In addition to their encomienda income, wealthy Spaniards owned sizeable farms and ranches in the Central Valley that were worked by Indians, slaves, and free mestizos and mulattos. Masters circulated both enslaved men and women within their families depending on the nature of the work required and where it was needed. For example, "seeing that his said father needed [someone] to attend his haciendas in the country," Father don Manuel José González Coronel arranged with Blas González Coronel to exchange Agustín, a young mulatto man, for Lorenza, a congo woman in her twenties, whom the young priest regarded as more useful for his own needs.[46] Less affluent Spaniards and castas depended on subsistence farming, and they, too, might own a slave or two.

Masters often kept both slaves and free servants. For example, Sebastiana, a free black woman, served in the home of doña Francisca de Chinchilla in 1671, along with the slaves Isabel, María, and the latter's young son, Juan.[47] Marta, a free mulatta, and her daughter, Gila, worked for Captain don Fernando de Salazar, who owned four slaves in 1678.[48] In 1700, Francisco Fernández and doña Eugenia Rodríguez owned one slave, Gaspar Rodríguez, and employed at least three free servants, Manuela, María, and Feliciana.[49] The same year, doña Sebastiana Calvo owned two female slaves, one male slave, and employed three free female servants (criadas).[50] Notwithstanding that he owned twenty slaves at the turn of the eighteenth century, don Miguel Calvo also employed Luis, a tributary Indian, as a criado on his Matina hacienda, no doubt paying his tribute obligations in exchange for his service.[51] In 1714, Gertrudis, a mulatta slave, lived on her master Captain Juan de Chávez's property in the Valley of Curridabat among several free mulatto workers and a young Talamanca Indian girl (very likely orphaned in the suppression of the failed rebellion of five years before).[52]

In this diversified, small-scale economy, there was little specialization of labor. Enslaved women of African descent worked at activities such as farming, and perhaps sold produce, in addition to caring for the homes and families of their owners. Slave men were usually "jacks of all trades," working at whatever task presented itself. Movement guaranteed that slave men especially developed varied work skills and encountered a broad range of people.

Unlike plantation societies, in which men and women generally worked together at back-breaking field labor, such as cutting cane or picking cotton, the work of enslaved men and women in Costa Rica followed a more or less strict division of labor.[53] Enslaved women worked at the myriad tasks of domestic service, cleaning, cooking, washing, and caring for the children of the master's home, among others. The term "domestic service" should be understood broadly in Costa Rica, however, as it might encompass agricultural work as well as household chores.[54] In a rare, explicit mention, doña Inés Pereira provided in her 1659 will for the manumission of her aged slave, Luisa de la Cruz, out of gratitude for "making some fields [*milpas*] and plantings for my sustenance."[55] In 1724, slave Eugenia reported that her masters "kept her occupied in caring for fields."[56] Few if any slaves, therefore, served their masters exclusively in the sphere of consumption, and living in the home of the master implied no superior status, especially for enslaved women.

Slave women carried much of the responsibility for raising their masters' children, a fact that the masters often recognized. Catalina Ruiz de las Alas of Esparza freed the creole Isabel some time before 1682. Ruiz had always thought of Isabel "in place of a mother, because [Isabel] raised her at her breasts" when Ruiz was a "little orphan girl."[57] Dominga, a mulatta, acquired her freedom in 1729 in compliance with a clause of her mistress's testament acknowledging that she had "served us with all fidelity, caring for our children."[58] In 1746, don Miguel de Ibarra freed the aged Micaela de Ibarra, a Yoruba (aná), "for having raised me." Having arrived on the *Christianus Quintus* or *Fredericus Quartus* in 1710 at the age of about fourteen, at least three of Micaela's own children had died by 1720.[59]

Some enslaved women earned money for themselves and their families as well as for their masters. Slaveholding widows especially relied on the income provided by slaves for their subsistence. The widow doña Juana Núñez de Trupira (elsewhere, Trujira) complained in 1692 of being the destitute mother of four children, with no other means to support herself than the earnings of her slave, María Manuela.[60] Referring to her slave María, the widow María Calvo admitted in 1720 that "with her work and my own I can scarcely maintain myself."[61] Doña Ana Rodríguez de Castro of the Valley of Aserrí declared in 1736 that "after the death of my said husband I have maintained myself by my own efforts alone [*sic*] and with the help of my said slave Efigenia."[62]

⋅ Unfortunately, the sources say little about exactly how enslaved women earned money, although they sometimes were able to accumulate considerable sums. By 1677, for example, Francisca de Montoya, a mulatta slave, had paid 320 pesos toward her own freedom.[63] A 1672 *real cédula* received in Cartago referred to masters' custom of sending their slave women to sell produce and wares on the streets of "the Indies," but there is little direct evidence to corroborate that they did so in Costa Rica.[64] María de Aguilar purchased her own freedom for 305 pesos in 1703 at the age of forty-three.[65] Doña Ana Rodríguez de Castro specified in 1739 that her slave Efigenia be freed after she had earned enough money to pay for thirty-six masses for her mistress's soul.[66] When he freed his slave María in 1741, Captain Luis de Morera specified that she had enabled him "to earn many pesos."[67] A few slave women developed lucrative skills, such as Clara Calvo, a dressmaker who sold clothes in her master's shop while she was still a slave. She ultimately attained her freedom and continued her craft, a businesswoman of modest means.[68]

Slave artisans were highly prized by their masters, who occasionally imported slave craftsmen from abroad. About 1706, Captain Lorenzo de Arburola sailed to Portobello intending to purchase, "among other things," a slave trained as a stonemason. After much persuasion, a secretary of the governor sold him Jacobo (or Jacob), a *mandinga* stonemason previously enslaved in Martinique.[69] In 1734, Captain don Dionisio Salmón Pacheco purchased Nicolás de la Calle, a zambo trained as a shoemaker, from a resident of Santiago de Veragua, Panama for the bargain price of 180 pesos.[70] Costa Rican slave masters also sometimes apprenticed enslaved youths to Cartago artisans. Learning a trade increased a slave's value exponentially, and some slave masters apparently regarded the training of their slaves as an investment in their own futures.[71] In 1660, Cristóbal de Vargas married doña Petronila Moreno, who brought Juan, a black creole boy, as part of her dowry. The same year, Vargas placed Juan as an apprentice with master tailor Diego Pérez. Juan must have seemed an especially promising student. Pérez agreed to teach him to "cut and sew any kind of clothes at all" within six months. If he failed, Pérez promised to pay four *reales* per day while Juan learned from another tailor.[72] In 1665, Captain don García de Alvarado purchased Juan Luis, a mulatto boy about eight years old, from doña Juana Moscoso for 250 pesos. The following year, Alvarado apprenticed Juan Luis to a tailor for a period of three years. Twenty-one years later, his mistress's dowry noted that he was a journeyman tailor (*oficial de sastre*) and valued him at the exceptionally high price of six hundred pesos.[73] Ignacio, a mulatto slave, had learned the trade of shoemaker by the time he was twenty-four years old. When his mistress authorized an agent to sell Ignacio, she insisted that he be sold for "a quantity that corresponds to his trade."[74]

There are clear indications that slaves and ex-slaves valued the skilled trades as avenues of mobility for their children, because the trades offered the best-paying and most prestigious livelihoods open to people of African descent. Free mulattos, many of whom had been slaves, made up a majority of the artisans in Cartago. These respected occupations promoted the assimilation of their sons into the free community of color. Mateo Rodríguez, a slave of Juan de la Cruz, and his wife Ana de Salazar, a free mulatta, apprenticed their son Manuel to a master stonecutter (*maestro de cantería*) in 1689.[75] Francisco Caamaño, a freedman of *casta arará* originally from the Slave Coast, and his wife Juana Valerino placed their son Juan with master shoemaker Miguel Pereira in 1718.[76] Juana Conga apprenticed her son Francisco, a free *pardo*, to blacksmith Tomás Calvo in 1730. In addition to planning for Francisco's future as a Cartago artisan, Juana must have taken pride in his choice, because in Kongo society, blacksmiths held an important status. The Kingdom of Kongo traced its origins to a wise blacksmith king who civilized his people by forging unity out of warring factions and providing them with the tools of agriculture. Ironically, Juana's enslavement allowed her son to enter a profession that in her African homeland remained largely the prerogative of the nobility.[77]

By the mid-seventeenth century, some Costa Rican Spaniards (and later, mestizos) turned to sugar cultivation, especially in the valleys of Aserrí and Barva, west of Cartago, and secondarily in the plains around the pueblo of Ujarrás, to the east.[78] In Costa Rica, sugar production always retained its small scale, primarily supplying the domestic market. According to historian Richard Dunn, in the seventeenth-century British Caribbean, a force of 100 slaves could produce about eighty tons (73 metric tons) of sugar per year for their masters.[79] In Brazil, the average *engenho* (sugar cane farm and mill) produced 6,000 Portuguese *arrobas* (92 tons/88 metric tons) per year by the early seventeenth century. The largest mills produced 8,000 to 10,000 *arrobas* (130 tons/118 metric tons to 162 tons/147 metric tons).[80] By contrast, in 1691, Costa Rica's largest sugar mill (*trapiche*) produced only 100 *arrobas* (1.25 tons/1.13 metric tons).[81] Despite the small quantities produced, however, by the early eighteenth century, raw sugar (*rapadura*) formed a basic article of consumption in Costa Rica.[82]

Where slaves were used in Costa Rican sugar production, they were usually supplemented by free workers. For example, planter Sergeant Major Blas González Coronel maintained just one slave at his sugar mill in 1719, generally relying on other "people of his service" for labor.[83] This was probably the case for much of the year, but in the critical days of cutting and grinding cane, larger groups of slaves could be mobilized. During three peak days of the harvest in 1702, for example, Alférez Pedro de Torres hired two mulatto slaves from doña María de Escobar Guijarro, borrowed another mulatto slave from his sister doña Francisca de Torres, and contracted a free mulatto to supplement the work of his own black slave.[84] Skilled slaves could form the core of the mill's labor force, and, in Costa Rica as elsewhere, planters sometimes chose slaves for the crucial position of the sugar master, who was charged with supervising the equally important tasks of boiling, cooling, and refining the sugar. On the sugar master depended the most critical moment of sugar making: *el punto*, the moment when cane syrup (*miel*) crystallized into granules.[85] Enslaved sugar masters were among the most expensive slaves sold in the colony. Twenty-eight-year-old creole sugar master José de Ibarra was valued at five hundred pesos in 1697, notwithstanding his propensity to run away.[86] As if to emphasize their utility in sugar production, occasionally slaves were sold with the other "equipment" necessary to a sugar mill. Salvador, a creole, was sold in 1719 along with the land, buildings, oxen, and two fields of "sweet cane" needed to operate a trapiche.[87]

In Costa Rica, sugar production never assumed the deadly characteristics often associated with the crop. Drawing on evidence from the Louisiana sugar industry, Michael Tadman has argued that "sugar planting brought together a lethal combination of factors that persistently and almost inevitably produced natural decrease among slaves."[88] Undoubtedly true in the late eighteenth and nineteenth-century Caribbean, this assertion ignores the vastly different conditions of sugar production in the centuries before.[89] Tadman qualifies his argument on the relationship between sugar cultivation and mortality by adding other necessary factors, namely the existence of slavery and access to the slave trade in a given locale. Costa Rica's access to the slave trade was sporadic, restricting the feasibility of slavery as a solution to the labor demands of sugar production. Even more important, however, were the technological conditions of sugar processing. For example, after his death in 1719, executors inventoried the property of planter Sergeant Major Blas González Coronel. González Coronel's cane fields in the Valley of Aserrí extended for fifty rows, probably measuring about fifty square yards. He owned a trapiche built of hardwood housed in a small building. Animals, usually oxen, supplied the power for almost all Costa Rican trapiches. González Coronel owned nine oxen, two designated specifically for powering the mill. Seven more oxen and a mule hauled firewood for boiling the cane.[90] The simple, animal-powered trapiche, like the primitive sugar-processing method itself, underwent no significant technological improvements during the length of the colonial period, and thus Costa Rica experienced none of the accelerations in production that later made work in Caribbean cane fields a virtual death sentence for African slaves.[91] *what was the work that made it so deadly?*

Notwithstanding the small scale of Costa Rica's sugar industry, slaves played a greater role in Costa Rican sugar production than historians have generally credited them with. In an important article on the colonial Costa Rican sugar industry, for example, historian Elizabeth Fonseca wrote that slaves participated only rarely in the cultivation and processing of cane.[92] From one perspective, she is undoubtedly correct. Of the more than 150 trapiches in operation by the mid-eighteenth century, only a small fraction used slave labor. On a closer look, however, it becomes apparent that slaves played an important role in overall output, constituting the main labor force used by some of Costa Rica's largest planters. As Fonseca shows, in 1691 (unfortunately the only year for which data on the amount of sugar produced are available), three growers, all members of the same extended family, accounted for more than half of all Costa Rican sugar production. Some of the same elite families who ruled livestock breeding and cacao production dominated sugar.[93] One of the three growers Fonseca mentions, don Sebastián de Sandoval Golfín, owned five slaves in 1697. This included a master sugar boiler who previously belonged to his relative Diego de Ibarra, the second of the three largest planters.[94] The third grower, don Francisco de Ocampo Golfín, owned twelve slaves by 1714 and fourteen by 1719. By 1734, his son and heir, the Licentiate don Francisco de Ocampo Golfín, owned sixteen slaves at the sugar hacienda in the Valley of Barva.[95] Although these data cannot retroactively establish that the 1691 yields were produced with slave labor, they do demonstrate that the largest planters also became slave owners, and large ones by the modest standards of Costa Rica. Although slave labor may have been marginal to sugar production generally, slaves did work on the mills with the largest outputs.

Doña Nicolasa Guerrero owned a more typical sugar complex in Ujarrás. Not far from Cartago, the plains around Ujarrás, well watered by the Agua Caliente and Paz rivers, proved ideal for the cultivation of sugar cane. Confronted with the irreversible decline of the local Indian population, the Spaniards of Ujarrás sought other sources of labor early on. One of the earliest Costa Rican inventories to list cane fields in Ujarrás, a 1646 dowry also included two slaves.[96] In 1717, Guerrero owned property that included a field of mature cane, probably measuring about a hundred square yards; seven slaves; and a grinding mill equipped with a 70 pound (32 kilogram) kettle for boiling cane juice. Such rudimentary equipment could not be used to produce refined sugar. Costa Ricans made do with the coarse brown sugar known as rapadura and conserved cane syrup for sweetening liquids. Guerrero's adobe houses, roofed with tiles rather than straw (an important distinction of wealth in colonial Costa Rica), adjoined the mill. Felipe and Francisco, both Yoruba, were Guerrero's only male slaves of working age. Felipe, Guerrero specified, worked cultivating cane. These African men surely shared duties with José Manuel, an orphan (son?) Guerrero had raised and selected to administer her property in case of her death. In addition to the sugar complex, Guerrero held substantial livestock in Ujarrás, including forty head of cattle, seven breeding mares, and fourteen other horses, including foals. When not clearing land, planting, weeding, cutting, hauling, grinding, or processing cane, the men surely tended the animals and grew food for the estate. A plantain field grew next to the cane.[97] At the time of the sugar harvest, Guerrero's female slaves, Catalina and María Gertrudis, no doubt joined in the work. Other local workers were almost certainly hired as well.

"Jacks of all trades," slaves went to work wherever their masters sent them and sometimes managed their masters' affairs. The work of enslaved men demanded that they be given broad freedom of movement, sometimes including long journeys outside Costa Rica. As one Nicoya master wrote in 1703, "there is nothing new in the train of mulatos and blacks, free and slave, who go from one province to another in the service of their masters."[98] Occasionally their travels afforded opportunities for slave men to negotiate with their masters for their freedom. Probably the best known of such slaves was José Cubero, a mulatto slave of Father Manuel Martínez Cubero.[99] Born in the home of the priest's parents, José first served his young master as a page. Around 1724, Father Cubero put José in charge of his mule train and trusted him to conduct his business in Nicoya, Bagaces, and the Landecho Valley. After José served as the priest's driver (mandador) for eight years,

Father Cubero sent him to Nicaragua to transport a cargo of tobacco, flour, and other dry goods. José continued to drive mules to and from Nicaragua for another seven or eight years, then in 1740 went to work on his master's cacao hacienda in Matina for a few months. After another trip to Nicaragua, his master sent him to carry forty loads of leaf tobacco to Panama, trusting him to return with the proceeds. When José returned, again earning his master's trust by bringing him the cash and jewelry he had been paid, Father Cubero sent him on four more trips to Panama. Each time, José returned with all the proceeds from the sales, whether they were in silver, gold ornaments, or merchandise.[100]

Eventually, Father Cubero allowed José to manage his affairs as if he were a free man and agreed to free him, for a price. While on journeys for his master, José began to sell bags of tobacco, as well as stockings his wife and her friends knitted, on his own account. Eventually José was able to accumulate enough money to buy his own mules and horses, and after many years of working and saving, amassed the sum of 380 pesos to purchase his manumission.[101] For enslaved men such as José Cubero, it made good sense to cultivate the confidence of their masters. Through years of loyal service and toil, José had secured the promise of freedom. In other cases, Costa Rican masters manipulated promises to gain the willing service of their slaves, especially those they placed in positions of authority. They could revoke their promises as easily as they made them. In the case of José, without a word of explanation, Father Cubero simply took the 380 pesos without granting manumission.[102]

Many enslaved men "traded and contracted" just as free men did, despite laws preventing them from assuming debts or engaging in commerce: Juan Ramiro, mulatto slave of Father don Alonso de Sandoval, sold a mare to Salvador de Acuña with his master's consent.[103] They could do so, however, only with their master's permission or if another free person guaranteed the debts they assumed.[104] Many slaves nevertheless managed to acquire money by earning wages, selling goods, or borrowing money. Luis Palacios, a mulatto slave of Gaspar Chinchilla, owed itinerant merchant Antonio Barela eight pesos two reales in silver in 1684.[105] Conversely, some slaves also extended credit in their dealings with Spaniards and other freemen. In 1682, Alférez Fernando Núñez Bejarano acknowledged that he owed a one-year-old colt to Nicolás Villegas, a mulatto slave of Captain Jerónimo Leal.[106]

At least a few slaves lived outside their master's homes and accumulated property. Although ostensibly belonging to their masters, they lived in most respects like free persons. In the mid- to late eighteenth century, Cayetano Chavarría, a mulatto slave born and raised in the home of his mistress María Calvo, worked as a day laborer, keeping a portion of his earnings. He also surrendered substantial sums to his mistress. By 1747, he had enough cash of his own to lend his mistress's son-in-law six pesos in silver. When she composed her will in 1762, María Calvo provided that Chavarría's market value be discounted by fifty pesos to facilitate self-purchase "because of how well he has served me."[107] Factors other than gratitude motivated Calvo's decision to lower Chavarría's price. Assessors considered him "old . . . and of no use."[108] Nevertheless, Chavarría never formally purchased his freedom. At the time of his death in Cartago ten years later, he lived in the free colored neighborhood of Puebla de los Pardos in a tile-roofed house. Chavarría could not, however, ultimately dispose of his property like a free person. Upon his mistress's death, his house reverted to María Calvo's estate.[109]

Specialization of labor, including skilled work, was exceptional. For an enslaved woman, particularly if she was her master's only slave, this might mean little more than an increased workload, including some farm labor in addition to cooking, cleaning, child care, running errands, and perhaps working for wages or selling goods outside the home for her master. Neither slave status nor occupation provided strong bases for the development of distinct slave identities. On the other hand, masters held the power to dictate the work slaves performed and, to a great extent, their opportunities for contact with other slaves. Masters organized production in their own interests in part by deciding where to allocate their slave laborers. Any opportunities for advancement that slaves enjoyed derived directly from their masters and could be withdrawn as easily as they had been granted. What property and earnings slaves acquired were never secure. In such circumstances, slaves had powerful incentives to cultivate close ties to the master. Slaves probably came to think of themselves first not just as slaves but as slaves of a particular master. The situation differed in Costa Rica's Caribbean region of Matina, where groups of African men lived largely separated from whites and more often made their own decisions regarding the organization of their time and production.

Cacao cultivation in Caribbean Costa Rica began with Indian labor, but planters relied on slave labor by the end of the seventeenth century. As profits rose, increased importations of captives led to a "re-Africanization" of Costa Rica's enslaved population, bringing men and women of diverse ethnic origins to the Central Valley as well as to the Caribbean lowlands. A unique combination of unusual circumstances combined to allow male slaves in the Caribbean Matina Valley an exceptional autonomy that was especially striking when compared to the brutal control exercised over slaves elsewhere in the Americas. Like slaves in some plantation societies, enslaved men in Matina worked largely free of white supervision and often organized their own time. Slave men managed all stages in the cultivation, processing, and sometimes sale of cacao, the colony's most important export. Unlike work in the cane fields of the Caribbean islands and Brazil or the rice swamps of South Carolina, however, cacao cultivation did not impose the murderous labor demands that often accompanied a measure of cultural autonomy. Other conditions, however, especially the exclusion of slave women from the region, coupled with the overwhelming tendency of slave men to marry free women, prevented the formation of slave families and, ultimately, the reproduction of a distinct slave culture. By negotiating arrangements with their masters or growing the valuable crop on their own account, several enslaved men were able to purchase their own freedom. This strategy, too, encouraged an individualism that undermined the development of a shared identity among slaves.

With the decline of the Central Valley's indigenous populations and the decline of the export trade with Panama, Costa Rican elites began searching for a new economic enterprise in the seventeenth century. Cacao seemed the perfect crop to develop for export. With ports on the Atlantic, a suitable climate, existing wild cacao groves, and a large if still unconquered Indian population, Costa Rica's Caribbean region seemed ideal for cacao cultivation. By the mid-seventeenth century, colonial governors had begun actively to promote the reconquest of Talamanca and the introduction of cacao cultivation. The twin projects offered foreseeable solutions to Costa Rica's major economic problems: cacao production would provide the colony with a valuable export crop, and the conquest of Talamanca would secure a new source of labor.

By the early 1670s, Spaniards had started to establish cacao haciendas in the Matina Valley. Urinama Indians, newly congregated in Franciscan missions in Talamanca, provided the haciendas with their first important source of labor. The hacendados soon began abusing the missions as bottomless reservoirs of Indian labor, enlisting the governors of Costa Rica and their lieutenants to remove the Urinamas from the missions, often by force. In 1675, Visitor General don Benito de Noboa Salgado prohibited Spaniards, mulattos, and mestizos from entering the Urinama pueblos except with the permission of the governor and for "good ends."[110] No doubt because the governor himself countenanced and benefited from them, the labor drafts continued. As long as work on the plantations did not interrupt evangelization, Franciscan friars found little objection to providing the hacendados with Indian workers. But as cacao production expanded, the needs of the haciendas clashed increasingly with the goals of the missionaries and placed ever greater demands on the Indians themselves. In 1678, the Urinamas revolted. Don Antonio Salmón Pacheco, a recent immigrant from Spain and the owner of a hacienda of four thousand cacao trees, led an expedition from Cartago to "punish" the rebels. His successful reconquest of the Urinamas paved the way for the reestablishment of the missions and the renewed exploitation of the Indians for the Matina cacao haciendas.[111]

In late 1689, Franciscan missionaries asked Governor don Miguel Gómez de Lara to send the Urinama laborers back to the missions "so that they could receive the sacraments." Not only did the governor refuse to return the natives already in Matina, but he asked the missionaries to send forty more Urinamas to the haciendas, provoking the friars to ask sarcastically "if they were his lieutenants."[112] In February 1690, Friar Diego Macotela, the Franciscan Provincial of Nicaragua and Costa Rica, petitioned the Audiencia of Guatemala to halt the removal of Urinamas to the haciendas of Matina. He held the governor of Costa Rica and his lieutenants primarily responsible for removing the Indians "for the *cacaotales* [cacao haciendas] of Matina." The Indians had been so terrorized by the "slavery that they experience" that when they heard the voice of the lieutenant governor, they fled the missions, and all the work the missionaries had undertaken was lost.[113] The Audiencia promptly acceded to the provincial's request, ordering in April 1690 that the governor and his lieutenants leave the Indians in the mission and not remove them "to Matina nor elsewhere, not for the reason of the benefit of the cacaotales, nor for any other."[114] In a second decree in May 1691, the Audiencia prohibited any "Spaniard, mestizo, black, or mulatto" from entering the missions without the express permission of the friars.[115]

Once the Audiencia prohibited the coercion of Urinama Indians into labor on cacao haciendas, planters considered and experimented with a number of labor sources. They did not switch to slave labor overnight. The transition from de facto Indian to de jure African slavery occurred over a period of decades. *Cacaoteros* experimented with workers of all racial categories and legal conditions, including the Urinamas, free wage laborers, sharecroppers, and African slaves. None of these groups proved wholly satisfactory from the planters' point of view, and they continued to use a mixed labor régime until the end of the colonial period. But as demand for cacao production grew, so did the need for stability and efficiency in the labor force. By the 1680s, many planters preferred slaves to other forms of labor.[116]

Living conditions in the Matina and Barbilla valleys were unpleasant and insecure. Throughout the colonial period and long after, the region suffered from a shortage of workers. Some of the same reasons that made Matina ideal for cacao cultivation, such as its heavy rainfall and high humidity, made Spanish colonists shun the area. In 1741, Governor don Juan Gemmir y Lleonart stated flatly that the Matina Valley was "uninhabitable" due to its "sickly, humid, and hot" climate.[117] A decade later, Bishop Pedro Agustín Morel de Santa Cruz agreed, noting that "it is extremely hot and humid, and the rains very continuous. . . . From these causes arise illnesses and fevers, so malignant that those who enter that country either die within a few short days, or if they escape with their lives, they lose their color entirely and contract a kind of paleness in their faces, which never leaves them."[118] The bishop's description probably referred to symptoms of malaria (*Plasmodium falciparum* and/or *Plasmodium vivax*), to which people of African descent demonstrate greater resistance than whites or Indians.[119] As Morel specified, "Only blacks enjoy good health in that intemperate climate."[120] Of course, Africans were not immune to disease, despite the mistaken beliefs held by whites such as the bishop. Luis, an enslaved African probably born on the Slave Coast, died of an "epidemic" in the Matina Valley in 1710 that affected others as well.[121]

Another threat came from other humans; more specifically, from the foreign predators who frequented Matina's shores. The British buccaneers Edward Mansfield and Henry Morgan landed on the Caribbean coast in 1666 with a multiethnic force of several hundred, sacking the haciendas and kidnapping resident workers. In 1687, the notorious pirate Lorencillo ravaged Matina for three months, killing several Spaniards.[122] Soon thereafter, in the 1690s, the Miskitu Zambos of Nicaragua and Honduras, newly allied with the British, began to attack Matina. The Miskitus preferred to sack the valley at the time of the cacao harvest, when they could make off with the crop as well as with prisoners.[123] In March 1705, the Miskitus attacked Matina at harvest time and kidnapped six slaves, along with some Spaniards.[124] When a force of five hundred Miskitu Zambos entered the Matina Valley in a surprise attack in April 1724, they took twelve slaves and twenty-one freemen (nineteen of them mulattos) prisoner.[125] After forcing the captives to carry up to a thousand *zurrones* (97 metric tons/107 tons) of cacao to their boats, the Miskitus sailed north with them to their territory in Nicaragua or Honduras.[126] The constant threat of military attack led Costa Rican masters to exclude slave women from the area, which had critical implications for the development of slave families and culture.

Factors such as the climate, the danger posed by wild animals, and especially the threat of attack and imprisonment by the Miskitus led free workers to successfully demand high wages for work in Matina. From the planter's perspective, the costs of hiring free people to work cacao haciendas were prohibitive. In 1703, cacao planter Captain Blas González Coronel claimed that during the cacao harvests, the free workers (*gente de servicio*) in Matina, "because there are no Indians, are composed of Spaniards, blacks, mulatos, [and] mestizos" and earned two pesos per day, paid either in cacao or in clothing and other goods.[127] González Coronel likely exaggerated; Captain Francisco Pérez del Cote cited a lower figure of one to one and a half pesos daily.[128] These wages were twice to four times as high as the half peso per day which one master sought as compensation for his slave's work in the Central Valley the same year.[129] Wages remained high throughout the first half of the eighteenth century, although they were always paid in cacao or merchandise, never in silver. Captain don José de Mier Cevallos noted that wage workers in Matina earned "a salary as high as twelve to fourteen pesos per month" in 1720.[130] By contrast, soldiers were paid just four pesos per month during an emergency the same year.[131] In 1724, prominent citizens of Cartago complained that since the recent attacks of the Miskitus, "no person can be found to go down to the cultivation of the cacao haciendas, except at double salary," because of their fear of being taken prisoner.[132] In 1736, Cartago's *Procurador Síndico* (city attorney) Captain Juan José de Cuende complained that hiring workers for the cacao haciendas was "extremely costly, because they are not content with earning a regular wage as in other places, but [want] exorbitance and serve [only] with reluctance."[133]

Although labor remained scarce and expensive, land in the Caribbean regions was abundant and, for all intents and purposes, free for the asking. Although masters listed Matina cacao trees in their testaments and inventories from the late 1650s, they never included the land itself, because they never bothered to secure legal title to it, as was customary in the Central and Pacific valleys. Nevertheless, they bought, sold, mortgaged, and bequeathed their haciendas in all respects as if they did own the land on which the plantations were established.[134] For much of the colonial period, the lands of the

Caribbean region officially remained Crown property (*tierras realengas*), and no law prevented an enterprising freeman from starting his own plantings on a piece of unclaimed land.

Using their influence with (or, just as frequently, as) colonial officials, hacendados strove to maintain exclusive control over the land and labor of the Matina Valley. Indeed, other than defense, control of workers constituted one of the only functions of an official presence in the region. Captain Luis Gutiérrez, an ex–lieutenant governor of Matina, said in 1719 that the duties of his former position consisted "only [of] that which is related to the defense of the port, and the orders given, and the obedience of the subjects who serve in that Valley, who are the servants of the haciendas."[135] Officials repeatedly issued edicts designed to prevent a free peasantry from establishing itself in Matina by ensuring that all people resident there were bound to a master. In 1704, Governor don Diego de Herrera Campuzano issued an order barring "idle and vagabond people" from the Matina Valley. He instructed his lieutenant, hacendado don Antonio de la Vega Cabral, to ensure that residents of Matina "work for a wage (*jornal*) on the haciendas of the *vecinos*, who will pay them for their labor according to custom." Those who refused to enter into contracts with the hacendados were to be expelled from the Valley.[136] Lieutenant Governor of Matina don Bernardo Marín issued a similar order in 1716. Marín ordered that all the "*vecinos hacendados*, sharecroppers, and black overseers" notify him of "the people each one has under contract." Anyone not bound by such a contract was to be expelled from Matina within three days.[137] Three years later, the *procurador general* (public attorney) of Cartago, cacao planter don Pedro de Moya, similarly petitioned the governor to expel any person in Matina found to be "independent of administration of hacienda or contract, or any others of those who go to the said Valley without a contract with the owners of the haciendas."[138] In 1737, Governor don Francisco Carrandi y Menán issued a related order directed against "vagabond persons" without "hacienda or contract with the owners of those haciendas."[139]

At an average price of approximately 315 pesos in the period 1651–1750, male slaves between the ages of sixteen and twenty-five constituted an expensive solution to the labor shortage.[140] Once planted, however, the labor requirements of cacao cultivation were relatively light, so there was no special need to purchase only men of prime working age. The strongest men could be used in clearing the thickly forested lands—"opening the bush," in the evocative phrase of one man who worked the cacaotales of the Barbilla Valley—and planting; those less robust could keep the plants watered, shaded, and free of weeds.[141] Older men could and did work, as did boys.[142] For example, a black man named José was sold in 1706 with a hacienda of 1,300 trees in the Barbilla Valley, reportedly at the age of fifty-five.[143] The black creole slave Juan Román labored on his master's haciendas until he was nearly sixty.[144] As Costa Rican historian Rina Cáceres has suggested, some elite Cartago families were able to survive the seventeenth-century depression by allocating enslaved workers to the cacao industry.[145] Cartago families who already owned slaves could send them to work in Matina without initially investing capital. As cacao exports increased, Costa Rican planters used profits to invest in more slave purchases. Registered slave sales in the 1680s rose 54 percent over the previous decade, 95 percent in the 1690s, then dropped sharply by 33 percent in the 1700s before rising 56 percent to peak in the 1710s.[146]

In a 1982 article, Costa Rican historian Carlos Rosés Alvarado wrote that the small-scale slave trade to Costa Rica was insufficient as a solution—even a passing one—to the chronic labor shortage that plagued cacao production.[147] More recently, North American Philip S. MacLeod drew attention to the variety of labor regimes employed on Caribbean cacao haciendas, including wage labor and sharecropping (*arrendamiento*), and suggested that slavery was of minor importance.[148] Both Rosés Alvarado

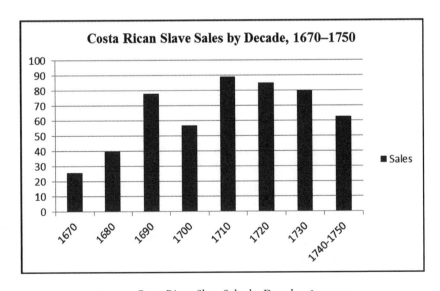

Figure 1. Costa Rican Slave Sales by Decade, 1670–1750

and MacLeod seemed to argue from an assumption that cacao production required a large labor force. This was not the case. The hacendados only recruited Urinamas on the order of thirty to sixty men at a time in the 1670s and 1680s.[149] When the agent of Antonio Salmón Pacheco presented a petition for labor to the Audiencia of Guatemala in 1691, he requested that twelve Urinama men be allocated to "the service and cultivation" of Salmón Pacheco's haciendas.[150] Apparently, he asked for more workers than he needed. In that year, Salmón Pacheco owned haciendas with a total of four thousand trees, and according to a 1721 Venezuelan text, it was "well known" that one slave could care for a thousand trees. According to the 1691 census, no planter in Costa Rica owned more than ten thousand trees in production, and the average cacao planter owned 1,894 trees.[151] Even owners of just one or two slaves, like many Costa Rican masters, could profitably cultivate cacao with slave labor, and many did.[152]

The generally low costs of starting a cacao hacienda allowed Cartago elites to diversify their economic enterprises at a time when their traditional activities had foundered. Although for most of the year the work was light, cacao trees required constant care. Most free workers found such work unattractive, and after the 1690 decree of the Audiencia, Indians could not legally be forced to do it. Slaves constituted the most expensive of the cacao hacienda's productive forces by far, but they soon were considered part of a hacienda's essential "equipment." Accordingly, enslaved men were sometimes transferred or sold as a package with the haciendas. In 1689, when doña Ana Margarita Escalante Paniagua married Captain don Juan Sáenz, her father don José de Escalante Paniagua gave the couple everything they needed for a successful future in the cacao business: a cacao hacienda in the Barbilla Valley, twelve mules, and Juan, a congo slave.[153] José, a black man about fifty-five years old in 1706, was sold with a hacienda in Barbilla for a combined price of five hundred pesos.[154] In March 1718, doña María Josefa de la Vega Cabral inherited a cacao hacienda and two slaves from her late father. A few months later, her husband don Juan José de Cuende sold a hacienda with Francisco and Sebastián, the two slaves who were "tied to said hacienda," along with the "shotgun, tools, . . . and other implements necessary to the work on the said hacienda."[155] In 1727, Diego de Angulo, born in West Central Africa, was auctioned off with the Matina hacienda he had worked for decades.[156]

Once purchased, maintenance costs for slaves in Matina were small. Slave men met virtually all of their needs themselves. They built their own houses, roofing them with palm thatch. Plantains, "which serve in place of bread," formed the most important part of their diet.[157] Fruits such as oranges, avocados, and *zapotes* added variety and nutrients.[158] Rice provided another staple. In 1733, the free cacao worker Miguel Solano remarked that creole slave Juan Román made his own "rice fields and other plantings" in the Barbilla Valley, "as other black slaves customarily" did in Matina as well.[159] Antonio Cabo Verde might have brought Old World knowledge of the crop to Costa Rica. His casta surname indicates an origin in Upper Guinea, where rice was the dietary staple, or in the Cape Verde Islands themselves, where it was also cultivated.[160] Wherever he learned to grow it, Antonio farmed rice successfully enough to sell a surplus to his free neighbors. He also raised chickens and pigs. Cattle raised in the Barbilla Valley provided the area with beef.[161] No doubt slave men also hunted—in 1721, don Diego de Barros y Carbajal complained that "my negro is asking for" his shotgun (*escopeta*), which was being repaired—and fished the nearby rivers.[162] Every year, the sea turtles that came to lay their eggs on the beaches provided another important source of meat, as they did on the Gold Coast and elsewhere in Western Africa.[163]

The high wages demanded by free workers, a desire to prevent the development of a free peasantry in Matina, and the minimal costs of maintaining a slave labor force go some distance toward explaining the cacaoteros' turn to slaves as a solution to their labor shortage. Spanish racial prejudices also played a role. Although most scholars agree that racism in the modern sense did not exist in this period, something approaching a modern conception of "race" was operating in the minds of Costa Rican planters by the late seventeenth and early eighteenth centuries. Masters sent black creoles to the haciendas in roughly equal numbers as they did bozales, but mulatto slaves, although as numerous as blacks, were seen less frequently on the haciendas. Despite equal numbers of mulattos in the slave population, planters purchased expensive Africans rather than send mulatto slaves to Matina. For reasons unrelated to culture—there were no cultural differences between black creole and mulatto slaves raised in identical surroundings—the hacendados considered "pure" blacks, especially Africans, best suited for what they considered arduous and unhealthy work. Ironically, their decision opened up opportunities to enslaved men in Matina that slaves in plantation societies of the Americas would have envied.

On the cacao haciendas of the Matina, Barbilla, and Reventazón Valleys, male slaves lived remarkably independent lives. More comfortable in the temperate Central Valley, hacendados generally left day-to-day operations in the hands of their slaves. Only once or twice a year did "some of the masters" come to supervise the harvest, traditionally around Christmas and the festival of Saint John in June, usually staying from two to three weeks. In 1744, Luis Díez Navarro reported to the Captain General of Guatemala that in the Caribbean lowlands near the Matina and Barbilla rivers, two or three black slaves lived year-round on cacao haciendas in thatch-covered huts. According to Díez Navarro, Central Valley masters left the slaves to cultivate, harvest, and transport the cacao to Cartago. Seven years later, Bishop Pedro Morel de Santa Cruz confirmed that the cacao planters came to Matina "only a few days" a year, leaving the haciendas in the care of their black slaves in the interim.[164] When masters or their agents arrived, they caused temporary disruptions not unlike those produced by the royal officials who collected tribute from Costa Rican Indian pueblos at the same times or even by the tax collectors who, as some of the enslaved men remembered, descended on the villages of the Kongo twice each year.[165]

The detailed inventories of the haciendas of doña Agueda Pérez de Muro provide evidence of slave life and work on a large cacao complex in the early eighteenth century. By 1722, when Pérez de Muro married for the second time, she owned four cacao haciendas in the Matina Valley, totaling 8,650 producing trees.[166] In the Barbilla Valley, she owned another hacienda of 1,150 trees, also already bearing fruit.[167] The combined value of the trees was assessed at 16,406 pesos in cacao, or 11,718 pesos 6 reales in silver—a sizeable fortune by Costa Rican standards. In addition, she owned another 600 trees, planted four or five years before, which had not yet borne fruit and were valued at 425 pesos cacao or 300 pesos in silver.[168] Five slaves administered her Matina haciendas. Two of them, José Congo and Nicolás Casasola, were described as "overseers" (mandadores). Another slave, Lorenzo, tended to the hacienda in Barbilla.[169]

The inventories provide a glimpse at the rustic conditions in which slaves lived and worked in Matina. The five men lived in three houses, "like those used in that Valley." Almost certainly, the men had built these themselves of local timber and palm thatch. Each was furnished with a grinding stone (*piedra de moler*) and a large iron pot used for cooking. For hunting and self-defense, they shared two "French shotguns."[170] To cut wood, keep the cacao groves free of weeds, split cacao pods at harvest time, and no doubt occasionally to protect themselves against snakes and other animals, they used four axes and eleven iron machetes, each of the latter weighing two and a half pounds. To pick cacao at the harvest, there were three *almaradas* (a tool consisting of a pole about one meter long, with a sharp, thin knife attached to one end). A *canoa* listed in the inventory was probably not a boat but rather a large trough used for fermenting cacao. To dry cacao, there were nineteen uncured cowskins and thirty-five more ready for use. In addition to the buildings used for housing, the hacienda had three terraces (*galeras*) used to "break cacao" and later to dry it in the sun. The men shared three needles, which they used to sew the leather bags in which cacao was transported and sold. A single pine box was probably kept by the overseers to store valuables, although it had no lock.[171]

Cacao was first planted as seedlings, which were transplanted at six to ten months.[172] About eight feet (2.4 meters) was allowed between cacao trees. Next to each, a plantain tree was planted to provide shade and shelter for the delicate plants.[173] Maintenance was relatively simple and required few workers; it consisted mainly of weeding and periodic planting. Mature plants were harvested twice a year, in late June and at Christmas.[174] The pods were lowered from the trees with almaradas (also called *cuchillones*). On the ground, the workers opened the pods with axes, machetes, or knives, then extracted the seeds and placed them in tubs (*bateas*) for fermentation. Later, the seeds were spread onto leather skins and dried in the sun—a step considered essential for the flavor of the cacao.[175] After drying, the cacao was sewn into leather bags (zurrones), each one purportedly holding about twenty thousand seeds and valued at twenty-five pesos.[176] Some of the cacao was then sent to Cartago, from where it was exported to Nicaragua, the only legal outlet for much of the colonial period. Many haciendas, however, had their own wharves (*embarcaderos*), and contraband trade with foreign smugglers was extensive.[177]

African slaves also worked in the transport of the crop, both to Cartago and to the coast, where it was sold illegally to customers, including the British and the Miskitu Zambos. In 1722, Francisco Plaza, a *mina* (from the Gold Coast or upper Slave Coast) slave of doña Luisa Calvo, brought a train of mules from Cartago to Matina to transport cacao.[178] (Far more often, however, muleteers were free mulattos, mestizos, and Indians.[179]) Some masters entrusted their slaves with illegal operations. On several occasions in the early eighteenth century, Gregorio Caamaño, the slave overseer of his mistress's haciendas, and fellow slave Juan Damián had brought a total of thirty-one zurrones (3 metric tons/3.3 tons) of cacao to the Caribbean coast by mule. There they traded it with smugglers for yards of cloth, hats, and finished articles of clothing, among other items, all of which they remitted to their mistress in Cartago.[180]

As on the cattle haciendas of the North Pacific, masters relied on black overseers (mandadores) to administer their Matina haciendas. Occasionally, planters hired Spanish overseers to supervise their slaves, but they far more commonly chose a driver from among the slaves themselves. Despite a 1708 decree requiring planters to employ a Spanish overseer on their haciendas, very few complied.[181] Most often, supervisors were Africans, as were the men they supervised. For example, Gregorio Caamaño, of Slave Coast (arará) origin, and José Congo both served at different times as mandadores of doña Agueda Pérez de Muro's haciendas. Manuel, a Yoruba (aná), and Antonio de la Riva, a mina (both survivors of the *Christianus Quintus* and/ or the *Fredericus Quartus*), were overseers at don Juan de Ibarra y Calvo's cacaotales.[182] Enslaved overseers reported to their masters on affairs of the haciendas, in at least one case by letter (probably dictated to a literate acquaintance).[183] Masters trusted these men with the equipment of the haciendas and, importantly, with calculating the number of trees on the properties. Taking an overseer's word for the number of trees on a hacienda amounted to relying on his assessment of the property's net worth. An undercount of the trees could allow slaves to appropriate and market the surplus for their own profit, and enslaved overseers were sometimes implicated in contraband trade.[184]

The rank of overseer brought material rewards. In some cases, masters clearly compensated their enslaved administrators with special privileges and incentives, the most important of which was the offer of eventual freedom. For example, in 1737, the mina slave Antonio de la Riva, overseer of his masters' haciendas, contracted with his masters to care for a newly planted cacao grove of 1,500 trees and to plant and care for a new grove of five hundred trees until all bore fruit. With full confidence that Antonio would fulfill the contract, don Juan José de Cuende and doña Manuela de Ibarra granted him his freedom in advance.[185] In 1745, de la Riva presented his masters not only with the two thousand trees previously agreed upon but, "of his spontaneous will," an additional five hundred trees "in recognition of the benefit" that they had shown him.[186] Mandador Gregorio Caamaño earned his freedom in exchange for raising five thousand young cacao trees until they bore fruit.[187] In return for such opportunities, drivers owed their masters demonstrable increases in production.

A circumstance particular to Costa Rica gave male slaves a rare bargaining power and enhanced their independence. From the early eighteenth century, cacao served as legal tender in the colony.[188] Because land in Matina was widely available, a number of slaves took the opportunity to plant and cultivate their own cacao groves. Some masters allowed this activity, provided slaves cultivated their own groves only "on feast days and without missing other days in the service of their masters."[189] With their own cacao, slaves could purchase needed items from vecinos and smugglers. Antonio Cabo Verde, an African slave of Captain Manuel García, purchased a mule from Juan Masís for one zurrón (97 kilograms/214 pounds) of cacao in 1718.[190] Although some Cartago merchants profited from selling merchandise to slaves, other planters inveighed against the practice, presumably reasoning that slaves paid for the items with stolen cacao. Despite prohibitions, the sales continued.[191] That masters spent little to dress their slaves can be inferred from the petition of one hacendado who sought to prohibit the passage of merchants to Matina because they sold clothing to the slaves.[192] Like "everyone in Matina," however, slaves traded cacao with smugglers for goods ultimately from Europe (particularly from England), especially cloth.[193] Their access to cacao allowed slave men to purchase needed goods and improve their material situation, and sometimes it offered a path to economic advancement and freedom itself.

Benefiting from exceptional arrangements, a few slaves became true entrepreneurs. About 1705, Benito, a black slave of don José Pérez de Muro, assumed the cultivation of a cacao hacienda owned by María de Zárate. With his master's permission, Benito kept half the produce and turned the other half over to Zárate.[194] In the early 1720s and with the permission of his master, *cabo verde* Diego García leased a Barbilla cacao hacienda from Juan González for fifty pesos in cacao per year. A relative of García's free wife, Manuela Gutiérrez, González leased the property "more out of love than for the two *zurrones* each year," because he "loved him as if the said Diego were his father." Unable to care for the hacienda personally because he had to attend his master's estate, García entrusted its cultivation to free mulatto Agustín de la Riva in return for a year's harvest.[195] De la Riva's stewardship proved so profitable to García that not only did he meet his obligations to González, but with a surplus of "many *zurrones* of cacao," lent money to Francisco Morales, the Spanish Captain of the Matina Valley.[196] Enterprising men such as Benito and Diego García, however, could pursue their economic activities only with the consent of their masters.

Such men hoped ultimately to raise enough cacao on their own account to purchase freedom from their masters. For example, Juan Román, a black creole slave nearly sixty years old in 1733, enlisted the help of his free son, José Nicolás, to cultivate a grove of five hundred trees adjoining the groves of his master, Captain Francisco Gutiérrez. Román hoped to sell the grove to his master in exchange for his freedom.[197] Such agreements resembled the practice of arrendamiento, a sharecropping arrangement whereby a renter agreed to pay a portion of the cacao harvest to the landowner. Lessees often agreed to plant new groves as well as care for those already existing. Obviously, this arrangement benefited the landowner as much as the contractor.[198] In the case of an aging slave such as Juan Román, a master improved his landholding at the same time as he recouped much of his initial investment in slave property. Masters granted privileges, such as permission for slaves to cultivate their own cacao groves, in order to increase productive yields. To masters, the relative freedom enslaved men enjoyed in Matina proved not only necessary but profitable.[199]

Slaves managed the cacao industry of Matina at every step. They grew the crop, packed it in leather bags, transported it to Cartago or to the coast, exchanged it for merchandise, and bought goods with it, sometimes even their own freedom. With only a few soldiers and officials in the entire valley, whites maintained only a token presence for most of the year. Overseers represented the interests of the masters, but they surely did so through negotiation and incentives rather than by force alone. Most of the time, slaves organized their time and production as they saw fit. A number of slaves earned their own freedom by cultivating cacao groves on their own account.

In the unusual circumstances of slavery in Matina, slave men combined in the same persons elements of the abstract categories of slave, sharecropper, and wage laborer. They worked both for their masters and for themselves, both from coercion and for material incentives.[200] Bound to masters and their lands, slave men surrendered the harvest twice a year like tributary Indians or Kongolese peasants, yet they traveled, "traded, and contracted" like free men—buying and selling produce, sometimes even leasing land. Owning nothing themselves, they created a domestic market, attracting merchants from the Central Valley, and even participated as principals in foreign trade with English smugglers. After gaining their freedom, some continued to live in Matina, working at the same activities they had worked at as slaves. In a host of ways, the lives of enslaved men in Matina blurred the line between slavery and freedom.

Yet slave men experienced the hardships of their condition in crucial ways that separated them from freemen. Far from Cartago, they lived a barracks-like existence, plagued by boredom, the threat of military attack, and a lack of female companionship. Indeed, armed with lances and firearms, slave men in Matina even mobilized for military service and provided the first line of defense against the Miskitu invaders.[201] Although they enjoyed greater control of their own time and greater access to money than other slaves, enslaved men in Matina could not spend their time or money with their wives and children. For them, freedom meant the freedom to live in family and community. "Only in the community, therefore, is personal freedom possible."[202]

Slaves in Costa Rica were scattered throughout the North Pacific, Central Valley, and Caribbean lowlands. Africans' opportunities for contact with people of similar background and experience varied along a continuum. There were few slaves on the cattle and mule ranches of the North Pacific region and even fewer who had been born in Africa. Chances to forge and pursue relationships with other Africans were greater in the capital, Cartago, and on the cacao haciendas of Matina. Groups of West Central Africans (congo and *angola*) as well as natives of the Gold Coast (mina), the Slave Coast (arará and *popo*), Yorubaland (aná), and Upper Guinea (mandinga), among others, could all be found in Cartago among more numerous creole and mulatto slaves. Members of the same groups all lived and worked in the Caribbean region as well. Cartago and Matina owed their strong African character not to the predominance of any particular "nation," however, but to their ethnic diversity. A small minority in the general population, Africans naturally formed their closest relationships with enslaved and free creole blacks and mulattos, with Indians, mestizos, and Spaniards, becoming part of the creole culture of Costa Rica.

CHAPTER SIX

Slave Resistance

✤ SLAVERY ITSELF CAUSED SLAVE RESISTANCE, AND SLAVES EVERY-
where resisted it. If slavery in Costa Rica did not seem the "undeclared war
between blacks and whites" that it did elsewhere, slave masters nonetheless
held no illusions about the struggle beneath a deceptively tranquil surface.[1]
Although they often claimed to have raised slaves as if they were their own
daughters and sons, they worried that slaves did not return their affections.[2]
In 1719, doña Agueda Pérez de Muro admitted that slaves and their masters
were "natural enemies."[3] Captain Manuel García de Argueta alleged in 1720
that slaves were "hidden enemies of their masters, as has been experienced
many times in this province; most of them are opposed to the Spaniards because of [their] oppression and subjection."[4]

But slave resistance in Costa Rica remained overwhelmingly individual, not collective, and therefore had a limited effect on the institution.
Many slaves fled in small groups, but most acted alone. There is little evidence of mass escapes or permanent runaway communities. Although
slaves sometimes lashed out against their masters with violence, they did
so individually rather than collectively. Rebellions were almost unheard of,
and even rumors of them were few. Slave resistance never posed a serious
threat to the slaveholding régime of Costa Rica, nor did slaves intend it to.
Rather, they used various strategies to improve the intolerable conditions
in which they lived as slaves. Within their limited objectives, they often
achieved some success.

Slave Flight

Flight formed the most basic and one of the most common forms of resistance to slavery. Africans fled from their masters almost as soon as they arrived in Costa Rica. As long as slavery existed, dozens of African- as well as
Costa Rican–born slaves took the chance and fled their masters. Their motives were both universal and highly personal. Fugitive slaves from other
colonies also regularly arrived in the colony, perhaps hoping that Costa
Rica's geography and sparse settlement would provide a "zone of refuge."[5]
Yet permanent *cimarrón* communities did not develop in Costa Rica, nor,
apparently, were significant numbers of fugitive slaves able to find asylum
among the unconquered Indians of the province. Cartago and Esparza were
too small to provide urban runaways with the anonymity common in larger
cities that hosted fugitives. In the absence of such zones of refuge, runaways
confronted potential betrayal on all sides, facing innumerable obstacles in a
colonial world that took the legitimacy of their enslavement for granted.
Spaniards, Indians, free blacks and mulattos, even fellow slaves, all cooperated in tracking down runaways. A fugitive's greatest chance for success lay
in leaving Costa Rica for another colony where he could claim to be free and
build a new life among strangers. A few succeeded in permanently escaping
from bondage, but most were recaptured. With their chances of permanent
escape limited, many would-be fugitives availed themselves of sympathetic
patrons who could offer at least temporary shelter and protection, using
flight as part of a strategy to escape, if not from slavery itself, then from situations that they could no longer endure.

Fugitives were overwhelmingly men, although a few, including some of
the most persistent runaways, were women. In proportion to their numbers,
the African-born attempted flight much more frequently than did creoles
and mulattos, making up more than half of all recorded fugitives. As scholars of other regions have found, creoles and Africans embraced different
modes of flight.[6] Africans were much more likely to escape in pairs or in
larger groups than were creole slaves, who usually absconded alone. Africans
quickly adapted to American life, however, and proved equally as sophisticated and resourceful as creoles in exploiting circumstances and manipulat-
ing patrons to effect escapes.

For recently arrived slaves, ethnicity played a key role in selecting partners with whom to escape. In October 1700, the ship *Nuestra Señora de la
Soledad y Santa Isabel* was forced by a storm to Costa Rica's Pacific port of

maybe b/c creole slaves were already
accustomed to the culture of Spaniards, so
they didn't have the same fears as African slaves,
especially those who hadn't acclimated.

La Caldera.[7] On November 6, local officials seized the ship's cargo of African slaves, and by the end of the month, the captives were being auctioned in Esparza.[8] At least one of the Africans preferred death to the miserable conditions in which he was being held, and within a few weeks, he got hold of a knife and killed himself.[9]

In February 1701, several of the captives from the *Nuestra Señora de la Soledad y Santa Isabel* fled.[10] Ethnic origins clearly influenced their choice of companions. After a few weeks of freedom, two men of *casta congo*, both about twenty-five years old, were found by two indigenous women in the pueblo of Tobosi near Cartago on February 20.[11] Two days later, the Indian Marcos Martínez captured four more young African men, described as of the same casta, and returned them to Esparza.[12] In April, a man and a woman, both described as of *casta carabalí*, escaped together, but were soon recaptured and sold.[13] Africans recently arrived in an alien world, with no knowledge of the country or its language, no local allies to whom they could turn, and few resources on which they could rely, often turned to fellow captives of similar ethnic and linguistic backgrounds when they attempted to escape.

In exceptional circumstances, larger groups of fugitives were able to unite according to identities based in Africa. When they fled into the forest near Costa Rica's Atlantic coast in March 1710, the former captives of the *Christianus Quintus* and *Fredericus Quartus* immediately reorganized themselves in groups that roughly corresponded to their ethnic origins. When Captain Juan Bautista Retana captured a group of forty-five Africans in late April, all were described as of *casta mina*, natives of the Gold Coast and perhaps the upper Slave Coast.[14] On the forced march to Cartago, three men and two women of the group managed to break away, but a *pardo* militia officer, Adjutant José de Chavarría, recaptured them four days later.[15] Around the same time, Captain don Juan Francisco de Ibarra captured another group of twenty-six Africans near Moín. When he brought sixteen of the captives to Cartago in June 1710, all were described as of *casta nangu*—Yoruba-speakers from modern Togo and Benin.[16] It seems clear that when Africans seized the chance to flee, they chose their companions with care, usually seeking out men and women of similar ethnic and linguistic background.

They also commonly reached out to Africans of other ethnicities, however, even in their first moments on Costa Rican shores. On the Middle Passage and in Africa itself, Africans had already begun to form bonds with men and women of different ethnic origins, and the process continued when Africans reached American shores.[17] When Captain Gaspar de Acosta

Arévalo recaptured a third group of former captives of the Danish slave ships, he apprehended eighteen men and women of Slave Coast (*arará*) origin in the company of two women from the Gold Coast or perhaps more probably the upper Slave Coast (*minas*), as well as two other men of an unknown but different ethnicity.[18]

Once in Costa Rica, the process of forming relationships and alliances with members of other ethnic groups accelerated. Africans continued to flee in groups, but their companions soon came to reflect the strength of the relationships they formed in Costa Rica, including people of other ethnic origins.[19] When he presided as judge over the confiscation of the Africans of the *Nuestra Señora de la Soledad y Santa Isabel* in 1700, the lieutenant governor of Esparza, don Gregorio Caamaño, illegally appropriated twelve of "the best of the lot" for his own use, concealing them at the hacienda of don José de la Haya Bolívar.[20] Caamaño soon sent these Africans of diverse ethnic origins to dive for pearls along the South Pacific coast of Chiriquí.[21] When a judge (*oidor*) of the Audiencia of Guatemala discovered Caamaño's fraud in 1702, all his property was ordered seized and auctioned, and Caamaño fled to Panama with his slaves.[22] Ten of the slaves took advantage of their master's legal troubles to flee, making their way to Cartago. Constituting the largest known group of fugitives during the period of this study, this group included three men of West Central African (*congo*) origin, four men from the Slave Coast (three *popos* and one *arará*), one man of Bight of Biafra origin (*carabalí*), one man described as of the unidentified *casta mora*, and a black creole.[23] The creole, Lorenzo José, must have urged the group to set out for Cartago, as there is no evidence that any of the African men had been there before.[24] Thrown together as shipmates on the *Nuestra Señora de la Soledad* after their arrival in Panama, these men had continued to bond at the hacienda of don José de la Haya Bolívar and, with a creole companion, on the boat they used when diving for pearls in the Pacific. Despite their diverse ethnic origins, they soon bonded as divers and, eventually, as fugitives. Running away together allowed for the formation of one of the most dramatic expressions of the close, cooperative relationships that soon developed between African and creole slaves.[25]

Over time, African slaves developed intimate relationships with members of other racial and ethnic groups, who might join them when they decided to flee. When Juan José, an African of Slave Coast (*arará*) origin, fled his master in 1705, his companions in flight reflected ties formed in both the Old and New Worlds. He fled with Miguel, a fellow *arará* and slave of the same master, but also with Tomasina, his mestiza wife.[26] When Antonio, a congo whose story is discussed in detail below, escaped from the Cartago jail in 1722, he absconded with José Antonio, a Tójar Indian.[27]

Cimarronaje

When the conquistador Hernán Sánchez de Badajoz established a short-lived settlement near the mouth of the Sixaola River in Talamanca in 1540, Pedro Gilofo, a slave of Senegambian origin, ran away from the Spanish settlement for more than twenty days, living among the "Indians of war."[28] Sánchez de Badajoz viewed such unauthorized relations between blacks and Indians with alarm, knowing that an alliance between the groups threatened the Spanish invasion. Sánchez de Badajoz judged that Pedro's flight merited the harshest punishment, "because there are other blacks and slaves in the encampment." He ordered that Pedro be shot with arrows until dead as an example to others who might flee. The execution was carried out on September 1, 1540.[29]

Pedro Gilofo provides an early example of *cimarronaje*, which may be provisionally defined as escape with the aim to reside permanently beyond the borders of effective colonial settlement, in Costa Rica. Whether among the Indians or with other fugitive slaves, *cimarrones* attempted to create or join independent communities.[30] In contrast to neighboring Panama, there is little evidence of such activity in Costa Rica in the early colonial period. Although group cimarronaje held the potential to undermine the economy of slavery and to serve as an example to other captives contemplating flight, individual flight by its very nature could do little to further the development of a collective slave consciousness.[31] Costa Rican history offers many examples of individual slaves who risked their lives to escape but, despite the ready availability of unoccupied land, only scant evidence of collective cimarronaje.

Individual cimarrón activity is documented for the late seventeenth and eighteenth centuries, and some almost certainly occurred earlier. María Manuela, a mulatta about twenty-five years old, eluded her mistress for more than a year in the mountains outside Cartago. When she was recaptured in 1692, she soon escaped again.[32] Antonio Civitola, a congo, remained at large for about six months in 1719 before he was found living in a small hut he had constructed on the outskirts of the capital.[33] Antonio, a mulatto, was reported to authorities as living "on the outskirts" of Cartago in 1730.[34] Fragmentary evidence suggests that self-liberated blacks established a more permanent community in the Matina Valley and that some lone runaways sought temporary refuge there. In 1720, Eugenia Vanegas, a middle-aged mulatta slave of don Juan Francisco de Ibarra, mentioned "having fled this city [Cartago] to the plaintain fields of the king, where she was for a year" about eight years before.[35] The "plantain fields of the king" (*platanares del Rey*) was most probably an area of unclaimed (*realenga* or "royal") lands planted with the crop. If Eugenia could live there undetected for a year, the area must have been both extensive and some distance from Cartago. During a visit to the area the following year, Governor don Francisco Antonio de Carrandi y Menán alluded to a creek called Cimarrones, although this is little more than a hint.[36] A group of seventeen black and Indian refugees arrived at the Reventazón River in October 1744, having escaped from the Miskitus and British of the island of San Andrés in the western Caribbean.[37] Today, near the Reventazón, a small river and township in the Canton of Siquirres, Limón Province, conserve the name Cimarrones, perhaps in commemoration of a long-vanished settlement of runaway slaves.[38]

Recapture

Dozens of slaves fled during the colonial period, but most were recaptured or voluntarily returned to their masters, often within a short period of time. Confident that their slaves would be captured, masters occasionally bought or sold slaves who were still at large.[39] Despite Costa Rica's challenging topography and sparse settlement, colonial officials mobilized their meager police and intelligence resources with surprising efficiency. Few passable roads, trails, or bridges traversed the mountains, rivers, and tropical forests of the interior. Colonial officials knew these well and covered them on horses or mules, aided by dogs in their search for runaways.[40] When congo slave Antonio escaped from the Cartago jail with an Indian companion in 1722, the governor immediately dispatched search parties to hunt for the fugitives at key crossings in the Pacific and Matina valleys. As they were intimately familiar with the Matina area, the pair eluded capture for a month, but pardo militiamen eventually overtook them.[41]

If escape into the countryside was difficult, blending into the cities was impossible. Local slaves on city streets were recognized immediately. They rarely enjoyed even a few days at liberty, as did Tomás and Antonio, slaves of don Gregorio de Caamaño, in 1705. Their master absent in Guatemala, the pair was sent from Cartago to Esparza with Caamaño's nephew but were observed "in the charge of no one, but rather at their will," for a couple of days before being arrested.[42]

Fugitive slaves were soon spotted by authorities if they stayed close to home, and runaways from other provinces drew attention just as quickly. No doubt seeking to start new lives in the anonymity of a new setting, fugitive slaves from other provinces regularly managed to make their way to Costa Rica, sometimes coming great distances. In striking contrast to fugitives within Costa Rica, runaways from other provinces captured in Costa Rica were overwhelmingly mulattos and creoles, which suggests that Africans were usually captured closer to home.[43] But like slaves of Costa Rican masters, fugitives from elsewhere were often identified and apprehended in a colony where people such as "Silvestre the Frenchman" or José Nicolás López, "a foreign mulato," tended to be referred to as outsiders even in everyday speech.[44] Slave masters from all over Central America had commercial and familial ties to Costa Rican elites and often drew on their connections to recover their fugitive slaves. Juan de Díaz, a mulatto also known as Juan de Herrera, escaped from his master in Nueva Segovia (now Ocotal), Nicaragua, near the modern border with Honduras. In November 1661, his master travelled to León, Nicaragua, where he authorized a Cartago resident to sell Juan despite his fugitive status, no doubt having heard that he was in Costa Rica. Juan was apprehended and sold in Cartago about four months later.[45] Salvador, a black creole, fled from his master in the Nicaraguan port town of Realejo more than a year before he was captured at El Salto in Costa Rica's Bagaces Valley in 1673.[46] This frontier area became a haven for runaway slaves and other outlaws. El Salto River formed the provincial border between Costa Rica and Nicoya, and authorities complained that fugitives crossed from one jurisdiction to the other at will, "whenever it strikes their fancy and they want to commit some evil, of the many they do customarily."[47] Costa Rican Governor don Juan López de la Flor brought Salvador to his home in Cartago, where he lent the disheveled fugitive some pants and a cape to wear while he went to send a message to the runaway's master. When the governor returned, he found that Salvador had broken open a chest and made off with more than two hundred pesos, as well as with his new suit of clothes. Salvador was recaptured soon after his bold gambit.[48] Domingo de la Trinidad was a mulatto purchased by an itinerant merchant in Guatemala City in 1676. Later transferred to the

Corregidor of Realejo, Domingo escaped, eventually to be captured and sold in Cartago in 1680.[49] In 1691, José Gómez Elgueros of Panama City learned that his escaped slave José de Ibarra, a black creole and master sugar boiler valued at five hundred pesos, had been spotted in Costa Rica. José, too, was eventually apprehended and sold to a Cartago master.[50]

One fugitive slave from another province succeeded in passing as a free man in Costa Rica—for a time. In 1732, the mulatto Diego Campuzano presented a petition to the parish priest of Cartago, seeking the proofs of eligibility he needed to marry Manuela de Padilla, a free mulatta. He claimed to be a free pardo from León, Nicaragua, and succeeded in persuading several friends to offer perjured testimony to support his petition.[51] Finding no impediment to the marriage, Father don Manuel López Conejo granted his approval in February 1732. Diego and Manuela soon married, probably in July 1732, and their son, Antonio Martín, was baptized in November 1733.[52]

Diego's life as a free man in Costa Rica lasted a little more than two years. In June 1734, don Juan Francisco de Ibarra learned that Campuzano was not a free pardo from Nicaragua but a fugitive slave of don Miguel de Zelaya of Comayagua, Honduras. When Diego admitted as much, he was arrested. Manuela "did not know, nor [had she] come to the understanding, in any way" that her husband was a slave, and she did not learn the truth until he was jailed as a fugitive.[53] A year later, she petitioned the ecclesiastical judge for an annulment. Although the outcome of her request was not recorded, her plea was forwarded to León, Nicaragua to be considered by the bishop.[54]

Although some fugitive slaves found free allies of other ethnic groups to aid them in their escapes, free people also cooperated in apprehending the runaways. As military men, members of the free pardo militias routinely apprehended fugitive slaves, and collected extra pay for these efforts. In 1710, pardo Adjutant José de Chavarría captured five African runaways from the *Christianus Quintus* and *Fredericus Quartus* and collected a twelve-peso reward for the service.[55] In April 1721, pardo Sergeant Cristóbal de Chavarría appeared before Governor don Diego de la Haya Fernández and turned over a fugitive African he had taken into custody in the Matina Valley. The following year, Andrés Calvo, the pardo ferryman at the Reventazón River, apprehended another escaped African slave and turned him in.[56] In May 1722, when the congo slave Antonio escaped from the Cartago jail with an Indian companion, Governor de la Haya dispatched two pardo militiamen to pursue the pair. José de Córdoba and Cristóbal Hidalgo enlisted the help of the same Andrés Calvo in an attempt to intercept the runaways at the Reventazón crossing. By June 18, the militiamen had overtaken the fugitives on the road to Matina and remanded them to the Cartago jail. The governor ordered that Córdoba and Hidalgo be paid "the customary quantity" for their service.[57]

Indians also occasionally joined in the apprehension of fugitive slaves. It is hard to know whether they lacked sympathy for fugitive slaves, whether they were tempted to capture them for financial incentives, or whether they feared pressure from the provincial authorities in Cartago to surrender the runaways. The indigenous pueblo of Tobosi, located near Cartago and along the road to Panama, made a tempting hideout for fugitives but provided little protection. Slave hunters (*cuadrilleros*) caught up with two runaways from Panama there in 1686.[58] In February 1701, two Indian women of the same pueblo turned over a pair of congo fugitives who had escaped from Esparza.[59] Two days later, the Indian Marcos Martínez arrived in Esparza with four more young African men, described as of the same casta. While collecting honey in the bush near the Pacific coast at La Herradura, Martínez had found them hiding, near starvation, in a small makeshift hut. After giving them some food, he lured them into accompanying him back to Esparza.[60] In the 1730s, a black slave of former governor don Baltasar de Valderrama escaped to the pueblo of Boruca in the South Pacific. Held for some days in the pueblo's jail, he was eventually brought to Cartago by two Indians, who demanded eight pesos each for their service.[61]

On occasion, slaves were employed to search for runaways, and they also received compensation. In October 1722, African-born slave Francisco Plaza was driving mules to Matina when he happened upon a mina fugitive, a countryman to whom "he spoke and understood his language." Plaza promptly turned the man over to the pardo ferryman at the Reventazón River.[62]

Runaways confronted severe obstacles in their attempts to escape, and although some succeeded in evading capture for a time, the available documentation suggests that most were eventually caught. Despite vast distances, primitive communications, and a limited state presence, fugitives were regularly apprehended. Mounted officials of the *Santa Hermandad* (rural constabulary) tracked fugitive slaves while patrolling the roads, hiring auxiliary slave catchers if the situation demanded.[63]

A fugitive's best chance for permanent freedom lay in leaving Costa Rica altogether to start a new life as a stranger in another province. A majority of Costa Rican slaves fleeing to other provinces went to Nicaragua. Diego Leal, a mulatto, fled his mistress in Aserrí, reportedly fleeing to Granada, in 1669.[64] Silvestre García, a black creole originally from Granada who had been sold to a Cartago master, was believed to have absconded to his former home in 1675.[65] Miguel, a congo, ran away from his mistress in Esparza in 1688 and was also believed to have been headed for the Granada area.[66] A few runaways succeeded in fleeing further. In 1640, Jerónimo de Retes of Cartago learned that his black creole slave, Francisco Valeriano, had been captured in Gracias a Dios, Honduras.[67] José de Arlegui, a mulatto about twenty-two years old in 1708, took the opportunity to flee from his Costa Rican master while traveling with him in Nicaragua. Manuel Antonio de Arlegui heard that José had made his way to Guatemala City, more than a thousand miles from Cartago. He was eventually apprehended there, but not until more than six years had passed.[68]

A handful of fugitives may have made it to freedom. By 1713, Gil de Salazar, a mulatto trained as a tailor, had avoided capture for eight or nine years.[69] In the same year, Antonio Morales, also a mulatto, had been reported as still a fugitive after a decade.[70] If they survived, these men probably succeeded in passing as free mulattos in the unknown provinces to which they had fled.

Flight and Patronage

Often, flight was not as simple as "fleeing slavery." To escape one master, slaves might flee to another. This could constitute an end in itself, or serve as a temporary measure, until the opportunity presented itself for a complete escape. Many would-be runaways risked the uncertainty of serving a new master rather than continuing to suffer with the old. New patrons could offer some protection from the authorities or from former owners but might turn out to be abusive masters themselves.

In July 1717, for example, Juan Damián and Gregorio Caamaño appeared before Governor don Pedro Ruiz de Bustamante to complain of "ill treatment" by their mistress, doña Agueda Pérez de Muro, and to ask to be sold to another owner. Because they also accused their mistress of smuggling, the governor immediately promised them the protection of "Royal Justice." He also demonstrated his complete lack of concern for their allegations of abuse by neglecting to question them on any subject other than the commercial activities of their mistress.[71] Nevertheless, Gregorio and

Juan Damián initially achieved their goal in being sold to another master. The governor confiscated the men from their mistress and, in September 1718, publicly auctioned both to Sergeant Major don Francisco de la Madriz Linares.[72] Pérez de Muro contested the confiscation of her slaves and appealed the case to the Royal Audiencia of Guatemala, which in March 1723 decreed that Gregorio and Juan Damián be returned to her.[73] A year later, Juan Damián was surrendered to Pérez de Muro's husband, don Francisco Garrido. Gregorio passed to Garrido's power in July 1724.[74]

Both Juan Damián and Gregorio Caamaño had fled other masters years before. Juan Damián was one of four congo youths who arrived on the *Nuestra Señora de la Soledad y Santa Isabel* in 1700 and had fled from Esparza in February 1701.[75] Gregorio, a popo, probably arrived in Costa Rica at the same time and was one of nine Africans who fled don Gregorio Caamaño around 1703. On that occasion, he had already succeeded in being sold to another master and was purchased by don Diego de Barros y Carvajal.[76] Fleeing to new masters formed a tactic both Juan Damián and Gregorio used at multiple times during their lives. By 1717, they had gained experience and developed relationships in Costa Rica that emboldened them to challenge their mistress before the governor and achieve their goal of sale to a new master. For Gregorio Caamaño, flight formed one strategy among several in his struggle for freedom. After a succession of owners, he finally obtained manumission in 1733.[77]

Antonio, a congo, also employed this tactic of fleeing from one master to another. Brought to Matina by English contrabandists around 1700, Antonio had been kidnapped just a few months after his arrival by the Miskitus and taken to a town he called Tita, probably on the coast of Nicaragua, where he became the slave of a Miskitu named "Llile" (Gilles?). Antonio explained that he had always wanted to escape from the Miskitus because of the "bad treatment they gave him," and when his master separated him from his wife, an enslaved Dorasque Indian, around 1719, he strengthened his resolve. Finally, in March 1722, Antonio escaped to Matina with José Antonio, a Tójar Indian and fellow slave of "Llile."[78] Considering that Antonio had originally been brought by smugglers, Costa Rican governor don Diego de la Haya Fernández declared him Crown property and ordered him auctioned as a slave.[79] Four days after the auctions began in Cartago's central plaza, Antonio and José Antonio fled the Cartago jail. A month later, they were recaptured by pardo soldiers in Matina.[80] On June 21, 1722, Antonio was sold to Francisco Javier Oreamuno, who divided his residence between

Cartago and Panama City. In 1724, Oreamuno sent Antonio to Esparza to be embarked for Panama. But from Esparza, Antonio escaped with a mulatto companion to Nicaragua.[81]

In May 1725, Antonio sought out the governor of Nicaragua, don Tomás Marcos Duque de Estrada, and appealed to him for his protection. Antonio related to the Nicaraguan governor a new and expanded narrative of his first escape that differed significantly from the one he had offered Costa Rican authorities. For twenty-two years, he now claimed, he had been a slave of the Miskitu governor Aníbal (Hannibal), eventually marrying one of Aníbal's daughters and two other women. No doubt having learned of royal *cédulas* promising freedom to slaves who fled from Spain's enemies,[82] Antonio claimed he had become "displeased with such a life, and remembering that he deserved the holy water of baptism, resolved to seek Christianity to comply with the divine precepts," fleeing "from those barbarians" to Matina. Not only were his motives pure, but Antonio now professed invaluable knowledge of Miskitu military strategy and tactics. He claimed to have accompanied the Miskitus on several raids on Nicaraguan territory, including an attack on Chontales and an expedition to Lake Nicaragua and the San Juan River in which the Miskitus had successfully evaded the Spanish garrison at the Castle of San Juan. Antonio knew all the routes and points of entry the Miskitus used for their incursions into Nicaragua, as well as the locations and populations of the Miskitu settlements themselves. He offered the governor his services as a guide and spy for any future surveillance or military operation against the Miskitus, asking only one thing in return: "the benefit of tranquility and freedom."[83]

Governor Duque de Estrada was particularly intrigued by Antonio's offer because he had just completed construction of a coast guard galliot "for the punishment of the said barbarians," and believed Antonio's knowledge could contribute to the success of a planned punitive expedition against the Miskitus. By January 1726, he had dispatched Antonio to the Castle of San Juan, where Antonio briefed the commander of the fort, don Pedro Marencos. Duque de Estrada concluded that the law favored Antonio for having "fled from the dominion of the enemy" and decided to "protect him and give him the security of freedom."[84]

Although surely exceptional, Antonio's story reflected a strategy used by many fugitive slaves. Antonio attempted to persuade a succession of patrons to grant him his freedom. If they disappointed him, he relied on his own resources to flee again. When he fled to Matina, Antonio hoped to be freed by the governor of Costa Rica.[85] In his March 1722 statement to Costa Rican governor don Diego de la Haya Fernández, Antonio said that he knew the Miskitu governor Aníbal well, but that his own master was the Miskitu "Llile." He related some details of Miskitu activities he had heard from Miskitu headmen Aníbal, Bernabé (Barnaby), and Pítar (Peter) while in his master's company, but these evidently failed to impress de la Haya. Of his motives for fleeing the Miskitus, Antonio mentioned "bad treatment" and separation from his wife, but said nothing of a yearning for Catholicism.[86] Antonio's Costa Rican master, Fermín de Oses, had long been dead, and when Oses's heirs failed to claim Antonio, Antonio must have been devastated when de la Haya ordered he be auctioned off as a slave.[87] He remained in Cartago until 1724, when his new master determined to send him to Panama. He then fled and sought another powerful patron, this time with much greater success.

Antonio's statement to Nicaraguan Governor don Tomás Marcos Duque de Estrada in 1725 reflected a more sophisticated knowledge of the factors likely to convince Spanish officials to extend freedom to a fugitive slave. After emphasizing his desire to live among Catholics, Antonio was baptized in the cathedral of Granada in November 1726.[88] More importantly, he refashioned himself as an expert in Miskitu military affairs, claiming to have been a slave and kinsman of the Miskitu governor Aníbal and to have participated (albeit unwillingly) in several Miskitu expeditions against the Spaniards. Francisco Javier de Oreamuno did not hesitate to describe these claims as false and "sinister."[89] Certainly Antonio's first and second statements showed contradictions, and his second declaration to the governor of Nicaragua enhanced his importance. On one level, Antonio's claim to have married a daughter of Aníbal and to have accompanied the Miskitus on raids in Nicaragua may have exaggerated his own stature and access to military secrets. On another, it illustrated Antonio's understanding of the importance of gaining the trust of and even intimacy with powerful patrons. If his subsequent behavior is any guide, over a period of twenty years, Antonio must have tried any number of ploys to convince his Miskitu masters to free him. When persuasion failed to achieve the desired result, Antonio fled, as he did later again and again before finally convincing the governor of Nicaragua to manumit him.

Victorino López, a mulatto, also escaped at least twice, biding his time for almost a decade between flights. Initially purchased in Villa de los Santos, Panama, Victorino was taken to Villa de Nicaragua (now Rivas) by traveling merchant Captain don Carlos Francisco de Sifuentes. In 1706, Victorino fled and made it as far as Cartago, where he was jailed.[90] Sold to Captain Blas González Coronel the same year,[91] Victorino remained in González Coronel's service until 1714, when a judge ordered González Coronel to surrender Victorino to Josefa Francisca Cartín, one of his creditors.[92] Recognizing a second chance, Victorino took advantage of the circumstances to flee. Rather than striking out on his own as he had in the past, he chose to hide out at the home of Pedro Martínez in the Valley of Aserrí.[93] Victorino's relationship to Martínez is unknown, but farmers in the valleys west of Cartago sometimes provided shelter to fugitives in exchange for their labor.[94] The problem became widespread enough that Governor don Lorenzo Antonio de Granda y Balvín issued an edict against hiding fugitive servants and slaves in 1707, an order repeated by Governor don Diego de la Haya more than a decade later.[95] In March 1715, however, Victorino was found out and returned to Cartín.[96]

A Choice of Masters: Flight as a Means of Influencing Sales

Although some runaways sought out patrons as a step on the path to permanent escape, other slaves resorted to flight to achieve more limited objectives, such as to convince a hated owner to sell them. In such cases, slaves fled precisely in order to seek out new patrons. Flight became a strategy not to "escape slavery" but to ameliorate the immediate conditions under which slaves lived.

Francisco, an African, was sent to work his master Pedro de Alvarado's hacienda in the Valley of Bagaces sometime around 1700. From there, Francisco fled to Nicaragua, "where he sought a master." The ploy proved successful. The son of Francisco's master, Gil de Alvarado, followed him to Nicaragua and decided to sell him to Andrés Arias of Granada rather than face future escape attempts.[97] Other slaves were forced to go to more drastic lengths. In 1692, María Manuela, a mulatta about twenty-five years old, had lived as a fugitive in the mountains near Cartago for more than a year. Her mistress, doña Juana Núñez Trupira (elsewhere Trujira), described María Manuela as "of such an evil nature that I have no profit from her at all." When Trupira succeeded in having her captured and returned to her house, María Manuela ran away again. She now refused to return to Trupira, and threatened that "if they compel her to do so she will have to take her own life."[98] Complaining of "bad treatment," María Manuela had repeatedly sought the intercession of civil authorities before presenting herself at the home of parish priest Agustín de Torres, asking for his protection until someone could be found to buy her.[99] Recognizing the "known danger to her life," *Alcalde* Nicolás de Céspedes ordered that María Manuela be sold. Juan Hidalgo purchased her the same day for four hundred pesos.[100] For María Manuela, flight was but one of the drastic means she used to try to relieve her own suffering at the hands of a cruel mistress. Similarly, in the 1720s, the mulatta Eugenia was sent by her master with an agent to be sold in Panama. Don Pedro de Castellanos was forced to return with Eugenia to La Caldera, as Eugenia had convinced him that she would flee or commit suicide if left in Panama. In her desperation to return to Costa Rica, Eugenia said that whatever Panamanian "gave his money [for her] would lose it, because she would have to hang herself." She demanded that authorities "put me in Cartago," because "I must not serve against my will."[101]

Desperation led some slaves to combine flight with other drastic actions. In April 1723, Captain Juan Cortés, a free mulatto who lived in the Valley of Barva west of Cartago, accused his slave, Antonia, a mulatta about forty years old, of having set a series of fires to his house, sugar mill, and cane field.[102] Antonia told judge Juan de Ugalde that she did not wish to be returned to Cortés. She asked instead that he concede her "a paper of sale to seek an owner to content her," in accordance with Spanish law.[103] On April 26, 1723, Cortés sold her to Governor don Diego de la Haya Fernández.[104]

Occasionally, slaves fled their masters and appealed directly to the governor of Costa Rica pleading for his protection. Francisco Caracata, a Slave Coast native of casta arará, was brought to Matina by English smugglers around the turn of the eighteenth century.[105] In Costa Rica, he became a confirmed runaway. By September 25, 1719, Caracata had eluded recapture for more than forty days. Don Manuel de Arburola's repeated attempts to find him had so far met with no success.[106] A few days later, Francisco was apprehended in Matina and surrendered to the overseer of his master's cacao hacienda.[107] When Caracata was brought to Cartago, his master imprisoned him in a room of his house. Although he was sick and chained, Caracata managed to break first one of his chains, then a bar on one of the windows to escape the house. Having searched the mountains and estates near Cartago to no avail, Arburola planned to look for him next in Matina.[108] Late on the night of January 17, 1721, Francisco appeared at the home of Governor don Diego de la Haya Fernández, still wearing a chain and lock around his right leg.[109] Francisco's body bore signs of ill health and probably abuse, such as swelling of the knees and abscesses on his chest and shoulder blades. Described as about fifty years old, he was probably much younger.[110] Although the governor did not bother to record what Francisco wanted of him, if he had sought to be sold to another master, he achieved his aim. In April 1722, the governor ordered Caracata sold to don Francisco Javier de Oreamuno for just one hundred pesos.[111]

Francisco Cubero, a mulatto, had lived all of his twenty years in the home of his mistress, doña Catalina González del Camino, who died in November 1745.[112] He must have known all of his mistress's children, and when he faced the prospect that one of them would soon become his new owner, Francisco fled.[113] A month after her other slaves had been distributed among her survivors, Francisco presented himself to the *alcalde provincial*, Sergeant Major don José Antonio de Oreamuno, requesting "that he might be sold to a master of his liking." Oreamuno conferred with González del Camino's heirs, and with their consent, Francisco was soon sold to don Francisco Fernández de la Pastora.[114]

Despite its rugged geography and mild climate—conditions which favored the growth of cimarrón communities elsewhere—unconquered areas of Costa Rica never provided a haven for significant numbers of fugitive slaves. Most slaves who struck out on the roads were soon captured and returned to their masters. Those who hid out in the woods were discovered or, in some cases, returned of their own accord. Little is known of the relationships between people of African descent and Costa Rica's indigenous peoples, but most fugitives apparently failed to find refuge among Indians. A few joined the Miskitu Zambos, but this was to risk enslavement by a new master. At least two African men repented of the decision and returned to Costa Rica years later. A slave's best chance of success lay in escaping to another Spanish province. Better able to blend into their new host societies posing as free men than were Africans, mulattos proved most successful at this strategy, but they, too, accounted for only a handful. With permanent escape offering slight chance of success, slaves often chose to flee not to "escape slavery" but to seek another master, who could provide protection against the old. Although this strategy alleviated some of the immediate problems confronting many slaves, ultimately, it reinforced and even enhanced the power of masters as a class by reaffirming their role as protectors of their social subordinates. In retrospect, slave flight, a permanent feature of Costa Rican slavery, might appear to have been little more than an ongoing nuisance. As many masters owned only one or two slaves, however, the flight of a slave could mean serious disruptions, for example, if slaves fled at the time of the cacao or sugar harvests, and sometimes economic hardship, as when widows relied on their slaves for income. When masters depended so immediately on their slaves, flight could prove more than an inconvenience.

Violent Resistance

Costa Rican documents keep remarkably silent about violent resistance by slaves. The scant evidence that exists appears most often as chance comment in documents about other matters. In 1678, for example, Captain don Francisco de Salazar recorded in his will that the previous year, his slave Segundo, a sixteen-year-old mulatto, had been garroted by Captain don José de Alvarado for "having resisted."[115] No record of the original charges against Segundo appears to have survived. Similarly, the following year, the *cabildo* of Cartago met to choose a new *Alguacil Mayor*. According to the cabildo's minutes, the acting *Alguacil*, Adjutant Francisco Sáenz de Espinoza, "is in bed because Juan Antonio, mulato slave of the Captain Juan Flores, treacherously stabbed him, as a result of which he has little hope of living."[116] No case file on Juan Antonio has been preserved. According to church records, Juan Antonio was executed by Alcalde Sebastián de Zamora and buried on August 10, 1679.[117] In 1687, doña Francisca Sánchez de Orozco petitioned the governor of Costa Rica to return to her the goods she had brought into her marriage as a dowry. Against her will, her husband had mortgaged two of her mulatto slaves, Santiago and Santamaría. The men were now imprisoned in Esparza, accused of complicity in the murder of Alonso Mateos, to whom they had been mortgaged.[118] Again, records of the criminal charges against Santiago and Santamaría cannot be located. Apparently, they were acquitted of those charges, as they appeared years later in the testament of Sánchez de Orozco's widowed husband.[119] Santiago, however, was later executed for murder, apparently as the result of another incident.[120] In other cases, not even the charges against the accused have survived, and only the names—sometimes not even those—of the black men and women executed remain. In 1681, an unnamed mulatta was hanged.[121] Antonio, a black, was executed in 1694.[122]

In contrast to the numerous, if poorly documented, cases of individual resistance, there is less direct evidence of slave rebellion in Costa Rica during the entire colonial period. Occasionally, however, slave masters made cryptic references to conspiracies among slaves that, again, went unrecorded in other documents. In 1720, Captain Manuel García de Argueta recalled that some slaves "have treacherously killed their masters . . . in this city, [and have been] hanged in the public square for such crimes and others."[123] Making these remarks decades after the events documented above, García must have referred to more recent incidents unrecorded in other documents. Most tantalizing of all, a 1732 letter from Governor don Baltasar Francisco de Valderrama to his lieutenant in Matina clearly referred to a slave uprising there:

> The thing about the blacks was looked at and has been looked at with the care and precaution that its nature and consequences demand, and already a provision was made for its remedy, as your relative Captain don Francisco Garrido, bearer of this [letter], will communicate to you; of this, in the end it is better that they should have been removed as Your Honor says . . . we would be free if at the first insolence Your Honor had hanged one, because in an uprising there is nothing better nor more lawful than to remove the leader [*cabeza*]; and because that did not happen, so that such boldness would not happen again, it is good that those who were the leaders be removed by their owners and they be given some punishment . . . because if it is tolerated there will be more and more . . . let the owners be advised for their compliance.[124]

Valderrama's reference to a verbal "provision" to be communicated by the bearer of the letter clearly indicates that the instructions for dealing with the slave uprising were oral and probably were never written down. Although the documents do not clarify the "nature and consequences" of this incident, rumblings of slave conspiracies in Matina continued more than two years later. José Felipe Bermúdez, lieutenant general in the Matina Valley, made another oblique reference in a 1734 letter to the governor: "Regarding the black slaves, I am informed of what I must do whenever it be necessary."[125]

Without better documentation, it is impossible to offer a definitive judgment on the impact of violent slave resistance. However, the everyday functioning of the Costa Rican slave system, including the broad freedom of movement accorded to male slaves, was not affected more than temporarily.

Honor among Slaves

Less dramatic examples of resistance occurred when slaves verbally demanded respect from their social superiors. Although enslaved, they refused to accept that they were inferior, despite laws that disadvantaged them as "common" or "vile people."[126] Through words alone, captives challenged the hierarchy of masters and slaves, implicitly refuting a major premise of slavery itself—that it was justified by black inferiority.[127] In the Mediterranean and in Latin America, furthermore, such verbal challenges, especially those uttered in public, threatened another fundamental concept underpinning the social order: honor.[128] Honor manifested itself in decidedly different ways for men and women, although a concern for reputation was paramount to both. For men, defending the public esteem of oneself and one's family mattered most. For women, the reputation of sexual purity as a virgin or faithful wife was most important and, in turn, reflected upon the family. Public insults to honor demanded public rectification, through violence or legal action. Ostensibly, only the honor of members of the Spanish ruling class was beyond reproach, but in practice, people at all levels of society laid claim to honor in varying degrees, and they sometimes proved bold enough to question the honor of their social superiors.[129]

To the disgust of Spaniards, this "arrogant" self-confidence and sense of self-worth extended even to slaves. For enslaved men, a sense of honor, independence, and even equality with white men sometimes developed from a knowledge of their importance in production. This sense proved especially strong in Matina, where enslaved men lived and worked largely free of the supervision or interference of whites. After building their own homes and managing the cacao haciendas in every way, some slave men understandably felt a sense of proprietorship and regarded the semiannual visits of the *hacendados* as unwelcome intrusions. In 1696, the Spanish Captain Juan de Bonilla traveled to Matina for the June harvest on an errand from doña Josefa de Santiago y Aguiar, who wished to ensure that no one collected cacao from her properties until her son arrived to supervise. Upon arrival, Bonilla found Francisco de Flores collecting cacao from doña Josefa's groves. When Bonilla asked him on whose authority he was picking the fruit, Flores replied that he had been sent by Gregorio Sanabria, the mulatto slave of doña Ambrosia de Echavarría Navarro. Sanabria had sent Flores to collect a debt of two *zurrones* (198 kilograms/436 pounds) that Benito Mejía, doña Josefa's slave, owed him.[130]

Infuriated by the slave's initiative, the next day, Captain Juan de Bonilla went with three servants to Echavarría Navarro's hacienda and called out to Gregorio, "Come here, mulato, where will your shamelessness end? On whose authority did you go to pick cacao?" Gregorio replied, "On [my] authority alone." When Bonilla called him a scoundrel (*desvergonzado*), Gregorio rejoined that the shameless one was Bonilla, "for coming to his [Gregorio's] house to treat him like that."[131] Bonilla then raised the stakes by calling Gregorio a dog. According to Mexicanist historian Javier Villa-Flores, "slaveholders often employed" this insult "as a prelude to a severe beating."[132] Gregorio warned Bonilla to "watch how he talked," and observed that "there were many kinds of dogs, there were Spanish dogs, too."[133] Enraged, Bonilla took a machete from his belt and was about to start at Gregorio when he thought better of it and "contained [himself] . . . as a Spaniard and a man of honor." He then told Gregorio, "Enough, man, let's stop it." Unsatisfied with the Spaniard's offer of a truce, Gregorio threw the contents of a cup of chocolate menacingly at Bonilla's feet and wished aloud that they were alone. Bonilla turned and made his exit, later to seek legal satisfaction for the insults. This led to Gregorio's imprisonment in the Cartago jail in July 1696.[134]

Captain Juan de Bonilla fully expected subordination from this mulatto slave, but Gregorio Sanabria refused to accept that his enslavement or color required him to submit to insults, even from a Spanish "man of honor." Insolent speech gave slaves the power to strike at their masters with the weapon of shame, and in this case Gregorio hit back.[135] By implying that Bonilla was a "Spanish dog," Gregorio rejected the idea that whites had honor by definition, and demanded respect even though he was a mulatto slave. By throwing down a cup of chocolate, Gregorio dared the Spaniard to try to subdue him by violence. At that critical moment, both the ideology and the reality of white superiority hung in the balance. If Gregorio succeeded in thrashing Bonilla, he would not only prove the falsity of white superiority but would momentarily defeat the violence that ultimately underpinned it.[136] Recognizing the stakes, already humiliated before his servants, Bonilla retreated to safer ground—the Spanish judicial system, where the odds were stacked overwhelmingly in his favor—and attempted to secure a legal restoration of his honor. The son of the mulatta slave María Sanabria, Gregorio had been born around 1662 and raised in the home of doña Juana Moscoso.[137] Although brought up in slavery and, beyond any doubt, aware of the Spanish American assumption of white superiority, Gregorio gave no indication that he accepted that premise. On the contrary, he openly scoffed at the implication that he owed this white man any special deference.

Like Gregorio Sanabria, the mulatta slaves Ana and Mauricia had grown up in the home of their mistress, daughter and granddaughter of the enslaved woman Juana.[138] As Gregorio challenged Captain Juan de Bonilla to defend his honor through violence, in 1755, Ana and Mauricia questioned the sexual purity of several Spanish women in their Cartago neighborhood. According to one witness, one Sunday after High Mass, doña Lucía de Alvarado, wife of don José Nicolás de Bonilla, for some reason called Ana "the biggest whore." Ana allegedly replied that she was no more a whore than doña Lucía, and that when her husband Bonilla was away, Alvarado went walking the streets.[139] With this rejoinder, the slave woman Ana, the single mother of Mauricia, compared her sexual reputation to that of a married Spanish woman and judged the behavior of the latter less reputable than her own. According to other accounts, Ana had made similar allegations against the honor of doña Lucía's unmarried younger sisters, charging that they had installed false bars in their windows that they removed at night to let men enter their bedrooms.[140] According to the indigenous servant Bernardo Campos, Ana and Mauricia had shouted the insults so loudly that he heard them from inside Bonilla's house, notwithstanding that he had been slaughtering a cow at the time.[141] No doubt to vindicate the honor of his household from such a public insult, don José Nicolás de Bonilla charged the slave women with slander, and Ana was held in the Cartago jail. The mulattas' accusations sufficiently piqued the curiosity of presiding judge don Tomás López del Corral that he made a special outing to Bonilla's house to inspect the windows in question. Evidently López del Corral did not reject the mulatta slaves' accusations out of hand—would he have dismissed the charges against them if he found that the windows could be removed? He found the windows, however, "fully secure, and with no sign of recent manufacture."[142]

In contrast to Gregorio Sanabria, Ana and Mauricia denied that they had challenged the honor of the Spanish women. In a lifetime of slavery, they had learned "verbal and nonverbal devices to mask their insolence."[143] When confronted with the statements of witnesses, Ana denied she "would ever have dared do such a thing" as insult doña Lucía de Alvarado.[144] Bonilla rejoined that Ana only denied her words because she was "afraid of punishment." He refused to accept Ana's retraction of the insults, because "this might be permissible when the words were proffered by a person of quality (*calidad*) and distinction, [but] not by a person so vile and of such low station as a mulata slave of bad origins."[145] Bonilla argued that her race and her tainted lineage meant that Ana could not undo the damage she had done with her public insults. Soon after, however, "persons of authority and respect, to whom I owe all [my] attention," persuaded Bonilla to drop the lawsuit if Ana and Mauricia would publicly disavow the aspersions they had cast on Bonilla's sisters-in-law.[146] *Alcalde Ordinario* Captain don Félix García de Casasola ordered Ana released forthwith. Aware of the "vexation and unpleasantness [*desazón y disgusto*]" between the two houses, García de Casasola warned their inhabitants, "masters as well as servants," to avoid any further nettlesome incidents.[147]

Insolent speech held no power to overthrow the slave system, but it did, if only fleetingly, call the bases of that system into question. By insulting their social superiors, slaves rejected the superiority of their masters. Through their verbal challenges, slaves vocally defied the justifications of their oppression. Such insolence hinted at a more pervasive discontent that was less often given voice. Although colonial society might attempt to reduce them to the status of "things," slaves never accepted that view of themselves.[148]

Conclusion

Slavery itself generated resistance, and slaves in Costa Rica resisted their oppression in myriad ways, ranging from verbal insolence to violence. At its most basic, their resistance showed that slaves refused to accept that their condition made them less human than others or condemned them to suffer inhuman treatment. This formulation does not vicariously impute to Costa Rican slaves a coherent desire to destroy the system of slavery but recognizes that they fought, even as slaves, to improve the conditions in which they lived. Such an elastic definition, however, can encompass muttered words or even secret thoughts, as well as concrete actions, threatening to render the concept of resistance meaningless by confusing intentions with consequences. Historians should strive toward a realistic understanding of whether various forms of resistance held the potential to improve the conditions in which slaves lived, which forms succeeded in doing so, and which failed.

Slave resistance in Costa Rica remained overwhelmingly at the individual level. Even when successful, individual resistance could do no more than a slave intended it to do—to ameliorate his or her own suffering. Although individual slaves might hope to solve personal problems through resistance, their actions could not directly lessen the plight of their fellow slaves and ultimately held no potential to threaten slavery in the colony. Verbal challenges could provide some psychological satisfaction and even restore a measure of dignity to slaves, but no more. For most slaves, the potential costs of insolence must have outweighed the benefits. Fugitive slaves, whether they escaped alone or in groups, were usually recaptured. Although sporadic and temporary, flight could still cause big problems for individual masters, but it posed only a minimal threat to the functioning of slavery in the colony. Furthermore, although the common strategy of fugitive slaves to seek out new patrons could undermine particular masters, it only increased the power of others. Even— perhaps especially—when successful at solving immediate problems, seeking new patrons discouraged slaves from relying on each other or forming common cause with members of other oppressed groups; instead, this tactic enhanced the power of the master class. Cimarrón communities and alliances with Indians, either of which could have presented a serious challenge to the slaveholding system, failed to materialize. In the few documented instances of slave violence, individual slaves struck at individual adversaries, no doubt for their own individual reasons. Their actions were rewarded with capital punishment. Although such desperate acts surely reflected a more general current of discontent among slaves, swift repression warned against similar incidents. The odds against slave uprisings were even greater; few went beyond the conspiracy stage.

Basic realities of slavery in Costa Rica conditioned the types of resistance that emerged there. Scattered and often isolated from their fellow slaves, Costa Rican slaves by and large failed to develop the collective consciousness that might have enabled them to threaten the slave system itself—not an entirely unrealistic notion in a colony with a relatively small investment in slavery. Although their attempts to improve their lives proved disruptive to individual masters, these attempts remained limited and containable. Ultimately, the Costa Rican colonial system proved well able to accommodate slave resistance.

CHAPTER SEVEN

More than Slaves

Family and Freedom

✝ LIKE OTHER AFRICANS, THE SURVIVORS OF THE *CHRISTIANUS Quintus* and the *Fredericus Quartus* began to form families and communities immediately upon arrival in Costa Rica and even before. In the fundamentally new contexts of American slavery, both the form and content of those families and communities differed radically from those the captives had known in the Gold Coast and the Slave Coast. Unfortunately, Costa Rican sources contain few descriptions of families among slaves other than those sanctioned by the Roman Catholic Church. They allow few glimpses of family forms that slaves might have organized partly according to their own distinct cultural values. However, as with associations based on ethnicity, place of residence, or shared labor, the ability to create and maintain a family depended on the concrete opportunities slaves had to forge and pursue relationships with others. In family life as in other aspects of their lives, Costa Rican slaves faced serious restrictions, threats, and obstacles. The nature of the relationships and families formed by enslaved people in Costa Rica varied according to several factors imposed by the unusual nature of slavery in the colony.

Family life under slavery was inherently unstable. Most slave mothers never saw their children grow to adulthood. High infant mortality claimed many of the children. Mothers were also separated from their children when their children were sold, mortgaged, given away, or even manumitted. Although Costa Rican masters frequently employed a discourse of paternalism, their actions indicated that they felt little reluctance to sepa-rate slave families, even those who had lived in their homes for generations. Masters tended to confine female slaves to their own homes, constraining their slaves' opportunities to pursue outside relationships. The disadvan-tages attending the condition of slavery meant that few solemnized their unions in the Catholic Church. A traditional Catholic family was almost impossible to attain, so slave women created other kinds of families. Although women and children achieved more success in attaining their freedom than did adult men, few were able to do so, and it was not unusual for three generations of slaves to reside in a master's home.

On the other hand, many men, especially Africans, enjoyed an excep-tional autonomy due to the nature of their work. Enslaved men developed strong relationships with free people, including free women, who were like-wise able to move at will. This contributed to enslaved men's overwhelming preference to marry free women, who were usually of other racial origins. Choosing exogamy, a strategy common to Africans and creoles, blacks and mulattos, reflected slave men's conscious strategy of ensuring that their chil-dren were born in freedom, but it also indicated their rejection of enslaved women. The gendered division of labor in Costa Rica, which tended to sepa-rate male and female slaves, posed an ultimately insuperable obstacle to the formation of slave families and the reproduction of a slave culture distinct from that of the masters.

Single Mothers and Their Children

Not long after their arrival in 1710, several of the African women brought on the *Christianus Quintus* and *Fredericus Quartus* gave birth. All of their cre-ole children were born out of wedlock. No priest, master, or public official bothered to record any information about the children's fathers, if they knew or cared. Petrona, a Yoruba (*aná*) sold to doña Cecilia Vázquez de Coronado of the Valley of Bagaces in October 1710, gave birth to María about 1712. A son, José Patricio, followed around 1714, and another son, Julián, was born about 1718.[1] María, also a Yoruba slave from the same household, saw her daughter Josefa baptized in May 1713.[2] Gertrudis, a Slave Coast native (*arará*) about twenty years old when the Danish ships brought her to Matina, soon had two sons, Toribio and Juan, both baptized in Cartago in 1714. Juan's baptismal record specified that his mother was unmarried (*soltera*), an observation that was unusual because single status was generally presumed in the case of slave women.[3]

As elsewhere in the Americas, the vast majority of children who were born in slavery in Costa Rica were born to legally single mothers. For most of those children, no information at all was recorded about their fathers. About thirty-eight of the 360 slaves baptized in the parish church of Cartago between 1595 and 1750 can be positively identified as adult Africans. Officials would not have recorded the paternity of these adults. Of the remaining 322 slaves, most of whom were children, 296 (92 percent) were listed without a father.[4] In Esparza, just thirteen slave children were baptized between 1708, the earliest year for which records survive, and 1750. Eleven were listed without attribution of paternity, but two slave children baptized in 1746 and 1748 were born to married slave couples.[5]

Although women of all racially subordinated groups gave birth to illegitimate children (*hijos naturales*) in disproportionately high numbers, the ratios of servant and slave children born out of wedlock were especially high.[6] In Cartago, the number of illegitimate births among free *casta* and Indian women showed only slight differences. Priests recorded 27 percent of Indian children, for example, as born illegitimately between 1599 and 1750. Twenty-nine percent

TABLE 7.1. Illegitimate Children by Race and Condition, Cartago, 1599–1750 (Percentages in parentheses)

RACE/CONDITION OF CHILD	TOTAL CHILDREN	ILLEGITIMATE CHILDREN
Black slave	72	63 (88)
Mulatto slave	82	76 (93)
Slave unidentified by color	168	158 (94)
Total slaves	322	297 (92)
Indian	414	110 (27)
Mestizo	678	197 (29)
Free mulatto	509	166 (33)
Spanish	1,191	34 (3)
Unidentified by color	4,021	1,515 (38)
Total children	7,135	2,319 (33)

TABLE 7.2. Illegitimate Children by Race and Condition, Esparza, 1708–1750 (Percentages in parentheses)

RACE/CONDITION OF CHILD	TOTAL CHILDREN	ILLEGITIMATE CHILDREN
Black slave	5	5 (100)
Mulatto slave	7	6 (86)
Slave unidentified by color	1	0 (0)
Total slaves	13	11 (85)
Indian	26	6 (23)
Mestizo	74	23 (31)
Free mulatto	318	55 (17)
Free Black	12	2 (17)
Zambo	30	4 (13)
Spanish	74	6 (8)
Unidentified by color	58	6 (10)
Total children	605	102 (17)

Source: ACM, Libros de Bautizos de Esparza (1706–1819)/FHL, VAULT INTL film 1223548, item 5.

of mestizo children baptized during the same period were noted as born out of wedlock. One-third of free mulatto children and nearly 40 percent of children unidentified by racial category were born to single mothers.[7] The percentage of enslaved mulatto children born out of wedlock in Cartago (93 percent), which was nearly three times greater than that of free mulatto children (33 percent), already suggests that "cultural" reasons cannot explain the prevalence of illegitimacy among slaves. Data from the North Pacific, a region where people of African descent comprised a majority of the population, reinforce this point. Baptismal records from Esparza indicate that illegitimacy was less than half that of Cartago (17 compared to 33 percent). The overwhelming majority (nearly 85 percent) of the 360 free mulatto, free black, and free zambo children baptized in the Esparza church between 1708 and 1750 were born to married couples. Almost all of the slave children were born out of wedlock.[8]

The near-total illegitimacy among children born to enslaved women can

TABLE 7.3. Illegitimate Children Born to Female Slaves and
Servants, Cartago, 1599–1750 (Percentage in parentheses)

RACE/CONDITION OF MOTHER	TOTAL CHILDREN	ILLEGITIMATE CHILDREN
Black slave	82	73 (89)
Mulatto slave	75	73 (97)
Slave unidentified by race	99	88 (89)
Total slaves	256	234 (91)
Indian criada	69	45 (65)
Mestiza criada	5	5 (100)
Criada unidentified by race	18	9 (50)
Total criadas	92	59 (64)

Note: The main reasons for discrepancies between the numbers of slave children and slave mothers are (1) baptized children were registered without mention of either parent and (2) children were described as of a different race than their mothers.
Sources: ACM, Libros de Bautizos de Cartago (1599–1750), nos. 1-6/FHL, VAULT INTL film1219701, items 1-5; film 1219702, items 1-3; (1706–1819)/ FHL, VAULT INTL film 1223548, item 5.

be attributed to slavery itself rather than simply to the conditions of domestic servitude. Free women specifically identified as domestic servants (*criadas*) in Cartago homes were mostly Indians. The number of out-of-wedlock children born to them was extremely high, but nonetheless, it was more than 25 percent lower than illegitimacy among slave children.[9] Although in many respects, slave and free servant women lived in identical conditions, even legally free servants were able to exercise greater control over their sexuality and family lives than were slaves.

Miscegenation, Slavery, and Freedom

Sexual relationships between masters and slaves were inherent to slavery itself. This form of *mestizaje* was *interracial sex, racial mixture*, and *miscegenation* of a different sort. With their "sterile, emotionless" sound, terms like these can "shroud acts of sexual submission characterized by violence and degradation."[10] Historians of antebellum United States slavery have estimated the mulatto slave population in the mid-nineteenth century at between 5 and 15 percent of the whole. Based on the low figure, they calculate that 58 percent of enslaved women faced a white man's sexual advances at some time between the ages of fifteen and thirty. Several factors demonstrably increased the likelihood of such contacts. Some, of course, were intangible, such as whether a particular white man found a particular slave woman attractive; others are susceptible to quantification.[11] In a detailed statistical analysis based on the 1850 U.S. census, Richard Steckel concluded that the proportion of mulattos among the slaves on 750 Southern properties (1) decreased with the size of the property, (2) increased on properties that had no separate dwellings for slaves, (3) decreased with the number of slaves per dwelling, and (4) increased with the number of adult white men in the area. In towns and cities and in homes without separate slave quarters, the probability that a slave child was mulatto was approximately twice as high as in the countryside.[12]

Considering Costa Rican slavery in the light of Steckel's conclusions suggests that master-slave miscegenation was extremely common. The vast majority of female slaves in Costa Rica lived in conditions where most if not all of Steckel's factors favoring miscegenation applied. Most enslaved women and girls lived in their masters' homes or in small buildings such as kitchens just outdoors—not in separate slave quarters at some distance from the "big house."[13] A majority lived in Cartago, where they were often the only slaves of their masters, and almost always one of just a handful. In the capital and on the small farms of the valleys surrounding it, virtually all slave women interacted daily with white men, including their masters, male family members and friends, and others. Simply put, it was the frequency and intensity of contacts between enslaved women and white men that promoted miscegenation. Any such contact could lead to an interracial sexual relationship, and the days and lives of slave women in Costa Rica were full of them.

Some contemporary critics charged that in Costa Rica, female slaves were prized as much for their reproductive capacity as for their labor. In 1684, Fray Juan de Rojas, Bishop of Nicaragua and Costa Rica, wrote to the king from León:

> The enormous greed of many [of Your] subjects who have unmarried slave women, Lord, they have the growth of their wealth and property in these [women]; because in order that the slaves multiply

through births, [the masters] allow them to live in licentiousness, so that from year to year there is no [slave woman] who does not give a male or female slave to her owner, whom they sell to enrich themselves, [the slave children] being able to serve. The fertile slave woman is the most esteemed and they sell for the highest prices like the mares in Spain, for she who has a womb is worth more than the others and so the slave women are more valued by those who buy them.[14]

Fray Juan never visited Costa Rica (although he did send a representative to tour the colony), and the applicability of his assertions to the province may be questioned.[15] Nevertheless, there is no doubt that Costa Rican slave owners valued and sometimes rewarded enslaved mothers who gave birth to many children. In July 1720, for example, Inés de Olivares freed her slave María de Brenes in a codicil to her testament, citing "the love that she has had for the said mulata María and [for] her good service, besides having given birth to twelve children [while] in [Olivares's] power." About sixty years old, María gained her freedom when her mistress died four days later.[16] Juana had six living children in 1697 when her mistress, Jerónima Barrantes, promised her freedom after Barrantes's death.[17] María Barquero likewise promised freedom to her "white mulata creole" slave Vicenta Josefa after her own death. Born about 1691, Vicenta had grown up in Barquero's family and given birth to many children, seven of whom survived in 1733.[18]

Costa Rican archives contain few traces of masters' sexual relationships with their female slaves, and even fewer documented instances conclusively prove their paternity of slave children. White masters almost never officially recognized their enslaved mulatto children. A well-known exception, don Miguel Calvo, recognized the four children of his former mulatta slave, Ana Cardoso, as his own in his 1715 testament.[19] Ana Cardoso was born to a slave mother owned by doña Ana Pereira Cardoso about 1650. When she was about twenty years old, Ana was purchased by don Tomás Calvo and his wife, doña Eugenia de Abarca, for four hundred pesos. Ana became involved in a sexual relationship with the couple's son, Miguel, when he returned from León, Nicaragua, where he had studied as a seminarian.[20] In the course of two decades, Ana bore at least five children who were fathered by don Miguel Calvo, and eventually she gained her freedom as a consequence of this relationship. In February 1687, doña Eugenia de Abarca sold her mulatto grandson Francisco to his father don Miguel, who freed the boy the same day.[21] Francisco's mother, however, remained a slave. In 1691, Abarca freed two more of Ana's daughters, María, born about 1682, and Feliciana, born some three years later. Ana herself was offered a nominal freedom in 1689, provided she remained in the home and service of Eugenia de Abarca until the latter's death. Two more children of Ana and don Miguel, Ana Micaela (did her name reflect the strength of the affection between her parents?) and José Felipe, were born legally free around 1691 and 1694.[22] Doña Eugenia died in 1702, leaving her freed grandchildren to grow up in the company of their father, don Miguel Calvo.[23] Their mother, Ana Cardoso, presumably acquired her freedom in fact as well as in law at that time.

Miguel Calvo's paternity of the mulatto children was well-known in Cartago. They grew up in their father's household in the central city, served by slaves and in all respects accustomed to the privileged lifestyle of the local elite. In 1715, María Calvo stated in an official document that "we and our father . . . always lived in the same house without any separation."[24] Five years later, she found occasion to remind the governor of Costa Rica that her "natural father" had been "one of the wealthiest" men in the province.[25] Don Miguel Calvo helped to establish his children as not only free but also wealthy members of Cartago society. He arranged marriages for his daughters with respectable free mulatto men and provided them with considerable sums of money. When María Calvo married Adjutant José de Chavarría, a free mulatto originally from León, in 1697, she brought a dowry of a declared value of 769 pesos.[26] Don Miguel Calvo provided "natural daughter" Feliciana with a sizeable dowry of six hundred pesos at the time of her marriage to Sergeant Francisco de Echavarría. In 1711, he gave Feliciana a mulatto slave boy, five-year-old Blas, as a gift.[27] Calvo recalled that he had given Ana Micaela goods worth more than a thousand pesos when she married mulatto silversmith Captain José de Carranza (this included the value of an enslaved woman, Juana).[28]

In 1715, Miguel Calvo composed his will, in which he provided for his children and their mother. He left little to the mother of his children. As a provision of Calvo's will, Ana Cardoso was to be allowed her choice of goods from his estate, not to exceed two hundred pesos in value.[29] In contrast, Calvo recognized all of his children as his natural heirs, ensuring that they would be able to inherit his wealth and "enjoy it with God's blessings."[30] Calvo bequeathed to his sons the means to succeed in agriculture or a trade. Each received an inheritance worth 884 pesos. As an unmistakable sign of status, Calvo bequeathed slaves to at least four of his five children. María, his favorite, received his home in the center of Cartago, confirming her status as a member of the local elite. In 1748, when María was an old woman, a priest flattered the ex-slave's pretensions by recording her name as "doña María Calvo."[31]

Miguel Calvo's recognition, manumission, and support of his children born to a slave mother were extraordinary, perhaps unique, in Costa Rican history. Masters virtually never recognized their enslaved children, at least not officially. Don Tomás de la Madriz recognized his paternity of five sons born to his wife's slave, María Josefa, only years after his wife's death. At an undetermined date between 1726 and 1730, doña Nicolasa Guerrero donated the mulatta María Josefa to her illegitimate daughter, doña Antonia de la Granda y Balvín.[32] Doña Antonia's marriage to don Tomás de la Madriz became acrimonious, and at some point don Tomás initiated sexual relations with María Josefa, whose feelings about the relationship will never be known. Doña Antonia reacted with jealousy. Claiming she needed money to buy clothing suitable for her family to attend Mass, doña Antonia mortgaged María Josefa's daughter Juana Manuela, just fifty days old, for one hundred pesos while her husband was away in Panama in 1737. No further record of Juana Manuela appears in Cartago notarial records.[33] Eight years later, doña Antonia donated two of María Josefa's sons, Francisco Justo and Isidro de la Paz, to her husband. In the next few years, María Josefa bore Madriz two more sons, Joaquín and Luis Fernando. In a final effort to punish her rival, doña Antonia stipulated in her 1746 will that María Josefa be sold to pay for the costs of her burial and funeral services. Don Tomás, however, failed to comply with her dying wish. In the three years after doña Antonia's death, he freed María Josefa, Joaquín, and Luis Fernando; both sons were around four at the time. Another son, José Ricardo, was born free after his mother's manumission. De la Madriz finally freed Justo and Isidro in 1757, when they were about eighteen years old. In his 1764 testament, don Tomás detailed his property and declared his sons, along with their mother, his sole heirs.[34]

Some white men probably freed their children quietly. In 1675, for example, Silvestre Lebat, a Frenchman living in Cartago, paid one hundred pesos to manumit two-year-old Juana, daughter of the mulatta slave María Sanabria. It seems plausible, but will probably never be known with certainty, that Lebat was the infant's father.[35] In another possible case, an anonymous male benefactor paid 125 pesos for the freedom of Benita Rosalía, a slave girl described as "white," in 1738. Named only as "a well-wisher who sponsors and favors the said little mulata," he might also have been her father.[36]

Most scholars of slave societies have concluded that women and children, particularly mulatto children, were more likely than adult men to be manumitted, estimating that women made up about two-thirds of slaves freed.[37] Some conclude that this proportion reflected masters freeing their enslaved sexual partners and children. Writers employ a simple procedure to derive the statistics on which they base such assertions: they categorize the manumitted slaves by gender, race, and age, count them, and divide the tallies by the total number of slaves manumitted.[38]

Applying this methodology to Costa Rica yields some intriguing results.[39] In total manumissions between 1648 and 1750, females enjoyed only a slight advantage over men (71 of 134, or 53 percent), much lower than the two-thirds majority reported for most areas of Latin America. In contrast to most slave societies, women did not win their freedom much more often than did men. In Costa Rica, however, among those women for whom race was recorded, mulattas were almost seven times as likely as black females to be manumitted (46 of 54, or 85 percent). At first glance, this appears to corroborate another thesis some authors have advanced: that mulattas were more attractive to white masters as sexual partners and benefited from such relationships by attaining freedom. Harmannus Hoetink, for example, famously suggested that mulattas more closely approximated an Iberian "somatic norm image," which not only appealed to white males but ultimately promoted the integration of people of mixed race into Latin American societies.[40] The Costa Rican case seems to conform to this pattern.

A closer look at the Costa Rican data, however, complicates the thesis that the sexuality of young mulattas directly contributed to their relative success in attaining freedom. As it turns out, twenty-four of the forty-six (52 percent) owners who manumitted enslaved mulattas were women themselves. In seven more cases (15 percent), mulatta slaves were manumitted by married couples. The documents show that only one-third of the manumissions of mulattas were by men alone. Although many studies have taken into account the gender of manumitted slaves, few have devoted attention to the gender of the masters and mistresses who did the manumitting. As Frank T. Proctor showed with Mexican data, cross-tabulating the gender of masters and freed slaves rather than looking at aggregate ratios yields results that force a reexamination of the nature of the master-slave relationships that contributed to manumission.[41] As in Mexico, Costa Rican widows proved especially likely to free their slaves: they were responsible for almost 12 percent of total manumissions (16 of 134) and more than 30 percent of all

TABLE 7.4. Slave Manumissions by Race and Gender,
Cartago, 1648–1750 (Percentages in parentheses)

RACE	FEMALES	MALES	TOTAL
Mulatto*	47* (35)	35 (26)	35 (61)
Black	7 (5)	13 (10)	20 (15)
Unknown	17 (13)	15 (11)	32 (24)
Total	24 (53)	63 (47)	134 (100)

*Includes one zamba.

Sources: ANCR, PC 801 (1607)–934 (1746); PH 572 (1723)–87 (1741);
PSJ 415 (1738); CC 3905 (1680), 3916 (1675), 3927 (1693), 4000 (1709);
Indice de los protocolos de Cartago, vols. 1–3.

manumissions by women (49 of 134). In some cases, these manumissions may have reflected women freeing their mulatto kin. In others, close but not necessarily familial relationships developed between female domestic slaves and their mistresses, encouraging mistresses to free enslaved women much more frequently than men. Given the gendered nature of slave labor in Costa Rica, this was likely the case. Access to the master or mistress played an obviously crucial role in a slave's ability to negotiate freedom, and gender strongly influenced whether someone enjoyed that access and benefited from such relationships in turn. Enslaved women generally lived and worked in closer proximity to their mistresses than did male slaves. Widows especially relied on their female slaves. Some freed them because they were financially able to do so; others without the means to maintain their slaves freed them to avoid having more mouths to feed. Male masters freed more than twice as many (38 of 63) male slaves as did mistresses and couples, in part because of their closer relationships to male slaves.

On the other hand, evidence clearly establishes that mulatto children benefited from manumission more frequently than any other group. Seventy-six of the 134 certificates of manumission noted the age of the individual freed. A full 22 percent of those (29) were children 10 years old or younger. Every child identified by race was described as mulatto (with the exception of one zamba, a term sometimes used interchangeably with mulatto), and an unknown number of these were the children of white master fathers. The fact that mulattos comprised 80 percent of all slaves freed whose race was recorded (82 of 102) might seem to bolster this suggestion. Men freed 52 percent

TABLE 7.5. Slave Manumissions by Race and Age, Cartago, 1648–1750
(Percentages in parentheses)

AGE GROUP OF SLAVES	MULATTOS*	BLACKS	UNKNOWN	TOTAL
0–5	12 (9)	0 (0)	6 (4)	18 (13)
6–10	9 (7)	0 (0)	2 (1)	11 (8)
11–15	1 (1)	0 (0)	1 (1)	2 (2)
16–20	2 (2)	1 (1)	0 (0)	3 (3)
21–30	14 (10)	1 (1)	3 (2)	18 (13)
31–40	13 (10)	1 (0)	0 (0)	14 (10)
41–50	3 (2)	1 (1)	1 (1)	5 (4)
51+	0 (0)	3 (2)	2 (1)	5 (4)
Subtotal	54 (41)	7 (5)	15 (11)	76 (57)
Unknown	29 (22)	11 (8)	18 (13)	58 (43)
Total	83 (62)	18 (13)	33 (25)	134 (100)

Sources: ANCR, PC 801 (1607)–934 (1746); PH 572 (1723)–587 (1741); PSJ 415 (1738); CC 3905 (1680), 3916 (1675), 3927 (1693), 4000 (1709); *Indice de los protocolos de Cartago*, vols. 1–3.

TABLE 7.6. Gender of Slave Owners Correlated with the Age of the Slaves They Manumitted, Cartago, 1648–1750

AGE GROUP	FEMALE	WIDOW	MARRIED COUPLE	MALE	TOTAL
0–5	1	5	1	11	18
6–10	2	2	3	4	11
11–15	0	1	0	1	2
16–20	1	0	0	2	3
21–30	3	3	3	9	18
31–40	3	2	3	6	14
41–50	0	0	2	3	5
51+	0	1	0	4	5
Unknown	20	3	3	32	58
Total	30	18	15	72	135

Sources: ANCR, PC 801 (1607)–934 (1746); PH 572 (1723)–87 (1741); PSJ 415 (1738); CC 3905 (1680), 3916 (1675), 3927 (1693), 4000 (1709); Indice de los protocolos de Cartago, vols. 1–3.

(15 of 29) of children aged 10 or younger; women freed just over one-third (10); and married couples manumitted 4 more children (14 percent). Direct proof of the paternity of the freed children, however, is lacking, as is evidence to suggest that enslaved women themselves benefited from these relationships. Manumission documents and lawsuits pertaining to inheritance are among our best sources on master-slave sexual relationships, but by their very nature, they reflect situations in which enslaved women enjoyed some success in turning such relationships to the advantage of their children and sometimes themselves. The documents keep silent about the enslaved women who endured years of sexual abuse and struggled determinedly for the freedom of their children only to see them mistreated and sold away.

The Destruction of Slave Families

Slave families could never be stable. Most slave women never knew the traditional family life that was the only one whites respected in Spanish American society. More to the point, chances were great that enslaved mothers would lose their children at a young age. Death; sale, gifts, or other transfers of ownership; the division of property following a master's death; or even manumission meant separation. The infant mortality that afflicted all sectors of colonial society killed many scores of slave children. Sale took many more. A tiny minority of slave children, almost always nursing infants, were sold with their mothers, but the overwhelming majority were torn away from them. Slave mothers also lost their children through other decisions by masters, such as charitable donations or dowries. Slave mothers often knew where such transactions had taken their children, however, and sometimes managed to stay in contact with them after separation.

As in other premodern societies, infant mortality in colonial Costa Rica was horrific. When asked about their children, individual slave women often recounted the names of the dead as well as the living. Isabel, a native of the Gold Coast or upper Slave Coast (*mina*), had three living children in 1718— Pablo José, Juan Manuel, and Petronila. Her twins Juana and José Antonio, she recalled, had died some years before.[42] Micaela de Ibarra, a Yoruba (*aná*), had three children—Juan, María Francisca, and Juana—before 1720. All died before their mother reached the age of twenty-four.[43] Manuela, also a mina, simply said that same year that she "did not have any [children] because all whom she had given birth to had died."[44] Lorenza, a native of the Slave Coast (ararà), told an especially heartbreaking story. When her master, don Antonio de la Riva Agüero, was bringing Lorenza from Cartago to his home in the Valley of Barva, her infant daughter drowned as they crossed a river. De la Riva had torn the dead infant, who had been named Juliana, from her mother's arms. Lorenza did not know where he had buried the baby, she later said.[45]

Millions of African mothers lost their children to the Atlantic slave trade. Although Europeans of the eighteenth century commonly believed that African parents willingly sold their children into slavery, experienced slave traders insisted that this rarely occurred.[46] According to the few available records, children comprised a large share of the African-born slaves who arrived in Costa Rica. Part of the reason derived from Costa Rica's disadvantaged position in the slave trade. British slave traders, for example, gave buyers in Jamaica first pick of "prime negroes." Most of those they rejected in these competitive markets, called "refuse," were sent on to Spanish America.[47] In Cartagena and Panama, wealthy Spaniards tended to buy up the strongest and healthiest of the arriving Africans. Some of these were sent on to the lucrative slave markets of Peru. Costa Rican slave buyers were often forced to accept the children, sick, and old Africans who had been passed up by wealthier slave buyers.

Children younger than twelve years old made up a significant proportion of captives imported to the Americas—nearly 14 percent of the Africans brought on 1,281 recorded slaving voyages between 1600 and 1750—and comprised up to one quarter of the enslaved Africans who arrived on the few slave ships that reached Costa Rica.[48] One cargo of Africans imported from Panama to Matina in 1702 included several children younger than ten years old, including a six-year-old girl suffering from a debilitating ulcer on her left foot.[49] Nine of the thirty-eight minas who arrived on the *Christianus Quintus* or *Fredericus Quartus* and were brought to Cartago by Juan Bautista Retana in 1710 were between the ages of eight and twelve years.[50]

The large proportion of children imported to the colony held powerful implications for the transmission of African ethnic identities in Costa Rica. At best, their knowledge of their home cultures was incomplete, and slaves who had arrived in Costa Rica as children often recalled nothing at all of Africa. In 1719, African-born Miguel specified that he did "not remember" his casta. Several other African men and women explained that they did not know their "nation" because they had arrived in Costa Rica when they were "small."[51] Diego de Angulo, about thirty years old when questioned in 1719, claimed that he "did not know any black men or women who could have come with him" from Africa, and that "he did not know where he came from because when he opened his eyes he found himself in the power of the master who owns him today."[52]

These men and women were far from unusual in remembering nothing of Africa. When asked directly, no fewer than 23 of 82 (28 percent) African-born slaves interviewed between 1719 and 1722 replied that they did "not know their *casta*," and 59 (72 percent) replied with a specific casta name. Africans who did "not know" their casta outnumbered those who claimed any single ethnic origin.[53] Antonia de Aguilar knew she had been born in Africa but did "not know her *casta* because she [did] not understand any language" spoken by other Africans.[54] She made clear that Africans spoke several languages in Cartago, but Antonia knew none of them and did not identify herself on the basis of any of the African ethnic groupings recognized in Costa Rica. Not surprisingly, age at the time of arrival played a crucial role in ethnic memory. Clearly, even under the best of circumstances, such women and men could pass on little of African culture to their children.

Many young slave children sold or otherwise transferred were Costa Rican–born. Indeed, sellers often specified that the children they offered for sale had been "born and raised" in their homes. Despite their use of language that conjured up images of hearth and family, masters showed little reluctance to tear even the youngest children away from their mothers. Separation from family figured among slaves' greatest fears, as masters surely knew; historian Norrece Jones has argued that because the temporary wounds of physical abuse hurt slaves much less than the permanent emotional pain of separation, the threat of separating slave families was "the most powerful long-term technique of control—short of death—that masters possessed."[55] Furthermore, the precarious financial situation of many Costa Rican masters led many to sell human property to liquidate debts, breaking up slave families in the process. In 1678, for example, the widow María Sagaste was forced to sell Gregorio, the sixteen-year-old son of her slave María Sanabria, born and raised in her home, in order to pay a three hundred–peso mortgage.[56] Almost one-fifth (109 of 618) of the slaves sold in Cartago for whom information on age is available between 1629 and 1750 were children younger than ten years old.[57]

Masters bought and sold children with little regard for the mother-child relationship, no matter if the mothers had been slaves of the master's family for decades. At bottom, masters simply refused to recognize kinship ties among slaves.[58] Nearly one quarter of slaves baptized were recorded in Cartago's parish registers without mention of either parent. The phrase "child of unknown parents" made sense in the case of African-born slaves, and priests surely applied the label when baptizing adult Africans. In the case of free persons, the notation "child of unknown parents" ostensibly meant "abandoned" (*expósito*), a more explicit classification, also common. For creole and mulatto slave children, however, the description formed a contradiction in terms, as only knowledge of the mother's condition could determine a child's slave status. Here the failure to record the name of either parent demonstrated that masters concerned themselves more with slave status than with kinship ties among the enslaved.[59] Masters and mistresses showed their disregard of slave families most clearly through their actions. Doña María Josefa de la Vega Cabral received Ambrosia as a gift from her parents when she married don Francisco de Betancourt in the early eighteenth century. Just eight days after Ambrosia gave birth to a son, Juan Elías, Vega Cabral sold the infant.[60] Juana, a mulatta slave, had grown up with doña Bernarda de Retes, and as part of her dowry, accompanied her mistress when she married. Years later, Juana watched as Retes sold her fourteen-year-old daughter María Nicolasa to Sergeant Juan González, who "took her by the hand . . . as his own thing, bought with his own money." Like other slave mothers, Juana surely dreaded the moment when her adolescent daughter "passed to his power" and González possessed all rights over her person.[61]

Masters also regarded slave infants as fine gifts for favorite relatives. Don Antonio de Moya, for example, designated in his 1702 will that as soon as he was "weaned from the breast" of his mother Isabel, ten-month-old Antonio was to be given to *Alférez* Diego de Santiago de Cárdenas.[62] A full one quarter (19) of the seventy-five slaves donated between 1630 and 1750 were younger than five years old. Another sixteen percent (12) were under ten.[63] In some respects, masters regarded slave children as investments no different than valuable inanimate objects, circulating them as a means of keeping sources of wealth within their extended families.[64] In several cases, slave owners donated enslaved children to poorer relatives or friends, stating explicitly that the human gifts should serve as security for the recipients' future. They often professed laudable intentions—without a thought, of course, to slave mothers or their young children. Father don Alonso de Sandoval gave five-year-old Juana Gregoria to his niece Mariana de Ocampo Golfín so that she would "be better able to take a position in keeping with the quality of her person," presumably as a wife or nun.[65] Father José de Lumbides likewise donated María Manuela, seven months old, and José, four, to doña Juana Núñez de Trujira (elsewhere Trupira) in 1668. Lumbides wished to ensure that the illegitimate and impoverished twelve-year-old girl, who had "served" him since the age of five, not fall into a wayward life. The slave children would help make up a dowry that would allow Trujira to marry or enter a convent in Guatemala, so that she would not "lose her virginity and offend God."[66] Doña Lorenza Vanegas made a gift of three-month-old Agustín, son of Eugenia, to her nephew Manuel González Coronel when he was four, again citing a wish that he "better have the wherewithal to sustain himself in keeping with the quality of his person." Years later, González Coronel was ordained a priest.[67] In such cases, Spanish family honor relied on the destruction of slave families.

Similarly, slave children were often included in dowries as investments for the couple's future and, in the case of infants and toddlers, as playmates for the couple's own future children. For example, Ramona, a black creole, formed part of doña María Josefa Maroto's dowry when Maroto married don Alfonso Ulloa in 1732. Doña Luisa Calvo had given Ramona, the daughter of her slave Luisa, as a gift to Maroto, her granddaughter, when both girls were about ten years old.[68] Of the 198 slaves transferred in dowries for whom age was recorded between 1639 and 1749, thirty (15 percent) were children younger than five years old. Another forty-one (21 percent) were under fifteen.[69] In Costa Rica, as elsewhere in Central America, slaves often comprised the most valuable property in bridal dowries. For example, Cecilia, a nine-year-old mulatta, accounted for 300 of the 470 pesos of doña Beatriz de Morales's dowry in 1695.[70] Three- or four-year-old Juana, assessed at 150 pesos, was worth five times as much as the next most valuable "item" in María Rodríguez de Sosa's pitiful dowry, a "wooden house on forked supports covered with straw" valued at thirty pesos in 1719.[71] Intended to spare their mistresses from housework, girls were more than twice as likely to be included in dowries as boys. Females comprised two-thirds of the seventy-one slave children (47) younger than fifteen years of age.[72] Girls as young as the six-year-old zamba Paula were designated specifically to "help carry the burdens of matrimony."[73]

As death confronted them, some masters worried about their eternal souls and made special bequests. For some slaves, the "pious works" of their masters translated into the heartbreaking destruction of their families. Not uncommonly, masters ordered that slaves be sold to pay for religious rituals. The imputed value of infants and young children made them convenient currency for the purpose. Doña Francisca Chinchilla had promised Juan to the confraternity of the Blessed Souls of Purgatory while he was still in his mother Isabel's womb. Upon Chinchilla's death, Juan was to be sold and a chaplaincy established in her name.[74] To pay for the celebrated preaching of the Franciscan friar Diego Caballero, doña Nicolasa Guerrero donated Cristóbal, the seven-year-old son of her African-born slave Catalina, in 1718.[75] Doña Inés de Sandoval Golfín designated a "white mulato" of four months of age to be given to the parish priest of Cartago to pay for her funeral.[76]

Enslaved mothers tried to keep track of the whereabouts of their children long after they had been sold. The arará Josefa's son Gabriel, for example, was sold away from her in 1718 when he was nine years old. No doubt hoping she would one day be reunited with him, two years later, Josefa recalled that he had been purchased by Sergeant Major don Pedro Martínez de Ugarrio, who took him to the Pueblo of El Viejo in Nicaragua.[77] She was unaware, however, that by then Ugarrio had already taken Gabriel to Guatemala City, where he had sold the boy to one don Guillermo Martínez de Pereda.[78] Other slaves were luckier. María Nicolasa was about fourteen when she was sold away from her mother and sisters, "but not for that did she cease to frequent the house" of her former owners to see her family.[79]

But as slavery destroyed families, it also gave rise to situations that created new ones. In 1720, Lorenza González, a *congo* from West Central Africa, declared that she had two children, María Josefa and José Manuel.[80] She said that María Josefa "was her daughter but she did not give birth to her."[81] About ten years before, Lorenza had delivered a child who died soon after birth. At about the same time, Juana, a fellow slave of Lorenza's master and mistress, gave birth to María Josefa but soon fell ill. As Lorenza was still lactating, she nursed María Josefa. Although Juana recovered from her illness, her breasts had ceased to produce milk, and María Josefa remained in Lorenza's care. Because Lorenza had nursed her, María Josefa and Lorenza always addressed each other as mother and daughter. Another of Juana's daughters, María Nicolasa González, considered María Josefa to be her sister no less than her other biological sisters, Eugenia and María Magdalena. From María Nicolasa's perspective, María Josefa had two mothers.[82] Official documents could not accommodate such complex realities in slave families. When he composed his testament in 1710, Sergeant Major Blas González had described Lorenza and María Josefa as mother and daughter, although María Josefa's baptismal certificate of the same year listed Juana as her mother.[83] "No one is unaware," Father Manuel José González Coronel explained, "that those who are raised at one's breasts are called [their] children."[84] Governor don Diego de la Haya, however, was not persuaded. He recognized only the biological bond of motherhood as legitimate.[85]

Marriages between Slaves

[handwritten annotation: the church relating to Christian or its clergy]

Both Spanish civil law and ecclesiastical law stipulated that slaves enjoyed the right to marry legally in the Catholic Church and could do so without the knowledge or consent, and even over the objections, of their masters.[86] "Neither bond nor free" could ignore a sacrament approved by Christ himself. One of the medieval Church's greatest theologians had stated categorically that "both freeman and bondsman enjoy the same liberty to marry in the faith of Christ Jesus," and further, a slave was "not subject to [the master] to the extent of being unable to marry freely."[87] For slaves no less than for other "qualified persons," the bond of marriage was indissoluble and required that husband and wife "live together throughout life."[88] Although the possibility that enslaved husbands and wives might belong to different masters was not entirely precluded, Spanish law and the Church alike required that masters ensure that married slaves be able to live together: "There is no marriage without inseparability." If distance prevented them from living conjugally, one of the spouses' masters had to sell his slave to the master of the other spouse.[89]

Early historians of comparative slavery assumed that the right of slaves to marry constituted one of the key differences between Latin and North American slave systems. More recently, researchers such as Herman Bennett and Christine Hünefeldt have confirmed that legally married slaves in urban areas of Spanish America as diverse as early colonial Mexico City and nineteenth-century Lima often successfully appealed to ecclesiastical courts to protect their families against separation by sale.[90] Even on Brazilian plantations, where masters might easily disregard the Church's directives, many slaves succeeded in having their unions consecrated by the Church. Although "typically slaves sought to marry, while masters denied permission and had to be entreated to fulfill their Christian duty," a growing number of masters did grant their approval—by the nineteenth century, between a quarter and a third of adult slaves on most Brazilian plantations were married and sometimes many more.[91]

As in so many other areas of slave life, Costa Rican slavery departed from the patterns documented for other Latin American slave and slaveholding societies. Parish registers show that slave marriages were rarely celebrated, suggesting a high degree of master control over slave family life. The small scale of slaveholdings in Costa Rica offers a partial explanation. In Brazil, for example, the overwhelming majority of married slaves lived on the same plantation; conversely, most single slaves lived on smallholdings. In Costa Rica, only a handful of masters owned slaves in numbers sufficient to provide a pool of potential spouses. Chances that a slave would marry another on his or her master's property were slim. Another reason that slave family life—whether legitimated by the Church or not—tended to be more stable on large properties was the relative absence of the master from the lives of his slaves. Field slaves residing on large plantations, who rarely came into contact with their masters, tended to enjoy more control over their family lives than those who lived on smallholdings or worked as domestic servants and frequently interacted with their masters. In Costa Rica, many if not most slaves, especially females, lived in or near their masters' homes, suffering their scrutiny and interference in most aspects of life.[92]

Marriages between slaves are exceedingly rare in ecclesiastical documents. Surviving marriage records from Cartago's parish church begin only in 1662, and only four marriages between slaves are recorded in the marriage registers during the entire period studied. The first record in which both spouses are identified as slaves does not occur until 1733. Antonio García, a mina from the Gold Coast or upper Slave Coast, and Agustina de Ibarra, a Yoruba (aná), both survived the Middle Passage on the *Christianus Quintus* and *Fredericus Quartus* and were eventually purchased by the same master. They married twenty-three years after arriving in Costa Rica; by then, shared experiences forged in American slavery, including the bonds between shipmates and slaves of the same master, meant more to them than their different ethnic origins.[93]

Not surprisingly, other documents establish that marriages were celebrated between slaves much earlier. Although also incomplete, Cartago baptismal registers date from the 1590s and provide evidence of six slave marriages in the 1610s, 1630s, and 1640s. Sebastián and Jerónima, slaves of Juan López, baptized their daughter Luisa in 1618. Pedro and Catalina, black slaves of Magdalena de la Portilla, were the parents of Paula, baptized in 1639, and Ursula, baptized the following year. Juan, son of Pedro and Antonia, and Nicolás de la Cruz, son of Francisco and Lucrecia, were baptized in 1639 and 1640, respectively. Both couples and their children were black slaves owned by Governor don Gregorio de Sandoval.[94] An imperfect measure, to be sure, still, combining all surviving marriage and baptismal records from between the years 1594 and 1749 provides evidence of ten marriages between enslaved men and enslaved women in the jurisdiction of Cartago, as well as two in Esparza between 1712 and 1750.

Consensual unions between slaves may well have been as enduring as legal marriages and were certainly much more common. María Victoria and José Cubero, both African-born slaves of Captain don José de Mier Cevallos and doña Catalina González Camino, lived in a stable union for many years. María Victoria, the mother of five living children in 1725, was described in a promissory note as the "wife" (*mujer*) of José, although there is no record of their marriage in Cartago's surviving marriage registers. The 1722 baptismal record of their son Juan Manuel noted that he was the "legitimate son" of José Cubero and Victoria Cubero, confirming that at some point they were married in the Church. Nevertheless, their union may not have been consecrated until years after the births of their first children. Miguel was born about 1706, Juana about four years later. When another son, Pablo Ramón, was baptized in 1713, Victoria was the only parent noted in the register, although another document dated twelve years later confirmed Pablo as the son of José Cubero.[95] José and María Victoria might have formalized their union in a church in the intervening years, or the slave José's paternity may simply have been omitted from the baptismal record of his son. Whatever the case, the absence of marriage records for slaves as well as the omission of slave fathers from the baptismal records of children leads to an underestimation of the extent of stable unions and families among slaves in Costa Rica.

There is no reason to assume that enslaved people spurned legal marriage because they rejected Christianity.[96] Legal marriage provided little protection to husbands and wives against separation by sale, and Costa Rican slaves knew it. Their failure to marry suggests that masters controlled the sexual and family lives of their slaves, especially those of the females who lived in their homes.

Exogamous Marriages

Costa Rican slave owners sharply limited the kinds of family life available to female slaves, but enslaved men faced fewer restrictions. Although they legally married relatively infrequently, records suggest they did so ten times as often as enslaved women. It may be that they encountered fewer obstacles in choosing spouses than did female slaves. The earliest available records suggest that slave men generally preferred to marry free women, a pattern that increased over time. The first Cartago baptism record to specify a father's slave status, from 1607, identifies Gaspar, black slave of doña Catalina de

Grados, and his wife Juana, an Indian, as the parents of the mulatto slave boy Juan.[97] This pattern of exogamy continued throughout the period under study and beyond, right up to the eve of abolition.[98] Slave men seldom celebrated legal marriages, but when they did, they almost always chose to marry free women. Although this tendency proved strong in many areas of Spanish America, the marriage patterns of enslaved men in Costa Rica exhibited several exceptional characteristics, perhaps unique in the Americas. Enslaved black men were far more likely to marry than were male mulatto slaves, and among black men, Africans married more frequently than did creoles.

Slave men in other areas of Spanish America also frequently sought free marriage partners. Researcher Edgar Love found that in the Mexico City parish of Santa Veracruz, for example, 48 percent of black male slaves and 80 percent of enslaved mulatto men married free women in the century between 1646 and 1746.[99] In the Sagrario Metropolitano parish of the same city, historian R. Douglas Cope found a similarly strong exogamous tendency in the late seventeenth century, although enslaved black men there married slave women more frequently. Seventy-nine percent of male mulatto slaves and one-third of black male slaves chose free partners between 1686 and 1690.[100] Christopher Lutz and Paul Lokken found that this pattern also pertained in Guatemala, which was probably the region of Central America with the largest slave population. In the capital city of Santiago, Lutz found that between 1660 and 1748, 64 percent of black slaves and 79 percent of enslaved mulattos married free spouses. (Unfortunately, Lutz does not specify genders.)[101] Focusing on rural Guatemala, Paul Lokken has identified what he terms a *strategy* of "marriage as slave emancipation" in the late seventeenth century; up to two-thirds of male slaves, he discovered, married free women.[102]

In Costa Rica, the unmistakable tendency of enslaved men to choose free women as wives proved even more pronounced, and male slave exogamy proved a permanent, structural feature of Costa Rican slavery. Of seventy-one marriages of slave men recorded in Cartago marriage registers between 1670 and 1750, a full sixty-six (93 percent) were to free women. With marriage to free women a viable option, slave men almost never married female slaves. Adding married couples with at least one slave partner from the baptism records beginning in 1607 does nothing to change the picture. Combining both sets of documents shows that 92 percent (118 of 128) of married enslaved men were married to free women. The near total exogamy of slave men persisted until the end of the colonial period.[103]

The disadvantages of marriage to an enslaved wife—foremost among them the birth of one's children in slavery—made slave women unattractive partners to free men as well as to male slaves. When Juan Antonio Chavarría, a free mulatto, married Manuela Cayetana, a slave of doña Francisca de Ibarra and don Tomás López del Corral, the choice cost him socially and materially. Chavarría's mother, the wealthy mulatta María Calvo, showered gifts on her other children but never gave Juan Antonio and Manuela Cayetana a thing, as her son "had married to my displeasure."[104] The Cartago marriage registers recorded only seven weddings of slave women during the entire period of study. Three of those enslaved women married free men. Nineteen more married enslaved women appear in the baptism records; all but Manuela Cayetana were married to slave men. In this small sample, enslaved women married free men in just 16 percent of cases.[105]

Historians of plantation societies have often cited the demographic structure of the slave trade as one reason enslaved men chose free spouses. In many regions, the skewed sex ratios of slave imports meant that there were simply not enough enslaved women to provide wives for most African men.[106] Other historians have also cited a large majority of males in the slave population to explain the exogamy of enslaved men in areas of Mesoamerica. R. Douglas Cope argued that in Mexico City, the gender imbalance proved "very persistent over time." A shortage of slave women thus led, indeed forced, a majority of enslaved men to marry free women.[107] Paul Lokken saw the same pattern in rural Guatemala, attributing the aggressive exogamy of enslaved men to the absence of slave women in the countryside.[108] More recently, Frank T. Proctor came up with different results that showed parity in the numbers of male and female slaves in several areas of colonial Mexico. The pronounced exogamy of slave men, he concludes, cannot be attributed to an unequal sex ratio among slaves. This myth, Proctor argues, "should be laid to rest."[109]

In Costa Rica, too, a demographic explanation for slave men's exogamy rings false. There were always plenty of female slaves for slave men to marry had they chosen to do so. Testaments, dowry inventories, promissory notes, and other documents suggest gender parity. The sparsity of the data for the decades before 1650 makes generalization difficult before the mid-seventeenth century. Only after 1680, when slave imports rose sharply in tandem with cacao production, did the number of male slaves in notarial documents clearly exceed the female, and even then it did not do so in all decades nor by a decisive margin at any time. On the contrary, the proportions of females and males showed a persistent parity. In the decades between 1630 and 1750, the proportion of females among slaves in notarial records never dropped below 45 percent.[110] The tendency of male slaves in Costa Rica to marry free women simply cannot be explained by a shortage of enslaved women. There was no such shortage.

Why, then, did slave men so overwhelmingly prefer to marry free women? As Paul Lokken, Herman Bennett, and many others have argued, the determination of enslaved men to secure stability for their families and freedom for their children immediately offers an explanation. Spanish law ostensibly protected slave marriages from separation by sale, providing a powerful incentive for slaves to marry. If masters used the threat of separating slave families as their "most effective long-term mechanism of control," as Norrece Jones has argued in the case of antebellum South Carolina, slave men's choice of free wives could deny masters their most powerful weapon.[111]

At times, however, officials in Costa Rica ignored not only the law against separating slave families by sale but the ancient one that dictated that the status of children follow the condition of the mother. Enslaved men could see their aspirations to ensure greater stability for their families and a better future for their children crushed when Costa Rican slave masters flagrantly violated the law. In the 1670s, some masters condemned the children of slave fathers and free mothers to a life of effective if not legal slavery. In 1675, Doctor don Benito de Noboa Salgado, a judge (*oidor*) of the Audiencia of Guatemala, visited Costa Rica and reported that Spanish masters frequently held children of slave men and indigenous women as slaves for life. Spanish landowners, Noboa Salgado wrote, "marry their slaves with the Indian women in their service and say that the children belong to them, and [the children] know no more of nature than their masters' homes."[112] In keeping with the age-old law dictating that the child follow the condition of his or her mother, Noboa Salgado identified children of indigenous mothers and African fathers as free. Local Spaniards, however, classified them as slaves, presumably because of their African ancestry, and claimed the right to their lifelong service. Noboa Salgado asserted, instead, that the children of tributary Indian women were tributary Indians. Concerned with the loss of tribute revenues and the depopulation of indigenous pueblos, the king attempted in 1676 to remedy the practice by prohibiting marriages between slave men and Indian women.[113]

Not surprisingly, marriages between slaves and Indians continued, notwithstanding the law, especially between slaves and Indian servants.

Although "mixed" marriages were most common in Cartago, small numbers of blacks and mulattos, both men and women, free and slave, also formed interracial families in indigenous villages, as they did elsewhere in Spanish America. In the Pueblo of Barva, for example, twenty-two-year-old Indian Ana María was married to an "old black man" in 1739. José Ramírez, an indigenous widower, was remarried to "a black woman on the outskirts of this village." Such families meant that despite the ideal segregation once envisioned by the Spanish Crown, there was no such thing as a "pure" Indian pueblo. Trying to classify people according to proper racial categories, officials sometimes scratched their heads. Eighteen-year-old Luisa Sánchez, noted a census taker, was a "zamba with kinky hair [*pelo torcido*]," but neighbors said she was "born from a marriage of Indian parents."[114]

The marriage choices available to enslaved men in Costa Rica differed from those found elsewhere in Mesoamerica in another important respect. In Mexico and Guatemala, mulatto slaves enjoyed substantially greater success in pursuing free wives than did enslaved black men—in Mexico City, mulattos married free women up to twice as often as blacks; in Guatemala, about 24 percent more often.[115] In Costa Rica, the reverse was true. Priests recorded the race of sixty-nine of the seventy-one slave bridegrooms in Cartago parish registers between 1662 and 1750. Fifty (72 percent) were black men; only eighteen (one-fourth) were mulattos.[116] The Costa Rican data challenge assumptions that free women found mulattos more attractive marriage partners than blacks, which should have been the case if blacks occupied a lower rung on the ladder of the racial hierarchy—long the accepted wisdom in Latin American historiography.

Whom did these slave men marry? In the marriage registers, priests failed to record the race of 42 percent (29 of 71) of the women who married enslaved men. They were certainly free women, however, because as far as is known, functionaries never omitted the fact that a bride was enslaved, and surely the overwhelming majority, if not all of them, were castas and possibly Indians, not Spanish women. When only free women of known race are included, free mulattas comprised almost half (15 of 35, or 43 percent) of the wives of slave men.[117] There are several explanations for the prominence of mulattas among free women who married slave men. Although there were adequate numbers of female slaves to make endogamy possible within the enslaved group, there were only a handful of free black women. If a black male slave wanted to marry a free woman, he had to choose a spouse outside his racial category.[118] Why mulattas, instead of free women of other castas?

According to Cope, in colonial Mexico City, "blacks and mulattas might normally be expected to intermarry," because castas tended to marry within "'parent groups' (blacks and Indians) and the associated intermediate groups (mulattas and mestizas, respectively)." High endogamy ratios prevailed within these "parent groups."[119] The prominence of mulattas among free women who married slave men may also suggest that women of ostensibly higher racial status married slave men more reluctantly. Mestiza and Indian women each accounted for about 13 percent of enslaved men's marriages. Two slave men married free black women. Only seven enslaved men (about 9 percent of the total) married other slaves.[120]

Some free women regarded marriage to slaves as a "misfortune" (*desgracia*), as the mestiza María de la Rosa Cuéllar stated in 1734 when discussing her own marriage to African-born Pedro de Rosas.[121] Mulatto Diego Campuzano lied about his slave status when he proposed to free mulatta Manuela Josefa de Padilla. When she learned the truth in 1735, after two years of marriage and the birth of a son, she sought an annulment.[122] Juana Paniagua refused to marry mulatto slave José Cubero until he secured a promise of eventual manumission from his master.[123] Why, then, would other free women choose to marry enslaved men? Part of the answer can be attributed to the unique position of African men in Costa Rica's cacao economy. Free women who married slaves counted on few resources of their own. A large majority of those for whom such information is available were of illegitimate birth and usually brought small dowries, if any. Diego García, a *cabo verde* born in West Africa who eventually earned his freedom, married twice while still a slave, each time to free women. When he composed his will in 1743, he stated plainly that "the said two women brought nothing at all to my possession."[124] For free women with few other marriage options, enslaved men living in Matina must have seemed viable marriage partners. Although they and all their property technically belonged to their masters, for all intents and purposes, African men in Matina lived in their own homes and grew provisions on their own land, just as poor farmers or ranchers did. Many enjoyed a decided advantage over some of the free poor. Because cacao was literally money, slave men in Matina had as ready access to cash as anyone in Costa Rica. When smugglers came to the coast, enslaved men purchased goods for the home, including iron pots and European cloth. Most importantly, cacao could provide the means to freedom itself and, ultimately, a path to financial and social advancement. Free wives must have seen a promise in their husbands that mitigated the men's slave status.

Although myriad individual circumstances influenced the decision to marry, slave men surely considered that marriage to free women could form part of a long-term strategy to acquire freedom itself. When free wives enlisted the support of friends and family members, they greatly increased their husbands' chances of eventual manumission. Juana de Paniagua, the free mulatta wife of slave José Cubero, recruited six of her friends to help her make and sell stockings and blue thread to earn money for her husband's freedom.[125] In 1742, mulatto slave Ramón Poveda proposed marriage to a free mulatta, María Nicolasa Geralda. Once the marriage was arranged, her father, a captain in the pardo militia, lent his daughter's suitor two hundred pesos toward the purchase of his freedom.[126] Juan Antonio de Cuéllar traded in mules and horses, earning 150 pesos to help his sister María de la Rosa obtain freedom for her husband, the African Pedro de Rosas.[127] Soon after his marriage to the free Manuela Gutiérrez in 1721, West African–born Diego García obtained permission from his master to lease a cacao hacienda for fifty pesos per year in cacao from an extended family member, Juan González. García was so successful that he was not only able to meet his obligation to González but raised a surplus of "many *zurrones* of cacao."[128]

But even with the help of free family members, it often took decades to amass the cacao necessary to buy freedom, if the enslaved ever gained it. Cartago notarial records contain no record of the manumission of Pedro de Rosas. Despite the exceptional opportunity extended to Diego García, he did not obtain his freedom for at least seventeen years after first leasing his kinsman's cacao hacienda. Diego Angulo, born in West Central Africa around 1690, married the free mulatta Felipa Chavarría in 1709. The couple eventually had four children, born in freedom.[129] Twenty-one years after their wedding, and with the help of his grown son Juan Manuel, working "on feast days and without missing other days in the service of [his] master," Angulo succeeded in amassing 375 pesos' worth of cacao and purchased his freedom in 1730.[130] Angulo owed his freedom and advancement in part to the help of his free family.

As difficult as it was for slave men to gain their freedom, even with the help of free family members and friends, it was harder for enslaved women. Isidora Zavaleta, a creole slave "born in the house" of her mistress doña Antonia de Oses, married mestizo Juan Méndez in June 1748. On October 24 of the following year, Méndez succeeded in purchasing his wife for three hundred pesos, although there is no record that he freed her.[131] In exceptional cases, slave women and their free husbands beat the odds and succeeded in building free lives together. In July 1720, Alférez Diego de la Cruz, a thirty-year-old free mulatto originally from Granada, Nicaragua, petitioned Cartago's ecclesiastical judge for permission to marry Josefa Micaela de la Vega Cabral, a "white mulata" slave. A royal mail carrier, de la Cruz had met Josefa in her master's home when he arrived in Cartago several months before. He was now about to depart for Guatemala City, where he would deliver top-secret papers from Governor don Diego de la Haya Fernández to the Audiencia, and wanted desperately to marry the twenty-two-year-old Josefa before he left. Father don Diego de Angulo Gascón acceded to his request.[132] In the event, Diego did not leave Cartago until January of the following year. After traveling "three hundred leagues" to Guatemala, Diego had to wait there until October 1721 for a response from the Audiencia. On the return to Cartago, he was detained another three weeks in Granada. Diego finally arrived in Cartago in February 1722, where he borrowed 150 pesos in cacao from the governor against the pay that was owed him.[133] On March 27, 1722, Diego purchased the freedom of his wife Josefa Micaela and her ten-year-old daughter Manuela Victoria for 300 pesos in silver and 150 pesos in cacao.[134]

The exceptional circumstances from which Diego and Josefa Micaela benefited are self-evident. De la Cruz worked at a high-paying job involving the highest responsibility. He enjoyed the trust of the most powerful officials in Costa Rica and, indeed, in all the Kingdom of Guatemala. Josefa Micaela's master, don Francisco de Betancourt, approved of her marriage to Diego and even offered testimony on his behalf before the ecclesiastical judge.[135] Diego could not only lay his hands on three hundred pesos in silver but also borrowed an additional six zurrones of cacao from the governor of Costa Rica. Although it was by no means easy, Diego could reasonably hope eventually to liberate Josefa Micaela and Manuela Victoria and to share a free life with them. Without such advantages, most free husbands of enslaved women could not.

Conclusion

Slavery shaped all aspects of the family life of those who lived under it. In Costa Rica, women and men experienced those effects in profoundly different ways. Masters controlled most directly the female slaves who lived in their homes, sharply limiting their options for marriage and family life.

Domestic slaves in general and female slaves in particular remained subject to the heightened vigilance, abuse, and manipulation of their masters. The overwhelming majority of children born to enslaved mothers was illegitimate, and we know almost nothing about the identity of the fathers. In homes where no adult male slaves lived, slave fathers cannot be assumed to have played important roles in the lives of their children—although they may have. Masters manipulated, controlled, and destroyed slave families at will, routinely selling, donating, and bequeathing children with no regard for the mother-child bond, let alone ties to other family members. Slave children were called *crías*, a word applied to the offspring of animals, and many were disposed of just as casually.[136]

Marriage in the Catholic Church promised protection from such devastating separations. Both civil and ecclesiastical law guaranteed the right of slaves to marry and theoretically protected slave couples from separation and sale.[137] These principles conflicted with the determination of slaveholders to dispose of their human property at will, however, and in Costa Rica, these protections were respected inconsistently at best. In any case, because slaves rarely wed and the law applied only to marriages celebrated in the Church, masters faced few restrictions in separating slave families. In large part because Spanish law mandated that the legal condition of children follow that of their mothers, few men saw advantages in taking enslaved women as wives.

Although legal matrimony sanctioned by the Church was the only family organization providing even a modicum of protection, there were many forms of slave family. Fewer than ten percent of slave children were born to couples married in the Catholic Church. Although only a few documented cases support it, some enslaved women maintained stable relationships with slave men, especially when both partners were owned by the same master. A small minority of female-headed families in Costa Rica also proved remarkably stable. A few enslaved children were lucky enough to remain with their mothers until they grew to adulthood. Several slave owners held three or even four generations of slaves in their homes.[138] As a result of short- or long-term relationships, and subject to varying degrees of coercion, some slave women bore children by their masters. A few slave owners freed their mulatto slave children, but few manumitted the children's mothers. There is little to suggest that enslaved women derived many benefits from sexual relationships with their masters, nor that they chose to remain single; rather, there is every reason to attribute their single status to structural characteristics of Costa Rican slavery.

Slave men married ten times more frequently than enslaved women, although only a small minority of enslaved men wed. Almost always, male slaves chose free women as wives. Unlike in other parts of Spanish America, African-born black men achieved far more success in pursuing free wives than did creole or mulatto slaves. Many African husbands worked cultivating cacao in the Matina Valley, where they exploited opportunities for advancement unavailable to other slave men. Their relatively independent lifestyle, access to cash and imported goods, and promise of eventual freedom overcame potential objections to their darker skin or cultural difference by the women they courted. For an enslaved man, marriage to a free woman guaranteed that his children would be born free, although this law was sometimes ignored, especially in the seventeenth century. For a free but poor woman, marriage to a Matina slave could mean an improvement of material condition if not of status. Free relatives, including wives, children, and in-laws, could help slave men eventually to gain their freedom. Those who remained slaves could look forward to a better life for their children. The freeborn children of married slave men found ready acceptance in the free community of color, learning artisans' trades, serving in the mulatto militias, and participating in religious confraternities.

The mobility provided by intermarriage, however, occurred on an individual basis and accepted rather than challenged the racial basis of the colonial hierarchy. African and other slave men married not only free but lighter-skinned women; "whitening" one's children was inseparable from freedom itself. Many mulatto children of slaves married mestizos. Children of such matches were usually considered mestizos, and their children in turn might be considered white, accomplishing the complete assimilation of Africans to Costa Rican society within a few short generations.[139]

Conclusions

⳨ THE SOUTHERNMOST PROVINCE OF THE KINGDOM OF GUATEMALA, Costa Rica was a remote, impoverished colony of the Spanish Empire, with no known mineral wealth and a comparatively small indigenous population. After a series of failed attempts at conquest, Spaniards showed minimal interest in settling the territory for much of the sixteenth century. Enslaved and free blacks, however, formed part of the earliest Spanish expeditions to Costa Rica. For the entire colonial period, effective Spanish control remained limited to the North Pacific and Central Valley regions. Militarily defeated, natives of these areas fell subject to the encomienda system. In the earliest decades of settlement, a small Spanish ruling class emerged, their wealth based primarily on their superexploitation of tributary Indians. Indigenous people never provided the elite with their only source of labor, however. The ruling Spanish families relied on a mixed labor force of Indians, mestizos, African and creole slaves, and a growing population of free people of African descent, especially in and around the colonial capital of Cartago. Costa Rican Spaniards marketed the produce grown in indigenous pueblos and on small haciendas worked by men and women of diverse racial origins in the nearby Isthmus of Panama, thereby amassing capital and consolidating their rule as merchant encomenderos.

In the early seventeenth century, however, two devastating crises confronted the ruling class of Costa Rica. Trade in Panama, which had provided Costa Rica with its major market, collapsed. At the same time, epidemics and overwork decimated Costa Rica's indigenous peoples, who had never been very populous. In some pueblos, not a single man, woman, or child survived. But African slaves could not provide a viable solution to local Spaniards' economic problems. Costa Rica's ruling class simply lacked sufficient capital or credit to compete successfully with buyers from wealthier areas of Spanish America. With the irreversible decline of the Indian population that had provided their main income and the destruction of the market that had furnished what capital they possessed, many Spaniards in Costa Rica retreated to their small country farms and haciendas. By and large, however, the merchant encomenderos never joined the self-reliant peasantry of Costa Rican lore.[1] Although mostly condemned to a life of mere subsistence, even the poorest Spaniards lived off the labor and produce of exploited Indians, mestizos, free mulattos, and slaves. And poverty remained relative: wealthier Spaniards often maintained several properties, such as cattle haciendas in the North Pacific; farms or small haciendas near Cartago; and, increasingly, cacao haciendas in the Caribbean lowlands.

By the 1650s, some members of Costa Rica's ruling elite looked to the Caribbean coast for a solution to their economic problems. They pursued cacao cultivation as their major economic activity, exporting to authorized markets in Spanish America and to illegal ones beyond. Although they first relied on the labor of Indians from newly established missions in Talamanca, indigenous resistance and eventually a prohibition from the Audiencia of Guatemala against the exploitation of Indians on the haciendas forced the *cacaoteros* to search for another source of labor. Wealthier Spaniards, particularly those who lived in Cartago, were able to move their slaves where they most needed them. With cacao profits, they acquired more Africans, both from the Asiento in Panama and from the smugglers who arrived on the Matina coast. By the last decade of the seventeenth century, the African population of Costa Rica boomed in tandem with increased cacao cultivation. Slaves comprised the sector of the labor force that provided the crucial links between the colony and Atlantic markets.

Both Costa Rica's sporadic access to the slave trade and the nature of slave labor in the colony uniquely conditioned the experience of enslaved Africans and creoles. Creolization, both in the sense of the creation of a colonial culture of diverse origins and in the procreation of an American-born slave population, occurred remarkably rapidly. Ethnic Africans had already joined people of other cultural and linguistic origins on the way to the coast and on the Middle Passage. Once arrived in Costa Rica, "seasoning" formed another key period of cultural exchange. From all major regions of West and West Central Africa, people of no single ethnic or regional group prevailed among slaves in any area of Costa Rica. Extreme diversity, not the demographic dominance of people of certain ethnic or cultural backgrounds, characterized the eighteenth-century "re-Africanization" of Costa Rica's slave population. Rather than ethnicity, the shipmate bond and/or ownership by a common master helped forge the strongest bonds for other Africans, who in general quickly adapted to the creole cultural patterns established long before. Although Africans formed small ethnic enclaves in Cartago and Matina and could sometimes maintain or forge relationships to people of similar cultural backgrounds, they never reached a critical mass sufficient to perpetuate ethnic cultures. There is little evidence that they transmitted ethnic languages, religions, or identities across the generations.[2] Spanish usually came to be the common language among African slaves, simultaneously facilitating the forging of relationships with people of other ethnic and racial origins. Official and popular Catholicism also encouraged the adaptation of Africans to their new environment. Compared to slaves in plantation societies, most slaves in Costa Rica lived in intimate proximity to their masters, and virtually all knew their masters personally. Such close contacts made slaves particularly vulnerable to their masters' abuse, although they could sometimes also provide exceptional opportunities.

Masters exercised a pervasive and stifling control over many slaves, particularly women. Slave labor in Costa Rica became starkly divided by gender, unlike in most American slave societies. Female slaves remained overwhelmingly concentrated in their masters' homes in the Central Valley and, to a lesser degree, in the North Pacific. Although female slaves proved able, to some extent, to maintain relationships with other slaves in the capital city of Cartago, masters intervened in most aspects of their lives. Occasionally, slave women proved able to persuade masters who had fathered their children to manumit them, but the mothers rarely gained their own freedom as a result of such relationships. On the other hand, enslaved women sometimes formed strong bonds with their mistresses, and when they won their own freedom, it was often due to these relationships. Physical and social mobility, however, usually remained tightly restricted for women.

Most Costa Rican masters relied on several economic activities for their incomes. Slaves worked in all of them but, except in the Caribbean zone, rarely as the main labor force. As a result, both enslaved men and women worked alongside and developed strong relationships with people of other racial origins. The variegated nature of their work meant that many enslaved men traveled about the province, shuttling between Matina and Cartago and sometimes going further afield to the North Pacific or even Panama and Nicaragua. Such physical mobility extended opportunities for them not only to forge extensive social networks but to accumulate their own property. Their prospects for material and social advancement made them more attractive potential husbands to free women than were slave men in many other parts of the Americas. Both poor, free women (often born out of wedlock) and enslaved men gained some security for themselves and their families through such mixed marriages, which favored the integration of their children into the broader creole culture. Developing relationships of patronage and kinship offered tangible opportunities. A slave's master, however, could withdraw an enslaved man's privileges to travel, accumulate property, and even keep a family together in a moment; doing everything possible to cultivate the master's good will made good sense. The ultimate prize, manumission, could be secured only by convincing the master to forfeit his rights to one's person, a process that usually took years of careful negotiations and—most often—waiting for the master's death. And although enslaved men could improve their social and material position in various ways, slave women usually stayed in the homes of their masters, with little prospect of freedom for themselves or their children.

All of these factors meant that enslaved men and women in Costa Rica identified strongly with free members of other racial groups and failed to develop the same solidarities among themselves that slaves did in other parts of the Americas. In the long term, neither ethnicity nor the condition of slavery itself led to the formation of a distinct identity for enslaved people in Costa Rica. For both slaves and servants, reliance on individual personal relationships diffused the potential for opposition and resistance. Patterns of residence and labor, decisively influenced by the nature of Costa Rica's economy, gender roles, and demographic realities, encouraged many slaves to acculturate and assimilate to the dominant culture. For women, this meant little more than taking their place among other domestic servants, sustaining the system of servitude through their forced labor and reproduction of the slave population. For men, close relationships with free people could lead to advancement all but unheard of for Africans in slave societies, sometimes even to freedom itself. Their cultivation of patronage ties with powerful Spaniards, however, although these offered real material and social advantages to individual slaves and free servants, discouraged the realization of their own class interests, thus serving the interests of the ruling Spaniards and ultimately reinforcing a colonial system founded on and perpetuated by the exploitation of racially subordinated Indians, mestizos, and people of African descent. Certainly individual slaves fought against their enslavement and oppression. But Costa Rica's economic

stagnation and the individualized, petty nature of exploitation during the colonial period retarded the development of racial and class consciousness and
real systemic change. Only the arrival of other people of African descent from
outside Costa Rica would begin the centuries-long, collective struggle against
racial oppression.

The study of slavery in Costa Rica holds implications for colonial Latin
American history beyond that small country's borders. Although slaves made
up only a small part of Costa Rica's population, their numbers did not reflect
their importance in the economic and social life of the colony. Slave men participated in the conquest and colonization of Costa Rica from the beginning,
as they did throughout the Americas. Slaves worked on the livestock ranches
of the North Pacific, the small farms and haciendas of the Central Valley, and
the cacao haciendas of the Caribbean region—precisely those sectors of the
economy that linked Costa Rica to the Atlantic world and allowed the small
ruling class to accumulate capital. To a considerable degree, the colonial elite
built its modest fortunes on slavery as well as on the oppression of indigenous
peoples.[3] Enslaved men especially occupied pivotal roles in production despite
their small numbers, which in some cases they were able to turn to their advantage. The social and economic mobility achieved by some slave men in
Costa Rica reveal the possibilities for and limitations on advancement in this
colonial society better than for any other group. Slavery in Costa Rica also
holds significance for our understanding of the roles of law and custom in the
colonies, including in frontier areas. In some ways, the law proved remarkably
open to slaves' interests, as in access to manumission. In others—such as in the
vicious rending of slave families—slave masters' interests overruled the law.
Viewing colonial Latin America through the prism of slavery allows us to dis-
cern new possibilities, including new perspectives of those societies in which
historians have viewed slavery as peripheral.

Slavery in Costa Rica was unique, but its history matters for comparative
studies of slavery as well. The conditions that promoted creolization in Costa
Rica surely occurred in other places and times in the Americas. Scholars of
North American slavery, for example, have found that slave societies that later
became heavily "Africanized" began with largely creole slave populations.[4]
Patterns established by early creole slaves, then, sometimes provided the context for the cultural adaptations of later African arrivals, as they did in Costa
Rica. Further research on slavery in the sixteenth and seventeenth centuries
may uncover similar findings for other regions of the Americas, including the
sugar islands later so heavily influenced by African-derived cultures.

Characteristics of Costa Rica's slave population raise other questions. Other parts of Central America, certainly, had mulatto slave majorities, equal sex ratios, and natural reproduction among slaves.[5] Historians of the United States South long emphasized that—unusually if not uniquely—the slave population of that region naturally reproduced itself, resulting in a creole majority by the early eighteenth century.[6] Mexico and Central America not only developed creole majority slave populations but did so more than half a century earlier than did the North American colonies.[7] The temporary closure of the slave trade in the 1640s and the relatively light physical demands of slave labor in Costa Rica likely played a role.[8] These factors and others require in-depth investigation—including intensive quantitative analysis—for the study of slave demography.

The importance and interaction of African and creole aspects of slave culture continue to occupy historians. A rich vein of scholarship has developed linking specific regions of West and West Central Africa to specific regions of the Americas, especially Brazil.[9] Historians have only begun, however, to trace identifiable groups of Africans from specific ports in Africa to specific ports in the Americas.[10] This research holds the potential to advance the "African-creolist" debate by moving beyond generalization to examine cultural continuity and change at a micro level, as studies of other groups of immigrants have been able to do for a long time.[11]

The stories of the women, men, and children who were loaded onto the *Christianus Quintus* and *Fredericus Quartus* in 1709 provide an opportunity "to understand the relationship between [African and creole] influences in specific historical contexts."[12] Akan, Ga-Adangme, Gbe, and Yoruba speakers, the veterans of the *Christianus Quintus* and *Fredericus Quartus* made the journey to Costa Rica surrounded by companions of similar linguistic and cultural backgrounds. They were not anonymous, atomized "crowds."[13] Their Middle Passage to the Americas was exceptionally harrowing even by the usual standards, but it was not a social death.[14] Although the highly specific, localized identities of Africa could not survive the Passage, immediately after being discharged on the beaches of Matina, the survivors of the *Christianus Quintus* and *Fredericus Quartus* began to reconstitute themselves in groups according to regional origins that would become the basis of diasporic ethnicities.[15] They had already begun to form other new identities on the Middle Passage itself that would only strengthen in the diaspora, extending their relationships to shipmates across ethnic lines. Shipmate ties could assume the force of kinship.[16] Through the process of "seasoning," those ties came to extend beyond shipmate and diasporic ethnic identities to companions on a new master's property. It was at work that these webs of relationships became broader still, as Africans encountered creole black and mulatto slaves, *ladino* Indians, mestizos, and free mulatto servants. Africans—especially in the city of Cartago and in the Caribbean Matina region—had the opportunity to maintain ties with people of similar ethnic and linguistic backgrounds, but relationships with creoles of all racial and social groups became just as, and ultimately more, important. Africans could not "recreate Africa" in Costa Rica. Creolization occurred in a unique way there. As historians continue to bring together both the African and American sides of the stories of enslaved people, our understanding of African cultures and creolization throughout the Americas will continue to advance.

Epilogue

✣ IN MARCH 1736, A SENTINEL SCANNED THE HORIZON FROM HIS POST
in the Spanish watchtower at Suerre on the Caribbean coast of Matina, Costa
Rica. Spying a Miskitu pirogue on the beach below, the watchman immediately sent a soldier to notify Capitan don Juan Díaz de Herrera y Garbanzo,
the lieutenant governor in charge of the Matina Valley.[1] After sending word
to the governor in Cartago, Díaz de Herrera sent Sergeant Baltazar de Vargas
and two soldiers to investigate. The soldiers found a group of four black men,
six Indian men, and several women and children on a small island at the
confluence of the Reventazón and Jiménez rivers. The black men were "well-
dressed with . . . linen shirts, and their silk sashes at the waist."[2] When the
soldiers asked them what they were doing there, the black men replied that

> they were coming to live there because they had fought with the
> Mosquitos and had killed five and had stolen a big pirogue from
> Ricardo and that there they were [now] safe and ready to do harm
> to the said Mosquitos which they would do neither to the [Matina]
> Valley nor to the Spaniards but only to [the Mosquitos] and that
> they would devastate and destroy them.[3]

As it turned out, two African men among the group had lived in Matina
years before. Nicolás had been a slave of José de Quirós, and Juan Bautista
had belonged to Marcos Zamora. About fifteen years before, Nicolás, a *mina*
born on the Gold Coast or upper Slave Coast, had arrived in Costa Rica as a
fugitive from his master, the governor of Portobello. Nicolás hid in the plantain fields of the Reventazón Valley from both Spaniards and Miskitus for

more than a year and a half before being captured and taken to Cartago. After being sold as a slave, he was sent to work on the cacao haciendas of José de Quirós in Matina. Later, he apparently fled to the Miskitus, but years later he repented of this decision and fled again. Nicolás must have remembered the Reventazón as a hospitable site for a settlement of *cimarrones* and exercised a strong influence in the choice of the runaways' destination.[4] Nicolás and Juan Bautista revealed their concern for their continued freedom when they immediately asked after their masters in Cartago. Juan Bautista learned that Zamora had died.[5]

When the soldiers returned and informed Díaz de Herrera of the camp, the lieutenant governor quickly inferred that the cimarrones posed a grave threat to Matina's slave régime. The settlement was "dangerous to this vicinity," he wrote to Governor don Baltasar Francisco de Valderrama, "even more so because most of the slaves of this Valley live [here] without masters." He emphasized that the settlement would prove "greatly damaging to the *vecinos* who have slaves here, because [the slaves] will go fleeing, seeking their freedom."[6] Governor Valderrama agreed, warning that "the said blacks could reproduce themselves and expand in people and forces, and [prove] to be of continual hostility to that Valley, and a refuge where the slaves of this Province would flee."[7] Governor Valderrama ordered reinforcements sent to the watchtower at the Reventazón, headed by *Alférez* Juan Carmona.[8]

In June, an extraordinary meeting took place in Cartago that included representatives from all sectors of Costa Rica's ruling class. The governor, members of Cartago's cabildo, the province's regular and noncommissioned army officers, and owners of Matina cacao haciendas met to discuss the fate of the refugees. Weighing their political and economic interests against their restricted military options, the council adopted a remarkable resolution. In a statement reflecting both realpolitik and lofty ideals, its members agreed

> unanimously by common accord and consent that it being so much to the service of God and the King our Lord (may God save him) to attend to the salvation of those souls and that those who are Catholics among them return to the union of our Holy Catholic Faith, and that the rest benefit from Holy Baptism, and to prevent them from returning to the Mosquitos and [to prevent] others from joining them, [and from] making and creating the core of a new population as began that of the Zambos Mosquitos; and as far as the slaves among them, in attention to [the fact] that their masters have

almost lost all right to them, and the impossibility of capturing them, and the risk of defense [against them] as they are a bandit people, for which reasons and because the slaves are the leaders [*cabezas*], it seems to [the council] very astute and that it will be much to the royal pleasure that in his royal name the said slaves be given the freedom for which they are asking, and that the others who are with them be pardoned so that they leave for this city under Royal Protection, and having left [the Reventazón] that they be given an appropriate settlement in which they may live.[9]

Nicolás and Juan Bautista, self-liberated slaves of Costa Rican masters and the spokesmen of the group, accepted and made their own statement remarkable in its time for its assertion of a doctrine of "original freedom."[10] Lieutenant General Díaz de Herrera reported their answer, which justified Nicolás and Juan Bautista's flight from Matina years before and explained why they now wanted to return:

If they had fled it was because they were free when they entered into our power, and we had enslaved them [*eran libres cuando vinieron a nuestro poder y que nosotros los habíamos esclavonizado*], for which reason they fled, but that they considered that they are Christians, and that they are living separated from the Church, and that if Your Lordship and the *vecinos* assure them of their freedom, they will leave [the Reventazón] and marry and live and die in the service of God and Our King and they will be his loyal vassals.[11]

The mina Nicolás, an orchestrator of the collective flight and no doubt a principal author of the statement, had never accepted enslavement—not by the governor of Portobello, nor by José de Quirós, nor by the Miskitus; not for himself and not for his fellow slaves. Insisting on the "original freedom" of Africans, including himself, who had been slaves of the Spaniards, he showed through his actions that his "self-liberation ethos" extended to all the enslaved. As far as is known, Nicolás never fled alone but always united with others in his various escapes.[12] Over the years, he had proved himself a master manipulator of those who sought to enslave him. Having once allegedly served as a guide to the Miskitus against the Spaniards, he now promised to help the Spaniards exterminate those very Miskitus. When sold to Quirós in 1725, Nicolás's bill of sale specified that he had never been baptized, but he now represented himself as a Catholic yearning for reunion with the Church. He surely knew of Spain's policy of offering freedom to slaves who fled from its enemies contingent on their acceptance of Catholicism, and he emphasized the desire of his fellow runaways to receive the sacraments.[13]

On June 23, 1736, the new governor don Antonio Vázquez de la Cuadra issued a letter in the name of the king, addressed to "the blacks and other persons who are living with them," promising freedom and royal protection to all "men as well as women."[14] In September, the party of twenty-two blacks and Indians arrived in Cartago, escorted by Alférez Juan Carmona, to face the *cabildo*. The cabildo immediately resolved that the non-Christians among them be instructed and baptized in the Catholic Church forthwith. Making good on its promise, the cabildo served Captain José de Quirós with a letter informing him that his former slave Nicolás, as well as Juan Bautista, had been freed in the name of the king.[15]

The crafty cabildo members kept to the letter of their promises but strictly circumscribed their meaning. Cartago's ruling citizens had no intention of letting the free blacks and Indians determine the meaning of their own freedom or of granting them autonomy in their promised settlement. Concerned that "they not be idle," the cabildo of Cartago placed the group in the continued custody of Juan Carmona, who should put them to work in "appropriate occupations" on his property in the Valley of Curridabat. Their promised freedom and settlement came in the form of forced service to a new master, performing whatever work he assigned to them—and the cabildo also charged Carmona with informing the authorities immediately should any of the free men and women take flight.[16]

Juan Carmona removed the blacks and Indians to the Valley of Curridabat, where he extracted even greater profits from their "free labor" than masters derived from slave labor. The conditions of Carmona's state-sponsored custody of the blacks and Indians allowed him to control them as masters controlled their slaves and appropriate the surplus product of their labor just as directly, yet he assumed few of the expenses for their upkeep. Like many slaveholders, Carmona provided the refugees with only rudimentary shelter and insufficient food, but unlike slave masters, he received reimbursement in cash from the state in addition to the refugees' labor. A year after arriving at Carmona's home, most of the twenty-two men, women, and children continued to live in "a crowded hut (*rancho*) that serves as a kitchen."[17] Carmona effectively collected twice on the value of the meager maintenance he provided for the blacks and Indians, as he dispensed the equivalent (according to him) of sixty pesos in beef and clothing to four black men and an Indian man in compensation for their work as axemen clearing the land around his home.[18] Carmona charged the state in cash and the refugees in labor for rations that were inadequate for their subsistence. The refugees incurred debts to other local Spaniards simply to feed themselves. Inocencio, one of the black refugees working for Carmona, was forced to borrow a *fanega* of corn from a local Spaniard in 1737.[19] Carmona super-exploited the black and Indian refugees for decades. By the 1760s, he had planted on his land more than forty-five square meters (forty-nine square yards) of sugar surrounded by a wood fence and a plantain grove of 112 trees and raised mules, horses, cattle, and oxen. His black and Indian charges had almost certainly cleared the land for his farm thirty years before. In 1738, the Audiencia of Guatemala ordered that the refugees be granted lands in the Valley of Aserrí. They built their own homes but continued to work for Carmona as late as 1755. They were known locally as "Carmona's blacks."[20]

Eight years later, on October 12, 1744, Captain don Esteban Ruiz de Mendoza, commander of the San Fernando Fort and lieutenant general in the Valley of Matina, made out two figures on the banks of the Suerre River gesturing for help. On the basis of past experience, Ruiz de Mendoza did not, this time, mistake them for Miskitu Zambos but assumed that they were prisoners escaped from the hated enemy. He dispatched six armed soldiers, who apprehended one of the two "shapes." It turned out to be a black creole woman named María Francisca, "ambassador for sixteen people who had been aboard a pirogue, . . . [and] who had been slaves of the English." María Francisca, who "expressed herself fairly well in the Spanish language," asked Ruiz de Mendoza "if I would protect them, . . . do them no harm, . . . and give them their freedom." In return, she and her party promised to become loyal "vassals of Our King and Lord." She explained that they had fled to the Spaniards because they knew them to be "Christians, and people of good heart, and that she was a Christian, and secondly, because the English punished them with much severity."[21] The group included seven young boys, each between three and seven years old; six adult men, five black and one an Indian; six adult women, two black and four Indian; and two female children, one five years and one just three weeks old—a total of twenty-two people. They had chests of clothes and several firearms.[22] Questioned by an interpreter, several of the fugitives explained that they had escaped from the English colony on the Island of San Andrés (Henrietta Island) in the western Caribbean, far off the coast of Nicaragua.[23] María

Francisca had recruited an *angola* named "Juamina" (Quamina), a practiced sailor, to pilot a craft to Matina.[24]

Considering that it "would be a shame that seventeen souls were lost to the union of the Catholic Church," Ruiz de Mendoza assured María Francisca that he would "protect them [and] take them in." When he designated a place for them to live, all shouted "Viva España!"[25] Learning of the arrival of the refugees, Governor don Juan Gemmir y Lleonart convened a special meeting of prominent Spanish vecinos at his home in Cartago. The council ratified the lieutenant general's decision to extend Spain's protection to the blacks.[26]

The party arrived in Cartago in late November. Governor Gemmir y Lleonart then promptly forced the black and Indian men to surrender their arms—eight shotguns and two sabers—their carpentry tools, including two large saws and several axes, and their clothing. He lodged the blacks and Indians at his own home on the plaza while the vicar of Cartago instructed them in Catholic doctrine, after which they were settled in Ujarrás.[27] The governor explained that their property would be returned to them, except for the weapons, which would not be returned "for now, because they were battered from the blows they took on the road" to Cartago. Instead, he remitted them to the Royal Armory.[28]

The governor ordered that the group be settled in the Valley of Escazú, west of Cartago, which would be "comfortable for them to make their fields" and close to a church where the non-Christians among them could receive instruction in Catholic doctrine. Like those who came in 1737, the refugees would live not like other peasants in the Central Valley but under close supervision. Gemmir y Lleonart turned over the black and Indian refugees to Juan Carmona, now a captain, "like others whom he has, who came in the same way as those in the year '37."[29] The governor charged Carmona to "take care of, watch over, and pay attention that the said black women and men are not bothered by anybody."[30] On March 29, 1745, the blacks and Indians arrived with Captain Juan Carmona at Villa Nueva de la Boca del Monte in the Valley of Aserrí, "where the other blacks are settled," on the exact site of Costa Rica's present capital, San José, thirty-three kilometers (twenty-one miles) west of Cartago. Outside the new settlement, Lieutenant General don Juan José de Cuende assigned them the plots of royal land on which they built their homes.[31]

More than a decade later, in early February 1755, Captain don Tomás López del Corral, *Alcalde Ordinario de Primer Voto* (chief magistrate) of Cartago, issued an order to the residents of the valleys west of Cartago. The alcalde mandated that owners of farms in the valleys build homes in the new settlement of Cubujuquí (now Heredia). "Those who do not have . . . haciendas to care for in the country," López del Corral ordered, "will tear up their houses, huts or shanties, . . . excepting no person," and leave the area around Villa Nueva.³²

Word of the order spread even before it was publicly announced, and many prepared to move. But on the night of February 12, Félix Durán, a free mulatto resident of the area, appeared at the home of Captain Nicolás de Zamora in the Valley of Aserrí to inform on a treacherous conspiracy. Confronted with the alcalde's order, "Carmona's blacks," Durán claimed, planned an uprising. Accustomed to living in the country "in the manner of a *palenque*," Durán alleged, the blacks had no intention of abandoning their savage lifestyle for the civilization of town. Free blacks Pedro Valerín and Francisco Guerrero planned to lead the blacks to Cartago, break into the royal armory and steal all the weapons, "kill three or four Spaniards . . . and their children," then go to Matina and incite all the black slaves there to rise up and abscond with them to the mountains, where they would live as allies of the Miskitu Zambos.³³

Juan Carmona confirmed that "many times" Pedro Valerín had tried to agitate the blacks to rise up and had always tried "to make himself the leader [*caudillo*] of the said blacks." His principal co-conspirators were his wife, the mulatta Juana Francisca; Francisco Guerrero; and "the black woman named María Francisca, whom all the blacks called the Captain." Valerín constantly caused trouble, was "always disobedient," and "had never had any peace with the rest of his companions." Valerín, Carmona continued, "had never come to obey him, nor come to his house [to work]," although he "always found all the others obedient." Most of the blacks, "hard-working, . . . good-natured, and peaceful," refused to listen to the admonitions of Valerín and his fellow agitators.³⁴ José Miguel Chavarría, one of the free blacks living outside Villa Nueva, told López del Corral that upon hearing of the order, he and most of the blacks and Indians who lived at Boca del Monte were preparing to move to the Puebla de los Angeles, Cartago's free colored neighborhood. But Pedro Valerín refused to leave his fields and the land where he had made his home. He insisted that "he was a man" and that "all the rest [who were leaving] were cowards."³⁵

When arrested and interrogated, Valerín denied all the charges as grotesque distortions of the truth, motivated by personal grudges. Carmona, Valerín explained, hated him because in all his years living in the mountains,

Valerín would never work for Carmona or "subject his freedom to the said Carmona's slavery." Because of Carmona's desire to exploit him and the other blacks, Valerín regarded Carmona with "great objection, loathing, and enmity."[36] He and the rest of the free blacks would leave the area, Valerín promised. They planned to take their families and property "to live wherever God would help them." First, he planned to go with his companions to Cartago, where they would ask for their weapons from Governor don Cristóbal Ignacio de Soria—the long guns and swords that they had surrendered to his predecessor eleven years before.[37] Don Tomás López del Corral acquitted Valerín and Guerrero of the charges, then evicted them from their homes in Boca del Monte.[38]

For the rest of the colonial period, black and Indian slaves continued occasionally to flee to Matina from British and Miskitu masters. For example, at about three o'clock one morning in October 1742, a guard surveilling the coast at Moín apprehended a black man he had spied skulking along the beach. José Manuel Sánchez, an African fluent in Spanish, had been a slave of cacao planter don Julián García de Argueta. He was working on one of his master's haciendas when the Miskitus invaded and took him prisoner in 1739. After some years, José Manuel and three of his fellow slaves stole a canoe and escaped. At the San Juan River, José Manuel abandoned the boat and fled to Matina on foot "seeking his country" and, as fugitives from the Miskitus invariably claimed, to return to the Catholic faith.[39]

By the 1770s, such arrivals had become almost routine. In February 1774, a mulatto and an Indian woman escaped the Miskitus and fled to Matina.[40] In June, two African slaves escaped from a Jamaican master and walked for nine days along the Reventazón River until they came to the main road from Matina to Cartago. The men assured Costa Rican officials that they came "only to obtain their freedom that they might be catechized."[41] The following year, free black Antonio Arizaga happened upon a black man, an indigenous man, an indigenous woman, and a mulatta at the Pacuare River, all fugitives from the Miskitus.[42] In 1777, a black woman unnamed in the documents arrived in a canoe with her six-year-old daughter, having fled the English settlement at Bluefields, Nicaragua.[43] Some decades later, around 1828, William Smith, an English-speaking black fisherman from Bocas del Toro, Panama, built his home at Cahuita Point, near the spot where the *Christianus Quintus* and *Fredericus Quartus* had arrived more than a century before. He was soon joined by other English-speaking "bachelors" from such places as Bocas del Toro, Nicaragua, and San Andrés, who started large families with local indigenous women and lived quiet, independent lives devoted to turtle fishing and coconut cultivation.[44]

In one of the first book-length monographs on Costa Rica's black population of West Indian descent, Michael D. Olien wrote in his 1967 dissertation that "there seems to be little or no continuity between the African Negro of the [colonial] period . . . and the West Indian Negro."[45] For the most part, he was right. By the late nineteenth century, virtually all of the descendants of the African slaves of the colonial period had been thoroughly assimilated into Costa Rica's popular classes. They preserved no culture, identity, or position in society distinct from the mestizo majority. That process of assimilation had begun centuries before, when the first Africans brought to the Spanish colony found themselves isolated from their countrymen and forced into close contact with members of other ethnic and racial groups. Most soon learned Spanish, adopted Catholicism, and became adept at carving out opportunities within a slave system that, by comparison with most in the New World, proved remarkably manipulable to their interests.

There were, however, exceptions to Olien's generalization who represent a tenuous continuity between the enslaved population of the colonial period and the later mass migrations of West Indian blacks to Costa Rica. English-speaking African and creole blacks such as Nicolás and Juan Bautista, "the Captain" María Francisca, and Pedro Valerín and Francisco Guerrero came to Costa Rica not as slaves but as self-liberated men and women. Unlike most African slaves, they were able to live together as a community for at least twenty years, maintaining the strong, culturally distinct, and oppositional identity they had forged in the crucible of other slave systems. Having struck and fought for their freedom against the Miskitus and English, some of these Anglophone black men and women jealously guarded their independence from the quasislavery of sugar planter Juan Carmona and the invasive directives of colonial officials. From the beginning, the independence of the outsiders worried royal governors and the ruling class of *hacendados*, who feared they might organize rebellions, ally with foreign invaders, or form the nucleus of a threatening enclave in the Atlantic region. After arriving on the Caribbean coast, these proud men and women established a tradition of resistance on the site that became the capital of an independent Costa Rica, where generations of West Indians and their descendants would continue to struggle.[46]

Appendix One

Fugitive Slaves, 1612–1746

TABLE A1.1 Some Fugitive Slaves of Costa Rican Masters, 1612–1746

NAME	CASTA	APPROXIMATE AGE	OWNER	ALONE?	NOTES	DATE OF DOCUMENT	DATE OF FLIGHT(S)	SOURCES
1. Francisco	Angola		Ambrosio de Brenes	Yes	Fled from at least three masters in Peru, Panama, and Costa Rica	1612	1608, 1610, 1611	ANCR, G. 34
2. Juan	Angola	35	The Crown	Yes	Described as habitual runaway	1624	1624	ANCR, G. 55
3. Francisco	Creole	27	Jerónimo de Retes	Yes	reported to be in Gracias a Dios, Honduras	1640	1640	Cáceres, Negros, mulatos, 86
4. Diego Leal	Mulatto		Doña Isidora Zambrano	Yes		1669	1669	ANCR, PC 817 bis, fols. 496–97
5. Andrés	Mulatto Creole	17	Lic. Pbo. don Alonso de Sandoval	Yes		1666	1666	ANCR, PC 817, fol. 140
6. Silvestre	Black Creole		Doña María de Sandoval	Yes	native of Granada, Nicaragua; donated while at large	1675	1675	ANCR, PC 824, fols. 13–14
7. Catalina	Black	20	Felipe Gómez Macotela	Yes	believed to be in Esparza	1675	1675	ANCR, PC 817, fol. 127

NAME	CASTA	APPROXIMATE AGE	OWNER	ALONE?	NOTES	DATE OF DOCUMENT	DATE OF FLIGHT(S)	SOURCES
8. Clemente	Mulatto	18	Lic. José de Lumbides	Yes	exchanged for another slave while at large	1677	1677	ANCR, PC 825, fols. 13–14
9. Antonio	Mina	21	Juan de Ugalde	Unknown	Described as habitual runaway	1680	Unknown	ANCR, PC 828, fols. 61–62
10. Andrés	Mina	23	Juan de Ugalde	Unknown	Described as habitual runaway	1680	Unknown	ANCR, PC 828, fols. 61–62
11. Melchora	Mulatta Zamba		don Diego de Ibarra	Yes	escaped from jail when accused of witchcraft; sold to don Lorenzo González Calderón in León, Nicaragua	1684	ca. 1677	AGN, Inquisición, vol. 650, exp. 3, fol. 576
12. Miguel	Congo		Isabel Vázquez Coronado	Yes		1688	1688	ANCR, PC 837, fols. 15–15v.
13. María Manuela	Mulatta	25	Doña Juana Núñez de Trupira	Yes	Described as habitual runaway	1692	1692	ANCR, PC 842, fols. 63–64v.
14. José de Ibarra	Black Creole	28	Alf. José Gómez Elgueros	Yes	master sugar maker	1692	1691	ANCR, PC 842, fols. 96v–98v
15. Antonio	Mulatto	18	Cap. Agustín Morales and Jerónimo de Morales	Yes	in custody of Alf. José Calderón	1694	1693	ANCR, PC 844, fols. 40–42v
16. Salvador	Black Creole	12	Don Miguel de Alvarado	Yes	Described as habitual runaway	1696	Unknown	ANCR, PC 848, fols. 28v–30
17. Juan Toribio	Mulatto	28	Doña Micaela Durán de Chávez	Yes	Fled in Mineral del Córpus, Honduras, after contracting to buy his freedom	1703	1695	ANCR, PC 857, fols. 5–5v

NAME	CASTA	APPROXIMATE AGE	OWNER	ALONE?	NOTES	DATE OF DOCUMENT	DATE OF FLIGHT(S)	SOURCES
18. Francisco	Bozal		don José de Alvarado	Yes	fled to Nicaragua from Valley of Bagaces	1719	ca. 1701	ANCR, C. 231, fol. 11
19. Unknown Male	Carabalí	16	The Crown	One of two	apprehended and auctioned to Alberto Pérez Parga	1701	1701	ANCR, C. 109, fol. 33
20. Unknown Female	Carabalí	16	The Crown	One of two	apprehended and auctioned to Alberto Pérez Parga	1701	1701	ANCR, C. 109, fol. 33
21. Luis	Congo	14	The Crown	One of four	apprehended and auctioned to José de Prado	1701	1701	ANCR, C. 109, fol. 27; AGI, AG 359, pieza 1, fols. 88v, 90
22. Juan	Congo	14	The Crown	One of four	apprehended and auctioned to José de Prado	1701	1701	ANCR, C. 109, fol. 27; AGI, AG 359, pieza 1, fols. 88v, 90
23. Cristóbal	Congo	14	The Crown	One of four	apprehended and auctioned to Juan de Escobar	1701	1701	ANCR, C. 109, fol. 29; ANCR, PC 860, fols. 10–12
24. Damián	Congo	14	The Crown	One of four	apprehended and auctioned to Juan de Escobar; repeat fugitive	1701	1701, 1717	ANCR, C. 109, fols. 27, 29; ANCR, PC 860, fols. 10–12, ANCR, CC 4111
25. Unknown female	Bozal		Fray Francisco de San José	Yes	fled immediately after arrival in Matina	1702	1702	AGI, AG 359, pieza 1, fols. 2v–3v

NAME	CASTA	APPROXIMATE AGE	OWNER	ALONE?	NOTES	DATE OF DOCUMENT	DATE OF FLIGHT(S)	SOURCES
26. Francisco Barrios	Congo		Diego de Barros y Carvajal	One of ten	fled from don Gregorio Caamaño; repeat fugitive	1719	1701, ca. 1703	ANCR, C. 265, fols. 2v, 3v
27. Gregorio	Popo	14	The Crown	One of ten	fled from don Gregorio Caamaño; repeat fugitive	1719	ca. 1703, 1717	ANCR, C. 265, fol. 3v; ANCR, CC 4111
28. Benito	Popo		The Crown	One of ten	fled from don Gregorio Caamaño	1719	ca. 1703	ANCR, C. 265, fol. 3v
29. Lorenzo José	Black Creole		The Crown	One of ten	fled from don Gregorio Caamaño	1719	ca. 1703	ANCR, C. 265, fol. 3v
30. Mateo Saca la Agua	Casta Mora		The Crown	One of ten	fled from don Gregorio Caamaño	1719	ca. 1703	ANCR, C. 265, fol. 3v; ANCR, C. 251, fol. 3v
31. Carlos	Popo		The Crown	One of ten	fled from don Gregorio Caamaño	1719	ca. 1703	ANCR, C. 265, fol. 3v
32. Manuel	Congo		The Crown	One of ten	fled from don Gregorio Caamaño	1719	ca. 1703	ANCR, C. 265, fol. 3v
33. Antonio	Arará		The Crown	One of ten	fled from don Gregorio Caamaño	1719	ca. 1703	ANCR, C. 265, fol. 3v
34. Pedro	Carabalí		The Crown	One of ten	fled from don Gregorio Caamaño	1719	ca. 1703	ANCR, C. 265, fol. 3v
35. Juan	Arará		Maestre de Campo don José de Casasola y Córdoba	One of two	fled to don Gregorio Caamaño	1705	1705	ANCR, PC 861, fols. 6–8; ANCR, CC 3798
36. Miguel	Arará	30	Maestre de Campo don José de Casasola y Córdoba	One of two	fled to don Gregorio Caamaño	1705	1705	ANCR, PC 861, fols. 6–8; ANCR, CC 3798

NAME	CASTA	APPROXIMATE AGE	OWNER	ALONE?	NOTES	DATE OF DOCUMENT	DATE OF FLIGHT(S)	SOURCES
37. José de Arlegui	Mulatto Creole	22	Alf. Manuel Antonio de Arlegui	Yes	apprehended in Santiago de Guatemala after at least six years at large	1714	1708	ANCR, PC 865, fols. 48–50; ANCR, PC 873, fols. 178–178v
38. Gil de Salazar	Mulatto		Cap. Diego Santiago de Cárdenas	Yes	trained as a tailor	1713	ca. 1704	Indice de los proto-colos de Cartago, 1:456, 2:235
39. Felipe de Oviedo	Mulatto		Doña Francisca Jiménez	Yes	escaped from jail	1715	1715	ANCR, CC 145
40. Antonio Civitola	Congo	50	María Calderón	Yes	at large at least six months	1719	1719	ANCR, C. 259, fols. 2v, 5
41. Francisco Caracata	Arará	50	Doña Josefa de Oses Navarro	Yes	at large at least forty days	1719	1719	ANCR, C. 232, fols. 4, 12
42. Eugenia Vanegas	Mulatta	40	Sarg. Mayor don Juan Francisco de Ibarra	Yes	slave of Fran-cisco Martínez at time of flight; at large one year in "Platanares del Rey"	1720	ca. 1712	ANCR, C. 241, fol. 28
43. Ramón Durán	Black Creole	50	María Calvo	Yes	at liberty in Chiriquí; described elsewhere as Cabo Verde	1720	ca. 1718	ANCR, PC 891, fols. 26–27; ANCR, PC 898, fols. 26–27
44. Nicolás	Mina		Governor of Portobello	One of two	various escapes	1721	1721	ANCR, C. 283
45. Francisco	Mina		Governor of Portobello	One of two	various escapes	1721	1721	ANCR, C. 283

TABLE A1.1. *(continued)*

NAME	CASTA	APPROXIMATE AGE	OWNER	ALONE?	NOTES	DATE OF DOCUMENT	DATE OF FLIGHT(S)	SOURCES
46. Antonio	Congo		Cap. don Francisco Javier de Oreamuno	One of two	various escapes	1722	1722, 1724	ANCR, C. 292; AGCA, A2 (6), exp. 193, leg. 12
47. Antonia	Mulatta	50	Juan Cortés	Yes	habitual runaway; accused of arson	1723	1723	ANCR, CC 5815
48. Juan Román	Black Creole	57	Cap. Francisco Gutiérrez	Yes	fled during manumission lawsuit	1733	1733	ANCR, CC 4292, fols. 13–13v, 32v
49. María Egipciaca	"White Mulatta" Creole	43	María Calderón	Yes		1724	1724	ANCR, PC 859, fol. 5v; PC 897, fols. 94v–95v
50. Ramón González	Mulatto	15	Manuel González	Yes	Described as mentally handicapped; pyromaniac	1726	1726	ANCR, CC 178, fol. 1
51. Antonio Camelo	Mulatto	45	José Felipe Calvo	Yes	master lived in Panama	1730	1730	ANCR, PC 903, fols. 18–19
52. Francisco Cubero	Mulatto	24	the late Doña Catalina González del Camino	Yes	fled on death of owner	1746	1746	ANCR, PC 934, fols. 66–68

Appendix Two

Slave Marriages, 1670–1750

TABLE A2.1. Marriages of Enslaved Black Men, 1670–1750*

RACE/ CONDTION OF WIFE	1670– 1679	1680– 1689	1690– 1699	1700– 1709	1710– 1719	1720– 1729	1730– 1739	1740– 1750	TOTAL (PER- CENT)
Indian	1	3		1	3				8 (16)
Mestiza	2			1			3		6 (12)
Slave, unidentified by race							1		1 (2)
Black slave							1	1	2 (4)
Free Black		2							2 (4)
Mulatta slave									0 (0)
Free mulatta**	1	2	1	2	1		4	3	14 (28)
Unidentified				1	5	4	2	5	17 (34)
Total	4	7	1	5	9	4	11	9	50 (100)

*In a few cases, other documents identified the racial origins of men and women for whom this information was omitted in the marriage registers.

**Includes mulatas libres, mulattas, one parda, and one zamba.

Sources: ACM, Libros de Matrimonios de Cartago, nos. 1–6/FHL, VAULT INTL film 1219727, Items 6–10.

TABLE A2.2. Marriages of Enslaved Mulatto Men, 1670–1750*

RACE/ CONDITION OF WIFE	1670– 1679	1680– 1689	1690– 1699	1700– 1709	1710– 1719	1720– 1729	1730– 1739	1740– 1750	TOTAL (PER- CENT)
Indian							1		1 (5)
Mestiza		1		1				1	3 (16)
Slave, unidentified by race								1	1 (5)
Black slave									0 (0)
Free Black									0 (0)
Mulatta slave		2							2 (0)
Free mulatta**								1	1 (21)
Unidentified		2		2	3	2		1	10 (53)
Total	0	5	0	3	3	2	1	4	18 (100)

*In a few cases, other documents identified the racial origins of men and women for whom this information was omitted in the marriage registers.

**Includes mulatas libres, mulattas, one parda, and one zamba.

Sources: ACM, Libros de Matrimonios de Cartago, nos. 1–6/FHL, VAULT INTL film 1219727, Items 6–10.

TABLE A2.3. Marriages of Enslaved Men Unidentified by Race, 1670–1750*

RACE/ CONDITION OF WIFE	1670– 1679	1680– 1689	1690– 1699	1700– 1709	1710– 1719	1720– 1729	1730– 1739	1740– 1750	TOTAL (PER- CENT)
Slave, unidentified by race							1		1 (33)
Mestiza									0 (0)
Free mulatta**									0 (0)
Unidentified		1						1	2 (67)
Total	0	1	0	0	0	0	1	1	3 (100)

*In a few cases, other documents identified the racial origins of men and women for whom this information was omitted in the marriage registers.

**Includes mulatas libres, mulattas, one parda, and one zamba.

Sources: ACM, Libros de Matrimonios de Cartago, nos. 1–6/FHL, VAULT INTL film 1219727, Items 6–10.

TABLE A2.4. All Marriages of Enslaved Men, Cartago, 1670–1750*

RACE/ CONDITION OF WIFE	1670– 1679	1680– 1689	1690– 1699	1700– 1709	1710– 1719	1720– 1729	1730– 1739	1740– 1750	TOTAL (PER- CENT)
Indian	1	3		1	3		1		9 (13)
Mestiza	2	1		2			3	1	9 (13)
Slave, unidentified by race							1	2	3 (3)
Black slave							1	1	2 (3)
Free Black		2							2 (3)
Mulatta slave		2							2 (3)
Free mulatta**	1	2	1	2	1	0	4	4	15 (21)
Unidentified		3		3	8	6	2	7	29 (41)
Total	0	1	0	0	0	0	2	1	71 (100)

*In a few cases, other documents identified the racial origins of men and women for whom this information was omitted in the marriage registers.

**Includes mulatas libres, mulattas, one parda, and one zamba.

Sources: ACM, Libros de Matrimonios de Cartago, nos. 1–6/FHL, VAULT INTL film 1219727, Items 6–10.

TABLE A2.5. All Marriages of Enslaved Women, Cartago, 1670–1750

RACE/ CONDITION OF HUSBAND	1670– 1679	1680– 1689	1690– 1699	1700– 1709	1710– 1719	1720– 1729	1730– 1739	1740– 1750	TOTAL (PER- CENT)
Slave	0	0	0	0	0	0	1	0	1 (13)
Black slave	0	0	0	0	0	0	2	1	3 (38)
Mulatto slave	0	0	0	0	0	0	0	1	1 (13)
Free mulatto	0	0	0	0	0	0	1	0	1 (13)
Unidentified	0	0	0	0	0	0	0	2	2 (25)
Total	0	0	0	0	0	0	4	4	8 (100)

Sources: ACM, Libros de Matrimonios, nos. 1–6/FHL, VAULT INTL film 1219727, Items 6–10.

TABLE A2.6. Marriages of Enslaved Black and Mulatta Women, Cartago, 1670–1750

RACE/ CONDITION OF HUSBAND	1670– 1679	1680– 1689	1690– 1699	1700– 1709	1710– 1719	1720– 1729	1730– 1739	1740– 1750	TOTAL (PER- CENT)
Enslaved Black women married to Black slaves							2	1	3 (100)
Enslaved mulatta women married to free mulattos							1		1 (100)
Total	0	0	0	0	0	0	3	1	4 (100)

Sources: ACM, Libros de Matrimonios, nos. 1–6/FHL, VAULT INTL film 1219727, Items 6–10.

TABLE A2.7. Marriages of Enslaved Women Unidentified by Race, Cartago, 1670–1750

RACE/ CONDITION OF HUSBAND	1670– 1679	1680– 1689	1690– 1699	1700– 1709	1710– 1719	1720– 1729	1730– 1739	1740– 1750	TOTAL (PER- CENT)
Slave unidentified by race							1		1 (25)
Mulatto slave								1	1 (25)
Unidentified								2	2 (50)
Total	0	0	0	0	0	0	1	3	4 (100)

Sources: ACM, Libros de Matrimonios, nos. 1–6/FHL, VAULT INTL film 1219727, Items 6–10.

Notes

INTRODUCTION

1. Sidney W. Mintz and Richard Price, *The Birth of African-American Culture: An Anthropolgical Perspective* (Boston, MA: Beacon Press, 1992), first published as *An Anthropological Approach to the Afro-American Past* (Philadelphia, PA: Institute for the Study of Human Issues, 1976), 7.

2. Mintz and Price, *Birth of African-American Culture*, 9, 18 (emphasis in original).

3. Ibid., 14 (emphasis in original).

4. Paul E. Lovejoy, "The African Diaspora: Revisionist Interpretations of Ethnicity, Culture and Religion Under Slavery," *Studies in the World History of Slavery, Abolition and Emancipation* 2, no. 1 (1997), http://ejournalofpoliticalscience.org/diaspora.html. See also Paul E. Lovejoy, "Identifying Enslaved Africans in the African Diaspora," in *Identity in the Shadow of Slavery*, ed. Paul E. Lovejoy (London: Continuum, 2000), 1–29, especially 12–21.

5. John K. Thornton, *Africa and Africans in the Making of the Atlantic World, 1400-1680*, 2nd ed. (Cambridge: Cambridge University Press, 1998), 192–97, quotations from 192, 195, 197.

6. Michael A. Gomez, *Exchanging Our Country Marks: The Transformation of African Identities in the Colonial and Antebellum South* (Chapel Hill: University of North Carolina Press, 1998).

7. Kristin Mann, "Shifting Paradigms in the Study of the African Diaspora and of Atlantic History and Culture," *Slavery & Abolition* 22, no. 1 (April 2001): 7, 6.

8. Carlos Monge Alfaro's *Historia de Costa Rica* appeared in mimeographed form in 1939 and was first published in 1947. Juan Rafael Quesada Camacho, *Historia de la historiografía costarricense, 1821–1940* (San José: Editorial de la Universidad de Costa Rica, 2001), 415n16.

9. Monge Alfaro, *Historia de Costa Rica*, 14th ed. (San José: Librería Trejos, 1978), 169.

10. "En Costa Rica no hubo esclavos ni sirvientes; todos fueron personas que hicieron valer su calidad de seres humanos. . . . Este interesante proceso de democratización, del cual arranca el sentido de vida costarricense, abarcó a todos los

habitantes por igual, fueran mestizos, criollos o españoles." Monge Alfaro, *Historia de Costa Rica*, 169.

11. Samuel Z. Stone, *La dinastía de los conquistadores* (San José: Editorial Universitaria Centroamericana [EDUCA], 1975).

12. Claudia Quirós Vargas, *La era de la encomienda* (San José: Editorial de la Universidad de Costa Rica, 1990).

13. Lowell Gudmundson K, "Mecanismos de movilidad social para la población de procedencia africana en Costa Rica colonial: Manumisión y mestizaje," *Revista de Historia* (Costa Rica) 2, no. 3 (1976): 131–82, http://www.revistas.una.ac.cr/index.php/historia/article/view/2150.

14. Carlos Meléndez, "El negro en Costa Rica durante la colonia," in Carlos Meléndez and Quince Duncan, *El negro en Costa Rica* (San José: Editorial Costa Rica, 1989); Mario Barrantes Ferrero, *Un caso de esclavitud en Costa Rica* (San José: Instituto Geográfico Nacional, 1968).

15. Oscar R. Aguilar Bulgarelli and Irene Alfaro Aguilar, *La esclavitud negra en Costa Rica: Origen de la oligarquía económica y política nacional* (San José: Progreso Editora, 1997).

16. Tatiana Lobo Wiehoff and Mauricio Meléndez Obando, *Negros y blancos: Todo mezclado* (San José: Editorial de la Universidad de Costa Rica, 1997).

17. Rina Cáceres, *Negros, mulatos, esclavos y libertos en la Costa Rica del siglo XVII* (Mexico City: Instituto Panamericano de Geografía e Historia, 2000).

18. Johannes Rask, *A Brief and Truthful Description of a Journey to and from Guinea*, vol. 1 of *Two Views from Christiansborg Castle*, trans. and ed. Selena Axelrod Winsnes (Accra: Sub-Saharan Publishers, 2009).

19. Ole Justesen, ed., *Danish Sources for the History of Ghana 1657–1754*, trans. James Manley, 2 vols. (Copenhagen: Det Kongelinge Danske Videnskabernes Selskab/ Royal Danish Academy of Sciences and Letters, 2005).

20. Georg Nørregård, "Forliset ved Nicaragua 1710" (The shipwreck off Nicaragua, 1710), in *Årbog 1948* (Helsingør, Denmark: Handels-og Søfartsmuseet på Kronborg, 1948, 67–98.

21. Costa Ricans of the colonial period rarely distinguished between *peninsulares* and *criollos*, instead referring to any person reputed to be exclusively of Spanish descent as a "Spaniard," regardless of place of birth. I follow them in using the term in this sense throughout this work.

22. Archivo Nacional de Costa Rica, San José (hereafter, ANCR), Sección Colonial Cartago (hereafter, C.) 182 (1710), 187 (1710); Archivo General de Centro América, Guatemala City (hereafter, AGCA), A1 (5), exp. 632, leg. 77 (1710); Archivo General de Indias, Seville (hereafter, AGI), Indiferente 2799 (1711–1714).

23. ANCR, C. 211 (1716–1719), 224 (1719), 229–46 (1719), 248–54 (1719), 256 (1719), 258–68 (1719), 273–78 (1720), 280 (1719), 283–84 (1721), 288–89 (1719–1720), 292 (1722); ANCR, Sección Colonial Guatemala (hereafter, G.) 173 (1719), 185–88 (1719).

24. The six questions asked of each slave are listed in ANCR, Sección Complementario Colonial 5837 (1719), fol. 43.

25. Wyatt MacGaffey, "Kongo Identity, 1483–1993," *South Atlantic Quarterly* 94, no. 4 (1995): 1028–29.

26. Orlando Patterson, *Slavery and Social Death* (Cambridge, MA: Harvard University Press, 1982); Fernando Henrique Cardoso, *Capitalismo e escravidão no Brasil meridional: O negro na sociedade escravocrata do Rio Grande do Sul*, 2nd ed. (Rio de Janeiro: Paz e Terra, 1977).

27. Douglas B. Chambers, "Tracing Igbo into the African Diaspora," in *Identity in the Shadow of Slavery*, ed. Paul E. Lovejoy (London: Continuum, 2000), 55.

28. Karl Marx, *Wage Labour and Capital*, in *Wage Labour and Capital* and *Value, Price and Profit* (New York: International Publishers, 1985), 27.

29. Barbara J. Fields, "Ideology and Race in American History," in *Region, Race, and Reconstruction: Essays in Honor of C. Vann Woodward*, ed. J. Morgan Kousser and James M. McPherson (New York: Oxford University Press, 1982), 151.

30. Eugenia Ibarra Rojas, *Las sociedades cacicales de Costa Rica* (San José: Editorial de la Universidad de Costa Rica, 1990); Quirós Vargas, *La era de la encomienda*; Philip S. MacLeod, "On the Edge of Empire: Costa Rica in the Colonial Era (1561–1800)" (PhD diss., Tulane University, 1999).

31. Bernardo A. Thiel, "Monografía de la población de Costa Rica en el siglo XIX," *Revista de Costa Rica en el Siglo XIX* 1 (1902): 1–52; Héctor Pérez Brignoli, *La población de Costa Rica según el obispo Thiel*, Avances de Investigación 42 (San José: Centro de Investigaciones Históricas, Universidad de Costa Rica, 1988).

32. See Lowell Gudmundson, "Materiales censales de finales de la colonia y principios del período republicano en Costa Rica," *Revista de Historia* (Costa Rica) 6, no. 11 (1985): 173–227.

33. Certificación de los vecinos e indios tributarios que tiene la provincia de Costa Rica, July 20, 1683, AGI, Contaduría 815, no. 1, fols. 91v–95v.

34. "Los vecinos del Valle de Bagases pretenden formar una villa, ciudad o lugar en dicho valle, con independencia del gobierno de la provincia de Costa Rica. Año de 1688," in *Colección de documentos*, ed. Leon Fernández (Barcelona: Imprenta Viuda de Luis Tasso, 1907), 8:477–501.

35. Padrón y memoria de los vecinos de Cartago, 1691–1692, ANCR, C. 83.

36. Relación geográfica de Costa Rica por el Gobernador don Juan Gemmir y Lleonart, Cartago, May 20, 1741, AGCA, A1.17, exp. 5016, leg. 210, fols. 252–53v.

37. Cáceres, *Negros, mulatos, esclavos*, 2–3; Aguilar Bulgarelli and Alfaro Aguilar, *La esclavitud negra en Costa Rica*; Lobo Wiehoff and Meléndez Obando, *Negros y blancos*.

38. Michael D. Olien, "Black and Part-Black Populations in Colonial Costa Rica: Ethnohistorical Resources and Problems," *Ethnohistory* 27, no. 1 (1980): 20.

39. Thiel, "Monografía de la población," 8.

40. Olien, "Black and Part-Black Populations," 18.

41. María C. Alvarez Solar, *La esclavitud como institución económica y social en Costa Rica, 1680–1725* (Kristiansand, Norway: Høyskoleforlaget, 1999), 73–74.

42. Certificación de los vecinos, fols. 91v–95v.

43. Visita apostólica de los pueblos de Nicaragua y Costa Rica hecha por el Illmo. Sr. don Pedro Morel de Santa Cruz, September 8, 1752, University of Texas at Austin, Benson Latin American Collection, Joaquín García Icazbalceta Collection, vol. 20, no. 7, fol. 58.

44. Visita apostólica.

45. Fields, "Ideology and Race," 161.

46. Cf. Herman L. Bennett, "A Research Note: Race, Slavery, and the Ambiguity of Corporate Consciousness," *Colonial Latin American Historical Review* 3, no. 2 (1994): 207–13; Bennett, *Africans in Colonial Mexico: Absolutism, Christianity, and Afro-Creole Consciousness, 1570–1640* (Bloomington: Indiana University Press, 2003); Bennett, *Colonial Blackness: A History of Afro-Mexico* (Bloomington: Indiana University Press, 2009).

47. Voyages Database, Voyages: The Trans-Atlantic Slave Trade Database, 2009, http://slavevoyages.org/tast/database/search.faces?yearFrom=1700&yearTo =1710.

CHAPTER ONE

1. Declaración de Alfonso Ramírez, Cartago, April 19, 1710, Archivo Nacional de Costa Rica, San José (hereafter ANCR), Sección Colonial Cartago (hereafter C.) 187, fols. 38v-42v, quoting from fol. 39v; Carta de Gaspar de Acosta Arévalo, Matina, March 13, 1710, ANCR, C. 187, fol. 3; Carta de Francisco Martínez, Matina, March 13, 1710, ANCR, C. 187, fol. 5.

2. Declaración de Nicolasa, negra de casta mina, Cartago, September 6, 1719, ANCR, C. 244, quoting from fol. 2; Declaración del Alf. Bernardo Pacheco, Cartago, June 18, 1720, ANCR, C. 244, fol. 17v.

3. Per O. Hernæs, *Slaves, Danes, and African Coast Society: The Danish Slave Trade from West Africa and Afro-Danish Relations on the Eighteenth-Century Gold Coast* (Trondheim, Norway: Department of History, University of Trondheim, 1995), 173–303; E. Gøbel, "Danish Trade to the West Indies and Guinea, 1671-1754," *Scandinavian Economic History Review* 33, nos. 1-3 (1985): 21; Georg Nørregård, "Forliset ved Nicaragua 1710" (The shipwreck off Nicaragua, 1710), in *Årbog 1948* (Helsingør, Denmark: Handels-og Søfartsmuseet på Kronborg, 1948), 69.

4. Gøbel, "Danish Trade," 24; Waldemar Westergaard, *The Danish West Indies Under Company Rule (1671–1754), with a Supplementary Chapter, 1755-1917* (New York: Macmillan, 1917), 149, 150.

5. Westergaard, *Danish West Indies*, 151; Jean Barbot, *Barbot on Guinea: The Writings of Jean Barbot on West Africa, 1678–1712*, ed. P. E. H. Hair, Adam Jones, and Robin Law, 2 vols. (London: Hakluyt Society, 1992), 2:560; Christopher DeCorse, "The Danes on the Gold Coast: Culture Change and the European Presence," *African Archaeological Review* 11 (1993): 153, 155; see also Extract from the Minutes of the Meeting of the Directors of the Chamber, Zeeland, February 7, 1730, Document 276, in A. Van Dantzig, ed., *The Dutch and the*

Guinea Coast, 1674-1742: A Collection of Documents from the General State Archive at The Hague (Accra: Ghana Academy of Arts and Sciences, 1978), 239.

6. Gøbel, "Danish Trade," 37; John J. McCusker, *Money and Exchange in Europe and America, 1600-1775: A Handbook* (Chapel Hill: University of North Carolina Press, 1992), 84-85, table 2.20.

7. Nørregård, "Forliset ved Nicaragua," 70.

8. Johannes Rask, *A Brief and Truthful Description of a Journey to and from Guinea*, vol. 1 of *Two Views from Christiansborg Castle*, trans. and ed. Selena Axelrod Winsnes (Accra: Sub-Saharan Publishers, 2009), [2, 36] (bracketed page numbers indicate the pagination of the original Danish edition).

9. Ludewig Ferdinand Rømer, *A Reliable Account of the Coast of Guinea (1760)*, trans. and ed. Selena Axelrod Winsnes (Oxford: Oxford University Press for the British Academy, 2000), [253-55] (bracketed page numbers indicate the pagination of the original Danish edition); Georg Nørregård, *Danish Settlements in West Africa, 1658-1850*, trans. Sigurd Mammen (Boston, MA: Boston University Press, 1966), 64-67; Nørregård, "Forliset ved Nicaragua," 70.

10. Rømer, *Reliable Account*, [254-55]; Gøbel, "Danish Trade," 29; Robin Law, *The Slave Coast of West Africa, 1550-1759* (Oxford: Clarendon Press, 1991), 43, 49-51, 181-82, 200-201.

11. Robin Law, *The Oyo Empire, c. 1600- c. 1836: A West African Imperialism in the Era of the Atlantic Slave Trade* (Oxford: Clarendon Press, 1977), 209; Law, *Slave Coast*, 199, 205; Gøbel, "Danish Trade," 30. Danish trader Ludewig Ferdinand Rømer, stationed on the Gold Coast in the 1740s, described the re-exported *slaplagerne* as "nothing but old, worn linen pieces. . . . I had seen people in Europe use better cloth to burn as tinder." Rømer, *Reliable Account*, [254].

12. Rask, *Brief and Truthful Description*, [6-15, 27-36]; Nørregård, "Forliset ved Nicaragua," 71.

13. Rask, *Brief and Truthful Description*, [37-39]; Nørregård, "Forliset ved Nicaragua," 71.

14. Lars Sundström, *The Exchange Economy of Pre-Colonial Africa* (New York: St. Martin's, 1974).

15. See the essays in Suzanne Miers and Igor Kopytoff, eds., *Slavery in Africa: Historical and Anthropological Perspectives* (Madison: University of Wisconsin Press, 1977).

16. G. Ugo Nwokeji, "African Conceptions of Gender and the Slave Traffic," *William and Mary Quarterly*, 3rd ser., 58, no. 1 (2001): 47-68; Herbert S. Klein, "African Women in the Atlantic Slave Trade," in *Women and Slavery in Africa*, ed. Claire C. Robertson and Martin A. Klein (Madison: University of Wisconsin Press, 1983), 28-38; Paul E. Lovejoy and David Richardson, "Competing Markets for Male and Female Slaves: Prices in the Interior of West Africa, 1780-1850," *International Journal of African Historical Studies* 28, no. 2 (1995): 261-94.

17. Joseph C. Miller, *Way of Death: Merchant Capitalism and the Angolan Slave Trade, 1730-1830* (Madison: University of Wisconsin Press, 1988), chap. 2; John K.

Thornton, *Africa and Africans in the Making of the Atlantic World, 1400–1680*, 2nd ed. (Cambridge: Cambridge University Press, 1998), chap. 3.

18. Thornton, *Africa and Africans*, 89–91; Law, *Slave Coast*, 167; Sandra E. Greene, *Gender, Ethnicity and Social Change on the Upper Slave Coast* (Portsmouth, NH: Heinemann, 1996), 23–24; Susan Herlin Broadhead, "Slave Wives, Free Sisters: Bakongo Women and Slavery c. 1700–1850," in *Women and Slavery in Africa*, ed. Claire C. Robinson and Martin A. Klein (Madison: University of Wisconsin Press, 1984), 179; Edna G. Bay, "Servitude and Worldly Success in the Palace of Dahomey," in *Women and Slavery in Africa*, ed. Claire C. Robinson and Martin A. Klein (Madison: University of Wisconsin Press, 1984), 354; Anne Hilton, *The Kingdom of Kongo* (Oxford: Clarendon Press, 1985), 188.

19. Claire C. Robertson, "Post-Proclamation Slavery in Accra: A Female Affair?" in *Women and Slavery in Africa*, ed. Claire C. Robertson and Martin A. Klein (Madison: University of Wisconsin Press, 1983), 225; John K. Thornton, *The Kingdom of Kongo: Civil War and Transition, 1641–1718* (Madison: University of Wisconsin Press, 1983), 22.

20. Rosalyn Terborg-Penn, "Women and Slavery in the African Diaspora: A Cross-Cultural Approach to Historical Analysis," *Sage* 3, no. 2 (1986): 11–14.

21. John K. Thornton, "Cannibals, Witches, and Slave Traders in the Atlantic World," *William and Mary Quarterly*, 3rd ser., 60, no. 2 (April 2003): 273–94; Walter Hawthorne, *From Africa to Brazil: Culture, Identity, and an Atlantic Slave Trade, 1600–1830* (Cambridge: Cambridge University Press, 2010), 81–90; Michael A. Gomez, *Exchanging Our Country Marks: The Transformation of African Identities in the Colonial and Antebellum South* (Chapel Hill: University of North Carolina Press, 1998), 154; Miller, *Way of Death*, 400–401; Clarence J. Munford, *The Black Ordeal of Slavery and Slave Trading in the French West Indies, 1625–1715*, 3 vols. (Lewiston, NY: Edwin Mellen Press, 1991), 2:296.

22. Joseph C. Miller, "Retention, Reinvention, and Remembering: Restoring Identities Through Enslavement in Africa and Under Slavery in Brazil," in *Enslaving Connections: Changing Cultures of Africa and Brazil During the Era of Slavery*, ed. José Curto and Paul E. Lovejoy (New York: Humanity Books, 2004), 83.

23. Law, *Slave Coast*, 224–28; Peter C. W. Gutkind, "The Canoemen of the Gold Coast (Ghana): A Survey and an Explanation in Precolonial African Labour History," *Cahiers d'Études Africaines* 29, nos. 3–4 (1989): 339–76; Patrick Manning, "Merchants, Porters and Canoemen in the Bight of Benin: Links in the West African Trade Network," in *The Workers of African Trade*, ed. Catherine Coquery-Vidrovitch and Paul E. Lovejoy (Beverly Hills, CA: Sage, 1985), 51–74.

24. Nørregård, "Forliset ved Nicaragua," 71; Rask, *Brief and Truthful Description*, [47].

25. Munford, *Black Ordeal*, 2:301–3; Westergaard, *Danish West Indies*, 143; Rømer, *Reliable Account*, quoting from [268], also see 199n30.

26. Governor Erich Lygaard, Christiansborg, to the Directors of the West India and Guinea Company, Copenhagen, May 3, 1709, Document V.18, in Ole Justesen, ed., *Danish Sources for the History of Ghana 1657–1754*, trans. James Manley, 2 vols.

(Copenhagen: Det Kongelinge Danske Videnskabernes Selskab/Royal Danish Academy of Sciences and Letters, 2005), 1:216.

27. Ray A. Kea, "'I Am Here to Plunder on the General Road': Bandits and Banditry in the Pre-Nineteenth Century Gold Coast," in *Banditry, Rebellion, and Social Protest in Africa*, ed. Donald Crummey (Portsmouth, NH: Heinemann, 1986), 121.

28. Kwame Yeboa Daaku, *Trade and Politics on the Gold Coast, 1600–1720: A Study of African Reaction to the European Trade* (Oxford: Clarendon Press, 1970), 5, but see also Hernæs's argument against the "gun-slave circle theory" in *Slaves, Danes, and African Coast Society*, 369–89.

29. Kea, "'I Am Here to Plunder,'" 119; Ray A. Kea, *Settlements, Trade, and Polities on the Seventeenth-Century Gold Coast* (Baltimore, MD: Johns Hopkins University Press, 1982), 36.

30. Barbot, *Barbot on Guinea*, 2:482–83; J. K. Fynn, *Asante and Its Neighbors, 1700–1807* (Evanston, IL: Northwestern University Press, 1971), 7, 13, 21; Daaku, *Trade and Politics*, 25, 27; Kea, *Settlements, Trade, and Polities*, 49, 50; John Parker, *Making the Town: Ga State and Society in Early Colonial Accra* (Portsmouth, NH: Heinemann, 2000), quoting from 6.

31. Greene, *Gender, Ethnicity and Social Change*, 24.

32. Erick Tilleman, *A Short and Simple Account of the Country Guinea and Its Nature (1697)*, trans. and ed. Selena Axelrod Winsnes (Madison: African Studies Program, University of Wisconsin–Madison, 1994), 25; Nørregård, *Danish Settlements*, 43–44; Ivor Wilks, "The Rise of the Akwamu Empire, 1650–1710," *Transactions of the Historical Society of Ghana* 3, no. 2 (1957): 104.

33. William Bosman, *A New and Accurate Description of the Coast of Guinea, Divided into the Gold, the Slave, and the Ivory Coasts* (London: James Knapton, 1709), 69, as corrected in Albert Van Dantzig, "English Bosman and Dutch Bosman: A Comparison of Texts, Part 2," *History in Africa* 3 (1976): 95; cf. Barbot, *Barbot on Guinea*, 2:431.

34. Barbot, *Barbot on Guinea*, 2:434; Rømer, *Reliable Account*, [215].

35. Johannes M. Postma, *The Dutch in the Atlantic Slave Trade, 1600–1815* (Cambridge: Cambridge University Press, 1990), 114–15.

36. C. C. Reindorf, *The History of the Gold Coast and Asante* (Basel, Switzerland: printed by author, 1895), 64; Reindorf, *The History of the Gold Coast and Asante*, 2nd ed. (Accra: Ghana Universities Press, 1966), 62.

37. Tilleman, *Short and Simple Account*, 28; Fynn, *Asante and Its Neighbours*, 21.

38. Daaku, *Trade and Politics*, 31.

39. Barbot, *Barbot on Guinea*, 2:436; Greene, *Gender, Ethnicity, and Social Change*, 20; Robin Law, "Between the Sea and the Lagoons: The Interaction of Maritime and Inland Navigation on the Pre-Colonial Slave Coast," *Cahiers d'Études Africaines* 29, no. 2 (no. 114) (1989): 213.

40. Nørregård, *Danish Settlements*, 67; Fynn, *Asante and Its Neighbours*, 22.

41. Rømer, *Reliable Account*, [122, 125–26]; Reindorf, *History of the Gold Coast*, 64; Kea, "'I Am Here to Plunder,'" 122.

42. Bosman, *New and Accurate Description*, 64; Kea, "'I Am Here to Plunder,'" 126–27; Daaku, *Trade and Politics*, 31.

43. Rømer, *Reliable Account*, quoting from [122, see also 131–32]; Reindorf, *History of the Gold Coast*, 73; 2nd ed., 62, 71; Fynn, *Asante and Its Neighbours*, 67.

44. Bosman, *New and Accurate Description*, 326; Lygaard, Christiansborg, to the Directors, Copenhagen, February 23, 1708, Document V.15, in Justesen, *Danish Sources*, 1:212; Lygaard to the Directors, July 14, 1708, Document V.16, in Justesen, *Danish Sources*, 1:214; Fynn, *Asante and Its Neighbours*, 67–68, quoting from 68; Nørregård, *Danish Settlements*, 67.

45. Lygaard to the Directors, May 3, 1709, Document V.18, in Justesen, *Danish Sources*, 1:216; Reindorf, *History of the Gold Coast*, 71; 2nd ed., 68–69; Nørregård, *Danish Settlements*, 67–68. See also Rømer, *Reliable Account*, [129–30].

46. Lygaard to the Directors, Christiansborg, May 3, 1709, Document V.18, in Justesen, *Danish Sources*, quoting from 1:216; Daaku, *Trade and Politics*, 155.

47. Reindorf, *History of the Gold Coast*, 71; 2nd ed., 69; Lygaard to the Directors, Christiansborg, May 3, 1709, Document V.18, in Justesen, *Danish Sources*, 1:216; Nørregård, *Danish Settlements*, 67; Nørregård, "Forliset ved Nicaragua," 72.

48. Lygaard to the Directors, Christiansborg, May 3, 1709, Document V.18, in Justesen, *Danish Sources*, quoting from 1:216, see also 217. Johannes Rask recorded that the *Fredericus Quartus* stopped at Fort Crevecoeur, the Dutch factory at Accra, on April 27, implying a slightly later arrival at Christiansborg. Rask, *Brief and Truthful Description*, [65].

49. Tilleman, *Short and Simple Account*, 34; Lygaard to the Directors, Christiansborg, May 3, 1709, Document V.18, in Justesen, *Danish Sources*, 1:216; Rask, *Brief and Truthful Description*, [66].

50. Nørregård, *Danish Settlements*, 42.

51. Gutkind, "Canoemen of the Gold Coast," 345.

52. John Barbot, *A Description of the Coasts of North and South Guinea, and of Ethiopia Inferior, Vulgarly Angola*, in *A Collection of Voyages and Travels*, ed. Awnsham Churchill and John Churchill, 6 vols. (London: By Assignment for Messrs. Churchill, 1732), 5:266. "Mina" refers to an African from the Gold Coast or possibly the upper Slave Coast.

53. Lygaard to the Directors, Christiansborg, August 19, 1709, Document V.20, in Justesen, *Danish Sources*, 1:222.

54. According to Rask, the *Fredericus Quartus* "weighed anchor and sailed from" Christiansborg on June 28 "in order to go farther along the coast where they might succeed in trading for some slaves," but returned on June 14 [*sic*; actually July], "having had little or no success in trade." *Brief and Truthful Description*, [67, 68].

55. Erich Lygaard to the Directors, Christiansborg, August 19, 1709, Document V.20, in Justesen, *Danish Sources*, 1:222; David Eltis, *The Rise of African Slavery in the Americas* (Cambridge: Cambridge University Press, 2000), 105.

56. Erich Lygaard to the Directors, Christiansborg, October 5, 1709, Document V.23, in Justesen, *Danish Sources*, 1:225.

57. Law, *Slave Coast*, 21, 219–20; Sandra E. Greene, "Cultural Zones in the Era of the Slave Trade: Exploring the Yoruba Connection with Anlo-Ewe," in *Identity in the Shadow of Slavery*, ed. Paul E. Lovejoy (London: Continuum, 2000), 92; S. Wilson, "Aperçu historique sur les peuples et cultures dans le Golfe du Bénin: Le cas des 'mina' d'Anécho," in *Peuples du golfe du Bénin: Aja-éwé (colloque de Cotonou)*, ed. François de Medeiros (Paris: Karthala, 1984), 133, 141.

58. Greene, "Cultural Zones," 88, 98; Greene, *Gender, Ethnicity, and Social Change*, 37; Law, "Between the Sea and the Lagoons," 217–18; Law, *Slave Coast*, 42.

59. Bosman, *New and Accurate Description*, 330; see also Greene, "Cultural Zones," 92, 97; Law, *Slave Coast*, 143.

60. Greene, *Gender, Ethnicity, and Social Change*, 35–37.

61. Governor Erich Lygaard, Christiansborg, to Directors of the West India and Guinea Company, Copenhagen, August 19, 1709, Document V.20, in Justesen, *Danish Sources*, 1:222; Nørregård, "Forliset ved Nicaragua," 74.

62. Voyages Database, Voyages: The Trans-Atlantic Slave Trade Database, 2009, http://slavevoyages.org/tast/database/search.faces?yearFrom=1699&yearTo=1709&mjbyptimp=60515&natinimp=.

63. Law, *Slave Coast*, 207–8.

64. Bosman, *New and Accurate Description*, 364.

65. Delbée, "Journal du voyage du Sieur Delbée," in *Relation de ce qui s'est passé dans les isles et Terre-ferme de l'Amerique pendant la dernière guerre avec l'Angleterre. . .* , ed. J. de Clodoré, 2 vols. (Paris: G. Clouzier, 1671), 2:436; Law, *Slave Coast*, 184.

66. Bosman, *New and Accurate Description*, 343; Law, *Slave Coast*, quoting from 185, 186; Law, *The Kingdom of Allada* (Leiden, Netherlands: Research School CNWS, School of Asian, African, and Amerindian Studies, 1997), 90, 101, 105.

67. Law, *Slave Coast*, 348.

68. Law, *Oyo Empire*, 219, 226; see also Robin Law and Paul E. Lovejoy, "Borgu in the Atlantic Slave Trade," *African Economic History* 27 (1999): 74–75.

69. Jan De Paauw to Assembly of Ten, Ouidah, February 11, 1709, Document 158, in Van Dantzig, *Dutch and the Guinea Coast*, 141.

70. Law, *Slave Coast*, 76.

71. Ibid., 90.

72. Robin Law, "Ideologies of Royal Power: The Dissolution and Reconstruction of Political Authority on the 'Slave Coast,' 1680–1750," *Africa* 57, no. 3 (1987): 337.

73. Law, *Slave Coast*, 91, 103, 255.

74. Law, *Kingdom of Allada*, 56; Law, *Slave Coast*, 254–55.

75. Law, *Slave Coast*, 252; Jan De Paauw to Assembly of Ten, Ouidah, September 6, 1709, Document 159, in Van Dantzig, *Dutch and the Guinea Coast*, 143.

76. Erich Lygaard, Christiansborg, to the Directors of the West India and Guinea Company, Copenhagen, October 5, 1709, Document V.23, in Justesen, *Danish Sources*, 1:225.

77. Eltis, *Rise of African Slavery*, 105; Erich Lygaard to the Directors, Christiansborg, January 14, 1710, Document V.25, in Justesen, *Danish Sources*, 1:227.

78. Rask, *Brief and Truthful Description*, quoting from [75–76]; Nørregård, "Forliset ved Nicaragua," 75; Nørregård, *Danish Settlements*, 89; Thomas Phillips, "A Journal of a Voyage Made in the *Hannibal* of London, 1693–1694," in *A Collection of Voyages and Travels*, ed. Awnsham Churchill and John Churchill (London: By Assignment for Messrs. Churchill, 1732), quoting from 6:219.

79. Erich Lygaard to the Directors, Christiansborg, January 14, 1710, Document V.25, in Justesen, *Danish Sources*, 1:227.

80. Ibid.; Rask, *Brief and Truthful Description*, [75].

81. John M. Janzen and Wyatt MacGaffey, *An Anthology of Kongo Religion: Primary Texts from Lower Zaïre* (Lawrence: University of Kansas Press, 1974), 34; Hilton, *Kingdom of Kongo*, 9.

82. Phillips, "Journal of a Voyage," 6:230–232; Bosman, *New and Accurate Description*, 399–400, 413; Nørregård, "Forliset ved Nicaragua," 76; Munford, *Black Ordeal*, 2:275, 277, 302.

83. Nørregård, "Forliset ved Nicaragua," 76.

84. Ibid., 76, 78.

85. Ibid., 78.

86. Ibid., 86–87.

87. Ibid., 78–79.

88. Voyages Database.

89. Nørregård, "Forliset ved Nicaragua," 81. The Danish sailors evidently believed they had landed in Nicaragua—an error repeated by Nørregård in the name of his article. "Punta Carreta" (sometimes "Punta Carreto") is another name for Punta Mona (Monkey Point) in Limón Province, Costa Rica. See *Costa Rica-Panama Arbitration: Documents Annexed to the Argument of Costa Rica . . .* (Rosslyn, VA: Commonwealth, 1913), 4:56–58. But see also Stephen J. Gluckman, "Preliminary Investigations of a Shipwreck, Pumpata Cahuita National Park, Costa Rica," in *Maritime Archaeology: A Reader of Substantive and Theoretical Contributions*, ed. Lawrence E. Babbits and Hans Van Tilburg (New York: Plenum Press, 1998), 453–67, for another possible site.

90. Nørregård, "Forliset ved Nicaragua," 79–83.

91. Ibid., 83–84, 88–89.

92. For a full account, see Carlos Roberto López Leal, "Una rebelión indígena en Talamanca: Pablo Presbere y el alzamiento general de 1709" (Licenciatura thesis, Universidad de San Carlos de Guatemala, 1973).

93. The best historical work on the Miskitu in this period is by Karl Offen, including "The Miskitu Kingdom Landscape and the Emergence of a Miskitu Ethnic Identity, Northeastern Nicaragua and Honduras, 1600–1800" (PhD diss., University of Texas at Austin, 1999); Offen, "The Sambo and Tawira Miskitu: The Colonial Origins and Geography of Intra-Miskitu Differentiation in Eastern Nicaragua and Honduras," *Ethnohistory* 49, no. 2 (2002): 319–72; Offen, "Creating Mosquitia: Mapping Amerindian Spatial Practices in Eastern Central America, 1629–1779," *Journal of Historical Geography* 33 (2007): 254–82; Offen, "Race and

Place in Colonial Mosquitia," in *Blacks and Blackness in Central America: Between Race and Place*, ed. Lowell Gudmundson and Justin Wolfe (Durham, NC: Duke University Press, 2010), 92–129.

94. Germán Romero Vargas, *Las sociedades del atlántico de Nicaragua en los siglos XVII y XVIII* (Managua: Fondo de Promoción Cultural–BANIC, 1995), 25, 27, 30; Troy S. Floyd, *The Anglo-Spanish Struggle for Mosquitia* (Albuquerque: University of New Mexico Press, 1967), 19.

95. Romero Vargas, *Sociedades del atlántico*, 41, 136, 150, 276, 310–11; Mary W. Helms, "Miskito Slaving and Culture Contact: Ethnicity and Opportunity in an Expanding Population," *Journal of Anthropological Research* 39, no. 2 (1983): 179–97.

96. Declaración del Cap. don José Pérez de Muro, Cartago, November 12, 1705, Archivo General de Indias (hereafter AGI), Escribanía 351B, pieza 1, fol. 165v.

97. Declaración de Suyntin, indio mosquito, Cartago, May 2, 1710, ANCR, C. 187, fols. 82v–83; Declaración de Antonio, indio mosquito, Cartago, May 2, 1710, ANCR, C. 187, fols. 86v–87, quoting from fol. 87.

98. For Miskitu slaving of the Talamanca and other indigenous peoples, see Helms, "Miskito Slaving and Culture Contact"; Romero Vargas, *Sociedades del atlántico*.

99. Declaración de Suyntin; Declaración de Antonio; Segunda declaración de Suyntin y Antonio, indios mosquitos, Cartago, May 3, 1710, ANCR, C. 187, fols. 91–94.

100. Declaración de Antonio, fols. 88–88v.

101. Figures calculated from Nørregård, "Forliset ved Nicaragua," 85.

102. John Alexander Holm, "The Creole English of Nicaragua's Miskitu Coast: Its Sociolinguistic History and a Comparative Study of Its Lexicon and Syntax" (PhD thesis, University of London, 1978), 186.

103. Declaración de Alfonso Ramírez, Cartago, April 19, 1710, ANCR, C. 187, fols. 38v–42v; Carta de Gaspar de Acosta Arévalo, Matina, March 13, 1710, ANCR, C. 187, fol. 3; Carta de Francisco Martínez, Matina, March 13, 1710, ANCR, C. 187, fol. 5.

104. Auto de noticia de 24 negros, Cartago, March 22, 1710, ANCR, C. 187, fol. 9; Declaración de Gaspar de Acosta Arévalo, Cartago, April 16, 1710, ANCR, C. 187, fols. 26–30; Declaración de Diego Oviedo, Cartago, April 16, 1710, ANCR, C. 187, fols. 30v–33v.

105. Avalúo de negros, Cartago, April 23, 1710, ANCR, C. 187, fols. 47–49.

106. Inventario de negros, Cartago, April 14, 1710, ANCR, C. 187, fols. 12–13v.

107. Depósito de los negros en Juan López de la Rea y Soto, Cartago, April 14, 1710, ANCR, C. 187, fols. 14–15.

108. Auto de la entrega de 10 negros por Gaspar de Acosta Arévalo, Cartago, May 2, 1710, ANCR, C. 187, fols. 52–52v; Inventario de los negros y su depósito en Juan López de la Rea y Soto, Cartago, May 2, 1710, ANCR, C. 187, fols. 53–54v.

109. Declaración de Antonio de Soto y Barahona, Cartago, May 1, 1710, ANCR, C. 187, fols. 77–79; Declaración de Juan Bautista Retana, Cartago, May 11, 1710, ANCR, C. 187, fol. 107v; Inventario de negros, Cartago, May 1, 1710, ANCR, C. 187, fols. 69v–70v.

110. Inventario de negros, Cartago, May 11, 1710, ANCR, C. 187, fols. 97–100v.
111. Carta de Juan Francisco de Ibarra y Calvo, Moín, April 27, 1710, ANCR, C. 187, fols. 64v–65.
112. Inventario de 16 negros y negras, Cartago, June 11, 1710, ANCR, C. 187, fols. 147–49.
113. Declaración de Juan Francisco de Ibarra y Calvo, Cartago, June 11, 1710, ANCR, C. 187, quoting from fol. 156v, see also fol. 157; Declaración de Bernardo Pacheco, Cartago, June 17, 1710, ANCR, C. 187, fol. 186.
114. Declaración de Matías Trejos, Cartago, November 6, 1719, ANCR, Sección Colonial Guatemala (hereafter G.) 185, fols. 81v–82v.
115. Nombramiento de Francisco de casta arará, esclavo del Cap. Francisco de la Madriz Linares, como intérprete, Cartago, April 14, 1710, ANCR, C. 187, fol. 17v.
116. Declaración de Juan, negro bozal, Cartago, April 16, 1710, ANCR, C. 187, fol. 18v.
117. Ibid., fols. 18v–19.
118. Ibid., fol. 19.
119. Ibid., fols. 18v–20v.
120. Compare the Declaración de Nicolás, negro bozal de casta arará, Cartago, April 16, 1710, ANCR, C. 187, fols. 21–23, and the Declaración de Miguel, negro bozal de casta arará, Cartago, April 16, 1710, ANCR, C. 187, fols. 23v–25v.
121. Declaración de Juan, fol. 19; Declaración de Nicolás, fol. 21v; Declaración de Miguel, fol. 24.
122. Declaración de Juan, fol. 19; Declaración de Nicolás, fol. 21v; Declaración de Miguel, fol. 24v.
123. Nørregård, "Forliset ved Nicaragua," 92, 96.
124. Memoria de los bienes del Cap. Pedro de Ibáñez, Cartago, May 16, 1702, ANCR, Mortuales Coloniales de Cartago 849, fol. 14; Testamento de doña Manuela de Quirós, otorgado por su marido el Sarg. Mayor Francisco de la Madriz Linares, Cartago, June 5, 1716, ANCR, Protocolos Coloniales de Cartago 878, fol. 85.
125. Declaración de Juan, fol. 19; Declaración de Nicolás, fol. 18v.
126. Declaración de Felipe Cubero, negro de casta congo, Matina, December 4, 1719, ANCR, C. 243, fol. 8v.
127. Declaración de Antonio Civitola, negro de casta congo, Cartago, December 18, 1719, ANCR, C. 259, fol. 5v.
128. Declaración de Micaela, negra de casta aná, Cartago, September 5, 1719, ANCR, G. 187, fol. 2.
129. See also "coger" in Real Academia Española, *Diccionario de autoridades*, 3 vols. (Madrid: Editorial Gredos, 1963, originally published in 1726 in 6 vols.), [2:397–98], 1:397–98 (1963 ed.).
130. Declaración de Miguel Largo, negro esclavo, Cartago, June 30, 1720, ANCR, C. 240, fol. 21.
131. Paul E. Lovejoy and David V. Trotman, "Enslaved Africans and Their Expectations of Slave Life in the Americas: Towards a Reconsideration of Models of 'Creolisation,'" in *Questioning Creole: Creolisation Discourses in Caribbean*

Culture, ed. Verene A. Shepherd and Glen L. Richards (Kingston, Jamaica: Ian Randle Publishers, 2002), 67–91.

132. See also "hurtar," "hurtado," and "hurto" in Real Academia Española, [4:194–98], 2:194–98.

133. Robin Law, *The Slave Coast of West Africa, 1550-1759* (Oxford: Clarendon Press, 1991), 111.

134. Ibid., 332; Melville J. Herskovits, *Dahomey: An Ancient West African Kingdom*, 2 vols. (New York: J. J. Augustin, 1938), 2:151, 153; P. Mercier, "The Fon of Dahomey," in *African Worlds: Studies in the Cosmological Ideas and Social Values of African Peoples*, ed. Darryl Forde (London: Oxford University Press, 1954), 213, 214; Geoffrey Parrinder, *West African Religion: A Study of the Beliefs and Practices of Akan, Ewe, Yoruba, Ibo and Kindred Peoples*, 2nd ed. (New York: Barnes & Noble, 1970), 31.

135. Albert de Surgy, *Le système religieux des évhé* (Paris: Éditions L'Harmattan, 1988), 111–12; Parrinder, *West African Religion*, 31–32.

136. Herskovits, *Dahomey*, 2:153; Surgy, *Système religieux*, 118; Parrinder, *West African Religion*, 32.

137. J. Omosade Awolalu, *Yoruba Beliefs and Sacrificial Rites* (London: Longman, 1979), 35–36.

138. Dana Lynn Rush provides examples and an interpretation in "Vodun Vortex: Accumulative Arts, Histories, and Religious Consciousnesses Along Coastal Benin" (PhD diss., University of Iowa, 1997), chap. 2.

139. Robin Law, "Ethnicity and the Slave Trade: 'Lucumi' and 'Nago' as Ethnonyms in West Africa," *History in Africa* 24 (1997): 210.

140. Parrinder, *West African Religion*, 32; Awolalu, *Yoruba Beliefs*, 35, 36, 38; Herskovits, *Dahomey*, 2:164; Marc Schiltz, "Yoruba Thunder Deities and Sovereignty: Ara Versus Sango," *Anthropos* 80 (1985): 67–84, especially 67, 80.

141. Joan Wescott and Peter Morton-Williams wrote of devotees of Shango in twentieth-century Nigeria: "Although the worshippers conform to the conventions of Yoruba behaviour in avoiding violence and destructiveness . . . , there is good evidence that they have fantasies of them and attribute to themselves the magical control of the destructive force of lightning." Joan Wescott and Peter Morton-Williams, "The Symbolism and Ritual Context of the Yoruba *Laba Shango*," *Journal of the Royal Anthropological Institute* 92 (1962): 25, 27.

CHAPTER TWO

1. Declaración de Miguel Largo, Cartago, September 7, 1719, Archivo Nacional de Costa Rica, San José (hereafter ANCR), Sección Colonial Cartago (hereafter C.) 240, fol. 3.

2. Auto del gobernador, Cartago, May 7, 1720, ANCR, C. 240, fol. 5v.

3. Declaración de Miguel Largo, Cartago, June 30, 1720, ANCR, C. 240, fol. 21.

4. Katia M. de Queirós Mattoso, *To Be a Slave in Brazil*, trans. Arthur Goldhammer (New Brunswick, NJ: Rutgers University Press, 1986), 133.

5. Simon Bockie, *Death and the Invisible Powers: The World of Kongo Belief* (Bloomington: Indiana University Press, 1993), chap. 1.

6. Julian Bromley and Viktor Kozlov, "The Theory of Ethnos and Ethnic Processes in Soviet Social Sciences," *Comparative Studies in Society and History* 31, no. 3 (1989): 425–38.

7. Cf. Richard N. Adams, "Internal and External Ethnicities: With Special Reference to Central America," in *Estado, democratización y desarrollo en Centroamérica y Panamá*, ed. Manuel Rivera, Giovani Duarte, and María Dolores Marroquín (Guatemala: Asociación Centroamericana de Sociología [ACAS], 1989), 478.

8. See Wyatt MacGaffey, "Kongo Identity, 1483–1993," *South Atlantic Quarterly* 94, no. 4 (1995): 1028–29. The question of ethnicity in precolonial Africa and the diaspora in the era of the slave trade remains one of the most contentious in the field. For a good overview of the issues, see Kristin Mann, "Shifting Paradigms in the Study of the African Diaspora and of Atlantic History and Culture," *Slavery & Abolition* 22, no. 1 (2001): 3–21. One sophisticated statement is Joseph C. Miller's "Retention, Reinvention, and Remembering: Restoring Identities Through Enslavement in Africa and Under Slavery in Brazil," in *Enslaving Connections: Changing Cultures of Africa and Brazil During the Era of Slavery*, ed. José Curto and Paul E. Lovejoy (New York: Humanity Books, 2004), 81–121.

9. See Femi J. Kolapo, "The Igbo and Their Neighbours During the Era of the Atlantic Slave Trade," *Slavery & Abolition* 25, no. 1 (2004): 114–33.

10. Miller, "Retention, Reinvention, and Remembering," 88.

11. Douglas B. Chambers, "Tracing Igbo into the African Diaspora," in *Identity in the Shadow of Slavery*, ed. Paul E. Lovejoy (London: Continuum, 2000), 55.

12. Douglas B. Chambers, "Ethnicity in the Diaspora: The Slave-Trade and the Creation of African 'Nations' in the Americas," *Slavery & Abolition* 22, no. 3 (2001): 33. See also Michael A. Gomez, *Exchanging Our Country Marks: The Transformation of African Identities in the Colonial and Antebellum South* (Chapel Hill: University of North Carolina Press, 1998), 7; Miller, "Retention, Reinvention, and Remembering," 87; John K. Thornton, "The Coromantees: An African Cultural Group in Colonial North America and the Caribbean," *Journal of Caribbean History* 32, nos. 1–2 (1998): 161–62.

13. Gomez, *Exchanging Our Country Marks*; Miller, "Retention, Reinvention, and Remembering."

14. Paul E. Lovejoy, "Methodology through the Ethnic Lens: The Study of Atlantic Africa," in *Sources and Methods in African History: Spoken, Written, Unearthed*, ed. Toyin Falola and Christian Jennings (Rochester, NY: Rochester University Press, 2003), 103–17.

15. ANCR, Protocolos Coloniales de Cartago (hereafter, PC) 801 (1607)–940 (1746); ANCR, Protocolos Coloniales de Heredia (hereafter, PH) 573 (1721)–94 (1749);

ANCR, Protocolos Coloniales de San José (hereafter, PSJ) 411 (1721)–15 (1738); *Indice de los protocolos de Cartago*, 6 vols. (San José: Tipografía Nacional, 1909–1930), vols. 1–3 (1909–1911); *Indice de los protocolos de Heredia, 1721–1851* (San José: Tipografía Nacional, 1904); *Indice de los protocolos de San José, 1721–1836*, 2 vols. (San José: Tipografía Nacional, 1905).

16. Russell Lohse, "Slave-Trade Nomenclature and African Ethnicities in the Americas: Evidence from Early Eighteenth-Century Costa Rica," *Slavery & Abolition* 23, no. 3 (2002): 73–92.

17. Kolapo, "Igbo and Their Neighbours"; Miller, "Retention, Reinvention, and Remembering," 86–87.

18. Paul E. Lovejoy, "The African Diaspora: Revisionist Interpretations of Ethnicity, Culture and Religion Under Slavery." *Studies in the World History of Slavery, Abolition and Emancipation* 2, no. 1 (1997), http://ejournalofpoliticalscience.org/diaspora.html; Lohse, "Slave-Trade Nomenclature," 74.

19. Joseph C. Miller, "Central Africa During the Era of the Slave Trade, c. 1490s–1850s," in *Central Africans and Cultural Transformations in the American Diaspora*, ed. Linda Heywood (Cambridge: Cambridge University Press, 2002), 22.

20. Miller, "Retention, Reinvention, and Remembering," 91.

21. For the concept of "charter generations" of black immigrants to the New World, see Ira Berlin, *Many Thousands Gone: The First Two Centuries of Slavery in North America* (Cambridge, MA: Belknap Press of Harvard University Press, 1998), chaps. 1–2; Berlin, *Generations of Captivity: A History of African-American Slaves* (Cambridge, MA: Belknap Press of Harvard University Press, 2003), chap. 1.

22. Nicolás Ngou-Mve, *El Africa bantú en la colonización de México (1595–1640)* (Madrid: Consejo Superior de Investigaciones Científicas, Agencia Española de Cooperación Internacional, 1994); Paul Lokken, "From the 'Kingdoms of Angola' to Santiago de Guatemala: The Portuguese Asientos and Spanish Central America, 1595–1640," *Hispanic American Historical Review* 93, no. 2 (2013): 171–203; Carlos Sempat Assadourian, *El tráfico de esclavos en Córdoba, de Angola a Potosí: Siglos XVI–XVII* (Córdoba, Argentina: Universidad Nacional de Córdoba, 1966).

23. See Paul E. Lovejoy, *Transformations in Slavery: A History of Slavery in Africa*, 2nd ed. (Cambridge: Cambridge University Press, 2000), chap. 3.

24. "Relación (hecha por Diego de Porrás) de la gente e navíos que llevó a descubrir el almirante don Cristóbal Colón" (November 1504?), in Academia de Geografía e Historia de Costa Rica, *Colección de documentos para la historia de Costa Rica relativos al cuarto y último viaje de Cristóbal Colón* (San José: Atenea, 1952), 51; Juan Carlos Solórzano Fonseca and Claudia Quirós Vargas, *Costa Rica en el siglo XVI: Descubrimiento, exploración y conquista* (San José: Editorial de la Universidad de Costa Rica, 2006), 57.

25. "Real cédula para quel thesorero de la contratación pague las partidas aquí conthenidas, a las personas en ella declaradas, que fueron en el postrer viaxe a las Indias con el almirante Colón" (Salamanca, November 2, 1505), in Academia de Geografía e Historia de Costa Rica, *Colección de documentos*, 102.

26. T. Bentley Duncan, *The Atlantic Islands: Madeira, the Azores, and Cabo Verde in the Seventeenth Century* (Chicago, IL: University of Chicago Press, 1972), 212; José da Silva Horta, "Evidence for a Luso-African Identity in 'Portuguese' Accounts on 'Guinea of Cape Verde' (Sixteenth-Seventeenth Centuries)," *History in Africa* 27 (2000): 103; Walter Hawthorne, *From Africa to Brazil: Culture, Identity, and an Atlantic Slave Trade* (Cambridge: Cambridge University Press, 2010), 101–2.

27. Referring to a slightly later period, Matthew Restall asserts that most "black conquistadors" were African born but had spent some time in the Caribbean or Iberia before joining Spanish military expeditions. Matthew Restall, "Black Conquistadors: Armed Africans in Early Spanish America," *The Americas* 57, no. 2 (2000): 189, 190. It is no exaggeration to speak of an explosion in the scholarship of Spanish slavery in recent decades, both in quantity and quality. For the literature through 2000, see the bibliography in Aurelia Martín Casares's comprehensive *La esclavitud en la Granada del siglo XVI: Género, raza, religión* (Granada, Spain: Editorial Universidad de Granada, 2000). For Portugal, see A. C. de C. M. Saunders, *A Social History of Black Slaves and Freemen in Portugal, 1441–1555* (Cambridge: Cambridge University Press, 1982).

28. Robin Blackburn, *The Making of New World Slavery: From the Baroque to the Modern, 1492–1800* (London: Verso, 1997), 52; Lutgardo García Fuentes, "Licencias para la introducción de esclavos en Indias y envíos desde Sevilla en el siglo XVI," *Jahrbuch für Geschichte von Staat, Wirtschaft und Gesellschaft Lateinamerikas* 19 (1982): 1–46.

29. Antonio Herrera y Tordesillas, *Historia general de los hechos de los castellanos en las islas y tierra firme del mar océano*, dec. 1, bk. 4, chap. 12; 17 vols. (Madrid: Real Academia de la Historia, 1934), 3:96.

30. "Real cédula para quel thesorero," 102.

31. Cf. James Lockhart, *Spanish Peru, 1532–1560: A Social History*, 2nd ed. (Madison: University of Wisconsin Press, 1994), 197, 206–7.

32. Eduardo Pérez Valle, ed., *Nicaragua en los cronistas de Indias: Oviedo* (Managua: Fondo de Promoción Cultural, Banco de América, 1976), 74, 383, 385.

33. Ibid., 73–75, quoting from 74, 75.

34. Restall, "Black Conquistadors," 183.

35. García Fuentes, "Licencias para la introducción."

36. Carlos Meléndez, ed., *Reales cédulas relativas a la provincia de Costa Rica (1540–1802)*, quoting from 115; Licencia de Diego de Artieda para llevar esclavos, Madrid, January 19, 1575, Archivo General de Indias, Seville (hereafter AGI), Indiferente 2055, no. 4 bis.

37. Visita de dos naos y un patache que don Diego de Artieda y Chirinos, gobernador de Costa Rica, lleva a esas provincias, Sanlúcar de Barrameda, April 4, 1575, AGI, Patronato 259, ramo 61.

38. For one example, see León Fernández, ed., *Colección de documentos para la historia de Costa Rica*, 10 vols. (San José: Imprenta Nacional [vols. 1–3], Paris: Imprenta Pablo Dupont [vols. 4–5], Barcelona: Imprenta Viuda de Luis Tasso [vols. 6–10], 1881–1907), 6:128.

39. Fernández, *Colección de documentos*, 2:129, 140.
40. Studies suggest that mulattos comprised a majority of the slaves in Honduras and Nicaragua as well. Melida Velásquez, "El comercio de esclavos en la Alcaldía Mayor de Tegucigalpa, siglos XVI al XVIII," *Mesoamérica*, no. 42 (2001): 204, 209; Germán Romero Vargas, *Las estructuras sociales de Nicaragua en el siglo XVIII* (Managua: Editorial Vanguardia, 1988), 289, 292.
41. Without question, the overwhelming majority of people of African and indigenous descent in the Central Valley were classified as "mulato." For just one example, see Partida del bautizo de Juan, mulato, hijo legítimo de Gaspar, negro esclavo de doña Catalina de Grados, y de Juana, su mujer, india, Cartago, January 13, 1607, Archivo de la Curia Metropolitana de San José, Costa Rica (hereafter, ACMSJ), Libros de Bautizos de Cartago, no. 1/Family History Library, Salt Lake City, Utah (hereafter, FHL), VAULT INTL film 1219701, item 1.
42. Contrast with Michael A. Gomez's assertion that "first generation African American" children were "socialized within the slave community according to the only set of principles and ideals known to their parents—African ones. For all practical purposes, then, these progeny were much more African in outlook and culture than American." Gomez, *Exchanging Our Country Marks*, 193.
43. In their pioneering essay, Sidney W. Mintz and Richard Price argued that the Saramaka Maroons established the basic and most important elements of their culture within the first two decades of their escape from slavery in Suriname. Sidney W. Mintz and Richard Price, *The Birth of African-American Culture: An Anthropological Perspective* (Boston, MA: Beacon Press, 1992), 49–50. Ira Berlin's elaboration of the "Atlantic creoles" and "charter generations" builds on their insights. Berlin, *Many Thousands Gone*, chaps. 1–2.
44. Alfonso Franco Silva, *Regesto documental sobre la esclavitud sevillana (1453–1513)* (Seville: Publicaciones de la Universidad de Sevilla, 1979); V. Cortés Alonso, "Procedencia de los esclavos negros en Valencia, 1482–1516," *Revista Española de Antropología Americana* 7 (1972): 123–51; P. E. H. Hair, "Black African Slaves at Valencia, 1482–1516: An Onomastic Inquiry," *History in Africa* 7 (1980): 120; Hair, "An Ethnolinguistic Inventory of the Upper Guinea Coast Before 1700," *African Language Review* 6 (1967): 32; Stephan Bühnen, "Ethnic Origins of Peruvian Slaves (1548–1650): Figures for Upper Guinea," *Paideuma* 39 (1993): 76.
45. Martin A. Klein, "Servitude Among the Wolof and Sereer of Senegambia," in *Slavery in Africa: Historical and Anthropological Perspectives*, ed. Suzanne Miers and Igor Kopytoff (Madison: University of Wisconsin Press, 1977), 336–37; Valentim Fernandes, quoted in Richard Jobson, *Discovery of the River Gambra (1623)*, ed. David P. Gamble and P. E. H. Hair (London: Hakluyt Society, 1999), 267; João de Barros, *Ásia, primeira década*, in Jobson, *Discovery*, 271; James F. Searing, *West African Slavery and Atlantic Commerce: The Senegal River Valley, 1700–1860* (Cambridge: Cambridge University Press, 1993), 10.
46. Boubacar Barry, *Senegambia and the Atlantic Slave Trade*, trans. Ayi Kwei Armah (Cambridge: Cambridge University Press, 1998), 35.

47. Jobson, *Discovery of the River Gambra*, 111n2; Boubacar Barry, *Le royaume de Waalo, 1659-1859: Le Sénégal avant la conquête* (Paris: François Maspero, 1972), 67.

48. Andrés Vega Bolaños, ed., *Colección Somoza: Documentos para la historia de Nicaragua*, 17 vols. (Madrid, 1945-1957), 6:495, 497.

49. Declaración de Leandro de Figueroa, corregidor de Pacaca, Cartago, October 9, 1609, Archivo General de la Nación, Mexico (hereafter AGN), Fondo Documental Inquisición (hereafter Inq.), vol. 292, exp. 25, fols. 92v-93v; Declaración de Juan de Buliaga, Santiago de Guatemala, March 16, 1610, AGN, Inq., vol. 474, exp. 6, fol. 333; Declaración de Francisco de Salas, Cartago, October 13, 1609, AGN, Inq., vol. 292, exp. 25, quoting from fol. 102v.

50. Partida de bautizo, January 6, 1619; ACMSJ, Libros de Bautizos de Cartago (hereafter, LBC), no. 1/FHL, VAULT INTL film 1219701, item 1; Partida de confirmación, Cartago, March 26, 1625, ACMSJ, Libro de Confirmaciones 1 (1609-1625)/ FHL, VAULT INTL film 1219727, item 2.

51. Sylviane Anna Diouf, "Devils or Sorcerers, Muslims or Studs: Manding in the Americas," in *Trans-Atlantic Dimensions of Ethnicity in the African Diaspora*, ed. Paul E. Lovejoy and David V. Trotman (London: Continuum, 2003), 139-41.

52. D. T. Niane, "Mali and the Second Mandingo Expansion," in *Africa from the Twelfth to the Sixteenth Century*, vol. 4 of *General History* of Africa, ed. D. T. Niane (Paris: UNESCO, 1984), 153-57.

53. Walter Rodney, "Upper Guinea and the Significance of Origins of Africans Enslaved in the New World," *Journal of Negro History* 54 (1969): 332-33, 335; Bühnen, "Ethnic Origins," 75, 76; José da Silva Horta, "La perception du mandé et de l'identité mandingue dans les textes européens, 1453-1508," *History in Africa* 23 (1996): 75-86; André Álvares de Almada, *Tratado breve dos rios de Guiné (c. 1594)*, in Jobson, *Discovery*, 281; Niane, "Mali and the Second," 4:119, 156.

54. Diouf, "Devils or Sorcerers," 148-151; Christopher Fyfe, *A History of Sierra Leone* (London: Oxford University Press, 1962), 6; Walter Rodney, "Jihad and Social Revolution in Futa Djalon in the Eighteenth Century," *Journal of the Historical Society of Nigeria* 4, no. 2 (1968): 273n2.

55. Gomez, *Exchanging Our Country Marks*, 39; Philip D. Curtin, *The Atlantic Slave Trade: A Census* (Madison: University of Wisconsin Press, 1969), 184-85; Rodney, "Upper Guinea," quoting from 335.

56. Gwendolyn Midlo Hall, *Africans in Colonial Louisiana: The Development of Afro-Creole Culture in the Eighteenth Century* (Baton Rouge: Louisiana State University Press, 1992), 41, 42; Searing, *West African Slavery*, 29; Paul Lovejoy, "Slavery, the Bilad al-Sudan and the Frontiers of the African Diaspora," in *Slavery on the Frontiers of Islam*, ed. Paul Lovejoy (Princeton, NJ: Markus Wiener, 2004), 14.

57. Gomez, *Exchanging Our Country Marks*, 39, quoting from 88, 88-89; Curtin, *Atlantic Slave Trade*, 184-85.

58. David Dalby, "Distribution and Nomenclature of the Manding People and Their

Language," in *Papers on the Manding*, ed. Carleton T. Hodge (Bloomington: Indiana University Press, 1971), 1–13.

59. Mervyn Hiskett, *The Development of Islam in West Africa* (New York: Longman, 1984), 30–31, 45, 139; Lamin O. Sanneh, *The Jakhanke Muslim Clerics: A Religious and Historical Study of Islam in Senegambia* (Lanham, MD: University Press of America, 1989), 12.

60. *Indice de los protocolos de Cartago*, 6 vols. (San José: Imprenta Nacional, 1909–1930), 1:169; Certificación del Cap. José Antonio de Espinosa, vecino de Panamá y tratante en Costa Rica, Cartago, February 3, 1716, ANCR, PC 875, fols. 38–39; Capital de bienes de doña Agueda Pérez del Muro en ocasión de su casamiento al Cap. don Francisco Garrido Berlanga, Cartago, April 16, 1722, ANCR, PC 895, fol. 51v; Venta de esclavo, Cartago, January 19, 1719, ANCR, PC 887, fols. 10–11v; Declaración del negro Jacob, esclavo del Cap. Antonio de Soto y Barahona, de casta mandinga, Cartago, October 2, 1719, ANCR, C. 233, fol. 5v; Petición del Cap. Antonio de Soto y Barahona, presentada en Cartago, May 20, 1720, ANCR, C. 233, fol. 34.

61. Venta de esclavo, Cartago, January 22, 1674, ANCR, PC 822, fols. 5–6; Partida de bautizo, Cartago, January 6, 1679, ACMSJ, LBC, no. 1/FHL, VAULT INTL film 1219701, item 1; Gonzalo Aguirre Beltrán, *La población negra de México, 1519–1810: Estudio etno-histórico*, 2nd ed. (Mexico City Fondo de Cultura Económica, 1972), 115. For an excellent analysis of the slave trade in the Guinea-Bissau region, including changes in the ethnic origins of those enslaved, see Walter Hawthorne, "The Production of Slaves Where There Was No State: The Guinea-Bissau Region, c. 1450–c. 1950," *Slavery & Abolition* 20 (1999): 97–124.

62. Hawthorne, *From Africa to Brazil*.

63. Alonso de Sandoval, *Un tratado sobre la esclavitud*, ed. Enriqueta Vila Vilar (Madrid: Alianza Editorial, 1987, originally published 1627), 137–38; Rodney, "Upper Guinea," 338.

64. P. E. H. Hair, "Ethnolinguistic Continuity on the Guinea Coast," *Journal of African History* 8, no. 2 (1967): 251.

65. If, as seems likely, the author of this document simply omitted the cedilla from the man's ethnic surname: Kris Lane and Herman Bennett recorded the casta name "Caçanga" in Quito, ca. 1600, and in Mexico City, 1615, respectively. Partida de confirmación de Catalina, mulata libre, hija de Juan Cacanga, Cartago, March 26, 1625, ACMSJ, Libro de Confirmaciones 1625/FHL, VAULT INTL film 1219727, item 2; Kris Lane, "Captivity and Redemption: Aspects of Slave Life in Early Colonial Quito and Popayán," *The Americas* 57, no. 2 (2000): 229; Herman L. Bennett, *Colonial Blackness: A History of Afro-Mexico* (Bloomington: Indiana University Press, 2009), 123. It is also possible in this case that "casanga" was the name of an Angolan ethnic group. Aguirre Beltrán, *Población negra*, 101. This seems unlikely, however, as West Central Africans were known in Costa Rica almost without exception simply as angolas or congos: the ethnic surnames of people from Upper Guinea reflected much greater specificity and diversity.

66. Bühnen, "Ethnic Origins," 77.

67. Aguirre Beltrán, *Población negra*, 295–96; Peter Boyd-Bowman, "Negro Slaves in Early Colonial Mexico," *The Americas* 26 (1969): 140, 141–42; Lane, "Captivity and Redemption," 229; Venta de cinco esclavos, Cartago, October 28, 1613, ANCR, G. 34, fol. 48; *Indice de los protocolos de Cartago*, 1:438, 449; Obligación del Lic. don Diego de Angulo Gascón y de doña Manuela Quirós, Cartago, August 20, 1705, ANCR, PC 861, fol. 45.

68. Hair, "Ethnolinguistic Continuity," 252; Hawthorne, "Production of Slaves," 114–18; Levi Marrero, *Cuba, economía y sociedad*, 11 vols. (Madrid: Editorial Playor, 1975), 2:360; Aguirre Beltrán, *Población negra*, 240, 241; Boyd-Bowman, "Negro Slaves," 140, 141; Robinson Herrera, "The African Slave Trade in Early Santiago," *Urban History Workshop Review* 4 (1998): 7; Carol F. Jopling, ed. *Indios y negros en Panamá en los siglos XVI y XVII: Selecciones de los documentos del Archivo General de Indias* (Antigua, Guatemala: Centro de Investigaciones Regionales de Mesoamérica, 1994), 242, 243, 248, 366, 373, 392, 413, 424, 449; David Pavy, "The Provenience of Colombian Negroes," *Journal of Negro History* 52, no. 1 (1967): 56; Miguel Acosta Saignes, *Vida de los esclavos negros en Venezuela* (Havana: Casa de las Américas, 1978), 96, 97; Lane, "Captivity and Redemption," 229; Frederick P. Bowser, *The African Slave in Colonial Peru, 1524–1650* (Stanford, CA: Stanford University Press, 1974), 40–43; Declaración de Juan Biafara, Nicoya, September 27, 1603, Archivo General de Centro América, Guatemala City (hereafter, AGCA), A3 (6), exp. 124, leg. 10.

69. Bühnen, "Ethnic Origins," 80; Rachel Sarah O'Toole, "From the Rivers of Guinea to the Valleys of Peru: Becoming a *Bran* Diaspora Within Spanish Slavery," *Social Text* 25, no. 3 (no. 92) (2007): 19–36.

70. Bühnen, "Ethnic Origins," quoting from 100; Partidas de bautizo, Cartago, March 29, 1639, November 15, 1640, [date incomplete] 1644, ACMSJ, LBC, no. 1/ FHL, VAULT INTL film 1219701, item 1; Testamento del Cap. José de Vargas Machuca, Cartago, April 30, 1684, ANCR, PC 833, fol. 25v.

71. Partidas de bautizo, Cartago, September 15, 1602, ACMSJ, LBC, no. 1/FHL, VAULT INTL film 1219701, item 1.

72. Lista de los milicianos negros, pardos, mulatos y mestizos bajos de Esparza, Cartago, November 9, 1726, ANCR, Sección Complementario Colonial (hereafter, CC) 3792, fol. 24v; Lista de las milicias de gente parda, Cartago, November 21, 1734, ANCR, CC 3798, fol. 34v; Lista de la compañía de pardos libres de Esparza, n.p., July 1, 1740, ANCR, CC 3864, fol. 24; Testamento del Cap. José Nicolás de la Haya, Cartago, May 2, 1747, ANCR, Mortuales Coloniales de Cartago (hereafter, MCC) 841, fol. 5v.

73. Manumisión de esclavo, Cartago, March 20, 1696, ANCR, PC 848, fols. 44v–45; Hawthorne, "The Production of Slaves," 102, 103, 111–14; Aguirre Beltrán, *Población negra*, 118; Rodney, "Upper Guinea," 331–32, 340.

74. Sandoval, *Tratado sobre la esclavitud*, 139, 412; Nicolas Ngou-Mve, "São Tomé et

la diaspora bantou vers l'Amérique hispanique," *Cahiers des Anneaux de la Mémoire*, no. 3 (2001): 66.

75. Duncan, *Atlantic Islands*, 211.

76. Sandoval, *Tratado sobre la esclavitud*, 139; António Carreira, *Cabo Verde: Formação e extinção de uma sociedade escravocrata, 1460–1878*, 2nd ed. (N.p.: Com o Patrocínio da Comissão da Comunidade Económica Europeia para o Instituto Caboverdeano do Livro, 1983), chap. 8.

77. Poder para aprehender a un esclavo, Cartago, November 27, 1720, ANCR, PC 891, fols. 26–27; Carta de manumisión, Cartago, April 10, 1725, ANCR, PC 898, fols. 21–22v.

78. Carta poder, Cartago, May 6, 1688, ANCR, PC 837, fols. 45–45v; Venta de esclavo, Cartago, 1692, ANCR, PC 842, fol. 143v; Venta de esclavo, Cartago, September 22, 1705, ANCR, PC 861, fols. 49v–52; Permuta de esclavos, Cartago, March 27, 1722, ANCR, PC 895, fol. 32v–35; Sandoval, *Tratado sobre la esclavitud*, 139; Aguirre Beltrán, *Población negra*, 114–15.

79. Asiento ajustado entre sus dos Majestades Católica y Cristianísima y la Real Compañía de Guinea de Francia, Madrid, September 27, 1701; Real Cédula, Buen Retiro, July 7, 1708, both in AGI, Indiferente 2779.

80. Hawthorne, *From Africa to Brazil*, 9n20, 11. Similarly, Alejandro de la Fuente García counted fifteen casta names of Upper Guinea origin in Cuban notarial documents from 1570–1699. Alejandro de la Fuente García, "Esclavos africanos en La Habana: Zonas de procedencia y denominaciones étnicas, 1570–1699," *Revista Española de Antropología Americana* 20 (1990): 141.

81. Vega Bolaños, *Colección Somoza*, 6:495, 497.

82. Declaración de Juan Biafara, Nicoya, September 27, 1603, AGCA, A3 (6), exp. 124, leg. 10.

83. Declaración de Leandro de Figueroa, corregidor de Pacaca, Cartago, October 9, 1609, AGN, Inquisición, vol. 292, exp. 25, fols. 92v–93v; Declaración de Juan de Buliaga, Santiago de Guatemala, March 16, 1610, AGN, Inquisición, vol. 474, exp. 6, fol. 333.

84. Declaración del negro Jacob, esclavo del Cap. Antonio de Soto y Barahona, de casta mandinga, Cartago, October 2, 1719, ANCR, C. 233, fol. 5v; Petición del Cap. Antonio de Soto y Barahona, presentada en Cartago, May 20, 1720, ANCR, C. 233, fol. 34.

85. Partida del bautizo de Raimundo, adulto negro esclavo de doña Micaela de Durán, Cartago, February 5, 1687, ACMSJ, LBC, no. 2/FHL, VAULT INTL film 1219701, item 2; Testamento del Cap. Miguel Calvo, Cartago, February 16, 1715, ANCR, PC 877, fol. 30v; Notificación en la casa del reo el Cap. José de Chavarría, Cartago, May 16, 1719; ANCR, G. 177, fol. 3v; Mortual del Cap. José de Chavarría, Cartago, April 22, 1720, ANCR, Mortuales Coloniales de Cartago (hereafter MCC) 733, fol. 14; Poder para aprehender a un esclavo, Cartago, November 27, 1720, ANCR, PC 891, fols. 26–27; Carta de manumisión, Cartago, April 10, 1725, ANCR, PC 898, fols. 21–22v.

86. Ngou-Mve, *Africa bantú*; Lokken, "From the 'Kingdoms of Angola'"; Sempat Assadourian, *Tráfico de esclavos*. But see also David Wheat's recent research on the continuing importance of natives of Upper Guinea during the period of the Portuguese Asientos: "The First Great Waves: African Provenance Zones for the Transatlantic Slave Trade to Cartagena de Indias, 1570–1640," *Journal of African History* 52, no. 1 (2011): 1–22.

87. Miller, "Central Africa," quoting from 44, 44–45n40.

88. Ibid., 28–29.

89. Ibid., 44, quoting from 46, 61.

90. Venta de esclavo, June 23, 1607, Cartago, ANCR, PC 801, fols. 46–47.

91. Permuta de esclavos, Cartago, March 10, 1612, ANCR, G. 34, fols. 51–53.

92. Testamento de Juan Martín de Montalvo, Astillero de Nandayure, Jurisdicción y Provincia de Nicoya, April 17, 1623, ANCR, MCC 918, fol. 7.

93. Jopling, *Indios y negros en Panamá*, 248; Partida de confirmación de Isabel Conga, Cartago, March 31, 1625, ACMSJ, Libro de Confirmaciones 1 (1609–1625)/FHL, VAULT INTL film 1219727, item 2; *Indice de los protocolos de Cartago*, 1:90.

94. John K. Thornton, *The Kingdom of Kongo: Civil War and Transition, 1641–1718* (Madison: University of Wisconsin Press, 1983), quoting from xv.

95. Anne Hilton, *The Kingdom of Kongo* (Oxford: Clarendon Press, 1985), 121–24.

96. Hilton, *Kingdom of Kongo*, 198; Wyatt MacGaffey, "Kongo Identity, 1483–1993," *South Atlantic Quarterly* 94, no. 4 (1995): quoting from 1027.

97. Sandoval, *Tratado sobre la esclavitud*, 139; Linda A. Newson and Susie Minchin, *From Capture to Sale: The Portuguese Slave Trade to Spanish South America in the Early Seventeenth Century* (Leiden, Netherlands: Brill, 2007), 121; Memorial de la Compañía Real de Guinea, Madrid, August 7, 1703, AGI, Indiferente 2783; Memorial de la Compañía Real de Guinea al Consejo de Indias, contestado por el Fiscal en Madrid, May 31, 1703, AGI, Indiferente 2783; Munford, *Black Ordeal*, 2:888.

98. John Atkins, *A Voyage to Guinea, Brazil, and the West Indies in His Majesty's Ships* The Swallow *and* Weymouth (London: Caesar Ward and Richard Chandler, 1735), 179.

99. David Eltis, *The Rise of African Slavery in the Americas* (Cambridge: Cambridge University Press, 2000), 252; Colin A. Palmer, *Human Cargoes: The British Slave Trade to Spanish America, 1700–1739* (Urbana: University of Illinois Press, 1981), quoting from 63. I have seen no document in which a Costa Rican master expressed a preference for one African ethnicity over another. On the other hand, of eighty-six slaves sold between 1607 and 1750 who were identified as African, eighty-three were identified by casta (97 percent), indicating that casta was indeed an important consideration for slave buyers. ANCR, PC 801 (1607)–940 (1746); ANCR, PH 573 (1721)–94 (1749); ANCR, PSJ 411 (1721)–15 (1738); *Indices de los protocolos de Cartago*, vols. 1–3; *Indice de los protocolos de Heredia*.

100. MacGaffey, "Kongo Identity," 1027.

101. Declaración del negro José, esclavo del Cap. Manuel de Arburola, Esparza, November 11, 1719, ANCR, C. 256, fols. 7–7v.

102. Robin Law, "Ethnicities of Enslaved Africans in the Diaspora: On the Meanings of 'Mina' (Again)," *History in Africa* 32 (2005): 247–67.

103. Thornton, *Africa and Africans*, 96; Ray A. Kea, *Settlements, Trade, and Polities on the Seventeenth-Century Gold Coast* (Baltimore, MD: Johns Hopkins University Press, 1982), 197–98, 399n147; John L. Vogt, "The Early São Tomé–Príncipe Slave Trade with Mina, 1500–1540," *International Journal of African Historical Studies* 6, no. 3 (1973): 453–67.

104. Pierre Verger, *Trade Relations Between the Bight of Benin and Bahia from the 17th to the 19th Century*, trans. Evelyn Crawford (Ibadan, Nigeria: Ibadan University Press, 1976), 3–4, 11; Stuart B. Schwartz, *Sugar Plantations in the Formation of Brazilian Society: Bahia, 1550–1835* (Cambridge: Cambridge University Press, 1985), 340; Hall, "African Ethnicities," 65.

105. Kea, *Settlements, Trade, and Polities*, 11; Lovejoy, *Transformations in Slavery*, 49. Africanists have largely abandoned assertions of a direct causal relationship between the importation of European firearms, African warfare, and the procurement of captives. For a strongly argued statement, see Per O. Hernæs, "The 'Gun-Slave' Circle Theory" in *Slaves, Danes, and African Coast Society: The Danish Slave Trade from West Africa and Afro-Danish Relations on the Eighteenth-Century Gold Coast* (Trondheim, Norway: Department of History, University of Trondheim, 1995), 369–84.

106. Thomas Phillips, "A Journal of a Voyage Made in the *Hannibal* of London, 1693–1694," in *A Collection of Voyages and Travels*, ed. Awnsham Churchill and John Churchill, 6 vols. (London: By Assignment for Messrs. Churchill, 1732), 6:214; K. G. Davies, *The Royal African Company* (London: Longman, Grion, 1957), 228; Eltis, *Rise of African Slavery*, 247, 252; Michael Craton, *Searching for the Invisible Man: Slaves and Plantation Life in Jamaica* (Cambridge, MA: Harvard University Press, 1979), 55; Thornton, "The Coromantees."

107. Venta de esclavo, Cartago, April 10, 1674, ANCR, PC 822, fols. 33–34v.

108. Venta de esclavos, Cartago, May 13, 1680, ANCR, PC 828, fols. 61–62.

109. Testamento de doña Micaela Durán de Chávez, Cartago, January 14, 1703, ANCR, PC 857, fol. 4v; Obligación de doña Juana Ruiz, Cartago, November 5, 1703, ANCR, PC 857, fols. 64v–66; Obligación del Cap. Blas González Coronel y su mujer doña Bárbara Fonseca, Cartago, September 30, 1706, ANCR, PC 860, fol. 94v; Testamento de doña Francisca Calvo, Cartago, September 30, 1706, ANCR, PC 863, fol. 110v; Obligación del Cap. Francisco López Conejo y su mujer doña María de Quirós, Cartago, 1709, ANCR, PC 867, fols. 163v–64v.

110. Nicoué Lodjou Gayibor, *Le Genyi: Un royaume oublié de la côte de Guinée au temps de la traite des noirs* (Lomé, Togo: Éditions HAHO, 1990); S. Wilson, "Aperçu historique sur les peuples et cultures dans le Golfe du Bénin: Le cas des 'mina' d'Anécho," in *Peuples du golfe du Bénin: Aja-éwé (colloque de Cotonou)*, ed. François de Medeiros (Paris: Karthala, 1984), 127–50.

111. Autos relativos a un esclavo de Pedro de Moya, Cartago, 1719, ANCR, C. 237; Autos relativos a una esclava de doña Ana Antonia de Acosta, Cartago, 1720, ANCR, C. 264; Autos relativos a varios esclavos de doña Luisa Calvo, Cartago, 1719, ANCR, C. 267; Autos relativos a varios esclavos de don Juan Francisco de Ibarra y Calvo, Cartago, 1719, ANCR, G. 187.

112. Lygaard to the Directors, Christiansborg, August 19, 1709, Document V.20 in Justesen, ed., *Danish Sources*, 1:222.

113. See Lohse, "Slave-Trade Nomenclature," 78–79.

114. Philip Bartle, "The Universe Has Three Souls: Notes on Translating Akan Culture," *Journal of Religion in Africa* 14 (1983): 85–114. See also Stephanie E. Smallwood, *Saltwater Slavery: A Middle Passage from Africa to American Diaspora* (Cambridge, MA: Harvard University Press, 2007), chap. 4.

115. Lovejoy, *Transformations in Slavery*, 50.

116. Albert Van Dantzig, "English Bosman and Dutch Bosman: A Comparison of Texts, Part 4," *History in Africa* 7 (1980): 285; Robin Law, *The Kingdom of Allada* (Leiden, Netherlands: Research School CNWS, School of Asian, African, and Amerindian Studies, 1997), 89.

117. Venta de esclavo, Cartago, August 29, 1677, ANCR, PC 828, fols. 12–15; Testamento del Pbo. don Domingo de Echavarría Navarro, Cartago, February 3, 1675, ANCR, PC 823, fol. 8; Venta de esclava, Cartago, July 27, 1696, ANCR, PC 848, fols. 111–12v; Certificación de venta celebrada en el 1 de noviembre de 1700, Cartago, August 24, 1701, ANCR, G. 188, fol. 10; Venta de esclava, Cartago, June 3, 1704, ANCR, PC 860, fols. 15–17; Obligación del Lic. don Diego de Angulo Gascón y doña Manuela Quirós, Cartago, August 20, 1705, ANCR, PC 861, fol. 45; Venta de esclavo, Cartago, September 22, 1705, ANCR, PC 861, fols. 49v–52; Obligación del Cap. Blas González Coronel y su mujer doña Bernarda de Fonseca, Cartago, September 30, 1706, ANCR, PC 860, fol. 94v.

118. Certificación de venta celebrada en el 1 de noviembre de 1700, Cartago, August 24, 1701, ANCR, G. 188, fol. 10.

119. Venta de cinco esclavos, Cartago, October 28, 1613, ANCR, G. 34, fol. 48.

120. Inventario de 16 negros y negras, Cartago, June 11, 1710, ANCR, C. 187, fols. 147–49.

121. Russell Lohse, "Africans in a Colony of Creoles: The Yoruba in Colonial Costa Rica," in *The Yoruba Diaspora in the Americas*, ed. Toyin Falola and Matt D. Childs (Bloomington: Indiana University Press, 2005), 131–34.

122. Biodun Adediran, *The Frontier States of Western Yorubaland, circa 1600–1889: State Formation and Political Growth in an Ethnic Frontier Zone* (Ibadan, Nigeria: Institut Français de Recherche en Afrique, 1994), 15; Adediran, "Yoruba Ethnic Groups or a Yoruba Ethnic Group? A Review of the Problem of Ethnic Identification," *África* [Centro de Estudos Africanos, Universidade de São Paulo] 7 (1984): 58; William Bascom, *The Yoruba of Southwestern Nigeria* (New York: Holt, Rinehart and Winston, 1969), 5.

Gonzalo Aguirre Beltrán included the "Aná" in his extensive catalogue of African ethnicities represented in Mexican colonial documents, asserting that they began to arrive in Mexico in the late sixteenth century, and precisely described their geographical origin as along the Ana tributary of the Mono River in southern Togo. However, he incorrectly identified the Ana as an Ewe-Fon-speaking group. Aguirre Beltrán, *La población negra de México*, 131. Costa Rican historian Carlos Meléndez followed Aguirre Beltrán in this misidentification; see "El negro en Costa Rica durante la colonia," in Carlos Meléndez and Quince Duncan, *El negro en Costa Rica* (San José: Editorial Costa Rica, 1989), 21. Jorge Castellanos and Isabel Castellanos also found "Aná" in Cuban documents, and likewise associated them with the Ewe-Fon in "The Geographic, Ethnologic, and Linguistic Roots of Cuban Blacks," *Cuban Studies* 17 (1987): 96–98.

123. Declaración de Antonia, negra esclava, Cartago, September 12, 1719, ANCR, C. 236, fol. 1v; Declaración de Antonia, negra esclava, Cartago, June 22, 1720, ANCR, C. 236, fol. 17.

124. Robin Law and Paul E. Lovejoy, "Borgu in the Atlantic Slave Trade," *African Economic History* 27 (1999): 74–75.

125. Almoneda de esclavos, Esparza, December 9, 1700, ANCR, C. 109, fols. 24–24v; Cuenta y relación de las almonedas de esclavos, inserta en una carta de Cartago, January 2, 1701, AGI, Audiencia de Guatemala 359, pieza 6, fol. 26v.

126. Declaración de Miguel Largo, Cartago, September 7, 1719, ANCR, C. 240, fol. 3; Auto del gobernador, Cartago, Cartago, May 7, 1720, ANCR, C. 240, fol. 5v.

127. Testimonio de la venta de una esclava, Cartago, September 3, 1716, ANCR, C. 236, fols. 7–11; Declaración de Antonia de casta barbá, Cartago, September 12, 1719, ANCR, C. 236, fol. 1v.

128. Declaración del Cap. Francisco de Bonilla, Cartago, May 25, 1720, ANCR, C. 232, fol. 19v; Declaración del Cap. Esteban de Zúñiga, Cartago, May 25, 1720, ANCR, C. 232, fol. 20; Declaración de Sebastián de Quirós, Cartago, May 27, 1720, ANCR, C. 232, fol. 20v; Careo en el cual las negras María y Petrona identifican a María Popo como una de sus carabelas, Cartago, October 5, 1720, ANCR, C. 267, fol. 59; Don Nicolás de Ocampo Golfín afianza a la negra María Popo, Cartago, February 25, 1722, ANCR, C. 288, fol. 71; Declaración de María negra de casta popó, Valle de Barva, November 12, 1719, ANCR, G. 188, fol. 7v.

129. Declaración de Juana, negra de casta popo, Cartago, September 9, 1719, ANCR, C. 232, fol. 2.

130. Kolapo, "The Igbo and Their Neighbours, 122.

131. David Northrup, *Trade Without Rulers: Pre-Colonial Economic Development in South-Eastern Nigeria* (Oxford: Clarendon Press, 1978), 51; Northrup, "Igbo and Myth Igbo: Culture and Ethnicity in the Atlantic World, 1600–1850," *Slavery & Abolition* 21, no. 3 (2000): 7–8; Hair, "Ethnolinguistic Continuity," 262, 262n54; Sandoval, *Tratado sobre la esclavitud*, 139.

132. Venta de cinco esclavos, Cartago, October 28, 1613, ANCR, G. 34, fol. 48.

133. Partida de bautizo, Cartago, 6 April 1622, ACMSJ, LBC, no. 1/FHL, VAULT INTL film 1219701, item 1.
134. Northrup, "Igbo and Myth Igbo," 8.
135. Ibid., quoting from 9, 10; Hair, "Ethnolinguistic Continuity," 262–63.
136. Testamento del Ayudante Juan Gómez Rico, Cartago, August 5, 1659, ANCR, PC 817 bis, fol. 276.
137. Carta dote de Francisco Gregorio de Govantes y Zúñiga a favor de Andrea González, Cartago, October 26, 1686, ANCR, PC 835, fol. 58v; Venta de esclava, Cartago, December 23, 1698, ANCR, PC 850, fols. 58v–61.
138. David Eltis, David Richardson, Stephen D. Behrendt, and Herbert S. Klein, eds., *The Trans-Atlantic Slave Trade: A Database on CD-ROM* (Cambridge: Cambridge University Press, 1999); E. J. Alagoa, "The Slave Trade in Niger Delta Oral Tradition and History," in *Africans in Bondage: Studies in Slavery and the Slave Trade*, ed. Paul E. Lovejoy (Madison: African Studies Program, University of Wisconsin–Madison, 1986), 127; G. Ugo Nwokeji, "The Biafran Frontier: Trade, Slaves, and Aro Society, c. 1750–1905 (PhD diss., University of Toronto, 1999), 51, 65; Northrup, *Trade Without Rulers*, 54, 55 fig. 1; Northrup, "Igbo and Myth Igbo," 14; Douglas B. Chambers, "The Significance of Igbo in the Bight of Biafra Slave-Trade: A Rejoinder to Northrup's 'Myth Igbo,'" *Slavery & Abolition* 23, no. 1 (2002): 110, 111.
139. Sandoval, *Tratado sobre la esclavitud*, 139; Declaración del negro Heredima, Cartago, December 3, 1744, C. 455, fol. 27; Declaración del negro Cocho, Cartago, December 5, 1744, C. 455, fol. 32.
140. Chambers, "The Significance of Igbo," 108–11.
141. Kolapo, "The Igbo and Their Neighbours," 114–33.
142. Ibid., 115.
143. Venta de cinco esclavos, Cartago, October 23, 1613, ANCR, G. 34, fol. 48; Partida del bautizo de Juan, Cartago, August 4, 1607; Partida del bautizo de Catalina, Cartago, December 26, 1638; Partida del bautizo de Nicolás Curridabat, Cartago, September 28, 1643; Partida del bautizo de Bartolomé, July 20, 1644, all in ACMSJ, LBC, no. 1/FHL, VAULT INTL film 1219701, item 1; Partida de confirmación de Magdalena de Turrialba, Cartago, January 1609; Partida de confirmación de Catalina, mulata, hija de Antón, negro, Cartago, March 26, 1625, both in ACMSJ, Confirmaciones de Cartago, Libro 1 (1609, 1625)/FHL, VAULT INTL film 1219727, item 2.
144. Auto de almoneda, Esparza, April 15, 1701, ANCR, C. 109, fols. 32v–33.
145. Testamento de doña Josefa de Ocampo, San José de Tenorio, Valle de Bagaces, December 10, 1732, ANCR, MCC 1052, fol. 8v; Inventario y avalúo de bienes de doña Josefa de Ocampo, San José de Tenorio, Valle de Bagaces, February 25, 1738, ANCR, MCC 1052, fol. 17v.
146. Ventas de esclavos, Cartago, August 16, 1746, ANCR, PC 934, fols. 64–68.
147. Robert W. Slenes, "The Great Porpoise-Skull Strike: Central African Water Spirits and Slave Identity in Early Nineteenth-Century Rio de Janeiro," in *Central*

Africans and Cultural Transformations in the American Diaspora, ed. Linda Heywood (Cambridge: Cambridge University Press, 2002), 186.

148. Hounkpatin Capo, "Le gbe est une langue unique," *Africa* 53, no. 2 (1983): 47–57; Law, *Slave Coast*, chaps. 1, 3.

149. Surgy, *Système religieux*, 118.

150. Adediran, *Frontier States of Western Yorubaland*, chap. 1.

151. Bartle, "The Universe Has Three Souls."

CHAPTER THREE

1. Rina Cáceres, "Costa Rica, en la frontera del comercio de esclavos africanos," *Reflexiones* (Costa Rica), no. 65 (1997): 6–7.

2. Lutgardo García Fuentes, "Licencias para la introducción de esclavos en Indias y envíos desde Sevilla en el siglo XVI," *Jahrbuch für Geschichte von Staat, Wirtschaft und Gesellschaft Lateinamerikas* 19 (1982): 1–46.

3. See Enriqueta Vila Vilar, *Hispanoamérica y el comercio de esclavos: Los asientos portugueses* (Seville: Escuela de Estudios Hispano-Americanos de Sevilla, 1977).

4. Matthew Restall, *The Black Middle: Africans, Mayas, and Spaniards in Colonial Yucatan* (Stanford, CA: Stanford University Press, 2009), 19.

5. Philip D. Morgan, "The Cultural Implications of the Atlantic Slave Trade: African Regional Origins, American Destinations and New World Developments," *Slavery & Abolition* 18, no. 1 (1997): 133–34.

6. Vila Vilar, *Hispanoamérica y el comercio*.

7. Colin A. Palmer, *Slaves of the White God: Blacks in Mexico, 1570–1650* (Cambridge, MA: Harvard University Press, 1976), chap. 1; Frederick P. Bowser, *The African Slave in Colonial Peru, 1524–1650* (Stanford, CA: Stanford University Press, 1974), chaps. 2–3.

8. Murdo J. MacLeod, *Spanish Central America: A Socioeconomic History, 1520–1720* (Berkeley: University of California Press, 1973), 50; María del Carmen Mena García, *La sociedad de Panamá en el siglo XVI* (Seville: Artes Gráficas Padura, 1984), 160.

9. Vila Vilar, *Hispanoamérica y el comercio*, 218–19; Marisa Vega Franco, *El tráfico de esclavos con América (Asientos de Grillo y Lomelín, 1663–1674)* (Seville: Escuela de Estudios Hispano-Americanos de Sevilla, 1984), 156, 185–88, 194–200; Colin A. Palmer, *Human Cargoes: The British Slave Trade to Spanish America, 1700–1739* (Urbana: University of Illinois Press, 1981), 110.

10. Vila Vilar, *Hispanoamérica y el comercio*, 169.

11. See tables 1–6 in Vila Vilar, *Hispanoamérica y el comercio*, 240–78.

12. Johannes M. Postma, *The Dutch in the Atlantic Slave Trade, 1600–1815* (Cambridge: Cambridge University Press, 1990), chap. 2; Postma, "The Dutch and the Asiento Slave Trade: African Slaves to the Spanish American Colonies, 1662–1715," in *De la traite à l'esclavage du Ve au XVIIIème siècle: Actes du Colloque International sur la traite des noirs, 1985*, 2 vols., ed. Serge Daget (Nantes: Centre de Recherche

sur l'Histoire du Monde Atlantique, 1988), 1:299–324; Vega Franco, *Tráfico de esclavos*, 194–201; Real cédula, Madrid, June 4, 1706, Archivo General de Indias, Seville (hereafter, AGI), Indiferente 2782; Palmer, *Human Cargoes*, 98–99; David Eltis, *The Rise of African Slavery in the Americas* (Cambridge: Cambridge University Press, 2000), 207–9.

13. Venta de siete esclavos, Portobello, October 12, 1689, Archivo Nacional de Costa Rica, San José (hereafter, ANCR), Protocolos Coloniales de Cartago (hereafter, PC) 839, fols. 20v–21.

14. For the sixteenth and early seventeenth centuries, see Bowser, *African Slave in Colonial Peru*, 61–62. Linda A. Newson and Susie Minchin detail the process in Cartagena, Portobello, and Panama City in *From Capture to Sale: The Portuguese Slave Trade to Spanish South America in the Early Seventeenth Century* (Leiden, Netherlands: Brill, 2007), 144–56, 188–95.

15. Auto de los Jueces Oficiales de la Real Hacienda, Portobello, June 10, 1666, AGI, Contaduría 264A, ramo 33, fols. 22v–24; Testimonio de los enfermos, Portobello, June 10, 1666, AGI, Contaduría 264A, ramo 33, fol. 24v; Tasación de las 110 piezas de esclavos, Panama, June 20, 1666, AGI, Contaduría 264A, ramo 33, fol. 27; Avaluación, Panama, July 18, 1666, AGI, Contaduría 264A, ramo 33, fol. 46v.

16. Unique voyage identification no. 75371, Voyages Database, Voyages: The Trans-Atlantic Slave Trade Database, http://slavevoyages.org/tast/database/search.face s?yearFrom=1514&yearTo=1866&voyageid=75371; Gastos en Portobelo por el navío *Mercader de Dunwich*, Panama, 1716, and Memoria de los muertos, Panama, 1716, both in AGI, Contaduría 267, leg. 5.

17. Vila Vilar, *Hispanoamérica y el comercio*, 218–19; Bowser, *African Slave*, 55.

18. Tasación de las 110 piezas de esclavos que tratan de comprar don Juan de Cevallos el caballero y el Alf. Francisco de Acosta, Panama, June 20, 1666, AGI, Contaduría 264A, ramo 33, fols. 27–27v.

19. Venta de esclavos, Panama, June 28, 1666, AGI, Contaduría 264A, ramo 33, fols. 29v–30v.

20. ANCR, PC 815 (1660–1662), 815 bis (1663), 816 (1664), 817 bis (1658, 1661), 818 (1664).

21. Bowser, *African Slave*, 344; *Indice de los protocolos de Cartago*, 6 vols. (San José: Imprenta Nacional, 1909–1930), 1:42.

22. *Indice de los protocolos de Cartago*, 1:86; Bowser, *African Slave*, 344.

23. Venta de esclavo, August 6, 1660, ANCR, PC 815, fols. 18–19v; Bowser, *African Slave*, 344. Calculations on slave prices use data from the following sources, all in the ANCR: Sección Colonial Cartago (hereafter, C.) 109 (1700), C. 113 (1702), C. 187 (1710), C. 211 (1713), C. 231 (1710), C. 233 (1710), C. 234 (1710), C. 243 (1719), 250 (1719); ANCR, Sección Complementario Colonial (hereafter, CC) 3919 (1686), CC 4111 (1718); CC 4121 (1720); ANCR, Sección Colonial Guatemala (hereafter, G.) 34 (1613), G. 55 (1624), G. 185 (1710), G. 187 (1716), G. 188 (1700, 1710); Mortuales Coloniales de Cartago 774 (1711); PC 801 (1607)–934 (1746); Protocolos Coloniales de Heredia (hereafter, PH) 573 (1721)–91 (1746); Protocolos Coloniales de San José (hereafter, PSJ) 411 (1721), 412 (1723); *Indice de los protocolos de Cartago*, vols. 1–3.

See also Lowell Gudmundson Kristjanson, "Mecanismos de movilidad social para la población de procedencia africana en Costa Rica colonial: Manumisión y mestizaje," in Lowell Gudmundson Kristjanson, *Estratificación socio-racial y económica de Costa Rica, 1700–1850* (San José: Editorial Universidad Estatal a Distancia, 1978), 23.

24. Jean-Pierre Tardieu, *El negro en Cusco: Los caminos de la alienación en la segunda mitad del siglo XVII* (Lima: Pontifícia Universidad Católica del Perú, 1998), 15, 25, 50.

25. *Indice de los protocolos de Cartago*, 1:33; Rina Cáceres, *Negros, mulatos, esclavos y libertos en la Costa Rica del siglo XVII* (Mexico City: Instituto Panamericano de Geografía e Historia, 2000), 58; Philip S. MacLeod, "On the Edge of Empire: Costa Rica in the Colonial Era (1561–1800)" (PhD diss., Tulane University, 1999), 153–54.

26. Declaración del Cap. José Antonio de Espinosa, Cartago, February 3, 1716, ANCR, PC 875, fols. 38–39.

27. Venta de cinco negros, Cartago, October 28, 1613, ANCR, G. 34, fols. 48–50.

28. Auto del Teniente de Contador y Tesorero Juez Oficial Real Juan de Morales, Cartago, January 17, 1643, ANCR, CC 3586, fol. 1. Unfortunately, only a few bills of sale survive from those years.

29. Venta de tres esclavos, Cartago, July 20, 1673, ANCR, PC 822, fols. 41–42; Cáceres, *Negros, mulatos*, 50.

30. Venta de esclavo, Cartago, April 10, 1674, ANCR, PC 822, fols. 33–34v; Venta de esclava, Cartago, April 10, 1674, ANCR, PC 822, fols. 36–37v.

31. Venta de esclavo, Cartago, November 22, 1688, ANCR, PC 837, fols. 94v–95v.

32. Venta de esclavo, Cartago, September 28, 1706, ANCR, PC 862, fols. 61v–63v.

33. Cáceres, *Negros, mulatos*, 50. For other examples, see Obligación del Alf. Sebastián de Aguirre y de su mujer doña Petronila de Grado y Moreno, Cartago, September 22, 1665, ANCR, PC 817, fols. 72v–74v; doña Eugenia Gertrudis de Abarca dona a su hijo el Cap. Miguel Calvo una negrita esclava que se ha de traer de Panamá, Cartago, July 9, 1689, ANCR, PC 838, fols. 85v–87v; doña María Ramírez, mujer del Alf. Juan Albo, da poder a éste para que compre en Esparza algunos esclavos o esclavas, Cartago, July 15, 1692, ANCR, PC 842, fols. 78–80v.

34. Obligación del Alf. Sebastián de Aguirre, Cartago, September 22, 1665, ANCR, PC 817, fols. 72v–74v.

35. Venta de siete esclavos, Portobello, October 12, 1689, ANCR, PC 839, fols. 20v–21.

36. Venta de esclavo, Cartago, February 22, 1690, ANCR, PC 839, fols. 22–24; Cáceres, *Negros, mulatos*, 51.

37. Joseph C. Miller, "Retention, Reinvention, and Remembering: Restoring Identities Through Enslavement in Africa and Under Slavery in Brazil," in *Enslaving Connections: Changing Cultures of Africa and Brazil During the Era of Slavery*, ed. José Curto and Paul E. Lovejoy (New York: Humanity Books, 2004), quoting from

88; Stanley M. Elkins, *Slavery: A Problem in American Institutional and Intellectual Life*, 3rd ed. (Chicago: University of Chicago Press, 1976).

38. MacLeod, *Spanish Central America*, chap. 18.

39. Oscar Aguilar Bulgarelli and Irene Alfaro Aguilar, *La esclavitud negra en Costa Rica: Origen de la oligarquía económica y política nacional* (San José: Progreso Editora, 1997), 86, 182–83; Mauricio Meléndez Obando, "Contrabando de esclavos," in Tatiana Lobo Wiehoff and Mauricio Meléndez Obando, *Negros y blancos: Todo mezclado* (San José: Editorial de la Universidad de Costa Rica, 1997), 102.

40. Declaración de doña Agueda Pérez de Muro, Cartago, July 15, 1720, ANCR, C. 240, fol. 27v.

41. Bowser, *African Slave*, 56.

42. Auto del Teniente de Contador y Tesorero Juez Oficial Real Juan de Morales, Cartago, January 17, 1643, ANCR, CC 3586, fol. 1.

43. Real cédula, Madrid, [date incompete] 14, 1673, ANCR, C. 1078, fols. 181–81v.

44. Declaración del Teniente Severino de Aguilar, Cartago, July 2, 1703, AGI, Audiencia de Guatemala (hereafter, AG) 359, pieza 1, fol. 19.

45. Declaración del Ayu. Luis de Salazar, Cartago, October 27, 1703, AGI, AG 359, pieza 3, fols. 46v, quoting from fol. 47, 47v.

46. Consulta del Juez Comisario al Presidente de la Real Audiencia de Guatemala, Cartago, June 20, 1703, AGI, AG 359, pieza 4, fol. 59.

47. Declaración de Pedro de Arburola, negro esclavo de doña Josefa de Oses, Matina, December 5, 1719, ANCR, C. 232, fols. 9v–10.

48. Declaración de José Morales, Cartago, October 12, 1703, AGI, AG 359, pieza 1, fol. 55; Declaración del Cap. Rafael Fajardo, Cartago, June 26, 1703, AGI, AG 359, pieza 1, fols. 5–5v, 8.

49. Declaración de Severino Aguilar, Cartago, July 2, 1703, AGI, AG 359, pieza 1, fol. 15; Declaración de José Morales, Cartago, October 12, 1703, AGI, AG 359, pieza 1, fol. 55; Declaración de Hipólito Trejos, Cartago, October 16, 1703, AGI, AG 359, pieza 1, fol. 61; Carta del MRP Fray Francisco de San José al Teniente de Jueces Oficiales de la Real Hacienda don José de Guzmán, Matina, August 14, 1702, ANCR, C. 113, fol. 1; also in AGI, AG 359, pieza 2, fols. 40–40v; Certificación del MRP Fray Francisco de San José, Matina, September 3, 1702, AGI, AG 359, pieza 1, fols. 21–21v.

50. Declaración de José Morales, Cartago, October 12, 1703, AGI, AG 359, pieza 1, fols. 55–56.

51. Carta del Cap. Andrés Verroterán y Aguirre al Gobernador de Costa Rica don Francisco Serrano de Reyna, Moín, July 17, 1702, AGI, AG 359, pieza 2, fols. 2–2v.

52. Declaración del Teniente Severino de Aguilar, Cartago, July 2, 1703, AGI, AG 359, pieza 1, fols. 14v, 15.

53. Respuesta del Gobernador al requerimiento del Teniente de Jueces Oficiales de la Real Hacienda don José Guzmán, Cartago, September 9, 1702, AGI, AG 359, pieza 2, fol. 44.

54. Comisión del Gobernador don Francisco Serrano de Reyna al Ayu. Lázaro de Robles, Cartago, August 15, 1702, AGI, AG 359, pieza 1, fols. 23–23v; Declaración de Domingo Guerrero, Cartago, July 11, 1703, AGI, AG 359, pieza 1, fols. 25–28.

55. Declaración del Ayu. Lázaro de Robles, Cartago, October 6, 1703, AGI, AG 359, pieza 1, fols. 41v–42, 47.

56. Declaración de Domingo Guerrero, Cartago, July 11, 1703, AGI, AG 359, pieza 1, fols. 25–28; Declaración del Ayu. Lázaro de Robles, Cartago, October 6, 1703, AGI, AG 359, pieza 1, quoting from 47v; Declaración de Manuel de Chavarría, Cartago, July 12, 1703, AGI, AG 359, pieza 1, fols. 31–31v; Declaración de Juan Ramón de la Cruz, Cartago, July 13, 1703, AGI, AG 359, pieza 1, fols. 32–33.

57. Declaración de Domingo Guerrero, Cartago, July 11, 1703, AGI, AG 359, pieza 1, fols. 25–28; Declaración del Ayu. Lázaro de Robles, Cartago, October 6, 1703, AGI, AG 359, pieza 1, quoting from 47v; Declaración de Manuel de Chavarría, Cartago, July 12, 1703, AGI, AG 359, pieza 1, fols. 31–31v; Declaración de Juan Ramón de la Cruz, Cartago, July 13, 1703, AGI, AG 359, pieza 1, fols. 32–33.

58. "Criminal contra los compradores de esclavos a los enemigos piratas. Año de 1702—Criminal de Comiso," *Revista de los Archivos Nacionales* (Costa Rica) 15, nos. 1–3 (1951): 14.

59. "Criminal contra los compradores," 15.

60. Ibid., 20.

61. Declaración del Ayu. Lázaro de Robles, Cartago, October 6, 1703, AGI, AG 359, pieza 1, fols. 47, 45v.

62. Petición del Lic. don Manuel José González Coronel, presentada en Cartago, July 30, 1720, ANCR, C. 224, fol. 55v.

63. "Título de Gobernador de Costa Rica de don José Antonio Lacayo de Briones—1713," *Revista de los Archivos Nacionales* (Costa Rica) 15 (1951): 23.

64. Declaración del Cap. Juan Gómez de Ocón y Trillo, Cartago, March 18, 1717, ANCR, C. 211, fol. 16.

65. Declaración de Francisco Alejandro Bonilla, Cartago, April 19, 1717, ANCR, C. 211, fols. 42, 42v.

66. Declaración de Catalina, negra esclava de doña Petronila Valerino, Cartago, November 13, 1720, ANCR, C. 244, fol. 6v.

67. Declaración del Cap. Manuel de Arburola, Cartago, June 18, 1720, ANCR, C. 233, fol. 49; Declaración de Jacob, negro de casta mandinga y esclavo del Cap. Antonio de Soto y Barahona, Cartago, October 2, 1719, ANCR, C. 233, fol. 5v; Razón de las declaraciones de la información, Cartago, July 20, 1720, ANCR, C. 232, fol. 43v.

68. Declaración de Isabel, negra esclava de María González, Cartago, September 23, 1719, ANCR, C. 253, fol. 1v.

69. Certificación de don Francisco Vicente García, Contador Oficial de la Real Hacienda de las Reales Cajas de Portobello, April 26, 1739, AGI, Panamá 364, fol. 130. For another example, see ANCR, C. 528 (1757).

70. For the concept of "re-Africanization" in another American colony with inter-mittent access to the slave trade, see Gwendolyn Midlo Hall, *Africans in Colonial*

Louisiana: The Development of Afro-Creole Culture in the Eighteenth Century
(Baton Rouge: Louisiana State University Press, 1992), chap. 9.

71. Auto de visita, Puerto de la Caldera, October 29, 1700, ANCR, C. 109, fol. 6v.

72. Auto de visita de la fragata *Nuestra Señora de la Soledad y Santa Isabel*, La Caldera, October 29, 1700, ANCR, C. 109, fols. 6v–7; AGI, AG 359, pieza 6, fols. 44v–46v.

73. Denunciación de negros de por alto, Esparza, November 6, 1700, ANCR, C. 109, fol. 7.

74. Diligencia, Esparza, November 6, 1700, ANCR, C. 109, fol. 7v; Sentencia de comiso, Esparza, November 21, 1700, ANCR, C. 109, fol. 14; Autos de almoneda, Esparza, November 30, 1700, December 2, 1700, December 5, 1700, December 12, 1700, December 9, 1700, December 25, 1700, February 24, 1701, April 15, 1701, ANCR, C. 109, fols. 16v–25v, 28v–29v, 32v–33.

75. Partición entre S.M., los jueces y denunciador de lo vendido hasta hoy, Esparza, March 2, 1701, ANCR, C. 109, fol. 31; Requerimiento, Esparza, September 30, 1701, ANCR, C. 109, fol. 57v.

76. Declaración de Juan Antonio Bogarín, Cartago, August 18, 1703, AGI, AG 359, pieza 5, fol. 21.

77. Ibid., fol. 26v.

78. Declaración del Cap. Francisco de los Reyes, Cartago, July 9, 1703, AGI, AG 359, pieza 5, fols. 2v–5.

79. Carta cuenta de los géneros que se dieron por de comiso de la fragata *Nuestra Señora de la Soledad y Santa Isabel*, n.p., January 2, 1701, AGI, AG 359, pieza 6, fol. 24v; Declaración de Juan Antonio Bogarín, Cartago, August 18, 1703, AGI, AG 359, pieza 5, fols. 28v–29v.

80. Declaración del Cap. Francisco de los Reyes, Cartago, July 9, 1703, AGI, AG 359, pieza 5, fols. 5v, 6v; Declaración de Juan Antonio Bogarín, Cartago, August 18, 1703, AGI, AG 359, pieza 5, fol. 25; Declaración de Juan Antonio Bogarín, Cartago, August 21, 1703, AGI, AG 359, pieza 5, fol. 32.

81. Declaración del Cap. Francisco de los Reyes, Cartago, July 9, 1703, AGI, AG 359, pieza 5, fol. 9.

82. Ibid., fol. 5.

83. Ibid., fols. 6v, 9–9v; Notificación de auto al Gobernador y su respuesta, Cartago, January 12, 1701, ANCR, C. 109, quoting from fol. 51v.

84. Auto de almoneda, Esparza, November 23, 1700, ANCR, 109, fols. 17–17v, quoting from fol. 17.

85. Declaración de Juan Antonio Bogarín, Cartago, August 21, 1703, AGI, AG 359, pieza 5, fols. 31v, quoting from fol. 32.

86. Declaración del Mre. de Campo don José de Casasola y Córdoba, Cartago, April 14, 1701, AGI, AG 359, pieza 4, fols. 33v–34; Declaración del Mtre. de Campo don José de Casasola y Córdoba, Cartago, November 9, 1703, AGI, AG 359, pieza 5, fol. 54v.

87. Partición entre S.M., los jueces y denunciador de lo vendido, Esparza, March 2, 1701, ANCR, C. 109, fol. 31; Declaración de Juan Antonio Bogarín, Cartago,

August 23, 1703, AGI, AG 359, pieza 5, fol. 43v; Parecer del Asesor el Lic. don Francisco de Carmona, Guatemala, December 5, 1701, AGI, AG 359, pieza 6, fol. 172; Requerimiento al Teniente de Gobernador don Gregorio de Caamaño y su respuesta, Esparza, September 30, 1701, ANCR, 109, fol. 57v.

88. Carta del Gobernador de Nicaragua don Pedro Luis de Colmenares al Presidente de la Real Audiencia de Guatemala, Masaya, Nic., January 25, 1702, AGI, AG 359, pieza 6, fol. 1v.

89. Decreto de la Real Audiencia, Guatemala, August 17, 1701, ANCR, C. 109, fol. 54v.

90. Auto del Juez Comisario el Lic. don Francisco de Carmona, Cartago, May 25, 1703, AGI, AG 359, pieza 4, fols. 3–3v; Consulta del Juez Comisario al Presidente de la Real Audiencia de Guatemala, Cartago, June 20, 1703, AGI, AG 359, pieza 4, quoting from fol. 56.

91. Decreto del Presidente de la Real Audiencia don Gabriel Sánchez de Berrospe, Guatemala, January 5, 1702, ANCR, C. 109, fols. 59v–60.

92. Sentencia pronunciada contra el Mtre. de Campo don Francisco Serrano de Reyna, Guatemala, December 24, 1705, Archivo General de Centro América, Guatemala City (hereafter, AGCA), A1.24, exp. 10216, leg. 1572, fols. [241–42v].

93. Sentencia pronunciada contra el Mtre. de Campo don Francisco Serrano de Reyna, Guatemala, October 23, 1706, AGCA, A1.24, exp. 10216, leg. 1572, fol. [246v].

94. León Fernández, ed., *Colección de documentos para la historia de Costa Rica*, 10 vols. (San José: Imprenta Nacional [vols. 1–3], Paris: Imprenta Pablo Dupont [vols. 4–5], Barcelona: Imprenta Viuda de Luis Tasso [vols. 6–10], 1881–1907), 9:64; MacLeod, "On the Edge of Empire," 374–75.

95. Consulta del Juez Comisario al Presidente de la Real Audiencia de Guatemala, Cartago, June 20, 1703, AGI, AG 359, pieza 4, fols. 55–64v, quoting from fols. 60v and 57.

96. Declaración del Ayu. Lázaro de Robles, Cartago, October 6, 1703, AGI, AG 359, pieza 1, fol. 47v.

97. Auto de los Sres. Presidente y Oidores de la Real Audiencia, Guatemala, August 9, 1703, AGI, AG 359, pieza 4, fol. 75v. This information was unavailable to Luz Alba Chacón de Umaña, who wrote in her *Don Diego de la Haya Fernández* that the Audiencia accepted Carmona's recommendation. Luz Alba Chacón de Umaña, *Don Diego de la Haya Fernández* (San José: Editorial Costa Rica, 1967), 87.

98. Chacón de Umaña, *Don Diego*, 87; MacLeod, "On the Edge of Empire," 374; Meléndez Obando, "Contrabando de esclavos," 104.

99. Sidney W. Mintz and Richard Price, *The Birth of African-American Culture: An Anthropological Perspective* (Boston, MA: Beacon Press, 1992, originally published as *An Anthropological Approach to the Afro-American Past*, Philadelphia, PA: Institute for the Study of Human Issues, 1976), 43, 44, 48. See also the different perspectives in Michael A. Gomez, *Exchanging Our Country Marks* (Chapel Hill: University of North Carolina Press, 1998), 165–66; Stephanie Ellen Smallwood, "Salt-Water Slaves: African Enslavement, Migration, and Settlement in the Anglo-Atlantic World, 1660–1700," (PhD diss., Duke University, 1999), 278–82.

100. For example, see the Declaración de Pedro, esclavo del Sarg. Mayor don Juan Francisco de Ibarra y Calvo, Cartago, November 7, 1719, ANCR, G. 187, fols. 12v–13.

101. Mintz and Price, *Birth of African-American Culture*, 43–44. For the importance of the shipmate relationship in other regions of the Americas, see Robert W. Slenes, "'*Malungu ngoma* vem!' África encoberta e descoberta no Brasil," *Revista USP* (Brazil), no. 12 (1991–1992): 48–67; Colin A. Palmer, "From Africa to the Americas: Ethnicity in the Early Black Communities of the Americas," *Journal of World History* (Honolulu) 6, no. 2 (1995): 230–31; Philip D. Morgan, *Slave Counterpoint: Black Culture in the Eighteenth-Century Chesapeake and Lowcountry* (Chapel Hill: University of North Carolina Press, 1998), 448–49; Walter Hawthorne, "'Being Now, as It Were, One Family': Shipmate Bonding on the Slave Vessel *Emilia*, in Rio de Janeiro and Throughout the Atlantic World," *Luso-Brazilian Review* 45, no. 1 (2008): 53–77; Rachel Sarah O'Toole, *Bound Lives: Africans, Indians, and the Making of Race in Colonial Peru* (Pittsburgh, PA: University of Pittsburgh Press, 2012), 53–55; Alex Borucki, "Shipmate Networks and Black Identities in the Marriage Files of Montevideo, 1768–1803," *Hispanic American Historical Review* 93, no. 2 (2013): 205–38.

102. Declaración de María, esclava de María Calvo, Cartago, September 10, 1719, ANCR, C. 242, fols. 1v, 2; Declaración de María Victoria, esclava del Cap. Don José de Mier Cevallos, Cartago, September 6, 1719, ANCR, C. 266, fol. 1v.

103. Declaración de María, negra de casta popo, Valle de Barva, November 12, 1719, ANCR, G. 188, fol. 7v.

104. Careamiento de esclavos, Cartago, October 2, 1720, ANCR, C. 267, fol. 56v; María de los Angeles Acuña, "Mujeres esclavas en la Costa Rica del siglo XVIII: Estrategias frente a la esclavitud," *Diálogos: Revista Electrónica de Historia* (Costa Rica) 5, nos. 1–2 (2004–2005), n42, http://www.historia.fcs.ucr.ac.cr/articulos/esp-genero/1parte/CAP1Marielos/CAP1Marielostexto.html.

105. Contrast with Mintz and Price's contention that the shipmate bond "already announced the birth of new societies founded on new kinds of principles." *Birth of African-American Culture*, 44.

106. Declaración de Pedro de Rosas, esclavo del Cap. Juan Sancho de Castañeda, Cartago, May 26, 1720, ANCR, C. 231, fol. 14v.

107. Declaración de Pedro, esclavo del Sarg. Mayor don Francisco de Ocampo Golfín, Valle de Barva, November 12, 1719, ANCR, G. 188, fol. 4.

CHAPTER FOUR

1. Pregón de negros, Cartago, May 4, 1710, Archivo Nacional de Costa Rica, San José (hereafter, ANCR), Sección Colonial Cartago (hereafter, C.) 187, fols. 58 and quoting from fol. 58v; Primer pregón de negros, Cartago, April 25, 1710, ANCR, C. 187, fols. 50–50v; Segundo pregón de negros, Cartago, April 28, 1710, ANCR,

C. 187, fols. 51–52v; Tercer pregón de negros, Cartago, May 1, 1710, ANCR, C. 187, fols. 51v–52.

2. Nombramiento y juramento de avaluadores, Cartago, April 23, 1710, ANCR, C. 187, fols. 44v–46.

3. Primer pregón de negros, Cartago, April 25, 1710, ANCR, C. 187, fols. 50–50v; Segundo pregón de negros, Cartago, April 28, 1710, ANCR, C. 187, fols. 51–52v; Tercer pregón de negros, Cartago, May 1, 1710, ANCR, C. 187, fols. 51v–52.

4. Declaración del Cap. Francisco de los Reyes, Cartago, July 9, 1703, Archivo General de Indias, Seville (hereafter, AGI), Audiencia de Guatemala (hereafter, AG) 359, pieza 5, fols. 6v, 9–9v; Notificación de auto al Gobernador don Francisco Serrano de Reyna y su respuesta, Cartago, January 12, 1701, ANCR, C. 109, fol. 51v.

5. Almoneda de negros, Cartago, May 5, 1710, ANCR, C. 187, fols. 59–60; Almoneda de negros, Cartago, May 18, 1710, ANCR, C. 187, fols. 63–64v.

6. Venta de esclavo, Cartago, June 22, 1710, ANCR, C. 187, fols. 203v–4.

7. Walter Johnson, *Soul by Soul: Life Inside the Antebellum Slave Market* (Cambridge, MA: Harvard University Press, 2000), 129.

8. Venta de esclavo, Cartago, September 28, 1706, ANCR, Protocolos Coloniales de Cartago (hereafter, PC) 862, fols. 61v–63v, quoting from fol. 62.

9. Katia M. de Queirós Mattoso, *To Be a Slave in Brazil, 1550–1888*, trans. Arthur Goldhammer (New Brunswick, NJ: Rutgers University Press, 1986), 93–97.

10. Silvia Hunold Lara, *Campos da violência: Escravos e senhores na capitania do Rio de Janeiro 1750–1808* (Rio de Janeiro: Editora Paz e Terra, 1988), 21, 54.

11. Diligencia, Extramuros de Cartago, January 1720, ANCR, C. 232, fol. 14.

12. Careamiento de negros, Cartago, October 2, 1720, ANCR, C. 267, fols. 55–56; Memoria de las personas que asistieron en la presa de negros, Cartago, August 12, 1710, ANCR, C. 182, fol. 45; Venta de esclavos, Barva, September 2, 1710, ANCR, Sección Colonial Guatemala (hereafter, G.) 187, fols. 27–27v; Tercer día de inventarios y avalúos de los bienes del Sarg. Mayor don Juan Francisco de Ibarra y Calvo, Cartago, March 15, 1737, ANCR, Mortuales Coloniales de Cartago (hereafter, MCC) 850, fols. 11v.

13. Declaración de Miguel, negro bozal de casta mina, León, Nic., May 5, 1722, ANCR, G. 198, fols. 3–3v; Tatiana Lobo Wiehoff, "La travesura de don Tomás," in *Negros y blancos: Todo mezclado*, by Tatiana Lobo Wiehoff and Mauricio Meléndez Obando (San José: Editorial de la Universidad de Costa Rica, 1997), 38–41.

14. Venta de esclavo, Cartago, January 26, 1660, ANCR, PC 815, fols. 59–60; Venta de esclavo, Cartago, September 19, 1675, ANCR, PC 823, fols. 30–33; Reconocimiento y avalúo de esclava, Cartago, September 23, 1719, ANCR, C. 253, fol. 2.

15. Tasación y avalúo de esclavos, Cartago, September 5, 1720, ANCR, C. 277, fol. 5.

16. For a recent example, see the autobiography of a young woman captured in Sudan in the 1980s: Mende Nazer, *Slave* (New York: Public Affairs, 2003), chap. 10.

17. John Barbot, *A Description of the Coasts of North and South Guinea, and of Ethiopia Inferior, Vulgarly Angola,* in *A Collection of Voyages and Travels,* ed. Awnsham Churchill and John Churchill, 6 vols. (London: By Assignment for Messrs. Churchill, 1732), 5:47.

18. Auto del notario del Santo Oficio de la Inquisición, Cartago, October 21, 1771, Archivo de la Curia Metropolitana de San José (hereafter, ACMSJ), Sección Fondos Antiguos, Serie Documentación Encuadernada (hereafter, SFASDE), Caja 27, quoting from fol. 324; Declaración de Juan Antonio González, Cartago, October 28, 1771, ACMSJ, SFASDE, Caja 27, fol. 325.

19. Don Gabriel de la Haya y Bolívar al Teniente de Gobernador Cap. don Bernardo Ruiz de Aviles, 1724, ANCR, Sección Complementario Colonial (hereafter, CC) 5816, fol. 1v.

20. Barbara Bush, *Slave Women in Caribbean Society, 1650–1838* (Bloomington: Indiana University Press, 1990), 44; Frank T. Proctor III, "Slavery, Identity, and Culture: An Afro-Mexican Counterpoint, 1640–1763" (PhD diss., Emory University, 2003), 153; Stanley J. Stein, *Vassouras: A Brazilian Coffee County, 1850–1890* (New York: Atheneum, 1970), 158; Eugene D. Genovese, *Roll, Jordan, Roll: The World the Slaves Made* (New York: Pantheon, 1974), 352–53; Richard H. Steckel, "Miscegenation and the American Slave Schedules," *Journal of Interdisciplinary History* 11, no. 2 (1980): 254–55.

21. Declaración de Felipa Arias, Bagaces, February 10, 1724, ANCR, CC 5816, fol. 7v.

22. Carlos Meléndez, "El negro en Costa Rica durante la colonia," in Carlos Meléndez and Quince Duncan, *El negro en Costa Rica* (San José: Editorial Costa Rica, 1989), 44.

23. Philip D. Morgan, *Slave Counterpoint: Black Culture in the Eighteenth-Century Chesapeake and Lowcountry* (Chapel Hill: University of North Carolina Press, 1998), 258–59; Lara, *Campos da violência,* chap. 2; Genovese, *Roll, Jordan, Roll,* 67–69, 124.

24. Asunción Lavrin, "Sexuality in Colonial Mexico: A Church Dilemma," in *Sexuality and Marriage in Colonial Latin America,* ed. Lavrin (Lincoln: University of Nebraska Press, 1989), 71–72.

25. Herman L. Bennett, *Africans in Colonial Mexico: Absolutism, Christianity, and Afro-Creole Consciousness, 1570–1640* (Bloomington: Indiana University Press, 2003).

26. V. I. Lenin, "The State," in *Collected Works,* 45 vols. (Moscow: Foreign Languages Publishing House, 1963–1970), 29:478.

27. Visita de cárcel pública, Cartago, December 24, 1700, ANCR, Municipal 483, fol. 13.

28. Michael A. Gomez, *Exchanging Our Country Marks: The Transformation of African Identities in the Colonial and Antebellum South* (Chapel Hill: University of North Carolina Press, 1998), 168.

29. David Eltis, *The Rise of African Slavery in the Americas* (Cambridge: Cambridge University Press, 2000), 156–57; Erik J. W. Hofstee, "The Great Divide: Aspects of

the Social History of the Middle Passage in the Trans-Atlantic Slave Trade" (PhD diss., Michigan State University, 2002), 180, 183.

30. Ernest Mandel, *An Introduction to Marxist Economic Theory* (New York: Pathfinder Press, 1970), 8.

31. Jacob Gorender, "Violência, consenso e contratualidade," in *A escravidão reabilitada* (São Paulo: Editora Ática, 1990), 27, 34–35, 38; Ernest Mandel, *Marxist Economic Theory*, trans. Brian Pearce (London: Merlin Press, 1968), 691.

32. Declaración de un negro bozal por medio de Francisco, negro de casta arará quien sirve de intérprete, Cartago, April 16, 1710, ANCR, C. 187, fol. 22v; Inventario de 16 negros y negras, Cartago, June 11, 1710, ANCR, C. 187, fol. 149.

33. Memoria de gastos presentada por el Alf. Juan Bautista Retana, presentada en Cartago, June 28, 1710, ANCR, C. 187, fols. 204v–5.

34. Memoria de los gastos para la manutención de los negros desde el 14 de abril hasta el 24 de julio de 1710, presentada en Cartago por el Cap. Juan López de la Rea y Soto, July 1710, ANCR, C. 182, fols. 43–43v.

35. Declaración de Jacinto de Rivera, Cartago, May 13, 1710, ANCR, C. 187, fol. 116.

36. Razón y memoria de los gastos para la manutención de los negros desde el 12 de mayo hasta el 17 de julio de 1710, presentada en Cartago por el Cap. don Antonio de la Vega Cabral, July 17, 1710, ANCR, C. 182, fol. 38.

37. Clarence J. Munford, *The Black Ordeal of Slavery and Slave Trading in the French West Indies, 1625–1715*, 3 vols. (Lewiston, NY: Edwin Mellen Press, 1991), 2:465.

38. Bowser, *African Slave*, 79; Munford, *Black Ordeal*, 2:465, 474; Ira Berlin, *Many Thousands Gone: The First Two Centuries of Slavery in North America* (Cambridge, MA: Belknap Press of Harvard University Press, 1998), 24.

39. Mattoso, *To Be a Slave*, chap. 4.

40. Declaración de Gaspar de Acosta Arévalo, Cartago, April 16, 1710, ANCR, C. 187, fol. 29v.

41. Parecer del fiscal, Madrid, March 12, 1708, AGI, Indiferente 2783.

42. E. Y. Egblewogbe, "Personal Names as a Parameter for the Study of Culture: The Case of the Ghanaian Ewe," in *Peuples du golfe du Bénin*, ed. François de Medeiros (Paris: Karthala, 1984), 209–19; Albert Tingbé-Azalou, "Rites de dation du nom initial de naissance chez les Aja-Fon du Bénin," *Anthropos* 85 (1990): 187–92.

43. A. B. Quartey-Papafio, "The Use of Names among the Gãs or Accra People of the Gold Coast," *Journal of the African Society* 13, no. 50 (1914): quoting from 169; C. C. Reindorf, *The History of the Gold Coast and Asante* (Basel, Switzerland: printed by the author, 1895), 23–24.

44. Barbot, *Barbot on Guinea*, 2:506; Philip Bartle, "The Universe Has Three Souls: Notes on Translating Akan Culture," *Journal of Religion in Africa* 14 (1983): 99, 101.

45. S. Wilson, "Aperçu historique sur les peuples et cultures dans le golfe du Bénin: Le cas des 'mina' d'Anécho," in *Peuples du golfe du Bénin: Aja-éwé (colloque de Cotonou)*, ed. François de Medeiros (Paris: Karthala, 1984), 148.

46. Melville J. Herskovits, *Dahomey: An Ancient West African Kingdom*, 2 vols. (New York: J. J. Augustin, 1938), 1:263; Wendy Schottman, "Baatonu Personal Names from Birth to Death," *Africa* 70, no. 1 (2000): 80.

47. For some early eighteenth-century stereotypes about African cultures, see Acuerdo de la Junta de Negros, [Madrid?], July 25, 1707, AGI, Indiferente 2782.

48. See, for example, Primera almoneda, Esparza, November 30, 1700, ANCR, 109, fols. 16v–18; Primera almoneda, Cartago, September 17, 1702, ANCR, C. 113, fols. 9–9v.

49. John K. Thornton, "Central African Names and African-American Naming Patterns," *William & Mary Quarterly*, 3rd ser., 50, no. 4 (1993): 727–42.

50. Declaraciones de tres negros bozales, Cartago, April 16, 1710, ANCR, C. 187, fols. 18v, 21v, 23v.

51. "Diego" was purchased in Esparza by the priest's brother, Antonio de Angulo Gascón, on November 30, 1700, ANCR, C. 109, fols. 18–18v; AGI, 359, pieza 6, fol. 26.

52. Venta de esclavo, Cartago, May 25, 1716, ANCR, G. 187, fols. 30v–33; Partida del matrimonio de Antonio de la Riva y Agüero, negro libre, y de Juana Antonia Sánchez, mestiza, Cartago, April 18, 1747, ACMSJ, Libros de Matrimonios de Cartago, no. 4/Family History Library, Salt Lake City, Utah (hereafter, FHL), VAULT INTL film 1219727, item 10.

53. I base this assertion on an examination of ANCR, PC 801 (1607)–934 (1746); ANCR, Protocolos Coloniales de Heredia 573 (1721)–94 (1749); ANCR, Protocolos Coloniales de San José 411 (1721)–15 (1738); ACMSJ, SFASDE, Caja 20 (1692, 1696, 1719); *Indices de los protocolos de Cartago*, vols. 1–3 (San José: Tipografía Nacional, 1909–1930); *Indice de los protocolos de Heredia, 1721–1851* (San José: Tipografía Nacional, 1904).

54. Trevor G. Burnard, "Slave Naming Patterns: Onomastics and the Taxonomy of Race in Eighteenth-Century Jamaica," *Journal of Interdisciplinary History* 31, no. 3 (2001): 325–46; Munford, *Black Ordeal*, 2:471.

55. Partida del bautizo de Bartolomé, Cartago, [October] 11, 1599, ACMSJ, Libros de Bautizos de Cartago, no. 1/FHL, VAULT INTL film 1219701, item 1.

56. R. Douglas Cope writes that "less than 6 percent of slaves used their masters' surnames" in seventeenth-century Mexico City but does not indicate that he researched the slaves' previous owners. R. Douglas Cope, *The Limits of Racial Domination: Plebeian Society in Colonial Mexico City, 1660–1720* (Madison: University of Wisconsin Press, 1994), 60–61, quoting from 61.

57. Codicilio de María de Ortega, Cartago, 1657, ANCR, PC 815 bis, fols. 287, 288; Venta de esclava, Cartago, January 10, 1677, ANCR, PC 825, fols. 60–61v; Testamento de Juan de la Cruz Fonseca, Cartago, May 17, 1689, ANCR, PC 838, fols. 59, 60–60v.

58. Declaración de Lorenza González, negra esclava del Cap. José Antonio Bermúdez, September 10, 1719, ANCR, C. 241, fols. 1v–2.

59. Testamento del Mtre. de Campo don Lorenzo Antonio de Granda y Balvín, Cartago, October 2, 1712, ANCR, PC 871, fols. 59v–60; Obligación del Cap. Juan Sancho de Castañeda y de su mujer doña Juana de Alvarado, Cartago, January

1713, in *Indice de los protocolos de Cartago*, 2:224; Testamento de doña Juana de Alvarado y Jirón, viuda del Cap. don Pedro Ortiz de Rosas y del Cap. don Juan Sancho de Castañeda, Cartago, April 6, 1737, ANCR, PC 916, fol. 91v; *Indice de los protocolos de Cartago*, 3:443.

60. Partida del bautizo de Isabel, Cartago, April 6, 1622, ACMSJ, Libros de Bautizos de Cartago, no. 1/FHL, VAULT INTL film 1219701, item 1; Testamento del Cap. Pedro de Ochoa Leguizamo, Cartago, February 12, 1611, ANCR, G. 34, fol. 56.

61. Defunciones de Cartago y cuentas presentadas por Juan de Chavarría Navarro del dinero a su cargo por concepto de entierros, Cartago, June 12, 1711, ACMSJ, SFASDE, Caja 9, fol. 86v; Concierto de aprendiz, Cartago, August 4, 1730, ANCR, PC 904, fols. 44–45; Lista general de gente y armas de Matina, Matina, January 23, 1719, ANCR, CC 3797, fol. 25.

62. Lista de los milicianos negros, pardos, mulatos y mestizos bajos de Esparza, November 9, 1726, ANCR, CC 3792, fol. 24v; Lista de las milicias de gente parda, Cartago, November 21, 1734, ANCR, CC 3798, fol. 34v; Lista de la compañía de pardos libres de Esparza, July 1, 1740, ANCR, CC 3864, fol. 24; Testamento del Cap. José Nicolás de la Haya, Cartago, May 2, 1747, ANCR, MCC 841, fol. 5v; Registro del entierro de un hijo de José Matamba, mulato, Cartago, September 10, 1688, ACMSJ, SFASDE, Caja 9, Libro 3, fols. 55–55v.

63. For the unusual case of colonial Colombia, see Germán de Granda Gutiérrez, "Datos antroponímicos sobre negros esclavos musulmanos en Nueva Granada," *Thesaurus* (Bogotá) 27, no. 1 (1972): 89–103, and Granda Gutiérrez, "Testimonios documentales sobre la preservación del sistema antroponímico twi entre los esclavos negros de la Nueva Granada," *Revista Española de Lingüística* 1, no. 2 (1971): 265–74, esp. 272–74.

64. Careamiento de esclavos, Cartago, October 2, 1720, ANCR, C. 267, fol. 56v; María de los Angeles Acuña, "Mujeres esclavas en la Costa Rica del siglo XVIII: Estrategias frente a la esclavitud," *Diálogos: Revista Electrónica de Historia* (Costa Rica) 5, nos. 1–2 (April 2004–February 2005), n42, http://www.historia.fcs.ucr.ac.cr/articulos/esp-genero/1parte/CAP1Marielos/CAP1Marielostexto.html.

65. Frederick P. Bowser, *The African Slave in Colonial Peru, 1524–1650* (Stanford, CA: Stanford University Press, 1974), 347; Stuart B. Schwartz, *Sugar Plantations in the Formation of Brazilian Society: Bahia, 1550–1835* (Cambridge: Cambridge University Press, 1985), 251; Douglas B. Chambers, "'He Is an African but Speaks Plain': Historical Creolization in Eighteenth-Century Virginia," in *The African Diaspora*, ed. Alusine Jalloh and Stephen E. Maizlish (College Station: Texas A&M University Press, 1996), 125n3; Stephanie E. Smallwood, *Saltwater Slavery: A Middle Passage from Africa to American Diaspora* (Cambridge, MA: Harvard University Press, 2007).

66. Declaración de Miguel, negro bozal mina, León, Nic., May 12, 1722, ANCR, G. 198, fol. 9.

67. Declaración de Antonia, negra esclava de Diego de Aguilar, Cartago, June 13, 1720, ANCR, C. 276, fol. 1v.

68. Notificación al Alf. José de Guevara y su respuesta, San Francisco del Salto, Valle de Bagaces, October 19, 1719, ANCR, C. 256, fol. 3.

69. Auto del gobernador, Cartago, January 3, 1720, ANCR, C. 240, fol. 5.

70. Venta de esclavo, Cartago, August 26, 1730, ANCR, PC 904, fols. 45–47v.

71. Declaración de José Feliciano de Acuña, Cartago, November 6, 1720, ANCR, G. 185, fol. 88; Declaración de Matías Quesada, Cartago, November 6, 1720, ANCR, G. 185, fol. 89.

72. Ray A. Kea, *Settlements, Trade, and Polities on the Seventeenth-Century Gold Coast* (Baltimore, MD: Johns Hopkins University Press, 1982), 12; Biodun Adediran, *The Frontier States of Western Yorubaland, circa 1600–1889: State Formation and Political Growth in an Ethnic Frontier Zone* (Ibadan, Nigeria: Institut Français de Recherche en Afrique, 1994), 4; Robin Law, *The Oyo Empire, c. 1600–c. 1836: A West African Imperialism in the Era of the Atlantic Slave Trade* (Oxford: Clarendon Press, 1977), 202; Robin Law, *The Slave Coast of West Africa, 1550–1759* (Oxford: Clarendon Press, 1991), 38–40.

73. Robin Law, "Between the Sea and the Lagoons: The Interaction of Maritime and Inland Navigation on the Pre-Colonial Slave Coast," *Cahiers d'Études Africaines* 29, no. 2 (no. 114) (1989): 212–13.

74. Adriano Parreira, *Economia e sociedade em Angola na epoca da rainha Jinga (século XVII)* (Lisbon: Editorial Estampa, 1990), 83; Anne Hilton, *The Kingdom of Kongo* (Oxford: Clarendon Press, 1985), 7.

75. Gomez, *Exchanging Our Country Marks*, 169; Munford, *Black Ordeal*, 2:467.

76. Declaración del Cap. Francisco de los Reyes, Cartago, July 9, 1703, AGI, AG 359, pieza 5, fols. 5v, 15v; Declaración de Juan Antonio Bogarín, Cartago, August 21, 1703, AGI, AG 359, pieza 5, fol. 32; Testimonio de venta de 10 negros, n.d. but ca. 1703, ANCR, C. 265, fol. 3v.

77. Alonso de Sandoval, *Un tratado sobre la esclavitud*, ed. Enriqueta Vila Vilar (Madrid: Alianza Editorial, 1987, originally published 1627), 382–84, 399, 412–13; T. Bentley Duncan, *The Atlantic Islands: Madeira, the Azores and the Cape Verdes in Seventeenth-Century Commerce and Navigation* (Chicago, IL: University of Chicago Press, 1972), 230–31, 233.

78. Partida de bautizo, Cartago, April 15, 1639, ACMSJ, Libros de Bautizos de Cartago, no. 1/FHL, VAULT INTL film 1219701, Item 1. Despite being strongly condemned by Church law, the administration of a second baptism was common in Costa Rica, usually to children on whom water "had been poured in case of necessity." See *Catechism of the Council of Trent for Parish Priests, Issued by Order of Pope Pius V*, trans. John A. McHugh and Charles J. Callan (Rockford, IL: TAN Books, 1982, originally published 1923), 200–202.

79. Inventario de 22 negros y negras traídos de Matina por el Cap. Gaspar de Acosta Arévalo, Cartago, April 14, 1710, ANCR, C. 187, fols. 12–13v; Declaración de Gaspar Acosta Arévalo, Cartago, April 17, 1710, ANCR, C. 187, fols. 27, 30.

80. Memoria de los gastos para la manutención de los negros desde el 12 de mayo hasta el 14 de abril hasta el 24 de julio de 1710, presentada en Cartago por el Cap. Juan López de la Rea y Soto, July 1710, ANCR, C. 182, fols. 43–43v.

81. León Fernández, *Historia de Costa Rica durante la dominación española 1502–1821* (Madrid: Tipografía de Manuel Ginés Hernández, 1889), 300, 308.

82. ACMSJ, Libros de Bautizos de Cartago, nos. 1–6 (1595–1738)/FHL, VAULT INTL film 1219701, items 1–5, VAULT INTL film 1219702, item 1. By contrast, it was extremely rare for adult Africans to remain unbaptized in colonial Rio de Janeiro. Mariza de Carvalho Soares, "Mina, Angola e Guiné: Nomes d'África no Rio de Janeiro setecentista," *Tempo* (Brazil) 3, no. 6 (1998): 82–83.

83. Partida del bautizo de Petrona, negra esclava del Cap. Salvador Suárez de Lugo; Partida del bautizo de María, negra bozal esclava del Cap. Salvador Suárez de Lugo, both Esparza, February 20, 1713, and both in ACMSJ, Libros de Bautizos de Esparza (1706–1819)/FHL, VAULT INTL film 1223548, item 5; Venta de esclavas, Esparza, October 10, 1710, ANCR, G. 185, fols. 14–16. Stuart Schwartz and Stephen Gudeman categorically state that in colonial Brazil, "masters never served as godparents to their own slaves." Stephen Gudeman and Stuart B. Schwartz, "Cleansing Original Sin: Godparenthood and the Baptism of Slaves in Eighteenth-Century Bahia," in *Kinship Ideology and Practice in Latin America*, ed. Raymond T. Smith (Chapel Hill: University of North Carolina Press, 1984), 44. In Costa Rica, masters serving as godparents was also unusual, but relatives of the master serving in that capacity was routine.

84. *Catechism of the Council of Trent*, 185.

85. See Takashi Maeyama, "The Masters Versus the Slaves Under the Plantation Systems in Brazil: Some Preliminary Considerations," *Latin American Studies* (University of Tsukuba, Japan) 3 (1981): 119.

86. Declaración de Pedro, esclavo del Sarg. Mayor don Juan Francisco de Ibarra y Calvo, November 7, 1719, ANCR, G. 187, fol. 12.

87. Bando de buen gobierno, Cartago, March 26, 1737, ANCR, C. 389, fol. 5v.

88. Fe de muerte de la negra María, Cartago, April 28, 1719, ANCR, C. 211, fol. 113. For his usage of "rudo," see Real Academia Española, *Diccionario de autoridades*, 3 vols. (Madrid: Editorial Gredos, 1963, originally published in 1726 in 6 vols.), [5:650] 3:650.

89. For example, see Robin Law, "Religion, Trade and Politics on the 'Slave Coast': Roman Catholic Missions in Allada and Whydah in the Seventeenth Century," *Journal of Religion in Africa* 21 (1991): 43–77.

90. Paul Lovejoy, "Slavery, the Bilad al-Sudan and the Frontiers of the African Diaspora," in *Slavery on the Frontiers of Islam*, ed. Paul Lovejoy (Princeton, NJ: Markus Wiener, 2004), 6, 7, 8; James H. Sweet, *Recreating Africa: Culture, Kinship, and Religion in the African-Portuguese World, 1441–1770* (Chapel Hill: University of North Carolina Press, 2003), 94.

91. Hilton, *Kingdom of Kongo*, 102; Sweet, *Recreating Africa*, 195–97. Almoneda de esclavo, Esparza, November 20, 1700, ANCR, C. 109, fols. 18–18v; Respuesta del Lic. don Diego de Angulo Gascón, Cartago, July 17, 1720, ANCR, C. 263, fol. 3v.

92. Inventario de los bienes del difunto Lic. don Diego de Angulo Gascón, Cartago, January 18, 1727, ANCR, MCC 451, fol. 16; Georges Balandier, *Daily Life in the Kingdom of the Kongo from the 16th to the 18th Century*, trans. Helen Weaver

(London: George Allen & Unwin, 1968), 112; Hilton, *Kingdom of Kongo*, 94, quoting from 102.

93. Inventario de los bienes del difunto Lic. don Diego de Angulo Gascón, Cartago, January 18, 1727, ANCR, MCC 451, fol. 7.

94. Adrian Hastings, "The Christianity of Pedro IV of the Kongo, 'the Pacific,'" *Journal of Religion in Africa* 28, no. 2 (1998), 149–50; Hilton, *Kingdom of Kongo*, 102; John K. Thornton, *Africa and Africans in the Making of the Atlantic World, 1400–1680*, 2nd ed. (Cambridge: Cambridge University Press, 1998), 257–58.

95. Inventario de los bienes del difunto Lic. don Diego de Angulo Gascón, Cartago, January 18, 1727, ANCR, MCC 451, fols. 17–18.

96. Partidas de confirmación, Cartago, March 25, 1625, ACMSJ, Confirmaciones de Cartago, Libro 1 (1609, 1625)/FHL, VAULT INTL film 1219727, item 2.

97. Testamento del Sarg. Mayor don Francisco de Ocampo Golfín, Cartago, October 3, 1714, ANCR, PC 874, fols. 21–21v; Declaración de Miguel, negro de casta congo, Valle de Barva, November 12, 1719, ANCR, G. 188, fol. 5; Declaración de Manuel, negro de casta congo, Valle de Barva, November 12, 1719, ANCR, G. 188, fol. 6; Linda M. Heywood, "The Angolan–Afro-Brazilian Cultural Connections," *Slavery & Abolition* 20, no. 1 (1999), 14; Sweet, *Recreating Africa*, 206–7.

98. Carta dote de don Bernardo García de Miranda a favor de doña Josefa de Casasola y Córdoba, Cartago, January 4, 1727, ANCR, PC 900, fols. 1v, 3–3v.

99. Declaración de Petrona, negra esclava del Sarg. Mayor don Salvador Suárez de Lugo, San Francisco de Tenorio, September 17, 1719, ANCR, G. 185, fols. 8v–9; Partida del bautizo de Petrona, Esparza, February 20, 1713, ACMSJ, Libros de Bautizos de Esparza, 1706–1819/FHL, VAULT INTL Film 1223548.

100. Declaración de Petrona, negra esclava del Sarg. Mayor don Salvador Suárez de Lugo, San Francisco de Tenorio, September 17, 1719, ANCR, G. 185, fol. 8.

Compare the second question of Jerónimo de Ripalda's *Exposición de la doctrina cristiana*, probably the most widely used Spanish-language catechism between the seventeenth and nineteenth centuries:

Q. Are you a Christian?
A. Yes, by the grace of Our Lord Jesus Christ.

Jerónimo de Ripalda, *Doctrina cristiana del P. Jerónimo de Ripalda e intento bibliográfico de la misma años 1591–1909*, ed. Juan M. Sánchez (Madrid: Imprenta Alemana, 1909), 3.

101. Declaración de Manuel García, esclavo del Cap. Manuel García, difunto, Cartago, December 20, 1733, ANCR, C. 325, fol. 240. "Miskitu" is the spelling preferred by the people themselves; "Mosquito" was invariably used in Spanish colonial documents.

102. Cf. Mariza de Carvalho Soares, *Devotos da cor: Identidade étnica, religiosidade e escravidão no Rio de Janeiro, século XVIII* (Rio de Janeiro: Civilização Brasileira, 2000).

103. Memoria de los bienes de Diego Angulo, presentada en Cartago, February 7, 1746, ANCR, MCC 462, fol. 3v.
104. Thornton, *Africa and Africans*, 267. Absolutely nothing suggests, however, a direct link between Kongo Christianity and the devotion to the Virgin of los Angeles, as Thornton seems to imply here. For the origins of the devotion, see Russell Lohse, "*La Negrita*, Queen of the Ticos: The Black Roots of Costa Rica's Patron Saint," *The Americas* 69, no. 3 (2013): 323–55.
105. Heywood, "Angolan–Afro-Brazilian Cultural Connections," 15.
106. Alonso de Sandoval, *Tratado sobre la esclavitud*, 139; António Carreira, *Cabo Verde: Formação e extinção de uma sociedade escravocrata, 1460–1878*, 2nd ed. (N.p.: Com o Patrocínio da Comissão da Comunidade Económica Europeia para o Instituto Caboverdeano do Livro, 1983), chap. 8.
107. Testamento de Diego García, negro libre, n.p., December 30, 1743, ANCR, PC 931, quoting from fol. 9, 10; Fundación de capellanía, Cartago, August 26, 1744, PC 931, fol. 83v.
108. Fundación de capellanía, Cartago, August 26, 1744, PC 931, fols. 81v–84, quoting from fol. 83v; Memoria de los aumentos de los bienes de la Cofradía de los Angeles, Cartago, October 29, 1737, ACMSJ, Sección Cofradías, Serie Cartago, Libro 16, fol. [93v] (burro, valued at thirty pesos); Carta dote, Barva, September 25, 1719, ANCR, PC 889, fols. 53–53v (house, valued at thirty pesos); Cuentas, división y partición de los bienes de doña Catalina González del Camino, Cartago, July 22, 1746, ANCR, MCC 797, fol. 94 (slave José, valued at thirty pesos).
109. Declaración de María Josefa Chávez, mulata esclava, Cartago, July 30, 1757, Archivo General de la Nación, Mexico City (hereafter AGN), Inquisición, vol. 929, exp. 25, fols. 364–64v.
110. Declaración de don Diego de Ibarra, Cartago, April 26, 1685, AGN, Inquisición, vol. 650, exp. 3, fol. 575; Padrón y memoria de los vecinos y moradores de Cartago, Cartago, March 27, 1691, ANCR, C. 83, fols. 4–4v.
111. *Indice de los protocolos de Cartago*, 1:452–53.
112. Testamento de María de Ortega, Cartago, April 30, 1655, ANCR, PC 815 bis, fol. 282; *Indice de los protocolos de Cartago*; Testamento de doña Ana de Retes, Cartago, April 20, 1704, ANCR, PC 859, fols. 21, 21v; Donación de una caballería de tierra, unas casas y tres esclavos, Cartago, November 25, 1704, ANCR, PC 859, fol. 44; Rina Cáceres, *Negros, mulatos, esclavos y libertos en la Costa Rica del siglo XVII* (Mexico: Instituto Panamericano de Geografía e Historia, 2000), 61.
113. Declaración de don Diego de Ibarra, Cartago, April 26, 1685, AGN, Inquisición, vol. 650, exp. 3, fol. 575, 575v.
114. For the similar case of an "Arda" slave discovering a mulatta's magic, see Sweet, *Recreating Africa*, 166–67; and for another case of an arará slave practicing divination to unmask malefactors in colonial Colombia, see Kathryn Joy McKnight,

"'En su tierra lo aprendió': An African Curandero's Defense Before the Cartagena Inquisition," *Colonial Latin American Review* 12, no. 1 (2003): 63–84.

115. Declaración de Leandro de Figueroa, corregidor de Pacaca, Cartago, October 9, 1609, AGN, Inquisición, vol. 292, exp. 25, fols. 92v–93v; Declaración de Juan de Buliaga, Guatemala, March 16, 1610, AGN, Inquisición, vol. 474, exp. 6, fol. 333.

116. Declaración de Leandro de Figueroa, corregidor de Pacaca, Cartago, October 9, 1609, AGN, Inquisición, vol. 292, exp. 25, fol. 93.

117. See Alonso de Sandoval's discussion of the "perverted sect of Mahoma" among the "*jolofos*" and other Senegambian peoples in *Tratado sobre la esclativud*, 118–20.

118. Declaración de Francisco de Salas, Cartago, October 13, 1609, AGN, Inquisición, vol. 292, exp. 25, fol. 102v.

119. Pereira's knowledge of Islam quickly exhausted, he passed on to suggestions that became more scandalous—and more dangerous—as they approached blasphemy. Pereira raised the stakes by offering Manuel a peso "to deny God, so that later they'll burn you." At that point, the table fell silent. His companions knew that Pereira had crossed a line, not only by inciting blasphemy but by ridiculing the Inquisition. Finally, Andrés López de Céspedes said mournfully, "I'd have given ten pesos if Gaspar Pereira hadn't said what he said." Declaración de Francisco de Salas, Cartago, October 13, 1609, AGN, Inquisición, vol. 292, exp. 25, fol. 102v. In February 1611, the Inquisition of Mexico took up the case of Pereira's "evil-sounding words." Carta del Comisario de la Inquisición de Niquinihomo y Nicaragua, unsigned and undated, recibida en el Santo Oficio, Mexico, February 7, 1611, AGN, Inquisición, vol. 292, exp. 25, fols. 85–86.

120. Michael A. Gomez argues that this was the case on Sapelo Island, Georgia in the antebellum United States. Michael A. Gomez, "Muslims in Early America," *Journal of Southern History* 60, no. 4 (1994): esp. 693–99.

121. Excluding the literature on the Malê rebellion in 1835 in Bahia, Brazil (a subgenre in itself), works on enslaved African Muslims in the New World have focused on North America and the British Caribbean. Of varying quality, they include Muhammad Abdul Jassan, "Muslim's [*sic*] Struggle Against Slavery and Their Efforts for Retention of Cultural Identity in the Caribbean Territories," *Hamdard Islamicus* (Pakistan) 21, no. 1 (1998): 75–84; Sultana Afroz, "The Unsung Slaves: Islam in Plantation Jamaica," *Caribbean Quarterly* 41, nos. 3–4 (1995): 30–44; Afroz, "The Manifestation of *Tawhid*: The Muslim Heritage of the Maroons in Jamaica," *Caribbean Quarterly* 45, no. 1 (1999): 27–40; Allan D. Austin, *African Muslims in Antebellum America: A Sourcebook* (New York: Garland, 1984); Austin, "Islamic Identities in Africans in North America in the Days of Slavery (1731–1865)," *Islam et Sociétés au Sud du Sahara* 7 (1993): 205–19; Sylviane Diouf, *Servants of Allah: African Muslims Enslaved in the Americas* (New York: New York University Press, 1998); Gomez, "Muslims in Early America"; Thomas C. Parramore, "Muslim Slave Aristocrats in North Carolina," *North Carolina Historical Review* 77, no. 2 (2000): 127–50; Brent Singleton, "The

Ummah Slowly Bled: A Select Bibliography of Enslaved African Muslims in the Americas and the Caribbean," *Journal of Muslim Minority Affairs* 22, no. 2 (2002): 401–12. Maureen Warner-Lewis demolishes fanciful exaggerations of Islamic influence in the Caribbean in "Jamaica's Muslim Past: Misrepresentations," *Journal of Caribbean History* 37, no. 2 (2003): 294–316. To my knowledge, the only work on colonial Spanish America remains Granda Gutiérrez, "Datos antroponímicos."

122. Diouf, *Servants of Allah*, 179–84.

CHAPTER FIVE

1. Much of this chapter was taken from K. Russell Lohse, "Cacao and Slavery in Matina, Costa Rica, 1650–1750," in Lowell Gudmundson and Justin Wolfe, eds., *Blacks and Blackness in Central America: Between Race and Place* (Durham, NC: Duke University Press, 2010), 57–91. Copyright, 2010, Duke University Press. All rights reserved. Reprinted by permission of the publisher.

2. Carlos Meléndez Chaverri, "El negro en Costa Rica durante la colonia," in Carlos Meléndez and Quince Duncan, *El negro en Costa Rica* (San José: Editorial Costa Rica, 1989), 36.

3. Lowell Gudmundson K, "Mecanismos de movilidad social para la población de procedencia africana en Costa Rica colonial: Manumisión y mestizaje," in *Estratificación socio-racial y económica de Costa Rica, 1700-1850* (San José: Editorial Universidad Estatal a Distancia [EUNED], 1978), quoting from 25; Mario Barrantes Ferrero, *Un caso de esclavitud en Costa Rica* (San José: Instituto Geográfico Nacional, 1968), quoting from 5–6.

4. Jacob Gorender, "Equívocos e mistificações sobre a variedade do ser escravo," in *A escravidão reabilitada* (São Paulo: Editora Ática, 1990), 90.

5. Testamento del Cap. Miguel Calvo, Cartago, February 16, 1715, Archivo Nacional de Costa Rica, San José (hereafter, ANCR), Protocolos Coloniales de Cartago (hereafter, PC) 877, fol. 30v.

6. "Inventario de los árboles de cacao de la costa y valle de Matina y Reventazón.— Año de 1682," in León Fernández, ed., *Colección de documentos para la historia de Costa Rica*, 10 vols. (San José: Imprenta Nacional [vols. 1–3], Paris: Imprenta Pablo Dupont [vols. 4–5], Barcelona: Imprenta Viuda de Luis Tasso [vols. 6–10], 1881–1907), 8:403; "Los vecinos del valle de Bagases pretenden formar una villa, ciudad ó lugar en dicho valle, con independencia de la provincia de Costa Rica.— Año de 1688," in Fernández, *Colección de documentos*, 8:485–86.

7. Ira Berlin refers to slaves in "societies with slaves" as "jacks of all trades" in *Many Thousands Gone: The First Two Centuries of Slavery in North America* (Cambridge, MA: Belknap Press, Harvard University Press, 1998), 68.

8. See Robin Blackburn, "Slave Exploitation and the Elementary Structures of Enslavement," in *Serfdom and Slavery: Studies in Legal Bondage*, ed. M. L. Bush (London: Longman, 1996), 163–64; Claude Meillassoux, *The Anthropology of*

Slavery: The Womb of Iron and Gold, trans. Alide Dasnois (Chicago, IL: University of Chicago Press, 1991), 304.

9. Eric R. Wolf and Sidney W. Mintz, "Haciendas and Plantations in Middle America and the Antilles," *Social and Economic Studies* (Jamaica) 6, no. 3 (1957): 81–91.

10. Venta de dos esclavas, Esparza, October 16, 1710, ANCR, Sección Colonial Guatemala (hereafter, G.) 185, fols. 14–16.

11. Murdo J. MacLeod, *Spanish Central America: A Socioeconomic History 1520–1720* (Berkeley: University of California Press, 1973), 274; Claudia Quirós Vargas de Quesada, "Aspectos socioeconómicos de la ciudad del Espíritu Santo de Esparza y su jurisdicción (1574–1878)" (Licenciatura thesis, Universidad de Costa Rica, 1976), 260–61.

12. See the census in "Los vecinos del Valle de Bagases pretenden formar una villa, ciudad o lugar en dicho valle, con independencia del gobierno de la provincia de Costa Rica. Año de 1688," in Fernández, *Colección de documentos*, 8:477–501; Claudia Quirós Vargas, *La era de la encomienda* (San José: Editorial de la Universidad de Costa Rica, 1990), 284.

13. John K. Thornton's assertion that Africans "could easily find others who spoke their language and shared their norms in the new environment, especially if they were on a large estate or in an urban area," did not hold true in the Bagaces Valley, nor indeed in Costa Rica generally. John K. Thornton, *Africa and the Africans in the Making of the Atlantic World, 1400–1680*, 2nd ed. (Cambridge: Cambridge University Press, 1998), 205.

14. Quirós Vargas de Quesada, "Aspectos socioeconómicos," 165.

15. Registro del bautizo de María y Petrona, negras esclavas de doña Cecilia Vázquez de Coronado, Esparza, February 20, 1713, Archivo de la Curia Metropolitana de San José, Costa Rica (hereafter, ACMSJ), Libros de Bautizos de Esparza, 1706–1819/Family History Library, Salt Lake City, Utah (hereafter, FHL) VAULT INTL Film 1223548.

16. Declaración de María, negra de casta lucumí, Cartago, September 25, 1720, ANCR, Sección Colonial Cartago (hereafter, C.) 267, fol. 50v; El Sarg. Mayor don Salvador Suárez de Lugo hace manifestación de sus esclavos, San Francisco de Tenorio, November 20, 1719, ANCR, C. 229, fols. 17v–18; ANCR, G. 185, fols. 19v–20.

17. Registro del bautizo de Mónica de la Cruz, hija de María Egipciaca, negra esclava de doña Cecilia Vázquez de Coronado, Esparza, May 19, 1729, ACMSJ, Libros de Bautizos de Esparza, 1706–1819/FHL, VAULT INTL Film 1223548; Venta de esclavos, Cartago, November 8, 1731, ANCR, PC 906, fols. 160v–64.

18. MacLeod, *Spanish Central America*, 51; Quirós Vargas, *La era de la encomienda*, 29–30, 145.

19. Linda A. Newson, "The Depopulation of Nicaragua in the Sixteenth Century," *Journal of Latin American Studies* 14, no. 2 (1982): 268.

20. Quirós Vargas, *La era de la encomienda*, 236.

21. MacLeod, *Spanish Central America*, 50. Luis Sibaja reviews the contentious debate on the scale of the Indian slave trade from Nicaragua in "Los indígenas de Nicoya bajo el dominio español, 1522–1560," *Estudios Sociales Centroamericanos* 11, no. 32 (1982): 27–29.

22. Libro de tasaciones de los naturales de las Provincias de Guatemala, Nicaragua, Yucatán y Comayagua, 1548–1551, Archivo General de Indias, Seville (hereafter, AGI), Audiencia de Guatemala (hereafter, AG) 128, fols. 234v–35, 285v; partially published in Andrés Vega Bolaños, ed., *Colección Somoza: Documentos para la historia de Nicaragua*, 17 vols. (Madrid, 1945–1957), 14:402–3, 467. See also Luis Sibaja, "La encomienda de tributo en el Valle Central de Costa Rica (1569–1683)," *Cuadernos Centroamericanos de Ciencias Sociales* (Universidad de Costa Rica) no. 11 (1984): 52.

23. Quirós Vargas, *La era de la encomienda*, 30; Fernández, *Colección de documentos*, 1:105.

24. Quirós Vargas de Quesada, "Aspectos socioeconómicos," 170.

25. Inventario de bienes del difunto Alf. José Maroto, Cartago, August 2, 1683, ANCR, Mortuales Coloniales de Cartago (hereafter, MCC) 927, fol. 6v; Inventario del hato del difunto Alf. José Maroto, n.p., August 4, 1683, ANCR, MCC 927, fols. 9–9v.

26. Prisión y embargo de bienes del Sarg. Mayor don Juan Francisco de Ibarra, Cartago, April 24, 1719, ANCR, C. 211, fol. 87v.

27. Lowell Wayne Gudmundson Kristjanson, "La ganadería guanacasteca en la época de la independencia: La hacienda de San Juan de Dios, 1815-1835," in *Estratificación socio-racial y económica de Costa Rica, 1700–1850* (San José: Editorial de la Universidad Estatal a Distancia [EUNED], 1978), 97.

28. Testamento del Sarg. Mayor don Francisco de Ocampo Golfín, Cartago, October 3, 1714, ANCR, PC 874, fol. 21v, 22; Declaración de Miguel, negro de casta congo, Valle de Barva, November 12, 1719, ANCR, G. 188, fol. 5v.

29. Quirós Vargas de Quesada, "Aspectos socioeconómicos," 156.

30. J. Vansina and T. Obenga, "The Kongo Kingdom and Its Neighbours," in *Africa from the Sixteenth to the Eighteenth Century*, ed. B. A. Ogot, vol. 5 of *General History of Africa* (Paris: UNESCO, 1992), 5:547; Georges Balandier, *Daily Life in the Kingdom of the Kongo from the 16th to the 18th Century*, trans. Helen Weaver (London: George Allen & Unwin, 1968, originally published as *La vie quotidienne au royaume de Kongo du XVIe au XVIIIe siècle* [Paris: Hachette, 1965]), 106–7.

31. Descargos dados por el apoderado del General don José Lacayo de Briones, Sebastián Vicente Alvarez, presentados en Cartago, August 29, 1719, AGI, Escribanía 353B, fol. 330v.

32. Quirós Vargas de Quesada, "Aspectos socioeconómicos," 156–59, 193.

33. Elizabeth Fonseca, *Costa Rica colonial: La tierra y el hombre*, 3rd ed. (San José: Editorial Universitaria Centroamericana [EDUCA], 1986), 266; Quirós Vargas de Quesada, "Aspectos socioeconómicos," 164.

34. Carlos Meléndez, "Formas en la tenencia de la tierra durante el régimen colonial," in Carlos Meléndez, *Costa Rica: Tierra y poblamiento en la colonia* (San José: Editorial Costa Rica, 1977), 76–77.

35. "Informe de don Diego de la Haya Fernández sobre la Provincia de Costa Rica," in Luz Alba Chacón de Umaña, *Don Diego de la Haya Fernández* (San José: Editorial Costa Rica, 1967), 171, 173; Juan Carlos Solórzano Fonseca, "El comercio exterior de Costa Rica en la época colonial (1690–1760)" (Licenciatura thesis, Universidad de Costa Rica, 1977), 10.

36. Testamento del Alf. Tomás de Chávez, Cartago, September 15, 1708, ANCR, PC 865, fol. 82.

37. "Los vecinos del valle de Bagases pretenden formar una villa, ciudad ó lugar en dicho valle, con independencia de la provincia de Costa Rica.—Año de 1688," in Fernández, *Colección de documentos*, 8:485–86. This document notes race and legal condition very inconsistently, perhaps in itself an indication that de facto relationship to the landowner prevailed over race or legal condition. The census notes individuals described only as "negra" or "mulata," without reference to legal condition, living on the properties of Spaniards, as well as persons clearly identified as "negro libre," "mulata esclava," and other designations. In no case were people of African descent noted as heads of household unless specifically described as free.

38. "Los vecinos del valle de Bagases," 8:487.

39. Ibid., 8:489.

40. ACMSJ, Libros de Bautizos de Esparza, 1706–1819/FHL, VAULT INTL film 1223548, item 6.

41. Razón del Teniente General don Diego de Barros de quien hubo su esclavo Francisco Congo, Cartago, May 30, 1720, ANCR, C. 265, fol. 2v; Reconocimiento del despacho presentado por don Diego de Barros, Cartago, June 3, 1720, ANCR, C. 265, fol. 3v; Declaracion de José Congo, negro esclavo de doña Agueda Pérez de Muro, Matina, December 5, 1719, ANCR, C. 251, fol. 3v.

42. Carlos Meléndez, *Conquistadores y pobladores: Orígenes de los costarricenses* (San José: EUNED, 1982), 79; Juan Carlos Solórzano Fonseca and Claudia Quirós Vargas, *Costa Rica en el siglo XVI: Descubrimiento, exploración y conquista* (San José: Editorial de la Universidad de Costa Rica, 2006), 234.

43. Expediente de confirmación de encomienda de Costa Rica a Diego del Cubillo, Guatemala, July 5, 1624, AGI, AG 98, no. 36.

44. Sibaja, "Encomienda de tributo"; Partida del bautizo de Cristóbal, hijo de María, negra esclava de doña Mayor de Benavides, Cartago, August 15, 1616, Partida del bautizo de Sebastián, hijo de Lucía, negra esclava de doña Mayor de Benavides, Cartago, August 16, 1616, Partida del bautizo de Salvador, hijo de Mariana, negra esclava de doña Mayor de Benavides, Cartago, April 29, [1618], Partida del bautizo de Juana, hija de Isabel, negra esclava de doña Mayor de Benavides, Cartago, May 3, 1625, all in ACMSJ, Libros de Bautizos de Cartago (hereafter, LBC), no. 1/ FHL, VAULT INTL film 1219701, item 1; Partida de las confirmaciones de Pedro y de Isabel, hija de otra Isabel, negros esclavos de doña Mayor de Benavides,

Cartago, May 26, 1625, ACMSJ, Confirmaciones de Cartago, Libro 1 (1609–1625)/ FHL, VAULT INTL Film 1219727, item 2.

45. For a recent assertion that Spaniards in the Central Valley owned slaves mainly for purposes of prestige, see Elizabeth Fonseca Corrales et al., *Costa Rica en el siglo XVIII* (San José: Editorial de la Universidad de Costa Rica, 2001), 51.

46. Razón dada en el Juzgado Eclesiástico por el Lic. don Manuel González Coronel, Cartago, May 21, 1720, ANCR, C. 241, fol. 12.

47. Testamento de doña Francisca de Chinchilla, Cartago, July 21, 1671, ANCR, PC 818, fols. 36–38v.

48. Testamento del Cap. don Fernando de Salazar, Cartago, January 14, 1678, ANCR, PC 825, fols. 64–69.

49. Testamento de Francisco Fernández y doña Eugenia Rodríguez, Cartago, August 8, 1700, ANCR, PC 854, fols. 14–18v.

50. Testamento cerrado de doña Sebastiana Calvo, Cartago, November 4, 1700, ANCR, PC 853, fols. 56, 58v.

51. Carta del Cap. Antonio de Soto y Barahona y de Felipe de Meza al Gobernador, Matina, August 15, 1727, ANCR, C. 325, fols. 16v–17.

52. Causa criminal contra Juan Eusebio Picón, mulato libre, por haber dado muerte accidentalmente con una escopeta a María, indiezuela de seis a siete años, natural de Talamanca, Cartago, 1714, ANCR, Sección Complementario Colonial (hereafter, CC) 141 (10 fols.); Carlos Roberto López Leal, "Una rebelión indígena en Talamanca: Pablo Presbere y el alzamiento general de 1709" (Licenciatura thesis, Universidad de San Carlos de Guatemala, 1973).

53. Hilary McD. Beckles, *Natural Rebels: A Social History of Enslaved Black Women in Barbados* (New Brunswick, NJ: Rutgers University Press, 1989), 29–43; Michael Craton, *Searching for the Invisible Man: Slaves and Plantation Life in Jamaica* (Cambridge, MA: Harvard University Press, 1979), 168–69; Bernard Moitt, *Women and Slavery in the French Antilles, 1635–1848* (Bloomington: Indiana University Press, 2001), chap. 3.

54. Rina Cáceres, "Costa Rica, en la frontera del comercio de esclavos africanos," *Reflexiones* (Facultad de Ciencias Sociales, Universidad de Costa Rica), no. 65 (1997): 11.

55. Testamento de doña Inés Pereira, Cartago, September 12, 1659, ANCR, PC 817 bis, fol. 278; Rina Cáceres, *Negros, mulatos, esclavos y libertos en la Costa Rica del siglo XVII* (Mexico City: Instituto Panamericano de Geografía e Historia, 2000), 73.

56. Certificación de don José de Mier Cevallos, Sitio de San Jerónimo, Jurisdicción de Esparza, February 8, 1724, ANCR, CC 4140, fol. 13v; María de los Angeles Acuña León, "Papel reproductivo y productivo de las mujeres esclavas en Costa Rica del siglo XVIII," *Revista de Historia* (Costa Rica), nos. 57–58 (2008): 153.

57. Testamento de Fernando López de Ascuña, Esparza, February 5, 1682, ANCR, Mortuales de Puntarenas 2473, fol. 6; Carta de libertad, Esparza, July 12, 1675, ANCR, CC 3916, quoting from fol. 5.

58. Carta de libertad, Cartago, December 15, ANCR, Protocolos Coloniales de Heredia (hereafter, PH) 580, fol. 89v.

59. Carta de libertad, Cartago, August 4, 1746, ANCR, PC 934, fol. 59; Razón de dos esclavas y los hijos que tienen, Cartago, October 5, 1720, ANCR, G. 185, fol. 45.

60. Petición de doña Juana Núñez de Trupira, presentada en Cartago, July 1, 1692, ANCR, PC 842, fol. 63.

61. Petición de María Calvo al Gobernador, presentada en Cartago, July 1, 1720, ANCR, C. 242, fol. 13v.

62. Carta de libertad, Cartago, June 5, 1736, ANCR, PC 915, fol. 26v.

63. Carta de libertad, Cartago, February 2, 1677, ANCR, PC 825, fols. 7–8v.

64. Real cédula, Madrid, December 12, 1672, ANCR, C. 1078, fol. 179.

65. Carta de libertad, Cartago, October 9, 1703, ANCR, PC 857, fols. 61v–63.

66. Carta de libertad, Cartago, December 11, 1739, ANCR, PC 921, fols. 90v–91v.

67. Carta de libertad, Valle de Barva, July 9, 1741, ANCR, PH 587, fol. 16v.

68. Memoria y testamento de Clara Calvo, mulata libre, esclava que fue de Miguel Calvo, Cartago, February 2, 1716, ANCR, PC 878, fols. 36–37v.

69. Declaración de Jacob, esclavo del Cap. Antonio de Soto y Barahona, Cartago, October 2, 1719, ANCR, C. 233, fols. 5v–6; Petición del Cap. Antonio de Soto y Barahona, presentada en Cartago, May 20, 1720, ANCR, C. 233, quoting from fol. 34; Declaración de Nicolás Briones, Puebla de los Angeles, Cartago, May 22, 1720, ANCR, fol. 35v.

70. Venta de esclavo, Cartago, March 8, 1737, ANCR, PC 916, fols. 41–45.

71. For a Mexican example of the potentially enormous profits that artisan slaves could generate, see Patrick J. Carroll, *Blacks in Colonial Veracruz: Race, Ethnicity, and Regional Development* (Austin: University of Texas Press, 1991), 66.

72. Carta dote, Cartago, 1660, ANCR, PC 815, fol. 67; Concierto de aprendiz, Cartago, August 9, 1660, ANCR, PC 815, fol. 195.

73. Venta de esclavo, Cartago, October 22, 1665, ANCR, PC 817, fols. 69–69v; Concierto de aprendiz, Cartago, December 18, 1666, ANCR, PC 817 bis, fol. 418; Carta dote del Cap. don Juan Plaza a favor de doña Juana de Salazar, Cartago, May 10, 1687, ANCR, PC 836, fol. 86; Partida del matrimonio de Domingo de Alvarado, negro esclavo de Juana de Salazar, y de María Clemencia, india de Güicasí, Cartago, May 4, 1682, ACMSJ, Libros de Matrimonios de Cartago, no. 1/ FHL, VAULT INTL film 1219727, Item 6.

74. Poder para vender a un esclavo, Cartago, May 15, 1711, PC 870, fol. 22v.

75. Concierto de aprendiz, Cartago, March 29, 1689, ANCR, PC 838, fols. 53–54v. María Elizet Payne Iglesias mistakenly included Manuel among enslaved apprentices in "Actividades artesanales, siglo XVII (Maestros, oficiales y aprendices)," in *Costa Rica colonial*, ed. Luis F. Sibaja (San José: Ediciones Guayacán, 1989), 48.

76. Declaración de Francisco Caamaño, negro libre, Cartago, February 12, 1705, ANCR, CC 3978, fol. 4; Concierto de aprendiz, Cartago, April 30, 1718, ANCR, PC 885, fols. 83v–84v.

77. Concierto de aprendiz, Cartago, August 4, 1730, ANCR, PC 904, fols. 44–45; Balandier, *Daily Life in the Kingdom*, 107–10.

78. Relación geográfica de Costa Rica por el Gobernador don Juan Gemmir y Lleonart, Cartago, May 20, 1741, Archivo General de Centro América, Guatemala City (hereafter, AGCA), A1.17, exp. 5016, leg. 210, fols. 252, 253v.

79. Richard S. Dunn, *Sugar and Slaves: The Rise of the Planter Class in the English West Indies, 1624–1713* (New York: W. W. Norton, 1972), 191.

80. Stuart B. Schwartz, *Sugar Plantations in the Formation of Brazilian Society: Bahia, 1550–1835* (Cambridge: Cambridge University Press, 1985), 23.

81. Padrón y memoria de todos los vecinos y moradores de Cartago, Cartago, March 27, 1691, ANCR, C. 83, fol. 3v.

82. María Elizet Payne Iglesias, "Organización productiva y explotación indígena en el área central de Costa Rica, 1580–1700" (Licenciatura thesis, Universidad de Costa Rica, 1988), 67.

83. Avalúo de los bienes de la hacienda de campo que fue del Sarg. Mayor Blas González Coronel, Valle de Aserrí, March 8, 1719, ACMSJ, Sección Fondos Antiguos, Serie Documentación Encuadernada (hereafter, SFASDE), Caja 20, fols. 160v–62; Petición de Cristóbal Cascante, presentada en Cartago, March 6, 1719, ACMSJ, SFASDE, Caja 20, quoting from fol. 166.

84. Declaración del Cap. Diego de San Martín y Soto, Cartago, December 20, 1702, ANCR, CC 3972, fol. 8.

85. Alejandro de la Fuente García, "Los ingenios de azúcar en La Habana del siglo XVII (1640–1700): Estructura y mano de obra," *Revista de Historia Económica* (Spain) 9, no. 1 (1991): 50.

86. Venta de esclavo, Cartago, August 8, 1692, ANCR, PC 842, fols. 96v–98v; Testamento de don Sebastián de Sandoval Golfín, Cartago, March 9, 1697, ANCR, PC 849, fol. 27.

87. Venta de esclavo, trapiche y otros bienes, Cartago, July 8, 1719, ANCR, PC 887, fols. 44v–47v.

88. Michael Tadman, "The Demographic Cost of Sugar: Debates on Slave Societies and Natural Increase in the Americas," *American Historical Review* 105, no. 5 (2000): 1534–75.

89. De la Fuente García, "Los ingenios de azúcar," 36.

90. Avalúo de los bienes de la hacienda de campo que fue del Sarg. Mayor Blas González Coronel, ACMSJ, SFASDE, Valle de Aserrí, March 8, 1719, Caja 20, fols. 161, 162. The assessors estimated González Coronel's cane field at "a little more than half a *suerte*"; the standard measure of a "suerte" of sugar cane corresponded to one hundred *varas* (roughly one hundred yards), in which were planted one hundred rows of cane. See Elizabeth Fonseca, "El cultivo de la caña de azúcar en el Valle Central de Costa Rica: Epoca colonial," in *Costa Rica colonial*, ed. Luis F. Sibaja (San José: Ediciones Guayacán, 1989), 88.

91. Fonseca Corrales et al., *Costa Rica en el siglo XVIII*, 122.

92. Fonseca, "Cultivo de la caña," 83.

93. Ibid., 84–85; Philip S. MacLeod, "On the Edge of Empire: Costa Rica in the Colonial Era (1561–1800)" (PhD diss., Tulane University, 1999), 200.

94. Testamento de don Sebastián de Sandoval Golfín, Cartago, March 9, 1697, ANCR, PC 849, fols. 27–27v; Poder para aprehender a un esclavo, Panamá, September 4, 1691, ANCR, PC 842, fols. 99–102; Venta de esclavo, Cartago, August 8, 1692, ANCR, PC 842, fols. 96v–98v.

95. Testamento del Sarg. Mayor don Francisco de Ocampo Golfín, Cartago, October 3, 1714, ANCR, PC 874, fols. 21v–22; Testamento del Sarg. Mayor don Francisco de Ocampo Golfín, Cartago, February 1, 1719, ANCR, PC 889, fols. 7–7v; Testamento del Lic. don Francisco de Ocampo Golfín, Cartago, ANCR, June 25, 1734, PC 912, fols. 26–27v.

96. Cáceres, Negros, mulatos, 60; Fonseca, "Cultivo de la caña," 82.

97. Testamento de doña Nicolasa Guerrero, Ujarrás, September 19, 1717, ANCR, PC 882. fols. 94–97v; Fonseca, "Cultivo de la caña," 88; Russell Lohse, "Africans in a Colony of Creoles: The Yoruba in Colonial Costa Rica," in The Yoruba Diaspora in the Americas, ed. Toyin Falola and Matt D. Childs (Bloomington: Indiana University Press, 2005), 130–56.

98. Petición del Cap. Antonio Mora Díaz de Silva, presentada en Guatemala, November 26, 1703, AGCA, A1.24 (6), exp. 10217, leg. 1573, fol. [496v].

99. See Tatiana Lobo Wiehoff, "José Cubero," in Tatiana Lobo Wiehoff and Mauricio Meléndez Obando, Negros y blancos: Todo mezclado (San José: Editorial de la Universidad de Costa Rica, 1997), 47–52; Franklin José Alvarado Quesada, ed., "Documentos relativos a la población afroamericana," special issue, Revista de Historia (Costa Rica), no. 39 (1999): 266–71.

100. Petición de José Cubero, presentada en Cartago, August 1, 1749, ACMSJ, SFASDE, Caja 18, fols. 455–56v. Paul Lokken recounts an example of a Santiago de Guatemala slave who similarly "traded far and wide on behalf of his master." Paul Lokken, "From Black to Ladino: People of African Descent, Mestizaje, and Racial Hierarchy in Rural Colonial Guatemala, 1600–1730" (PhD diss., University of Florida, 2000), 232.

101. Petición de José Cubero, presentada en Cartago, August 1, 1749, ACMSJ, SFASDE, Caja 18, fols. 456v–58.

102. Ibid., fol. 458.

103. Memoria testamental de don Alonso de Sandoval, Cartago, May 10, 1692, ANCR, CC 3927, fol. 10v.

104. Declaración del Sarg. Antonio de Umaña, Cartago, April 10, 1744, ANCR, CC 6219, fol. 5; Declaración de Felipe de Umaña, Cartago, April 10, 1744, ANCR, CC 6219, fols. 5v–6.

105. Memoria de Antonio Barela, Cartago, January 10, 1684, ANCR, PC 831, fol. 5v.

106. Testamento del Alf. don Fernando Núñez Bejarano, Cartago, March 23, 1682, ANCR, PC 831, fol. 4.

107. Testamento de María Calvo, Cartago, September 6, 1762, ANCR, PC 950, quoting from fol. 43; Petición de don Félix Joaquín Meneses, albacea de María Calvo,

presentada en Cartago, June 7, 1774, ANCR, MCC 648, fol. 27; Testamento del
Cap. José Nicolás de la Haya, Cartago, May 2, 1747, ANCR, MCC 841, fol. 5;
Gudmundson, "Mecanismos de movilidad," 26.

108. Certificación y agregación de bienes al inventario, Cartago, June 17, 1774, ANCR,
MCC 648, fol. 30v.

109. Avalúo de bienes del difunto Cayetano de Chavarría, Puebla de los Pardos, June 16,
1774, ANCR, MCC 648, fol. 34v; Auto, Cartago, June 16, 1774, MCC 648, fol. 34.

110. "Real cédula que aprueba las ordenanzas dictadas en favor de los indios por el
Dr. don Benito de Noboa Salgado, oidor de la Audiencia de Guatemala y visitador
de la provincia de Costa Rica.—Año de 1676," *Revista de los Archivos Nacionales*
(Costa Rica) 1, nos. 3–4 (1937): 147, quoting from 148.

111. MacLeod, "On the Edge of Empire," 231; Fernández, *Colección de documentos*,
5:353, 8:376.

112. Carta de Fr. Sebastián de las Alas al Provincial Fr. Diego Macotela, San Bartolomé
de Ycarurú, December 10, 1689, AGI, AG 297, fols. 13v–14, in Fernández, *Colección
de documentos*, 8:503.

113. Carta de Fr. Diego Macotela a la Audiencia de Guatemala, León, Nic., February 20,
1690, AGI, AG 297, fol. 9v, in Fernández, *Colección de documentos*, 9:7–8.

114. Auto del Presidente de la Audiencia de Guatemala don Jacinto de Barrios Leal,
Guatemala, April 4, 1690, AGI, AG 297, fols. 12v–13v, quoting from fol. 13.

115. Respuesta del fiscal, May 12, 1691, AGI, AG 297, fol. 28; Despacho de la Real
Audiencia, Guatemala, May 22, 1691, AGI, AG 297, fol. 30.

116. See Russell R. Menard and Stuart B. Schwartz, "Why African Slavery? Labor
Force Transitions in Brazil, Mexico, and the Carolina Lowcountry," in *Slavery in
the Americas*, ed. Wolfgang Binder (Würzburg: Königshausen & Neumann,
1993), 89–114.

117. Relación geográfica de Costa Rica por el Gobernador don Juan Gemmir y
Lleonart, May 21, 1741, AGCA, A1.17, exp. 5016, leg. 210, fols. 252v–53, in Fernández,
Colección de documentos, 9:370.

118. Visita apostólica de los pueblos de Nicaragua y Costa Rica hecha por el Illmo.
Sr. don Pedro Morel de Santa Cruz, September 8, 1752, University of Texas, Nettie
Lee Benson Latin American Collection, Joaquín García Icazbalceta Collection,
vol. 20, no. 7, fol. 57v.

119. Kenneth F. Kiple, *The Caribbean Slave: A Biological History* (Cambridge:
Cambridge University Press, 1984), 14–21. For possible malaria in colonial Costa
Rica, see Tulio von Bülow, "Apuntes para la historia de la medicina en Costa Rica
durante la colonia," *Revista de los Archivos Nacionales* (Costa Rica) 9 (1945): 137,
471. David P. Adams offers an interesting thesis in "Malaria, Labor, and
Population Distribution in Costa Rica: A Biohistorical Perspective," *Journal of
Interdisciplinary History* 27, no. 1 (1996): 75–85. Unfortunately, numerous and
substantial errors on Costa Rican history compromise his article.

120. Visita apostólica de los pueblos de Nicaragua y Costa Rica hecha por el Illmo.
Sr. don Pedro Morel de Santa Cruz, September 8, 1752, University of Texas, Nettie

Lee Benson Latin American Collection, Joaquín García Icazbalceta Collection, vol. 20, no. 7, fol. 58.

121. Petición del Cap. Felipe de Meza, presentada en Cartago, October 18, 1720, ANCR, C. 275, fol. 9; Auto de sentencia, Cartago, November 22, 1720, ANCR, C. 275, fol. 15.

122. "Fragmentos del testimonio de los autos hechos con motivo de la invasión de la provincia de Costa Rica por los piratas Mansfelt y Henry Morgan en 1666," *Revista de los Archivos Nacionales* (Costa Rica) 1, nos. 1–2 (1936): 5–33; Declaración del Cap. Lucas Cervantes, Cartago, October 22, 1691, ANCR, C. 85, fol. [14v].

123. Germán Romero Vargas, *Las sociedades del atlántico de Nicaragua en los siglos XVII y XVIII* (Managua: Fondo de Promoción Cultural–BANIC, 1995), 80.

124. Declaración del Cap. don José Pérez de Muro, Cartago, November 12, 1705, AGI, Escribanía 351B, pieza 1, fol. 165v.

125. Declaración de Diego Sánchez, pardo libre, Cartago, May 8, 1724, ANCR, C. 303, fols. 68v–69v; Memoria de los prisioneros libres y esclavos, Matina, May 1, 1724, ANCR, C. 303, fols. 66–66v.

126. Declaración de Diego Sánchez, pardo libre, Cartago, May 8, 1724, ANCR, C. 303, fols. 68v–69.

127. Declaración del Cap. Blas González Coronel, Cartago, October 15, 1703, AGI, AG 359, pieza 3, fol. 17v.

128. Declaración del Cap. Francisco Pérez del Cote, Cartago, October 17, 1703, AGI, AG 359, pieza 3, fol. 28.

129. Petición de Nicolás Granajo en nombre del Cap. don Antonio Mora Díaz de Silva, presentada en Guatemala, November 26, 1703, AGCA, A1.24 (6), exp. 10217, leg. 1573, fol. [498].

130. Petición del Cap. don José de Mier Cevallos, presentada en Cartago, July 11, 1720, ANCR, C. 266, fol. 31v.

131. Auto del Gobernador don Diego de la Haya Fernández, Pacaca, February 20, 1720, AGCA, A2 (6), exp. 3, leg. 1, fol. 25.

132. Junta de Guerra, Cartago, February 10, 1724, AGI, AG 455, fol. 534.

133. Petición del Cap. Juan José de Cuende, Procurador Síndico presentada en Cartago, March 14, 1736, ANCR, Municipal 772, fol. 94v, in Fernández, *Colección de documentos*, 9:209.

134. MacLeod, "On the Edge of Empire," 206, 208; Oscar R. Aguilar Bulgarelli and Irene Alfaro Aguilar, *La esclavitud negra en Costa Rica: Origen de la oligarquía económica y política nacional* (San José: Progreso Editora, 1997), 177; Fonseca, *Costa Rica colonial*, 228–30.

135. Petición de descargos del Cap. Luis Gutiérrez, Cartago, August 20, 1719, AGI, Escribanía 353B, fol. 628.

136. Auto del gobernador, Cartago, July 1, 1704, ANCR, C. 127, fols. 1–1v.

137. Auto de buen gobierno, Matina, August 8, 1716, ANCR, C. 205, fols. 1–1v.

138. Petición del Cap. don Pedro de Moya, presentada en Cartago, April 21, 1719, ANCR, C. 269, fol. 2.

139. Bando de buen gobierno, Cartago, March 26, 1737, C. 389, fols. 5v–6.

140. Gudmundson, "Mecanismos de movilidad," 23.

141. Declaración de Miguel Solano, Cartago, August 26, 1733, ANCR, CC 4292, fol. 20; Robert J. Ferry, "Encomienda, African Slavery, and Agriculture in Seventeenth-Century Caracas," *Hispanic American Historical Review* 61, no. 4 (1981): 631.

142. Notificación a Efigenia Brenes y su respuesta, Puebla de los Pardos, May 7, 1752, ANCR, MCC 629, fol. 20.

143. Venta de esclavo, Cartago, October 25, 1706, ANCR, PC 862. fols. 73v–75v.

144. Petición del negro esclavo Juan Román al Teniente de Gobernador don José Mier de Cevallos, presentada en Cartago, July 27, 1733, ANCR, CC 4292, fol. 1v.

145. Cáceres, *Negros, mulatos*, 40.

146. Number of sales in the 1670s, 26; in the 1680s, 40; in the 1690s, 78; in the 1700s, 57; in the 1710s, 89. Calculations based on ANCR, PC 601 (1607)–PC 940 (1750); PH 573 (1721)–94 (1749); Protocolos Coloniales de San José 411 (1720)–15 (1738); *Indice de los protocolos de Cartago*, 6 vols. (San José: Imprenta Nacional, 1909–1930), vols. 1–3.

147. Carlos Rosés Alvarado, "El ciclo del cacao en la economía colonial de Costa Rica, 1650–1794," *Mesoamérica* 3, no. 4 (1982): 235.

148. "Few cacaoteros used slaves on their haciendas, given their expense and scarcity in this peripheral society." MacLeod, "On the Edge of Empire," 255.

149. "Real cédula que aprueba las ordenanzas dictadas en favor de los indios por el Dr. don Benito de Noboa Salgado, oidor de la Audiencia de Guatemala y visitador de la provincia de Costa Rica.—Año de 1676," *Revista de los Archivos Nacionales* (Costa Rica) 1, nos. 3–4 (1937): 147, 148; Carta de Fr. Sebastián de las Alas al Provincial Fr. Diego Macotela, San Bartolomé de Ycarurú, December 10, 1689, AGI, AG 297, fols. 13v–14, in Fernández, *Colección de documentos*, 8:503.

150. Petición de Manuel de Farinas, apoderado de don Antonio Salmón Pachecho, presentada en Guatemala, January 16, 1691, AGI, AG 297, fol. 19v.

151. Padrón y memoria de todos los vecinos y moradores de Cartago, March 27, 1691, ANCR, C. 83, fols. 4v, 3–7; Eugenio Piñero, "Accounting Practices in a Colonial Economy: A Case Study of Cacao Haciendas in Venezuela, 1700–1770," *Colonial Latin American Historical Review* 1, no. 1 (1992): quoting from 41.

152. In a recent study, Eduardo Madrigal Muñoz confirms that the Caribbean cacao haciendas "operated in the main with slave labor. . . . Nevertheless, . . . in most cases, the cacao planters studied owned few slaves, in reality, because . . . this type of crop requires little manpower." Eduardo Madrigal Muñoz, "Los lazos sociales en la dinámica de un grupo subordinado en una sociedad colonial periférica: Los cacaoteros de Costa Rica, 1660–1740," *Mesoamérica*, no. 53 (2011): 124, 124n54.

153. Carta dote, Cartago, September 10, 1689, ANCR, PC 838, fol. 110; Poder para vender a un esclavo, Cartago, August 20, 1693, ANCR, PC 843, fols. 65–67.

154. Venta de esclavo, Cartago, October 25, 1706, PC 862, fols. 73v.–75v.

155. Venta de esclavos, Cartago, June 21, 1718, ANCR, PC 885, fols. 109–13v, quoting from fol. 110v.

156. Petición de Diego de Angulo, negro esclavo, presentada en Cartago, September 12, 1729, ANCR, CC 4259, fol. [2].

157. Auto del Gobernador don Diego de la Haya Fernández, Esparza, April 28, 1720, AGCA, A2 (6), exp. 3, leg. 1, fol. 39v.

158. Carta de libertad, Cartago, March 2, 1733, ANCR, PC 910, fol. 8.

159. Declaración de Miguel Solano, Cartago, August 27, 1733, ANCR, CC 4292, quoting from fol. 20, 21v. See also Declaración de Juan de Salazar, Cartago, May 7, 1715, ANCR, CC 4036, fol. 4v. These documents establish that rice was grown widely in Matina in the early eighteenth century, not introduced to Costa Rica in the late nineteenth, as Fonseca Corrales et al. wrote in *Costa Rica en el siglo XVIII*, 146.

160. Walter Hawthorne, "Nourishing a Stateless Society During the Slave Trade: The Rise of Balanta Paddy-Rice Production in Guinea-Bissau," *Journal of African History* 42, no. 1 (2001): 1–24; Hawthorne, *Planting Rice and Harvesting Slaves: Transformations Along the Guinea-Bissau Coast, 1400–1900* (Portsmouth, NH: Heinemann, 2003); T. Bentley Duncan, *The Atlantic Islands: Madeira, the Azores, and Cabo Verde in the Seventeenth Century* (Chicago, IL: University of Chicago Press, 1972), 167, 168.

161. Petición del Sarg. Cristóbal de Chavarría, presentada en Cartago, August 1, 1719, ANCR, CC 4075, fol. 10v; Memoria de los gastos presentada por el Alf. Juan Bautista Retana, presentada en Cartago, June 28, 1710, ANCR, C. 187, fol. 205.

162. Don Diego de Barros y Carbajal al Ayudante Matías Masís en Cartago, July 16, 1721, ANCR, MCC 941, fol. 16.

163. For a reference to turtling (*tortugueando*) during the colonial period, see Declaración del Cap. Juan Cayetano Jiménez, Cartago, March 18, 1717, ANCR, C. 211, fol. 13v. For hunting turtle on the Gold Coast, see Johannes Rask, *A Brief and Truthful Description of a Journey to and from Guinea*, vol. 1 of *Two Views from Christiansborg Castle*, trans. and ed. Selena Axelrod Winsnes (Accra: Sub-Saharan Publishers, 2009), [43] (bracketed page numbers indicate the pagination of the original Danish edition).

164. Declaración del Cap. de Caballos don Antonio de la Vega Cabral, Cartago, June 28, 1703, AGI, AG 359, pieza 1, fol. 10v; "Informe sobre la Provincia de Costa Rica presentado por el Ingeniero don Luis Díez Navarro al Capitán General de Guatemala don Tomás de Rivera y Santa Cruz.—Año de 1744," *Revista de los Archivos Nacionales* (Costa Rica) 3, nos. 11–12 (1939), quoting from 583; Visita apostólica de los pueblos de Nicaragua y Costa Rica hecha por el Illmo. Sr. don Pedro Morel de Santa Cruz, September 8, 1752, University of Texas, Nettie Lee Benson Latin American Collection, Joaquín García Icazbalceta Collection, vol. 20, no. 7, quoting from fol. 58.

165. Quirós Vargas, *Era de la encomienda*, 181; Autos del remate de los tributos vacos, para formar el fondo de gastos de guerra (1687), AGCA, A1 (6), exp. 1041, leg. 68;

Tasación de los tributos de Garabito, Ujarrás y Curridabat (1693), ANCR, G. 118 bis; Balandier, *Daily Life in the Kingdom*, 129, 156.

166. Inventario de las haciendas de cacao de doña Agueda Pérez de Muro, Matina, April 20, 1722, ANCR, PC 895, fols. 94, 94v.

167. Inventario de las haciendas de cacao de doña Agueda Pérez de Muro, Barbilla, April 22, 1722, ANCR, PC 895, fol. 95v.

168. Avalúo de las haciendas de cacao de doña Agueda Pérez de Muro, Cartago, May 12, 1722, ANCR, PC 895, fol. 100v; Razón dada por el negro Nicolás, esclavo de doña Agueda Pérez de Muro, Cartago, May 4, 1722, ANCR, PC 895, fol. 99.

169. Inventario de las haciendas de cacao de doña Agueda Pérez de Muro, Matina, April 23, 1723, ANCR, PC 895, fols. 95v–96; Petición del Cap. don Francisco Garrido, presentada en Cartago, May 2, 1722, ANCR, PC 895, fol. 97v.

170. Razón dada por el negro Nicolás, esclavo de doña Agueda Pérez de Muro, Cartago, May 4, 1722, ANCR, PC 895, fol. 99, 99v.

171. Ibid.

172. For a reference to replanting, see Declaración de José Guerrero, pardo libre, Cartago, September 4, 1733, ANCR, CC 4292, fol. 29.

173. Thus, cacao groves were referred to as "plantained" (*plataneadas*). See Arrendamiento de cacaotal, June 15, 1715, ANCR, PC 877, fol. 103; Arrendamiento de cacaotal, Cartago, May 9, 1731, ANCR, PC 905, fol. 1; Arrendamiento de cacaotal, Cartago, October 31, 1730, ANCR, PC 905, fol. 17v.

174. Declaración del Cap. Rafael Fajardo, Cartago, October 10, 1703, AGI, Guatemala 359, pieza 3, fol. 9; Testimonio de arrendamiento de cacaotal, Cartago, April 17, 1724, ANCR, MCC 700, fol. 12; Carta de libertad, Cartago, October 3, 1733, ANCR, PC 910, fol. 72.

175. See Prisión y embargo de bienes del Cap. Felipe de Meza, Matina, May 15, 1721, ANCR, C. 211, fol. 135; Testamento del Teniente don Pedro Jiménez de Mondragón, Cartago, July 30, 1732, ANCR, PC 908, fol. 38v; Inventario de los bienes del Sarg. Mayor don Juan Francisco de Ibarra, Matina, March 23, 1737, ANCR, MCC 850, fol. 18; Inventario de los bienes de Agustín de la Riva, mulato libre, Matina, March 4, 1740, ANCR, MCC 1165, fol. 4v; Inventario de los bienes de Francisco Guerrero, Matina, December 30, 1743, ANCR, MCC 795, fol. 6v.

176. Carta de libertad, Barva, November 19, 1693, ANCR, PC 844, fol. 2.

177. See Información tomada a los arrieros que vienen de Matina, 1724, ANCR, C. 304.

178. Auto del Gobernador don Diego de la Haya Fernández, Cartago, November 2, 1722, ANCR, C. 283, fol. 9v; Declaración de Nicolás, negro de casta mina, Cartago, April 25, 1723, ANCR, C. 283, fol. 11.

179. Cuaderno de registro de las recuas procedentes de Matina que llegan a Cartago, Cartago, 1724, ANCR, C. 285.

180. Declaración de Juan Damián, negro esclavo, Cartago, August 14, 1717, ANCR, CC 4111, fols. 3–5; Declaración de Gregorio Caamaño, negro esclavo, Cartago, August 14, 1717, ANCR, CC 4111, fols. 5–8; Confesión de Juan Damián, esclavo que fue de doña Agueda Pérez de Muro, Cartago, May 11, 1719, ANCR, G. 181, fol. 2v.

181. Auto de buen gobierno, Cartago, July 14, 1708, ANCR, C. 166, fol. 5. For references to Spanish mandadores, see Declaración del Alf. Jacinto de Rivera, Cartago, May 31, 1720, ANCR, C. 237, fol. 14v; Declaración de Pedro Mina, negro esclavo del Sarg. Mayor don Juan Francisco de Ibarra y Calvo, Cartago, June 6, 1720, ANCR, C. 237, fol. 14v.

182. Declaración de José Congo, mandador de haciendas, Matina, April 23, 1722, ANCR, PC 895, fol. 95v; Indice de los protocolos de Cartago, 2:231–32; Declaración de Gregorio Caamaño, negro esclavo y mandador de haciendas, Cartago, August 14, 1717, ANCR, CC 4111, fol. 6; Declaración de Antonio de la Riva, negro de casta mina y mandador de haciendas, Valle de Matina, March 22, 1737, ANCR, MCC 850, fol. 17.

183. Carta del negro esclavo José de Moya a su amo el Cap. don Pedro de Moya, Matina, August 16, 1720, ANCR, C. 237, fols. 25–25v.

184. Declaración de Juan Damián, negro esclavo y ladino de doña Agueda Pérez de Muro, Cartago, August 14, 1717, ANCR, CC 4111, fol. 3v; Confesión de Antonio Mina, negro esclavo del Cap. Manuel García de Argueta, Cartago, December 2, 1721, ANCR, CC 5805, fol. 2.

185. Carta de libertad, Cartago, September 18, 1737, ANCR, PC 916, fol. 166v.

186. Carta de libertad, Cartago, June 15, 1745, ANCR, PC 933, fol. 55.

187. Carta de libertad, Cartago, March 2, 1733, ANCR, PC 910, fols. 7v–9.

188. "Se dispone que el cacao corra en la provincia de Costa Rica para la compra de víveres por no haber en ella moneda de plata. Año de 1709," Revista de los Archivos Nacionales (Costa Rica) 1, nos. 9–10 (1937): 600–603.

189. Declaración de Antonio Masís, negro libre, Cartago, August 26, 1733, ANCR, CC 4292, fol. 16.

190. Petición de Juan Masís, presentada en Cartago, August 14, 1719, ANCR, CC 4075, fol. 18v; Petición del Sarg. Cristóbal de Chavarría, presentada en Cartago, August 1, 1719, ANCR, CC 4075, fol. 10v.

191. Auto del Gobernador don Diego de la Haya Fernández, Cartago, January 8, 1720, ANCR, CC 160, fols. 1–1v.

192. Petición del Sarg. Mayor don Antonio de Utrera, vecino y Procurador General de Cartago, presentada en Cartago, April 25, 1727, ANCR, C. 323, fols. 1–1v.

193. Confesión de Juan Damián, esclavo que fue de doña Agueda Pérez de Muro, Cartago, May 11, 1719, ANCR, G. 181, fol. 2v, quoting from fol. 3; Declaración de Pablo José de Alvarado, indio ladino, Cartago, October 18, 1703, AGI, AG 359, pieza 1, fols. 65v, 67v; Declaración de Francisco Alejandro Bonilla, Cartago, April 19, 1717, ANCR, C. 211, fol. 42v.

194. Testamento de María de Zárate, Cartago, October 21, 1705, ANCR, PC 861, fols. 59v–60.

195. Petición de Diego de Casasola [Diego García], negro esclavo, presentada en Cartago, November 20, 1724, ANCR, CC 4148, fol. 1; Declaración de Antonio Masís, Cartago, November 21, 1724, ANCR, CC 4148, quoting from fol. 2v;

Declaración del Teniente Jacinto de Campos, Cartago, November 23, 1724, ANCR, CC 4148, fol. 4.

196. Declaración de Tomás Rivera, mulato libre, Cartago, November 24, 1724, ANCR, CC 4148, fol. 4v.

197. Petición de Juan Román, negro esclavo, presentada en Cartago, July 27, 1733, ANCR, CC 4292, fol. 1v.

198. For example, Arrendamiento de cacaotal, Cartago, March 23, 1718, ANCR, PC 885, fols. 41v–43v; Arrendamiento de cacaotal, Cartago, October 8, 1731, ANCR, PC 906, fols. 119v–20v; Arrendamiento de cacaotal, Cartago, May 29, 1733, ANCR, PC 910, fols. 40v–42.

199. Cf. Stuart B. Schwartz, "Sugar Plantation Labor and Slave Life," in *Slaves, Peasants, and Rebels: Reconsidering Brazilian Slavery* (Urbana: University of Illinois Press, 1992), 54.

200. Sidney W. Mintz, "Was the Plantation Slave a Proletarian?" *Review* 2, no. 1 (1978): 91–95; O. Nigel Bolland, "Proto-Proletarians? Slave Wages in the Americas," in *From Chattel Slaves to Wage Slaves: The Dynamics of Labour Bargaining in the Americas*, ed. Mary Turner (London: James Currey, 1995), 126.

201. Gente y armas del Valle de Matina: Negros esclavos asistentes, Matina, January 23, 1719, ANCR, CC 3797, fol. 26v–27.

202. Karl Marx and Frederick Engels, *The German Ideology*, ed. C. J. Arthur (New York: International Publishers, 1995), 83.

CHAPTER SIX

1. Trevor Burnard, *Mastery, Tyranny, and Desire: Thomas Thistlewood and His Slaves in the Anglo-Jamaican World* (Chapel Hill: University of North Carolina, 2004), quoting from 138; Norrece T. Jones, Jr., *Born a Child of Freedom, Yet a Slave: Mechanisms of Control and Strategies of Resistance in Antebellum South Carolina* (Hanover, CT: Wesleyan University Press, 1990), 10.

2. Such language was particularly common in letters of manumission; for one of many examples, see Carta de libertad de 5 esclavos, Cartago, March 28, 1726, Archivo Nacional de Costa Rica, San José (hereafter, ANCR), Protocolos Coloniales de Cartago (hereafter, PC) 899, fols. 24–25.

3. Petición de doña Agueda Pérez de Muro, presentada en Cartago, January 9, 1719, ANCR, Sección Complementario Colonial (hereafter, CC) 4111, fol. 36.

4. Petición del Cap. Manuel García de Argueta, presentada en Cartago, July 13, 1720, ANCR, Sección Colonial Cartago (hereafter, C.) 243, fols. 25–25v.

5. Rina Cáceres, "Costa Rica, en la frontera del comercio de esclavos africanos," *Reflexiones* (Facultad de Ciencias Sociales, Universidad de Costa Rica), no. 65 (1997): 12.

6. Gerald W. Mullin, *Flight and Rebellion: Slave Resistance in Eighteenth-Century Virginia* (New York: Oxford University Press, 1972), 39–47; John Hope Franklin

and Loren Schweninger, *Runaway Slaves: Rebels on the Plantation* (New York: Oxford University Press, 1999), 232–33.

7. Auto de visita, Puerto de la Caldera, October 29, 1700, ANCR, C. 109, fol. 6v.

8. Auto de comiso de 41 negros y negras, Esparza, November 6, 1700, ANCR, C. 109, fol. 7; Auto de depósito de 41 negros y negras, Esparza, November 7, 1700, ANCR, C. 109, fol. 8; Auto de almoneda, Esparza, November 30, 1700, ANCR, C. 109, fol. 16v. Although the initial proceedings generated by the judges don Gregorio de Caamaño y Juan Antonio de Bogarín referred to forty-one blacks, Bogarín later revealed that the *Nuestra Señora de la Soledad y Santa Isabel* actually brought fifty-four Africans. Declaración de Juan Antonio Bogarín, August 18, 1703, Archivo General de Indias, Seville (hereafter, AGI), Audiencia de Guatemala (hereafter, AG) 359, pieza 5, fols. 29v. Caamaño falsified the documents to conceal his own appropriation of "a dozen of the best blacks." Declaración del Cap. Francisco de los Reyes, Cartago, July 9, 1703, AGI, AG 359, pieza 5, fol. 5v.

9. Carta de don José de Guzmán al Presidente de la Audiencia de Guatemala, Cartago, January 2, 1701, AGI, AG 359, pieza 6, fol. 5v; Requerimiento al Gobernador de Costa Rica don Francisco Serrano de Reina, y su respuesta, Cartago, January 12, 1701, ANCR, C. 109, fol. 51v.

10. Petición del Alf. Ambrosio Hernández, presentada en Esparza, March 12, 1701, ANCR, C. 109, fol. 32; AGI, AG 359, pieza 6, fol. 107.

11. Auto de los jueces don Gregorio de Caamaño y Juan Antonio de Bogarín, Esparza, February 20, 1701, ANCR, C. 109, fol. 27. But see also the later statement of Bogarín, when he claimed that these slaves were illegally concealed by Caamaño, leaving doubt as to whether they actually fled. Declaración de Juan Antonio Bogarín, Cartago, August 21, 1703, AGI, AG 359, pieza 5, fol. 38.

12. Auto de manifestación de 4 negros, Esparza, February 22, 1701, ANCR, C. 109, fol. 28.

13. Auto de almoneda, Esparza, April 15, 1701, ANCR, C. 109, fols. 32v–33.

14. Inventario de los cinco negros traídos de Matina por el Cap. Antonio de Soto y Barahona, Cartago, May 1, 1710, ANCR, C. 187, fols. 69v–70v; Inventario de los 38 negros traídos de Matina por el Teniente Juan Bautista Retana, Cartago, May 11, 1710, ANCR, C. 187, fols. 97–100v.

15. Memoria de los gastos en el mantenimiento de los negros, presentada por Juan López Carrera y Soto, Cartago, July 24, 1710, ANCR, C. 182, fol. 43v; Aprecio de los negros, Cartago, August 18, 1710, ANCR, C. 182, fol. 58; Inventario de los cinco negros traídos de Matina por el Cap. Antonio de Soto y Barahona, Cartago, May 1, 1710, ANCR, C. 187, fols. 69v–70v.

16. Inventario de 16 negros y negras, Cartago, June 11, 1710, ANCR, C. 187, fols. 147–49. For the identification of the "nangu" with the Ana subgroup of the Yoruba, see Russell Lohse, "Africans in a Colony of Creoles: The Yoruba in Colonial Costa Rica" in *The Yoruba Diaspora in the Americas*, ed. Toyin Falola and Matt D. Childs (Bloomington: Indiana University Press, 2005), 131–34.

17. Sidney W. Mintz and Richard Price, *The Birth of African-American Culture: An Anthropological Perspective* (Boston, MA: Beacon Press, 1992).

18. Inventario de 22 negros y negras traídos de Matina por el Cap. Gaspar de Acosta Arévalo, Cartago, April 14, 1710, ANCR, C. 187, fols. 12-13v. The two men were called carabalí by their new captors, indicating an origin in the Bight of Biafra, but this identification was clearly mistaken, as neither ship obtained Africans east of Ouidah in modern Benin.

19. Philip Morgan notes groups containing both African and creole slave fugitives in colonial South Carolina, as does Brenda E. Stevenson in colonial Virginia, who makes an argument similar to that presented here. Philip Morgan, *Slave Counterpoint: Black Culture in the Eighteenth-Century Chesapeake and Lowcountry* (Chapel Hill: University of North Carolina Press, 1998), 448; Brenda E. Stevenson, *Life in Black and White: Family and Community in the Slave South* (New York: Oxford University Press, 1996), 169-70.

20. Declaración del Cap. Francisco de los Reyes, Cartago, July 9, 1703, AGI, AG 359, pieza 5, quoting from fol. 5v, fol. 9.

21. Razón del Teniente General don Diego de Barros de quien hubo su esclavo Francisco Congo, Cartago, May 30, 1720, ANCR, C. 265, fol. 2v; Reconocimiento del despacho presentado por don Diego de Barros, Cartago, June 3, 1720, ANCR, C. 265, fol. 3v.

22. Decreto de don Gabriel Sánchez de Berrospe, Presidente de la Real Audiencia, Guatemala, January 5, 1702, ANCR, C. 109, fols. 59-60; Auto del Lic. don Francisco de Carmona, juez comisario, Cartago, May 31, 1703, ANCR, G. 128, fol. 6v; Auto del Lic. don Francisco de Carmona, juez comisario, Cartago, May 25, 1703, AGI, AG 359, pieza 4, fol. 3; Respuesta del Gobernador don Francisco Serrano de Reina, Cartago, May 30, 1703, ANCR, G. 128, fol. 4.

23. Razón del Teniente General don Diego de Barros de quien hubo su esclavo Francisco Congo, Cartago, May 30, 1720, ANCR, C. 265, fol. 2v; Reconocimiento del despacho presentado por don Diego de Barros, Cartago, June 3, 1720, ANCR, C. 265, fol. 3v; Declaracion de José Congo, negro esclavo de doña Agueda Pérez de Muro, Matina, December 5, 1719, ANCR, C. 251, fol. 3v.

24. Philip Morgan argues that in colonial South Carolina, "creoles were often the dominant partners" in groups of runaways that included both Africans and creoles. Morgan, *Slave Counterpoint*, 462.

25. Michael A. Gomez, *Exchanging Our Country Marks: The Transformation of African Identities in the Colonial and Antebellum South* (Chapel Hill: University of North Carolina Press, 1998), 195-97.

26. Petición del Maestre de Campo don José de Casasola y Córdoba, presentada en Cartago, February 12, 1705, ANCR, CC 3978, fol. 2.

27. Autos del gobernador, Cartago, March 19, 1722, ANCR, C. 292, fols. 6, 8.

28. "Juicio promovido por Rodrigo de Contreras contra Hernán Sánchez de Badajoz en la costa del Mar del Norte, al cual se acumularon los procesos entablados por Juan de Bastidas y Juan Luis contra el dicho," 1540, in Andrés Vega Bolaños, ed.,

Colección Somoza: Documentos para la historia de Nicaragua, 17 vols. (Madrid, 1945–1957), 6:495, 497.

29. Ibid., 6:495, quoting from 6:496, 497.

30. See Richard Price, "Introduction: Maroons and Their Communities," in *Maroon Societies*, ed. Richard Price, 2nd ed. (Baltimore, MD: Johns Hopkins University Press, 1979), 1–30; João José Reis and Flávio dos Santos Gomes, "Introdução: Uma história da liberdade," in *Liberdade por um fio*, ed. João José Reis and Flávio dos Santos Gomes (São Paulo: Companhia das Letras, 1996), 9–25.

31. Clarence J. Munford, *The Black Ordeal of Slavery and Slave Trading in the French West Indies, 1625–1715*, 3 vols. (Lewiston, NY: Edwin Mellen Press, 1991), 3:924.

32. Petición de doña Juana Núñez de Trupira, presentada en Cartago, July 1, 1692, ANCR, PC 842, fol. 63.

33. Auto de aprehensión del negro Antonio Civitola, Cartago, December 27, 1719, ANCR, C. 259, fol. 5.

34. Poder para vender a 2 esclavos, Cartago, October 31, 1730, PC 903, fols. 18–18v.

35. Declaración de Eugenia, mulata esclava del Sarg. Mayor don Juan Francisco de Ibarra, Cartago, September 7, 1720, ANCR, C. 241, fol. 28.

36. "Relación del viaje del gobernador D. Francisco de Carrandi y Menán al valle y costa de Matina en 1737.—Año de 1738," in León Fernández, ed., *Colección de documentos para la historia de Costa Rica*, 10 vols. (San José: Imprenta Nacional [vols. 1–3], Paris: Imprenta Pablo Dupont [vols. 4–5], Barcelona: Imprenta Viuda de Luis Tasso [vols. 6–10], 1881–1907), 9:309.

37. Carta de Esteban Ruiz de Mendoza al Gobernador de Costa Rica, Fuerte de San Fernando de Matina, October 15, 1744, ANCR, C. 455, fols. 1–2v; see also Tatiana Lobo Wiehoff, "Primeros fundadores de San José," in Tatiana Lobo Wiehoff and Mauricio Meléndez Obando, *Negros y blancos: Todo mezclado* (San José: Editorial de la Universidad de Costa Rica, 1997), 24–39.

38. Carlos Meléndez, "El negro en Costa Rica durante la colonia," in Carlos Meléndez and Quince Duncan, *El negro en Costa Rica* (San José: Editorial Costa Rica, 1989), 26; Tatiana Lobo Wiehoff, "Cimarrones," in Tatiana Lobo Wiehoff and Meléndez Obando, *Negros y blancos: Todo mezclado* (San José: Editorial de la Universidad de Costa Rica, 1997), 34.

39. See Permuta de esclavos, Cartago, March 10, 1612, ANCR, G. 34, fol. 52; Venta de esclavo, Cartago, April 28, 1612, ANCR, G. 34, fol. 17; Poder para vender a una esclava, Cartago, September 30, 1724, ANCR, PC 897, fols. 94v–95v.

40. Segunda declaración de Suyntin y Antonio, zambos mosquitos, Cartago, May 3, 1710, ANCR, C. 187, fol. 93v.

41. Auto del Gobernador don Diego de la Haya Fernández, Cartago, May 19, 1722, ANCR, C. 292, fols. 5v–6; Carta de Bernardo Pacheco al Gobernador, Matina, May 23, 1722, ANCR, C. 292, fol. 7v; Auto del gobernador, Cartago, June 18, 1722, ANCR, C. 292, fol. 10.

42. Carta del Cap. Alvaro de Nava, Esparza, February 28, 1705, ANCR, CC 3978, fol. 8.

43. Gad J. Heuman notes that in nineteenth-century Barbados, mulatto slaves succeeded in remaining at large for periods three times longer than Africans; black creoles went unrecovered for twice as long. Gad J. Heuman, "Runaway Slaves in Nineteenth-Century Barbados," *Slavery & Abolition* 6, no. 3 (1985): 103.

44. Defunciones de Cartago y cuentas presentadas por concepto de entierros [1677–1678], Archivo de la Curia Metropolitana de San José (hereafter, ACMSJ), Sección Fondos Antiguos, Sección Documentación Encuadernada (hereafter, SFASDE), Caja 9, fol. 17v; Declaración de Ana María Solano del Carmen de Villalobos, Cartago, August 5, 1757, Archivo General de la Nación, Mexico (hereafter, AGN), Grupo Documental Inquisición, vol. 929, exp. 25, fol. 368.

45. Juan Tercero de Montalvo, vecino de Nueva Segovia, da poder a don Salvador Jirón para vender un esclavo, León, Nic., November 16, 1661, ANCR, PC 815, fols. 199–200; Venta de esclavo, Cartago, March 22, 1662, ANCR, PC 815, fols. 202–3.

46. Obligación de don José de Escalante Paniagua, Cartago, December 12, 1673, ANCR, PC 821, fol. 28.

47. Declaración de José de la Cerda, San Francisco del Higuerón, January 25, 1715, AGI, Escribanía 353B, fol. 666; Carta requisitoria del Teniente de Gobernador de Esparza don Francisco Duque de Estrada al Alcalde Mayor de Nicoya, San Francisco del Higuerón, January 25, 1715, AGI, Escribanía 353B, quoting from fol. 670.

48. Obligación de don José de Escalante Paniagua, Cartago, December 12, 1673, ANCR, PC 821, fol. 28.

49. Venta de esclavo, Cartago, November 19, 1680, ANCR, PC 830, fols. 20–22v; José Gómez de Villalobos sustituye un poder en el Cap. don José de Escalante Paniagua, Realejo, Nic., May 20, 1680, PC 830, fol. 25.

50. El Alf. José Gómez Elgueros da poder al Cap. don Matías González Camino para aprender y vender a un esclavo, Panama, September 4, 1691, ANCR, PC 842, fols. 99–102; Venta de esclavo, Cartago, August 8, 1692, ANCR, PC 842, fols. 96v–98v; Testamento de don Sebastián de Sandoval Golfín, Cartago, March 9, 1697, ANCR, PC 849, fol. 27.

51. Petición de Diego Campuzano, presentada en Cartago, January 26, 1732, ACMSJ, SFASDE, Caja 14, fol. 284.

52. Auto de aprobación, Cartago, February 1, 1732, ACMSJ, SFASDE, Caja 14, fol. 287. The recorded marriage of "José Campuzano" to "María Padilla" by Fr. José Antonio Díaz de Herrera in Cartago on July 4, 1732, almost certainly refers to this marriage. ACMSJ, Libros de Matrimonios no. 3/Family History Library, Salt Lake City, Utah (hereafter, FHL), VAULT INTL film 1219727, item 8. Partida de bautizo de Antonio Martín, hijo de Diego Campuzano y de Manuela Padilla, Cartago, November 13, 1733, ACMSJ, Libros de Bautizos de Cartago, no. 5/FHL, VAULT INTL film 1219701, item 5.

53. Petición del Sarg. Mayor don Juan Francisco de Ibarra, presentada en Cartago, June 28, 1734, ACMSJ, SFASDE, Caja 15, fol. 47; Declaración de Diego Campuzano, June 28, 1734, ACMSJ, SFASDE, Caja 15, fols. 47–47v; Declaración

de Manuela Josefa de Padilla, Cartago, June 28, 1734, ACMSJ, SFASDE, Caja 15, fol. 48.

54. Auto de remisión, Cartago, June 30, 1735, ACMSJ, SFASDE, Caja 15, fols. 48–48v.

55. Tercera liquidación de los gastos par la manutención de los negros, Cartago, August 18, 1710, ANCR, C. 182, fol. 58.

56. Auto del recibo de un negro, Cartago, April 8, 1721, ANCR, C. 283, fol. 2v; Auto sobre haber traído a este juzgado el canoero Andrés Calvo un negro que salió aquel paraje del Reventazón, Cartago, November 2, 1722, ANCR, C. 283, fol. 9v.

57. Auto para despachar órdenes, Cartago, May 19, 1722, ANCR, C. 292, fols. 5v–6; Auto del gobernador, Cartago, June 18, 1722, ANCR, C. 292, fol. 10; Orden del gobernador, Cartago, June 5, 1722, Archivo General de Centro América, Guatemala City (hereafter, AGCA), A1 (6), exp. 1057, quoting from leg. 73.

58. Petición del Ayu. Francisco Hernández Barquero, presentada en Cartago, September 16, 1687, ANCR, CC 3925, fol. 1.

59. Auto de los jueces don Gregorio de Caamaño y Juan Antonio de Bogarín, Esparza, February 20, 1701, ANCR, C. 109, fol. 27.

60. Auto de manifestación de 4 negros, Esparza, February 22, 1701, ANCR, C. 109, fol. 28.

61. "Informe del gobernador D. Francisco de Carrandi y Menán al presidente de Guatemala sobre el estado de las misiones en la provincia de Costa Rica.—Año de 1737," in Fernández, Colección de documentos, 9:260–61.

62. Auto sobre haber traído a este juzgado el canoero Andrés Calvo un negro que salió aquel paraje del Reventazón, Cartago, November 2, 1722, ANCR, C. 283, quoting from fol. 9v; Declaración de Nicolás, negro de casta mina, Cartago, April 25, 1723, ANCR, C. 283, fol. 11.

63. Petición del Ayudante Francisco Hernández Barquero, presentada en Cartago, September 16, 1687, ANCR, CC 3925, fol. 1.

64. Doña Isidora Zambrano da poder a don Pedro de Colina, su hijo, para que en Granada pueda prender, asegurar y vender un esclavo, Aserrí, July 1, 1669, ANCR, PC 817 bis., fols. 496–97.

65. Doña María de Sandoval da poder a los Capitanes don Francisco Navarrete y Jerónimo de Villegas, vecinos de Granada, para que persigan, recobren y vendan un esclavo, Cartago, May 16, 1675, ANCR, PC 824, fols. 13–14.

66. El Cap. Rodrigo Vázquez Coronado da poder al Cap. don Fernando Pérez de Vera, vecino de Granada, para que venda a un esclavo, Cartago, March 30, 1688, ANCR, PC 837, fols. 15–15v.

67. Indice de los protocolos de Cartago, 6 vols. (San José: Tipografía Nacional, 1909–1930), 1:79; Rina Cáceres, Negros, mulatos, esclavos y libertos en la Costa Rica del siglo XVII (Mexico City: Instituto Panamericano de Geografía e Historia, 2000), 86.

68. El Alf. Manuel Antonio de Arlegui da poder al Mtre. de Campo don José de Casasola y Córdoba para reclamar a un esclavo, Cartago, April 9, 1708, ANCR, PC 865, fol. 48v; Doña Gracia Gertrudis de Hoces Navarro otorga poder para que

don Félix Esteban de Hoces Navarro, estante en Guatemala, venda a un esclavo, Cartago, December 24, 1714, ANCR, PC 873, fols. 179–80.

69. Testamento del Cap. don Fernando de Salazar, Cartago, January 14, 1678, ANCR, PC 825, fol. 65v; Carta dote, Cartago, August 13, 1699, ANCR, Mortuales Coloniales de Cartago (hereafter, MCC) 797, fol. 29; *Indice de los protocolos de Cartago*, 2:235.

70. Ibid., 2:239.

71. Auto del Mtre. de Campo don Pedro Ruiz de Bustamante, Gobernador de Costa Rica, Cartago, July 14, 1717, ANCR, CC 4111, fols. 1–1v, 2v; Declaración de Juan Damián, negro esclavo ladino de doña Agueda Pérez de Muro, Cartago, August 14, 1717, ANCR, CC 4111, fols. 3–5; Declaración de Gregorio Caamaño, negro esclavo de doña Agueda Pérez de Muro, Cartago, August 14, 1717, ANCR, CC 4111, fols. 5v–8. The castas of the men are identified in Confesión de Juan Damián, negro esclavo de casta congo, ANCR, G. 181, fol. 2; Razón del Teniente General don Diego de Barros de quién hubo su esclavo Francisco Congo, Cartago, May 30, 1720, ANCR, C. 265, fol. 2v.

72. Almoneda de dos esclavos, Cartago, September 25, 1718, ANCR, CC 4111, fol. 24v.

73. Petición de doña Agueda Pérez de Muro, presentada en Cartago, January 9, 1719, ANCR, CC 4111, fols. 35–36v; Real Provisión, Guatemala, March 11, 1723, ANCR, CC 4142, fols. 1v–2v.

74. Notificación al Sarg. Mayor don Francisco de la Madriz Linares y su respuesta, Cartago, March 6, 1724, CC 4142, fol. 5v; Recibo del negro Gregorio Caamaño por el Cap. don Francisco Garrido, Cartago, July 19, 1724, ANCR, CC 4142, fol. 9.

75. Auto de almoneda, Esparza, February 20, 1701, ANCR, C. 109, fol. 27; Almoneda de dos esclavos, Esparza, February 24, 1701, C. 109, fol. 29; Venta de dos esclavos, Cartago, May 2, 1704, PC 860, fols. 10–12.

76. Razón del Teniente General don Diego de Barros de quien hubo su esclavo Francisco Congo, Cartago, May 30, 1720, ANCR, C. 265, fol. 2v; Reconocimiento del despacho presentado por don Diego de Barros, Cartago, June 3, 1720, ANCR, C. 265, fol. 3v.

77. Carta de libertad, Cartago, March 2, 1733, ANCR, PC 910, fol. 8.

78. Declaración del negro Antonio Congo, Cartago, March 8, 1722, ANCR, C. 290, quoting from fol. 2, fol. 2v.

79. Auto de sentencia sobre el negro Antonio Congo, Cartago, May 12, 1722, ANCR, C. 292, fols. 3v–4.

80. Almoneda de esclavo, Cartago, May 15, 1722, ANCR, C. 292, fols. 5–5v; Auto para despachar órdenes, Cartago, May 19, 1722, ANCR, C. 292, fols. 5v–6; Auto del gobernador, Cartago, June 18, 1722, ANCR, C. 292, fol. 10.

81. Razón de almoneda de esclavo, Cartago, June 21, 1722, ANCR, C. 292, fols. 11–11v; Petición de don Francisco Javier de Oreamuno, presentada en Cartago, September 28, 1725, AGCA, A2 (6), exp. 193, leg. 12, fol. 6.

82. Real cédula, Campo Real de Castel David, July 1, 1704, AGCA, A1.23, leg. 1524, fols. 158–59. See also the survey of intercolonial slave flight in Julius S. Scott, "The

Common Wind: Currents of Afro-American Communication in the Era of the Haitian Revolution" (PhD diss., Duke University, 1986), 92–103.

83. Auto del Almirante don Tomás Marcos Duque de Estrada, Gobernador de Nicaragua, Masaya, Nic., January 12, 1726, AGCA, A2 (6), exp. 193, leg. 12, fol. 12.

84. Auto del Almirante don Tomás Marcos Duque de Estrada, Gobernador de Nicaragua, Masaya, Nic., January 12, 1726, AGCA, A2 (6), exp. 193, leg. 12, fols. 12, 12v. Francisco Javier de Oreamuno appealed his ownership of Antonio to the Audiencia of Guatemala. The case continued in 1727, but its final outcome was not recorded. AGCA, A2 (6), exp. 193, leg. 12.

85. Auto del Almirante don Tomás Marcos Duque de Estrada, Gobernador de Nicaragua, Masaya, Nic., January 12, 1726, AGCA, A2 (6), exp. 193, leg. 12, fol. 12.

86. Declaración de Antonio Congo, Cartago, March 8, 1722, ANCR, C. 290, fols. 2–3.

87. Entrega de los autos mortuales de Fermín de Oses, Cartago, April 29, 1722, ANCR, C. 292, fol. 2; Notificación al albacea el Cap. Antonio de Soto y Barahona, y su respuesta, Cartago, May 11, 1722, ANCR, C. 292, fols. 3–3v; Auto de sentencia sobre el negro Antonio Congo, Cartago, May 12, 1722, ANCR, C. 292, fols. 3v–4.

88. Fe del bautizo de Antonio Luis, negro adulto que se huyó del enemigo, Granada, Nic., November 15, 1726, AGCA, A2 (6), exp. 193, leg. 12.

89. Petición de don Francisco Javier de Oreamuno, presentada en Cartago, September 28, 1725, AGCA, A2 (6), exp. 193, leg. 12, fols. 6, 6v.

90. Poder para aprehender a un esclavo, Granada, Nic., May 19, 1705, ANCR, PC 862, fols. 55v, 56–57v, 58–59v.

91. Venta de esclavo, Cartago, September 7, 1706, ANCR, PC 862, fols. 58–59v.

92. Testamento del Sarg. Mayor Blas González Coronel, Cartago, August 2, 1710, ANCR, PC 868, fol. 72v; Testamento del Sarg. Mayor Blas González Coronel, Cartago, July 19, 1714, ANCR, PC 873, fol. 89; Venta de esclavo, Cartago, April 15, 1715, ANCR, PC 887, fols. 65v–68v.

93. Auto del gobernador, Cartago, March 5, 1715, AGI, Escribanía 353B, fol. 104.

94. For an example, see the Declaración de Juan Ramírez y de Paula Sánchez, su mujer, naturales del Pueblo de Tobosi, Cartago, August 20, 1726, ANCR, CC 169, fols. 26v–27.

95. Auto de buen gobierno, Cartago, May 2, 1707, ANCR, C. 157, fol. 7v; Auto, Aserrí, August 26, 1720, ANCR, Protocolos Coloniales de San José (hereafter, PSJ) 411, fol. 40.

96. Auto del gobernador, Cartago, March 5, 1715, AGI, Escribanía 353B, fol. 104.

97. Declaración de Antonio de Rosas, negro esclavo del Cap. Juan Sancho de Castañeda, Matina, December 6, 1719, ANCR, C. 231, quoting from fol. 11; Razón dada por don Gil de Alvarado sobre el negro Francisco, Cartago, July 11, 1720, ANCR, C. 231, fol. 26.

98. Petición de doña Juana Núñez de Trupira, presentada en Cartago, July 1, 1692, ANCR, PC 842, fol. 63.

99. Auto del Alf. Nicolás de Céspedes, Regidor Perpetuo y Alcalde Ordinario Más Antiguo de Cartago, Cartago, July 1, 1692, ANCR, PC 842, fol. 64; Petición de doña Juana Núñez de Trupira, presentada en Cartago, July 1, 1692, ANCR, PC 842, fols. 63–63v.

100. Auto del Alf. Nicolás de Céspedes, Regidor Perpetuo y Alcalde Ordinario Más Antiguo de Cartago, Cartago, July 1, 1692, ANCR, PC 842, fol. 64; Venta de esclava, Cartago, July 1, 1692, ANCR, PC 842, fols. 56v–58v.

101. Certificación de don José de Mier Cevallos, Sitio de San Jerónimo, February 8, 1724, ANCR, CC 4140, fol. 13v, 14; María de los Angeles Acuña, "Mujeres esclavas en la Costa Rica del siglo XVIII: Estrategias frente a la esclavitud," *Diálogos: Revista Electrónica de Historia* (Costa Rica) 5, nos. 1–2 (April 2004–February 2005): 13, http://www.historia.fcs.ucr.ac.cr/articulos/esp-genero/1parte/CAP1Marielos/CAP1Marielostexto.html.

102. Auto del Cap. Juan de Ugalde, Teniente de Gobernador y Juez del Campo del Valle de Barva, Cartago, April 14, 1723, ANCR, CC 5815, fol. 1; Notificación al Alf. Juan Cortés y su respuesta, Cartago, May 19, 1720, ANCR, C. 248, fol. 3v; Venta de esclava, Barva, January 7, 1723, ANCR, PSJ 412, fols. 4–5; Confesión de Antonia, mulata esclava, Cartago, April 14, 1723, ANCR, CC 5815, fol. 1v.

103. Notificación a Antonia, mulata esclava, y su respuesta, Cartago, April 24, 1723, ANCR, CC 5815, fol. 9.

104. Diligencia y entrega de Antonia, mulata esclava del Cap. Juan Cortés, al suso dicho, Cartago, April 25, 1723, ANCR, CC 5815, fol. 10v; Venta de esclava, Cartago, April 26, 1723, ANCR, PC 896, fols. 46–47v.

105. Declaración de Francisco Caracata, negro esclavo de casta arará, Cartago, January 18, 1720, ANCR, C. 232, fol. 12.

106. Notificación al Cap. don Manuel de Arburola, y su respuesta, Cartago, September 25, 1719, ANCR, C. 232, fol. 4.

107. Razón dada por Jacinto de Rivera sobre el negro Francisco, Cartago, September 30, 1719, ANCR, C. 232, fol. 4v.

108. Auto sobre el negro Francisco y respuesta del Cap. Manuel de Arburola, Cartago, November 10, 1719, ANCR, C. 232, fol. 6v; Auto para que el Cap. Manuel de Arburola ponga en el Juzgado el negro Francisco, quien respondió haberse huido, Cartago, November 20, 1719, ANCR, C. 232, fol. 7v; Diligencia en la que dice doña Josefa de Oses no afianza el negro por estar enfermo y ser cimarrón, Cartago, January 1720, ANCR, C. 232, fol. 14.

109. Diligencia en la que consta haber parecido el negro Francisco Caracata en la puerta de la casa del Gobernador, Cartago, January 18, 1720, ANCR, C. 231, fol. 12.

110. Reconocimiento y avalúo del negro Francisco, Cartago, January 18, 1720, ANCR, C. 232, fol. 13.

111. Razón del remate del negro Francisco Caracata, Cartago, April 22, 1722, ANCR, C. 232, fol. 54.

112. Inventario de los bienes de doña Catalina González del Camino, Cartago, November 19, 1745, ANCR, MCC 797, fol. 18.

113. Petición del Lic. don Manuel Francisco Martínez Cubero y de don José de Mier Cevallos, presentada en Cartago, July 15, 1746, ANCR, MCC 797, quoting from fol. 84v; Cuentas, división y partición de los bienes de doña Catalina González del Camino, Cartago, July 22, 1746, MCC 797, fol. 88v.

114. Venta de esclavo, Cartago, August 16, 1746, ANCR, PC 934, fols. 66–68, quoting from fol. 66.

115. Testamento del Cap. don Fernando de Salazar, Cartago, January 14, 1678, ANCR, PC 825, fol. 68.

116. Nombramiento de Alguacil Mayor, Cartago, July 5, 1679, ANCR, C. 1143, fol. 52.

117. Razón del entierro de Juan Antonio, mulato esclavo, Cartago, August 10, 1679, ACMSJ, SFASDE, Caja 9, fol. 22v.

118. Declaración de doña Francisca Sánchez de Orozco, Cartago, September 19, 1687, ANCR, CC 3914, fol. 2v.

119. Testamento del Alf. José de Quesada, Cartago, January 13, 1716, ANCR, PC 878, fol. 10.

120. Testamento del Alf. José de Quesada, Cartago, April 12, 1723, ANCR, PSJ 412, fols. 16–16v.

121. Razón del entierro de una mulata que ahorcaron, Cartago, August 11, 1681, ACMSJ, SFASDE, Caja 9, fol. 29.

122. Razón del entierro de Antonio, negro que ajusticiaron, Cartago, January 14, 1694, ACMSJ, SFASDE, Caja 9, fol. 57v.

123. Petición del Cap. Manuel García de Argueta, presentada en Cartago, July 13, 1720, ANCR, C. 243, fols. 25–25v.

124. Gobernador don Baltasar Francisco de Valderrama al Teniente General de Matina don Diego de Barros y Carbajal, Cartago, March 21, 1732, ANCR, C. 325, fols. 212–12v.

125. Carta del Teniente General José Felipe Bermúdez al Gobernador Valderrama, Cartago, April 28, 1734, ANCR, C. 325, fols. 248–48v.

126. Petición del Sarg. Mayor don Juan Francisco de Ibarra, presentada en Cartago, November 4, 1720, ANCR, G. 185, quoting from fol. 85.

127. William E. Wiethoff, *The Insolent Slave* (Columbia: University of South Carolina Press, 2000), 1.

128. J. G. Peristiany, introduction to *Honour and Shame: The Values of Mediterranean Society*, ed. J. G. Peristiany (Chicago, IL: University of Chicago Press, 1966), 9–18; Julian Pitt-Rivers, "Honour and Social Status," in *Honour and Shame: The Values of Mediterranean Society*, ed. J. G. Peristiany (Chicago, IL: University of Chicago Press, 1966), 19–77.

129. Patricia Seed, *To Love, Honor and Obey in Colonial Mexico: Conflicts over Marriage Choice, 1574–1821* (Stanford, CA: Stanford University Press, 1988), 137; Ann Twinam, "Honor, Sexuality, and Illegitimacy in Colonial Spanish America," in *Sexuality and Marriage in Colonial Latin America*, ed. Asunción Lavrin (Lincoln: University of Nebraska Press, 1989), 123–24; Lyman L. Johnson and Sonya Lipsett-Rivera, eds., *The Faces of Honor: Sex, Shame, and Violence in*

Colonial Latin America (Albuquerque: University of New Mexico Press, 1988), esp. Sandra Lauderdale Graham's chapter, "Honor Among Slaves," 201–28.

130. Querella por el Cap. Juan de Bonilla, presentada en Cartago, July 17, 1686, ANCR, CC 6403, fol. 1.

131. Ibid., fols. 1, 1v; Declaración de Manuel de Mora, Cartago, August 30, 1696, ANCR, CC 6403, fol. 6.

132. Javier Villa-Flores, "'To Lose One's Soul': Blasphemy and Slavery in New Spain, 1596–1669," *Hispanic American Historical Review* 82, no. 3 (2002): 448.

133. Declaración de Francisco de Flores, Cartago, August 30, 1696, ANCR, CC 6403, fol. 5v.

134. Querella por el Cap. Juan de Bonilla, presentada en Cartago, July 17, 1696, ANCR, CC 6403, fol. 1v; Declaración de Manuel de Mora, Cartago, August 30, 1696, ANCR, CC 6403, fol. 6; Prisión del mulato esclavo Gregorio Sanabria, Valle de Matina, July 25, 1696, ANCR, CC 6403, fols. 3–3v.

135. Wiethoff, *Insolent Slave*, 1.

136. Compare the famous fight between Frederick Douglass and the "nigger-breaker" Edward Covey. Frederick Douglass, *Narrative of the Life of Frederick Douglass*, in *The Classic Slave Narratives*, ed. Henry Louis Gates (New York: Signet, 2002), 383, 393–95; William S. McFeely, *Frederick Douglass* (New York: W. W. Norton, 1991), 44–48.

137. Donación de esclavos, Cartago, May 29, 1665, ANCR, PC 817, fol. 15; Testamento de María Sagaste, Cartago, November 19, 1690, ANCR, PC 839, fols. 114v, 115.

138. Testamento de doña Ana María Maroto, Cartago, February 28, 1737, ANCR, PC 916, fol. 22v.

139. Declaración de José Antonio Pérez, Cartago, May 27, 1755, ANCR, CC 6229, fol. 6v.

140. Petición de José Nicolás Bonilla, presentada en Cartago, May 26, 1755, ANCR, CC 6229, fols. 1–2.

141. Declaración de Bernardo Campos, indio natural del pueblo de Curridabat, Cartago, May 27, 1755, ANCR, CC 6229, fols. 3v–4.

142. Auto del Alcalde Ordinario don Tomás López del Corral, Cartago, May 26, 1755, ANCR, CC 6229, quoting from fol. 3, fol. 8v.

143. Wiethoff, *Insolent Slave*, 7.

144. Confesión de Ana Miranda, mulata esclava, Cartago, May 31, 1755, ANCR, CC 6229, fols. 10–10v; Petición de doña Francisca de Miranda al Alcalde Ordinario, presentada en Cartago, June 28, 1755, ANCR, CC 6229, fol. 17.

145. Petición de don José Nicolás de Bonilla al Alcalde Ordinario y Teniente de Gobernador, presentada en Cartago, June 10, 1755, ANCR, CC 6229, fols. 12–12v; Petición de don José Nicolás de Bonilla al Alcalde Ordinario y Teniente de Gobernador, presentada en Cartago, June 16, 1755, ANCR, CC 6229, fol. 15v.

146. Petición de don José Nicolás de Bonilla al Alcalde Ordinario y Teniente de Gobernador, presentada en Cartago, June 29, 1755, ANCR, CC 6229, fol. 20v.

147. Sentencia del Alcalde Ordinario Cap. don Félix García de Casasola, Cartago, July 5, 1755, ANCR, CC 6229, fol. 25v.

148. Jacob Gorender, "Violência, consenso e contratualidade," in *A escravidão reabilitada* (São Paulo: Editora Ática, 1990), 22–23.

CHAPTER SEVEN

 1. Manifestación de crías, San Francisco de Tenorio, November 20, 1719, Archivo Nacional de Costa Rica (hereafter, ANCR), Sección Colonial Guatemala (hereafter, G.) 185, fol. 20.
 2. Partida del bautizo de Josefa, Esparza, May 29, 1713, Archivo de la Curia Metropolitana de San José, San José (hereafter, ACMSJ), Libros de Bautizos de Esparza (1706–1819)/Family History Library, Salt Lake City, Utah (hereafter, FHL), VAULT INTL film 1223548, item 5.
 3. Partida del bautizo de Toribio, Cartago, July 20, 1714, and Partida del bautizo de Juan, Cartago, August 6, 1714, both in ACMSJ, Libros de bautizos de Cartago (hereafter, LBC), no. 4/FHL, VAULT INTL film 1219701, item 4.
 4. ACMSJ, LBC, nos. 1–6 (1594–1738)/FHL, VAULT INTL film 1219701, items 1–5, VAULT INTL film 1219702, item 1.
 5. ACMSJ, Libros de Bautizos de Esparza (1708–1819)/FHL, VAULT INTL film 1223548, items 5–6.
 6. For illegitimacy in the late colonial period, see Héctor Pérez Brignoli, "Deux siècles d'illégitimité au Costa Rica, 1770–1974," in *Marriage and Remarriage in Populations of the Past*, ed. J. Dupâquier et al. (London: Academic Press, 1981), 481–93.
 7. ACMSJ, LBC (1599–1750), nos. 1–6/FHL, VAULT INTL film1219701, items 1–5; film 1219702, items 1–3.
 8. ACMSJ, Libros de Bautizos de Esparza (1706–1819)/FHL, VAULT INTL film 1223548, items 5–6.
 9. ACMSJ, LBC (1599–1750), nos. 1–6/FHL, VAULT INTL film 1219701, items 1–5; film 1219702, items 1–3.
10. Brenda E. Stevenson, *Life in Black and White: Family and Community in the Slave South* (New York: Oxford University Press, 1996), 240.
11. Ann Patton Malone, *Sweet Chariot: Slave Family and Household Structure in Nineteenth-Century Louisiana* (Chapel Hill: University of North Carolina Press, 1992), 219.
12. Richard H. Steckel, "Miscegenation and the American Slave Schedules," *Journal of Interdisciplinary History* 11, no. 2 (1980): 253, 260.
13. María de los Angeles Acuña León, "Papel reproductivo y productivo de las mujeres esclavas en Costa Rica del siglo XVIII," *Revista de Historia* (Costa Rica), nos. 57–58 (2008): 154.
14. Carta del Obispo de Nicaragua y Costa Rica Fr. Juan de Rojas al Rey, León, Nic., January 31, 1684, Archivo General de Indias, Seville (hereafter, AGI), Audiencia de Guatemala (hereafter, AG) 162, fol. 459; Germán Romero Vargas, *Las estructuras sociales de Nicaragua en el siglo XVIII* (Managua: Editorial Vanguardia, 1988), 290.

15. Ricardo Blanco Segura, *Obispos, arzobispos y representantes de la Santa Sede en Costa Rica* (San José: Editorial Universidad Estatal a Distancia, 1984), 46.

16. Codicilio al testamento de Inés de Olvidares, Cartago, July 8, 1720, ANCR, Protocolos Coloniales de Cartago (hereafter, PC) 892, fols. 17v–18v; Carta de libertad, Cartago, July 12, 1720, ANCR, PC 892, fols. 22v–23.

17. Testamento de Jerónima Barrantes, Cartago, January 30, 1697, ANCR, PC 849, fols. 6v, 7.

18. Testamento del Ayu. Francisco Hernández Barquero, Cartago, August 10, 1698, ANCR, PC 850, fol. 13; Testamento de María Barquero, Cartago, October 28, 1733, ANCR, PC 909, fol. 101v; Donación de 8 esclavos, Cartago, June 5, 1741, ANCR, PC 926, fol. 17.

19. Several scholars have written about Miguel Calvo, Ana Cardoso, and their children, the subjects of the best-known case of racial mixture in the Costa Rican historiography. See Pedro Pérez Zeledón, "Fusión de sangres," in *Gregorio José Ramírez y otros ensayos* (San José: Editorial Costa Rica, 1971, originally published 1918), 89–94; Lowell Gudmundson K, "Mecanismos de movilidad social para la población de procedencia africana en Costa Rica colonial: Manumisión y mestizaje," *Revista de Historia* (Costa Rica) 2, no. 3 (1976): 29, http://www.revistas.una.ac.cr/index.php/historia/article/view/2150; Mauricio Meléndez Obando, "Los Calvo," in Tatiana Lobo Wiehoff and Mauricio Meléndez Obando, *Negros y blancos: Todo mezclado* (San José: Editorial de la Universidad de Costa Rica, 1997), 137–39.

20. Pérez Zeledón, "Fusión de sangres," 89; Meléndez Obando, "Los Calvo," 138. I have been unable to locate the document cited by Pérez Zeledón recording Ana's sale.

21. Venta de esclavo, Cartago, February 10, 1687, ANCR, PC 836, fols. 1–1v; Manumisión de esclavo, Cartago, February 10, 1687, ANCR, PC 836, fols. 2–2v.

22. Manumisión de esclava (Ana Cardoso), Cartago, May 27, 1689, ANCR, PC 838, fols. 63–64v; Manumisión de esclavas (María y Francisca), Cartago, January 14, 1691, ANCR, PC 841, fols. 3v–5; Testamento del Cap. don Miguel Calvo, Cartago, February 16, 1715, ANCR, PC 877, fols. 34–34v; Pérez Zeledón, "Fusión de sangres," 90–91.

23. Testamento cerrado de doña Eugenia de Abarca Alatras, Cartago, June 28, 1702, ANCR, PC 856, fols. 87–91v; Manumisión de esclava, Cartago, July 3, 1715, ANCR, PC 877, fols. 123v–24.

24. Carta de libertad, Cartago, July 3, 1715, ANCR, PC 877, fol. 123.

25. Petición de María Calvo, parda libre, al Gobernador don Diego de la Haya Fernández, 1 July 1720, ANCR, C. 242, fol. 11.

26. Carta dote, Cartago, April 8, 1697, ANCR, PC 849, fols. 31–33; Carta dote, Cartago, April 27, 1697, ANCR, Mortuales Coloniales de Cartago (hereafter, MCC) 733, fols. 1–5v.

27. El Sarg. Francisco de Echavarría reconoce recibo de 1.484 pesos y 6 maravedíes, Cartago, August 29, 1715, ANCR, MCC 707, fols. 13–16; Donación de esclavo, Cartago, February 25, 1711, ANCR, PC 870, fols. 9–10v, quoting from fol. 9.

28. Testamento del Cap. don Miguel Calvo, Cartago, February 16, 1715, ANCR, P.C. 877, fol. 35.
29. Ibid., fol. 36.
30. Ibid., fol. 38.
31. Adjudicación de bienes de don Miguel Calvo, Cartago, June 1715, ANCR, MCC 733, fols. 73–79; Petición de María Calvo, parda libre, presentada en Cartago, May 20, 1720, ANCR, C. 242, fol. 5; Declaración de Juana, negra de casta mina, Cartago, September 14, 1719, ANCR, C. 248, fol. 1v; Testamento del Cap. don Miguel Calvo, Cartago, February 16, 1715, ANCR, PC 877, fol. 35v; Partida del bautizo de María Fernanda, hija de Cayetano, esclavo de doña María Calvo, Cartago, July 22, 1748, ACMSJ, LBC, no. 8/FHL, VAULT INTL film 1219702, item 3.
32. Permuta de esclavos, Cartago, June 17, 1723, ANCR, PC 896, fols. 66–68v; Testamento de doña Nicolasa Guerrero, Cartago, November 24, 1726, ANCR, PC 899, fol. 129v; Testamento de doña Nicolasa Guerrero, Cartago, February 20, 1730, ANCR, PC 903, fol. 7.
33. Petición hecha por Tomás de la Madriz ante el Juez eclesiástico a fin de que se anule su matrimonio con Antonia de la Granda y Balvín, presentada en Cartago, October 17, 1727, ACMSJ, SFASDE, Caja 13, fols. 384–91; Obligación de doña Antonia de la Granda y Balvín, Cartago, August 12, 1734, ANCR, PC 912, fols. 50v–51; Mauricio Meléndez Obando, "Los Madriz," in Tatiana Lobo Wiehoff and Mauricio Meléndez Obando, Negros y blancos: Todo mezclado (San José: Editorial de la Universidad de Costa Rica, 1997), 134–35.
34. Donación de esclavos, Cartago, September 17, 1742, ANCR, PC 927, fol. 73v–77; Indice de los protocolos de Cartago, 6 vols. (San José: Tipografía Nacional, 1909–1930), 3:434–35, 443, 455, 4:64; Meléndez Obando, "Los Madriz," 136–37; Testamento de doña Antonia de Granda y Balvín, Cartago, July 14, 1746, ANCR, PC 934, fol. 52v. See also María de los Angeles Acuña León, "Mujeres esclavas en la Costa Rica del siglo XVIII: Estrategias frente a la esclavitud," Diálogos: Revista Electrónica de Historia (Costa Rica) 5, nos. 1–2 (April 2004–February 2005), http://www.historia.fcs.ucr.ac.cr/articulos/esp-genero/1parte/CAP1Marielos/CAP1Marielostexto.html.
35. Carta de libertad, Cartago, August 3, 1675, ANCR, PC 824, fols. 27v–28v.
36. Carta de libertad, Cartago, July 9, 1738, ANCR, PC 919, fol. 59v.
37. Herbert S. Klein, African Slavery in Latin America and the Caribbean (Oxford: Oxford University Press, 1986), 227, 229; Stuart B. Schwartz, "The Manumission of Slaves in Colonial Brazil: Bahia, 1684–1745," Hispanic American Historical Review 54 (1974): 611; Schwartz, Sugar Plantations in the Formation of Brazilian Society: Bahia, 1550–1835 (Cambridge: Cambridge University Press, 1985), 331, 410.
38. See, for example, Schwartz, "Manumission of Slaves," 611–19; Gudmundson K, "Mecanismos de movilidad," 27–30.
39. Calculations using manumissions are based on cartas de libertad in ANCR, PC 815 (1654–1655, 1664–1667)–934 (1746); Protocolos Coloniales de Heredia

(hereafter, PH) 572 (1723)–87 (1741); Protocolos Coloniales de San José (hereafter, PSJ) 415 (1738); Sección Complementario Colonial (hereafter, CC) 3905 (1680), CC 3916 (1675), CC 3927 (1693), CC 4000 (1709); *Indice de los protocolos de Cartago*, vols. 1–3.

40. H. Hoetink, *Caribbean Race Relations: A Study of Two Variants* (Oxford: Oxford University Press for the Institute of Race Relations, 1967), 176.

41. Frank T. Proctor III, "Gender and the Manumission of Slaves in New Spain," *Hispanic American Historical Review* 86, no. 2 (2006): 309–36.

42. Obligación del Cap. Blas González Coronel y su mujer doña Bernarda de Fonseca, Cartago, September 30, 1706, ANCR, PC 860, fol. 94v; Testamento del Sarg. Mayor Blas González Coronel, Cartago, August 2, 1710, ANCR, PC 868, fols. 72v, 74v; Declaración de Isabel, negra, Cartago, September 22, 1720, ANCR, C. 284, fol. 13v.

43. Declaraciones de 3 negros, Cartago, October 5, 1720, ANCR, G. 185, fol. 45.

44. Razón dada por la negra Manuela de no tener crías, Cartago, September 2, 1720, ANCR, C. 258, fol. 22v.

45. Razón dada por la negra Lorenza, Cartago, September 2, 1720, ANCR, C. 260, fol. 21v.

46. William Bosman, *A New and Accurate Description of the Coast of Guinea, Divided into the Gold, the Slave and the Ivory Coasts* (London: James Knapton, 1705), 364; Ludwig Ferdinand Rømer, *A Reliable Account of the Coast of Guinea (1760)*, trans. and ed. Selena Axelrod Winsnes (Oxford: Oxford University Press for the British Academy, 2000), [132] (bracketed page numbers refer to the original pagination).

47. Stephanie E. Smallwood, *Saltwater Slavery: A Middle Passage from Africa to American Diaspora* (Cambridge, MA: Harvard University Press, 2007), 172–73.

48. Voyages Database, Voyages: The Trans-Atlantic Slave Trade Database, http://slavevoyages.org/tast/database/search.faces?yearFrom=1600&yearTo=1750.

49. Razón de 14 negros, Cartago, September 10, 1702, ANCR, C. 113, fol. 4v; Auto del gobernador, Cartago, September 30, 1702, ANCR, C. 113, fol. 10v.

50. Inventario de los 5 negros traídos de Matina por el Cap. Antonio de Soto y Barahona, Cartago, May 1, 1710, ANCR, C. 187, fol. 70.

51. Declaración de Miguel, esclavo de doña Luisa Calvo, Cartago, November 15, 1719, ANCR, C. 267, fol. 7; Declaración de Magdalena, esclava de doña Josefa de Oses, Cartago, September 9, 1719, ANCR, C. 232, fol. 2v; Declaración de María, esclava del Sarg. Mayor Antonio de Soto y Barahona, Cartago, September 14, 1719, ANCR, C. 233, fol. 1v; Declaración de Teresa, esclava del Sarg. Mayor Antonio de Soto y Barahona, Cartago, September 14, 1719, ANCR, C. 233, fols. 2–2v; Declaración de Manuela, esclava del Cap. Francisco de Flores, Cartago, September 28, 1719, ANCR, C. 254, fol. 1v.

52. Declaración de Diego de Angulo, esclavo del Beneficiado don Diego de Angulo Gascón, Valle de Matina, December 9, 1719, ANCR, C. 263, fol. 1v.

53. These figures are derived from statements by African slaves in ANCR, C. 211 (1716–1719), C. 224 (1719), C. 229–46 (1719), C. 248–54 (1719), C. 256 (1719), C. 258–68 (1719), C. 273–78 (1720), C. 280 (1719), C. 283–84 (1721), C. 288–89 (1719–1720), C. 292 (1722); ANCR, G. 185–88 (1719).

54. Declaración de Antonia, negra esclava de Diego de Aguilar, Cartago, June 13, 1720, ANCR, C. 276, fol. 1v.

55. Norrece T. Jones Jr., *Born a Child of Freedom, Yet a Slave: Mechanisms of Control and Strategies of Resistance in Antebellum South Carolina* (Hanover, CT: Wesleyan University Press, 1990), 3.

56. Donación de esclavos, Cartago, May 29, 1665, ANCR, PC 817, fol. 15; Almoneda, Cartago, December 15, 1679, ANCR, CC 3903, fol. 16; Testamento de María Sagaste, Cartago, November 19, 1690, ANCR, PC 839, fols. 114v, 115.

57. ANCR, PC 801 (1607)–934 (1746), 927 (1742); ANCR, PH 573 (1721)–91 (1746); PSJ 411 (1721)–12 (1723); *Indice de los protocolos de Cartago*, vols. 1–3.

58. Orlando Patterson, *Slavery and Social Death* (Cambridge, MA: Harvard University Press, 1982), 5–10.

59. For examples, see Partida del bautizo de Juan Benito, mulato esclavo de padres no conocidos, Cartago, August 30, 1705, and Partida del bautizo de Agustín, mulato esclavo del Lic. don Diego de Campos, Cartago, May 7, 1706, both in ACMSJ, LBC, no. 3/FHL, VAULT INTL film 1219701, item 3.

60. Venta de esclavo, Cartago, April 3, 1738, ANCR, PC 919, fols. 38v–40.

61. Venta de esclava, Cartago, September 4, 1690, ANCR, PC 839, fols. 91–93.

62. Testamento del Sarg. Mayor don Antonio de Moya, Cartago, June 28, 1702, ANCR, PC 856, fol. 84v.

63. ANCR, PC 815 (1655, 1663)–927 (1742); ACMSJ, SFASDE, Caja 20, fols. 225–27; *Indice de los protocolos de Cartago*, vols. 1–3.

64. Rina Cáceres, *Negros, mulatos, esclavos y libertos en la Costa Rica del siglo XVII* (Mexico City: Instituto Panamericano de Geografía e Historia, 2000), 59; Cáceres, "El trabajo esclavo en Costa Rica," *Revista de Historia* (Costa Rica), no. 39 (1999): 40; Melida Velásquez, "El comercio de esclavos en la Alcaldía Mayor de Tegucigalpa, siglos XVI al XVIII," *Mesoamérica*, no. 42 (2001): 208.

65. Donación de esclava, Cartago, January 3, 1666, ANCR, PC 817, fol. 142.

66. Donación de esclavos, Cartago, July 18, 1668, ANCR, PC 817 bis, fol. 444.

67. Licencia para vender a un esclavo, Cartago, August 20, 1696, ACMSJ, SFASDE, Caja 20, fol. 223v; Donación de esclavo, Cartago, August 22, 1696, ACMSJ, SFASDE, Caja 20, fol. 225v.

68. Donación de esclava, Cartago, June 14, 1718, ANCR, PC 885, fols. 102v–3v; Carta dote, Cartago, May 20, 1732, ANCR, PC 908, fols. 19–19v; Mauricio Meléndez Obando, "Los Ulloa," in Tatiana Lobo Wiehoff and Mauricio Meléndez Obando, *Negros y blancos: Todo mezclado* (San José: Editorial de la Universidad de Costa Rica, 1997), 128.

69. ANCR, PC 815 (1660, 1662)–934 (1746); ANCR, CC 3914, fols. 4–7 (1683); ANCR, PH 577 (1726)–78 (1727); ANCR, MCC 733 (1697), MCC 797 (1699); ACMSJ, SFASDE, Caja 20 (1692); *Indice de los protocolos de Cartago*, vols. 1–3.

70. Carta dote, Cartago, September 9, 1695, ANCR, PC 846, fol. 46; Velásquez, "El comercio de esclavos," 218.

71. Carta dote, Barva, September 25, 1719, ANCR, PC 889, fols. 53–53v.

72. ANCR, PC 815 (1660, 1662)–934 (1746); ANCR, CC 3914, fols. 4–7 (1683); ANCR, PH 577 (1726)–78 (1727); ANCR, MCC 733 (1697), MCC 797 (1699); ACMSJ, SFASDE, Caja 20 (1692); *Indice de los protocolos de Cartago*, vols. 1–3.

73. Carta dote, Cartago, February 6, 1691, ANCR, PC 841, fol. 66v.

74. Testamento de doña Francisca de Chinchilla, Cartago, July 21, 1671, ANCR, PC 818, fol. 37.

75. Venta de esclavo, August 6, 1718, Cartago, ANCR, PC 886, fols. 17v–19.

76. Testamento de doña Inés de Sandoval Golfín, Cartago, November 3, 1729, ANCR, PC 902, fol. 81.

77. Razón dada por la negra Josefa de tener dos crías, Cartago, September 2, 1720, ANCR, C. 273, fol. 12v.

78. Auto del gobernador, Cartago, January 4, 1721, ANCR, C. 273, fol. 17v; Carta del Gobernador de Costa Rica al Presidente de la Real Audiencia, Cartago, January 10, 1721, AGCA, A1.1, exp. 74, leg. 4.

79. Venta de esclava, Cartago, September 4, 1690, ANCR, PC 839. fols. 91–93; Declaración de María Nicolasa González, mulata libre, Cartago, September 16, 1720, ANCR, C. 241, fols. 47–48, quoting from 47v.

80. Razón dada por la negra Lorenza de tener dos crías, Cartago, September 2, 1720, ANCR, C. 241, fol. 22v; Tasación de negro, Cartago, September 3, 1720, ANCR, C. 241, fol. 23.

81. Declaración de la negra Lorenza, Cartago, August 6, 1720 (*sic:* actual date September 6, 1720), ANCR, C. 241, fol. 26v.

82. Declaración de María Nicolasa González, mulata libre, Cartago, September 16, 1720, ANCR, C. 241, fols. 47–48.

83. Testamento del Sarg. Mayor Blas González Coronel, Cartago, August 2, 1710, ANCR, PC 868, fol. 72v; Diligencia, Cartago, September 18, 1720, ANCR, C. 241, fol. 49v; Partida del bautizo de María Josefa, hija de Juana, mulata esclava del Sarg. Mayor Blas González Coronel, Cartago, March 2, 1710, ACMSJ, LBC, no. 4/ FHL, VAULT INTL film 1219701, item 4.

84. Petición del Lic. don Manuel José González Coronel, presentada en Cartago, September 20, 1720, ANCR, C. 241, fol. 51.

85. Razón del remate de la negra Lorenza y su hijo, Cartago, April 11, 1722, ANCR, C. 241, fol. 57.

86. Robert I. Burns, ed., *Las Siete Partidas*, trans. Samuel Parsons Scott (Philadelphia: University of Pennsylvania Press, 2001), 4:901 (Part. IV, Tit. V, Law I); Thomas

302   NOTES TO PAGES 188–190

Aquinas, The "Summa Theologica" of St. Thomas Aquinas, trans. Fathers of the English Dominican Province, 22 vols. (London: Burns Oates & Washbourne, 1920), 19:174–79 (Suppl., q. 52, a. 1c, a. 2c, a. 2 ad 2, a. 3c).

87. Gal. 3:28, cf. 1 Cor. 12:13, Col. 3:11; Aquinas, Summa Theologica, 19:177 (Suppl., q. 52, a. 2c).

88. Catechism of the Council of Trent for Parish Priests, Issued by Order of Pope Pius V, trans. John A. McHugh and Charles J. Callan (Rockford, IL: TAN Books, 1982, originally published 1923), quoting from 363, 367–68, 373–75.

89. Aquinas, Summa Theologica, quoting from 19:150 (Suppl., q. 49, a. 3c), 19:178 (Suppl., q. 52, a. 2, ad 4); Burns, Siete Partidas, 4:901–2 (Part. IV, Tit. V, Laws I–II); Concilio III Provincial Mexicano celebrado en el año de 1585, confirmado en Roma por el Papa Sixto V, y mandado observar por el gobierno español en diversas reales órdenes (Mexico City: Eugenio Maillefert, Editores, 1859), 347.

90. Frank Tannenbaum, Slave and Citizen: The Negro in the Americas (New York: Vintage, 1946), 64; Stanley M. Elkins, Slavery: A Problem in American Institutional and Intellectual Life, 2nd ed. (Chicago: University of Chicago Press, 1968), 53–54; Herbert S. Klein, Slavery in the Americas: A Comparative Study of Virginia and Cuba (Chicago, IL: University of Chicago Press, 1967), 95–97; Herman L. Bennett, Africans in Colonial Mexico: Absolutism, Christianity, and Afro-Creole Consciousness, 1570–1640 (Bloomington: Indiana University Press, 2003), chap. 4; Hünefeldt, Paying the Price of Freedom, 149–66.

91. Sandra Lauderdale Graham, Caetana Says No: Women's Stories from a Slave Society (Cambridge: Cambridge University Press, 2002), quoting from 27, 30, 31, 32–33; Robert W. Slenes, Na senzala uma flor: Esperanças e recordações na formação da família escrava: Brasil sudeste, século XIX (Rio de Janeiro: Editora Nova Fronteira, 1999), 74–78.

92. Schwartz, Sugar Plantations, 383, 390; Alida Metcalf, Family and Frontier in Colonial Brazil: Santana de Parnaíba, 1580–1822 (Berkeley: University of California Press, 1992), 168–69, 173.

93. Partida del matrimonio de Antonio García y de Agustina, los dos esclavos del Sarg. Mayor don Juan Francisco de Ibarra, Cartago, May 3, 1733, ACMSJ, Libros de Matrimonios de no. 3/FHL, VAULT INTL film 1219727, item 8.

94. Partida del bautizo de Luisa, hija de Sebastián y de Jerónima, esclavos de Juan López, Cartago, March 11, [1618]; Partida del bautizo de Paula, negra del Comisario Baltazar de Grado, hija de Pedro y de Catalina, su mujer, negros de Magdalena de la Portilla, Cartago, April 18, 1639; Partida del bautizo de Juan, hijo de Pedro, negros de don Gregorio de Sandoval, Gobernador y Cap. General de Costa Rica, Cartago, May 22, 1639; and Partida del bautizo de Nicolás de la Cruz, hijo de [roto: Francisco] y de Lucrecia, su mujer, negros esclavos del Gobernador de Costa Rica, Cartago, September 30, 1640, all in ACMSJ, LBC, no. 1 /FHL, VAULT INTL film 1219701, item 1.

95. Obligación del Cap. don José de Mier Cevallos y de su mujer doña Catalina González Camino a la Real Caja, Cartago, April 18, 1725, ANCR, PC 898, fol. 27;

Partida del bautizo de Juan Manuel, hijo legítimo de José Cubero y de Victoria Cubero, esclavos del Cap. don José de Mier Cevallos, Cartago, June 7, 1722, ACMSJ, LBC, no. 5/FHL, VAULT INTL film 1219701, item 5; Mauricio Meléndez Obando, "Manumisión," in Tatiana Lobo Wiehoff and Mauricio Meléndez Obando, *Negros y blancos: Todo mezclado* (San José: Editorial de la Universidad de Costa Rica, 1997), 108–9.

96. As James H. Sweet has argued for colonial Brazil: see James H. Sweet, *Recreating Africa: Culture, Kinship, and Religion in the African-Portuguese World, 1441–1770* (Chapel Hill: University of North Carolina Press, 2003), 36, 43.

97. Partida del bautizo de Juan, mulato, Cartago, January 13, 1607, ACMSJ, LBC, no. 1/FHL, VAULT INTL film 1219701, item 1.

98. See María de los Angeles Acuña León and Doriam Chavarría López, "Endogamia y exogamia en la sociedad colonial cartaginesa," *Revista de Historia* (Costa Rica), no. 23 (1991): 107–44; Acuña León and Chavarría López, "Cartago colonial: Mestizaje y patrones matrimoniales 1738–1821," *Mesoamérica*, no. 31 (1996): 157–79.

99. Edgar F. Love, "Marriage Patterns of Persons of African Descent in a Colonial Mexico City Parish," *Hispanic American Historical Review* 51, no. 1 (1971): 87–89.

100. R. Douglas Cope, *The Limits of Racial Domination: Plebeian Society in Colonial Mexico City, 1660–1720* (Madison: University of Wisconsin Press, 1994), 81–82, 82 table 4.10.

101. Christopher H. Lutz, *Santiago de Guatemala, 1541–1773: City, Caste, and the Colonial Experience* (Norman: University of Oklahoma Press, 1994), 177–78.

102. Paul Lokken, "Marriage as Slave Emancipation in Seventeenth-Century Rural Guatemala," *The Americas* 58, no. 2 (2001): 175–200.

103. ACMSJ, LMC, nos. 1–6/FHL, VAULT INTL film 1219727, items 6–10; ACMSJ, LBC, nos. 1–8 (1594–1749)/FHL, VAULT INTL film 1219701, items 1–5, VAULT INTL film 1219702, items 1–3; Acuña León and Chavarría López, "Endogamia y exogamia," 132–33, 136.

104. Testamento de María Calvo, Cartago, September 6, 1762, ANCR, PC 950, fol. 41v; Traslado de causa a María Cayetana Corrales, coheredera de María Calvo, y su respuesta, Cartago, June 14, 1774, ANCR, MCC 648, fol. 32v.

105. ACMSJ, LMC, nos. 1–6/FHL, VAULT INTL film 1219727, items 6–10; ACMSJ, LBC, nos. 1–8 (1594–1749)/FHL, VAULT INTL film 1219701, items 1–5, VAULT INTL film 1219702, items 1–3.

106. For example, Klein, "African Women," 37; Schwartz, *Sugar Plantations*, 383–84; Metcalf, *Family and Frontier*, 161; Trevor Burnard, *Mastery, Tyranny, and Desire: Thomas Thistlewood and His Slaves in the Anglo-Jamaican World* (Chapel Hill: University of North Carolina, 2004), 163.

107. Cope, *Limits of Racial Domination*, 81–82, quoting from 81.

108. Lokken, "Marriage as Slave Emancipation," 178, 181, 190–91.

109. Proctor, "Slavery, Identity, and Culture," 146–147, quoting from 156.

110. ANCR, PC 801 (1607)–3 (1629), 815 (1654–1655, 1664–1667)–50 (1698), 853 (1697, 1699, 1700, 1701)–65 (1708), 867 (1709)–71 (1712), 873 (1714)–17 (1737), 919 (1738)–24 (1740), 926 (1741)–34 (1746); ANCR, PH 573 (1721)–81 (1730), 583 (1733)–86 (1739), 588 (1742)–94 (1749); ANCR, PSJ 411 (1721)–15 (1738); ACM, SFASDE, Caja 20 (1692, 1696, 1719); *Indices de los protocolos de Cartago*, vols. 1–3; *Indice de los protocolos de Heredia.*
111. Jones, *Born a Child of Freedom*, 37.
112. "Carta al rey del oidor doctor don Benito de Noboa Salgado," *Revista de los Archivos Nacionales* (Costa Rica) 3, nos. 5–6 (1939): 227–28.
113. "Real cédula que aprueba las ordenanzas dictadas en favor de los indios por el Dr. Benito de Noboa Salgado, oidor de la Audiencia de Guatemala y visitador de la provincia de Costa Rica.—Año de 1676," *Revista de los Archivos Nacionales* (Costa Rica) 1, nos. 3–4 (1937): 152.
114. Padrón del Pueblo de San Bartolomé de Barva, July 9, 1739, AGCA, A3.16 (6), leg. 68.
115. Love, "Marriage Patterns," 87–89; Cope, *Limits of Racial Domination*, 81–82, 82 table 4.10; Lutz, *Santiago de Guatemala*, 88–89, 177–78.
116. ACMSJ, LMC, nos. 1–6/FHL, VAULT INTL film 1219727, items 6–10.
117. Ibid.
118. Acuña León and Chavarría López, "Endogamia y exogamia," 133, 136.
119. Cope, *Limits of Racial Domination*, chap. 4, quoting from 82.
120. ACMSJ, LMC, nos. 1–6/FHL, VAULT INTL film 1219727, items 6–10.
121. Petición de María de la Rosa Cuéllar, presentada en Cartago, August 26, 1734, ANCR, CC 4293, fol. 2.
122. Auto de remisión, Cartago, July 30, 1735, ACMSJ, SFASDE, Caja 15, fols. 48–48v.
123. Petición de José Cubero, mulato, presentada en Cartago, [August 1, 1749], ACMSJ, SFASDE, Caja 18, fol. 456v.
124. Testamento de Diego García, negro libre, Cartago, December 30, 1743, ANCR, PC 931, fol. 10.
125. Petición de José Cubero, fol. 457.
126. Declaración del Cap. José Nicolás de la Haya, mulato libre, Cartago, April 22, 1744, ANCR, CC 6219, fols. 2–2v; Testamento del Cap. José Nicolás de la Haya, Cartago, May 2, 1747, ANCR, MCC 841, fol. 2v.
127. Petición de María de la Rosa Cuéllar, presentada en Cartago, August 26, 1734, ANCR, CC 4293, fol. 2.
128. Declaración de Tomás Rivera, mulato libre, Cartago, November 24, 1724, ANCR, CC 4148, fol. 4v.
129. Partida del matrimonio de Diego Angulo, negro esclavo, y de Felipa Chavarría, mulata, October 16, 1709, ACMSJ, Libros de Matrimonios de Cartago, no. 3/FHL, VAULT INTL film 1219727, ítem 8; Auto, Puebla de los Angeles, February 8, 1746, ANCR, MCC 462, fol. 4v.
130. Declaración de Antonio Masís, negro libre, Cartago, August 26, 1733, ANCR, CC 4292, fol. 16; Carta del Teniente don Antonio de Angulo, Cartago, September 9, 1729, ANCR, CC 4259, fol. [1]; Diligencia de haber entregado los 325 pesos de

cacao y recibo de ellos, Cartago, September 29, 1729, ANCR, CC 4259, fols. [9v–10]; Carta de libertad, Cartago, February 20, 1730, ANCR, PC 903, fols. 1v–4.

131. Partida del matrimonio de Juan Méndez y de Isidora Zavaleta, esclava de doña Antonia de Oses, Cartago, June 21, 1748, ACMSJ, Libros de Matrimonios de Cartago, no. 4/FHL, VAULT INTL film 1219727, item 10; Indice de los protocolos de Cartago, 3:455.

132. Petición del Alf. Diego de la Cruz, Cartago, July 17, 1720, ACMSJ, SFASDE, Caja 9, Libro 3, fol. 147; Testimonio del Cap. don Francisco de Betancourt, Cartago, July 18, 1720, ACMSJ, SFASDE, Caja 9, Libro 3, fols. 148–48v; Auto del Juez Eclesiástico, Cartago, July 25, 1720, ACMSJ, SFASDE, Caja 9, Libro 3, fol. 149v; Carta de libertad, Cartago, March 27, 1722, ANCR, PC 895, fol. 35–37.

133. Recibo de Diego de la Cruz, correo, del cajoncito de cuadernos de autos, Cartago, January 13, 1721, ANCR, CC 5837, fols. 112–13v; Ajuste y liquidación del viaje que executó el Alf. Diego de la Cruz, Guatemala, October 8, 1721, AGCA, A1 (6), exp. 1057, leg. 73; Obligación de Diego de la Cruz y de su mujer Josefa Micaela de la Vega Cabral, Cartago, March 27, 1722, ANCR, PC 895, fols. 37–38v.

134. Carta de libertad, Cartago, March 27, 1722, ANCR, PC 895, fol. 35–37.

135. Testimonio del Cap. don Francisco de Betancourt, Cartago, July 18, 1720, ACMSJ, SFASDE, Caja 9, Libro 3, fols. 148–48v.

136. For example, Razón dada por la negra Isabel de no tener crías, Cartago, September 2, 1720, ANCR, C. 253, fol. 8v.

137. Burns, Siete Partidas, 4:901–2 (Part. IV, Tit. V, Laws I–II); Aquinas, Summa Theologica, 19:174–79 (Suppl., q. 52, a. 1c, a. 2c, a. 2 ad 2, a. 2 ad 4, a. 3c).

138. Testamento de doña Bárbara Rodríguez Altamirano, Cartago, March 5, 1711, ANCR, PC 870, fol. 13; Testamento del Cap. Miguel Calvo, Cartago, February 16, 1715, ANCR, PC 877, fol. 30v; Carta de manumisión, Cartago, February 20, 1720, ANCR, PC 890, fols. 29v–30; Testamento de doña Mariana Solano, fallecida el 19 octubre 1729, otorgado por sus apoderados su marido y el Sarg. Mayor don Francisco de la Madriz Linares, Cartago, November 3, 1729, ANCR, PC 902, fol. 78; Testamento de doña Ana María Maroto, Cartago, February 28, 1737, ANCR, PC 916, fol. 22v; Donación de 8 esclavos, Cartago, June 5, 1741, ANCR, PC 926, fols. 16–17; Inventario y avalúo de los bienes de doña Catalina González Camino, Cartago, November 19, 1745, ANCR, MCC 797, fols. 18v–19.

139. See Gudmundson K, "Mecanismos de movilidad"; Acuña León and Chavarría López, "Endogamia y exogamia" and "Cartago colonial"; and Mauricio Meléndez Obando's detailed family trees in Tatiana Lobo Wiehoff and Mauricio Meléndez Obando, Negros y blancos: Todo mezclado (San José: Editorial de la Universidad de Costa Rica, 1997).

CONCLUSIONS

1. Claudia Quirós Vargas and Margarita Bolaños Arquín, "El mestizaje en el siglo XVII: Consideraciones para comprender la génesis del campesinado criollo del

Valle Central," in *Costa Rica colonial*, ed. Luis F. Sibaja (San José: Ediciones Guayacán, 1989), 61–78.

2. For one example, see the Declaración de Juana, negra de casta popo, Cartago, September 9, 1719, Archivo Nacional de Costa Rica, San José (hereafter, ANCR), Sección Colonial Cartago (hereafter, C.) 232, fol. 2.

3. Oscar R. Aguilar Bulgarelli and Irene Alfaro Aguilar, *La esclavitud negra en Costa Rica: Origen de la oligarquía económica y política nacional* (San José: Progreso Editora, 1997).

4. Gwendolyn Midlo Hall, *Africans in Colonial Louisiana: The Development of Afro-Creole Culture in the Eighteenth Century* (Baton Rouge: Louisiana State University Press, 1992); Ira Berlin, *Many Thousands Gone: The First Two Centuries of Slavery in North America* (Cambridge, MA: Belknap Press of Harvard University Press, 1998); Philip D. Morgan, *Slave Counterpoint: Black Culture in the Eighteenth-Century Chesapeake and Lowcountry* (Chapel Hill: University of North Carolina Press, 1998).

5. Melida Velásquez, "El comercio de esclavos en la Alcaldía Mayor de Tegucigalpa, siglos XVI al XVIII," *Mesoamérica*, no. 42 (2001): 199–222; Germán Romero Vargas, *Las estructuras sociales de Nicaragua en el siglo XVIII* (Managua: Editorial Vanguardia, 1988), 289–95.

6. See Peter Kolchin's review of the historiography in *American Slavery, 1619–1877* (New York: Hill and Wang, 1993), 37–40.

7. K. Russell Lohse, "Mexico and Central America," in *The Oxford Handbook of Slavery in the Americas*, ed. Robert L. Paquette and Mark M. Smith (Oxford: Oxford University Press, 2010), 47, 51.

8. See Michael Tadman, "The Demographic Cost of Sugar: Debates on Slave Societies and Natural Increase in the Americas," *American Historical Review* 105, no. 5 (2000): 1534–75.

9. For two model studies, see James H. Sweet, *Recreating Africa: Culture, Kinship, and Religion in the African-Portuguese World, 1441–1770* (Chapel Hill: University of North Carolina Press, 2003), and Walter Hawthorne, *From Africa to Brazil: Culture, Identity, and an Atlantic Slave Trade, 1600–1830* (Cambridge: Cambridge University Press, 2010).

10. One example is Sylviane Diouf, *Dreams of Africa in Alabama: The Slave Ship Clotilda and the Story of the Last Africans Brought to America* (Oxford: Oxford University Press, 2007).

11. For a colonial Latin American example, see Ida Altman, *Transatlantic Ties in the Spanish Empire: Brihuega, Spain, and Puebla, Mexico, 1560–1620* (Stanford, CA: Stanford University Press, 2000).

12. Kristin Mann, "Shifting Paradigms in the Study of the African Diaspora and of Atlantic History and Culture," *Slavery & Abolition* 22, no. 1 (2001): 6, 7.

13. Sidney W. Mintz and Richard Price, *The Birth of African-American Culture: An Anthropological Perspective* (Boston, MA: Beacon Press, 1992, originally published

as *An Anthropological Approach to the Afro-American Past* [Philadelphia, PA: Institute for the Study of Human Issues, 1976]), 18.

14. Orlando Patterson, *Slavery and Social Death* (Cambridge, MA: Harvard University Press, 1982); Stephanie E. Smallwood, *Saltwater Slavery: A Middle Passage from Africa to American Diaspora* (Cambridge, MA: Harvard University Press, 2007).

15. Inventario de los cinco negros traídos de Matina por el Cap. Antonio de Soto y Barahona, Cartago, May 1, 1710, ANCR, C. 187, fols. 69v–70v; Inventario de los 38 negros traídos de Matina por el Teniente Juan Bautista Retana, Cartago, May 11, 1710, ANCR, C. 187, fols. 97–100v; Douglas B. Chambers, "Ethnicity in the Diaspora: The Slave-Trade and the Creation of African 'Nations' in the Americas," *Slavery & Abolition* 22, no. 3 (2001): 25–39.

16. Declaración de María negra de casta popo, Valle de Barva, November 12, 1719, ANCR, Sección Colonial Guatemala 188, fol. 7v; Mintz and Price, *Birth of African-American Culture*, 14.

EPILOGUE

1. Carta del Cap. don Juan Díaz de Herrera al Gobernador don Baltasar Francisco de Valderrama, n.p., March 19, 1736, Archivo Nacional de Costa Rica (hereafter, ANCR), Sección Colonial Cartago (hereafter, C.) 325, fols. 265–65v.

2. Carta del Cap. don Juan Díaz de Herrera al Gobernador, Matina, April 14, 1736, ANCR, C. 325, fol. 268v; Declaración de José Nicolás Román, Cartago, April 16, 1736, ANCR, C. 325, quoting from fol. 271.

3. Carta del Cap. don Juan Díaz de Herrera al Gobernador, Matina, April 14, 1736, ANCR, C. 325, fols. 268, quoting from fol. 268v, Declaración de José Nicolás Román, Cartago, April 16, 1736, ANCR, C. 325, fol. 271.

4. Razón dada por el negro Francisco de casta mina, Cartago, April 15, 1721, ANCR, C. 283, fols. 3–4; Declaración de Nicolás, negro de casta mina, Cartago, April 25, 1723, ANCR, C. 283, fols. 10–11.

5. Venta de esclavo, November 17, 1725, ANCR, Protocolos Coloniales de Cartago (hereafter, PC) 898, fols. 168–70; Obligación, January 22, 1727, ANCR, PC 900, fols. 12–13; Declaración de José Nicolás Román, Cartago, April 16, 1736, ANCR, C. 325, quoting from fol. 271v; Declaración del Cap. Sebastián de Guillén, Cartago, August 26, 1733, ANCR, Sección Complementario Colonial (hereafter, CC) 4292, fol. 15.

6. Carta del Cap. don Juan Díaz de Herrera al Gobernador, Matina, April 14, 1736, ANCR, C. 325, fol. 268v.

7. Junta sobre el nuevo aviso del Teniente General de Matina, Cartago, April 16, 1736, ANCR, C. 325, fol. 269.

8. Carta del Gobernador al Teniente General de Matina, Cartago, April 17, 1736, ANCR, C. 325, quoting from fols. 272v, 273.

9. Junta de vecinos, Cartago, June 7, 1736, ANCR, C. 325, fols. 274–74v, quoting from fol. 274v; Auto del cabildo de Cartago, ANCR, Municipal 772, fols. 106v–7v.

10. See José C. Curto, "The Story of Nbena, 1817–1820: Unlawful Enslavement and the Concept of 'Original Freedom' in Angola," in *Trans-Atlantic Dimensions of Ethnicity in the African Diaspora*, ed. Paul E. Lovejoy and David V. Trotman (London: Continuum, 2003), 43–64.

11. Carta de Juan Díaz de Herrera al Gobernador don Antonio Vázquez de la Cuadra, Matina, June 3, 1736, ANCR, C. 325, fols. 275–75v; Petición del Alf. Juan de Carmona, presentada en Cartago, September 12, 1736, ANCR, Municipal 772, fol. 110v.

12. Razón dada por el negro Francisco de casta mina, Cartago, April 15, 1721, ANCR, C. 283, fols. 3–4; Declaración de Nicolás, negro de casta mina, Cartago, April 25, 1723, ANCR, C. 283, fols. 10–11; Hilary McD. Beckles, "Caribbean Anti-Slavery: The Self-Liberation Ethos of Enslaved Blacks," *Journal of Caribbean History* 22, nos. 1–2 (1990): 1–19.

13. Declaración de José Alejos Fernández, prisionero que vino de los Mosquitos, Cartago, July 17, 1727, ANCR, C. 325, fol. 12v; Venta de esclavo, Cartago, November 17, 1725, ANCR, PC 898, fols. 168–70; Real cédula, Campo Real de Castel David, July 1, 1704, Archivo General de Centroamérica, Guatemala City, A1.23, leg. 1524, fols. 158–59. See also the survey of intercolonial slave flight in Julius S. Scott, "The Common Wind: Currents of Afro-American Communication in the Era of the Haitian Revolution" (PhD diss., Duke University, 1986), 92–103.

14. Carta del Gobernador a los negros y demás personas quienes habitan con ellos, Cartago, June 23, 1736, ANCR, C. 325, quoting from fol. 278, fol. 278v.

15. Auto del cabildo de Cartago, September 3, 1736, ANCR, C. 325, fols. 282, quoting from fol. 283; Vista ocular de los negros y demás personas, Valle de Aserrí, May 16, 1737, ANCR, Sección Colonial Guatemala (hereafter, G.) 250, fols. 9–9v.

16. Auto del cabildo de Cartago, September 12, 1736, ANCR, Municipal 772, quoting from fol. 111v; Notificación al Alf. Juan de Carmona, Cartago, September 5, 1736, ANCR, Municipal 772, fols. 113–13v.

17. Respuesta de Juan de Carmona, Cartago, May 4, 1737, ANCR, Municipal 772, fols. 7v–8v; Vista ocular de los negros y demás personas, Valle de Aserrí, May 16, 1737, ANCR, G. 250, fol. 10.

18. Respuesta de Juan de Carmona, Cartago, May 4, 1737, ANCR, Municipal 772, fol. 8.

19. Memoria testamental de Josefa Nicolasa de Ibarra, March 16, 1737, ANCR, PC 916, fol. 57.

20. Testamento de Juan Carmona, December 27, 1765, ANCR, Protocolos Coloniales de San José 422, fols. 54–57v; Petición del Cap. don Manuel Cayetano de Guevara, presentada en Cartago, April 5, 1755, ANCR, CC 6231, fol. 23; Decreto del Presidente de la Real Audiencia, Guatemala, May 10, 1738, ANCR, C. 413, fols. 4–4v; Auto del Alcalde Provincial de la Santa Hermandad, Valle de Barva, February 14, 1755, CC 6231, quoting from fol. 4.

21. Carta de Esteban Ruiz de Mendoza al Gobernador don Juan Gemmir y Lleonart, Fuerte de San Fernando, October 15, 1744, ANCR, C. 450, fols. 1, 1v.
22. Ibid., fols. 1v, 2.
23. Diligencia de reconocimiento, Cartago, November 25, 1744, ANCR, C. 455, fols. 10v–12; Auto del gobernador, Cartago, December 6, 1744, ANCR, C. 455, fol. 36v.
24. Declaración de Juamina, Cartago, December 2, 1744, ANCR, C. 455, fols. 22v–24, quoting from fol. 23; Declaración de Guinza, Cartago, December 2, 1744, ANCR, C. 455, fol. 25.
25. Carta de Esteban Ruiz de Mendoza al Gobernador don Juan Gemmir y Lleonart, Fuerte de San Fernando, October 15, 1744, ANCR, C. 450, fols. 1v, 2.
26. Junta de vecinos, Cartago, October 21, 1744, ANCR, C. 455, fols. 4–7, quoting from fol. 5; Diligencia de reconocimiento, Cartago, November 25, 1744, ANCR, C. 455, fol. 10v.
27. Auto del gobernador, Cartago, November 25, 1744, ANCR, C. 455, fols. 9–10v; Razón de cría de india, Cartago, November 25, 1744, ANCR, C. 455, fol. 12.
28. Diligencia de reconocimiento, Cartago, November 25, 1744, ANCR, C. 455, fols. 10v–12, quoting from fol. 11v; Auto del gobernador, Cartago, December 6, 1744, ANCR, C. 455, fol. 36v.
29. Auto del gobernador, Cartago, December 6, 1744, ANCR, C. 455, fols. 36v–38, quoting from fols. 37 and 37v; Auto del gobernador, Cartago, March 26, 1745, ANCR, C. 455, fol. 39. In her fictionalized retelling of the arrival of the 1744 refugees, novelist Tatiana Lobo wrote that "the document that speaks of those who arrived in 1737 does not exist or it is not possible to find it." On the contrary, there are three major sources for these arrivals, which are the basis of my discussion in the text above. Tatiana Lobo Wiehoff, "Primeros fundadores de San José," in Tatiana Lobo Wiehoff and Mauricio Meléndez Obando, *Negros y blancos: Todo mezclado* (San José: Editorial de la Universidad de Costa Rica, 1997), 28.
30. Auto del gobernador, Cartago, March 26, 1745, ANCR, C. 455, fols. 38–40, quoting from fol. 40.
31. Auto del Capitán don Juan José de Cuende Teniente General Juez Político de Cartago, Villa Nueva de la Boca del Monte y Valle de Aserrí, March 29, 1745, ANCR, C. 455, fols. 40–41, quoting from fol. 40v.
32. León Fernández, ed., *Colección de documentos para la historia de Costa Rica*, 10 vols. (San José: Imprenta Nacional [vols. 1–3], Paris: Imprenta Pablo Dupont [vols. 4–5], Barcelona: Imprenta Viuda de Luis Tasso [vols. 6–10], 1881–1907), 9:507; Declaración de Juana María, Cartago, May 6, 1755, ANCR, CC 6231, fol. 40v.
33. Auto del Alcalde Ordinario de Primer Voto Cap. don Tomás López del Corral, Valle de Aserrí, February 13, 1755, ANCR, CC 6231, quoting from fol. 1; Declaración del Cap. Nicolás de Zamora, Valle de Aserrí, February 13, 1755, ANCR, CC 6231, fol. 1v; Declaración de Félix Durán, pardo libre, Valle de Aserrí, February 13, 1755, ANCR, CC 6231, fols. 2–2v; Auto del Alcalde Provincial de la Santa Hermandad Sarg. Mayor don José Manuel de Saborío, Valle de Barva, February 14, 1755,

ANCR, CC 6231, quoting from fol. 4; Petición del Cap. Diego de Cárdenas, presentada en Cartago, March 10, 1755, ANCR, CC 6231, quoting from fol. 17v.

34. Declaración de Juan Carmona, Valle de Aserrí, February 17, 1755, ANCR, CC 6231, fols. 10v–11v.

35. Declaración de José Miguel Chavarría, Boca del Monte, February 16, 1755, ANCR, CC 6231, fol. 7v; Declaración de José Miguel Chavarría, Cartago, April 21, 1755, ANCR, CC 6231, fol. 36; Declaración de Pablo García, indio ladino, Cartago, April 22, 1755, CC 6231, fol. 38; Declaración de Juana María, Cartago, May 6, 1755, ANCR, CC 6231, fol. 40v.

36. Petición del Cap. Manuel Cayetano de Guevara, presentada en Cartago, April 5, 1755, ANCR, CC 6231, quoting from fol. 23v; Petición del Cap. Manuel Cayetano de Guevara, presentada en Cartago, April 15, 1755, ANCR, CC 6231, quoting from fol. 28.

37. Declaración de Pedro Valerín, Boca del Monte, February 16, 1755, ANCR, CC 6231, fols. 6–6v, quoting from fol. 6; Auto del Alcalde de la Santa Hermandad, Valle de Aserrí, February 27, 1755, ANCR, CC 6231, fol. 19v.

38. Sentencia pronunciada, Cartago, June 9, 1755, ANCR, CC 6231, fol. 47v.

39. Declaración de José Manuel Sánchez, Matina, October 1742, ANCR, C. 451, fols. 1–2v, quoting fol. 1; Declaración de José Manuel Sánchez, Cartago, October 18, 1742, ANCR, C. 451, fols. 3v–5v, quoting from fol. 4v.

40. ANCR, C. 609 (1774).

41. Auto del gobernador, Cartago, June 28, 1774, ANCR, CC 354, fols. 1v–2, quoting from fol. 2.

42. ANCR, C. 640 (1775).

43. ANCR, C. 659 (1777); Tatiana Lobo Wiehoff, "La negra marinera," in Tatiana Lobo Wiehoff and Mauricio Meléndez Obando, *Negros y blancos: Todo mezclado* (San José: Editorial de la Universidad de Costa Rica, 1997), 22–24.

44. Paula Palmer, *"What Happen": A Folk-History of Costa Rica's Talamanca Coast*, 2nd ed. (San José: Publications in English, 1993), 15–16, quoting from 28.

45. Michael D. Olien, "The Negro in Costa Rica: The Ethnohistory of an Ethnic Minority in a Complex Society" (PhD diss., University of Oregon, Eugene, 1967), 86.

46. For an excellent study, see Ronald N. Harpelle, *The West Indians of Costa Rica: Race, Class, and the Integration of an Ethnic Minority* (Montreal: Ian Randle, 2001).

Glossary

Terms are Spanish unless otherwise noted.

alcabala: Royal tax on all sales.

Alcalde Ordinario: Municipal magistrate; justice of the peace; judge of first instance.

Alcalde Ordinario de Primer Voto: Chief magistrate.

Alcalde de la Santa Hermandad: Chief of the rural constabulary.

Alcaldía Mayor: An administrative province or district, such as the Alcaldía Mayor of Nicoya.

Alférez: Second lieutenant; royal standard bearer.

Alguacil: Constable, police officer; jailer.

Alguacil Mayor: Chief constable.

almarada: Pole with hook or knife attached to one end, used for picking cacao.

aná: Identified with the Ana, a western group of Yoruba-speaking people in modern Togo and Benin.

angola: A captive exported from Luanda.

arará: Generic term for peoples originating from the Slave Coast.

arrendamiento: Lease; sharecropping arrangement.

arrendatario: Lessee; sharecropper.

arroba (Portuguese): Unit of weight equivalent to 14.7 kilograms/32 pounds.

arroba (Spanish): Unit of weight equivalent to 11.34 kilograms/25 pounds.

asentista: Holder of an asiento.

asiento: Royal contract granting exclusive rights to transport African slaves to Spanish America, awarded to an individual or company for a specified period.

Audiencia de Guatemala: Administrative district that included modern Guatemala, Chiapas (Mexico), El Salvador, Honduras, Nicaragua, and Costa Rica, also known as the Kingdom of Guatemala; the High Court with jurisdiction over this area.

balandra: Sloop (a one-masted sailing boat with a mainsail and jib rigged fore and aft).

barbá: From *Bariba*, the Yoruba-language name given by the Oyo to their neighbors in the kingdoms of Borgu, including a western group in the north of modern Benin and Togo.

batea: Tub used for fermenting cacao.

biojo: European term for both the Bijagó (an ethnic group indigenous to the Bijagós [Bissagos] Islands just off the coast of Guinea-Bissau at the mouth of the Geba River) and their victims, including Biafaras, Balantas, and Nalus.

bozal: African-born slave.

bran: Captives from several ethnic groups now known as Brame, Manjak, Papel, and Mankanya.

caballería: Area equivalent to 45 hectares/111.1 acres.

cabildo: Municipal council.

cabo verde: Captive exported from Cape Verde.

cacaotal: Cacao hacienda.

cacaotero: Cacao planter.

canoa: Boat about 13 meters (42.6 feet) long; also a trough used for fermenting cacao, making cheese, and so on.

capellanía: Chantry or chaplaincy; a bequeathal of private property, in Costa Rica usually a cacao hacienda, to the Church in return for the performance of religious services such as the saying of memorial masses; property donated in capellanías was rented (usually at 6 percent interest) but not sold to administrators, and the money helped fund the training of seminarians.

carabalí: Term applied to a large number of ethnic groups in the Bight of Biafra hinterland.

carabela: Caravel (a small, fast ship); shipmate.

casta: Racial category; as applied to Africans, "national" or ethnic origin.

casta aná: From Yorubaland.

casta arará: From the Slave Coast.

casta carabalí: From the Bight of Biafra.

casta mina: From the Gold Coast or possibly the upper Slave Coast.

cimarrón: Runaway slave, maroon.

cofradía: Religious confraternity.

congo: Captive from West Central Africa, the Kongo.

corregidor: Crown agent in charge of Indians of a certain administrative district.

corregimiento: An administrative district usually composed of indigenous communities.

creole: Person of foreign ancestry born in the Americas, whether African or European.

criada, criado: Legally free, live-in household servant.

criollo: A person born in the New World to parents of Spanish origin.

cuadrillero: Officer or deputy employed in apprehending runaway slaves.

cuchillón: See almarada.

depositario: Trustee, custodian.

diputado: Elected officer in a religious confraternity.

encomendero: Holder of an encomienda.

encomienda: Royal grant of access to tribute and labor of Indians in a specified area, later modified to include tribute payments only.

estancia: Large estate dedicated to livestock ranching.

fanega: Unit of volume equivalent to 54.5 liters/14.4 gallons.

fiscal: Crown attorney.

géneros de la tierra: Local produce.

grumete: Cabin boy; common seaman.

hacendado: Owner of a hacienda.

hacienda: Landed estate dedicated to agriculture and/or livestock breeding.

hato: Small ranch dedicated to livestock breeding.

ibo: Person of Igbo origin.

jolofo (also *gelofe, gilofo, jalof, jolof,* and other variations): A subject of the Jolof Empire.

jornal: Daily wage.

ladino: Spanish-speaking African or Indian.

league (legua): Unit of distance equivalent to 5.5 kilometers/3.4 miles.

lucumí: Captive from the Bight of Benin.

maestro: Master artisan.

mandador: Overseer, driver, supervisor, administrator.

mandinga: Portuguese term for people from all areas of West Africa still under the influence of Mali, especially the states along the River Gambia; also, along the Atlantic coast, captives called mandinga came from an area extending from the north bank of the Gambia to the Rio Cacheu in Guinea-Bissau or to the Biafara territories along the Geba River.

maravedí: ⅟₃₄ of a real.

merced: Royal land grant.

mestizo: A person ostensibly of mixed Indian and European ancestry; in reality, often a person of partial African ancestry who might or might not have indigenous ancestors.

milpa: Small field, usually planted with corn.

mozo: Legally free, live-in male servant; a ranch hand.

mulatto, mulato: A person ostensibly of mixed African and European descent; in reality, sometimes a person of African and indigenous ancestry.

mulato blanco: A light-skinned person of African and European descent.

nación: "Nation"; during the colonial period, an ethnic group defined by common language and culture, without reference to statehood; applied to Africans as well as Europeans, in the former case used interchangeably with casta.

nación de los ríos (also casta de los ríos): Captives from the area between the Senegal and Geba rivers (encompassing the modern states of Senegal, The Gambia, and Guinea-Bissau).

oficial: Journeyman artisan.

oidor: Judge (auditor) of the Audiencia.

orisha: Divinity (Yoruba).

palenque: Settlement of *cimarrones*.

pardo: A more polite term for a mulatto.

peninsular: New World resident "Spaniard" born in Spain.

perito: Expert hired to evaluate slaves.

pieza de Indias: Unit equivalent to one ideal healthy adult male slave.

pirogue: Large dugout canoe (French; in Spanish, *piragua*).

popo: A captive embarked at Little Popo (Aneho, Anécho) or Great Popo.

pregonero: Crier.

Procurador Síndico: City attorney.

pueblo: Legally chartered, tribute-paying Indian village or town.

rancho: Hut.

rapadura: Raw sugar.

real: One-eighth of a Spanish peso.

real cédula: Royal decree.

Real Hacienda: Royal Treasury.

Regidor: Cabildo member, municipal councilman.

rixdollar (Danish): Unit of Danish money worth approximately two shillings English money.

Santa Hermandad: Rural constabulary.

seasoning (English): Process by which newly arrived Africans were adapted to new disease, cultural, and work environments.

sistema de castas: Caste system.

Spaniard: In Costa Rica, a person ostensibly of exclusively European descent, whether born in Spain or the Americas.

suerte: Unit applied to plantings of sugar cane, equivalent to 100 rows or a fourth of a caballería; about 11.3 hectares/27.8 acres.

trapiche: Small animal-, water-, or human-powered sugar mill.

vaquiada: Annual cattle roundup.

vara: Unit of length equivalent to 83.5 centimeters/39.2 inches.

vecina, vecino: Urban resident and property owner with full legal rights.

visitador: Official inspector, whether civil or ecclesiastical.

vodun: Divinity (Gbe).

Wolof: Ethnic group that dominated the territory of the Jolof Empire, demographically and politically.

zambo: A person ostensibly of African and indigenous ancestry; in the Central Valley, such people were far more frequently referred to as mulattos.

zurrón: Leather bag containing 214 pounds/97 kilograms of cacao, officially equivalent to twenty-five pesos in silver.

Bibliography

Archives

Costa Rica

Archivo Nacional de Costa Rica, San José (ANCR).
Archivo de la Curia Metropolitana de San José (ACMSJ; now Archivo Histórico Arquidiocesano "Bernardo Augusto Thiel").

Guatemala

Archivo General de Centroamérica, Guatemala City (AGCA).

Mexico

Archivo General de la Nación, Mexico City (AGN).

Spain

Archivo General de Indias, Seville (AGI).

United States

Family History Library, Salt Lake City, Utah (FHL).
University of Texas, Nettie Lee Benson Latin American Collection, Rare Books and Manuscripts.

Databases

Voyages: The Trans-Atlantic Slave Trade Database. 2009. http://slavevoyages.org/tast/index.faces.

Published Primary Sources

Academia de Geografía e Historia de Costa Rica. *Colección de documentos para la historia de Costa Rica relativos al cuarto y último viaje de Cristóbal Colón*. San José: Atenea, 1952.

Alvarado Quesada, Franklin José, ed. "Documentos relativos a la población afroamericana." Special issue, *Revista de Historia* (Costa Rica), no. 39 (1999): 249–324.

Aquinas, Thomas. *The "Summa Theologica" of St. Thomas Aquinas*. Translated by the
Fathers of the English Dominican Province. 22 vols. London: Burns, Oates and
Washbourne, 1920–1942.

Atkins, John. *A Voyage to Guinea, Brazil, and the West Indies in His Majesty's Ships
The Swallow and Weymouth*. London: Caesar Ward and Richard Chandler,
1735.

Barbot, Jean. *Barbot on Guinea: The Writings of Jean Barbot on West Africa 1678–1712*.
Edited by P. E. H. Hair. 2 vols. London: Hakluyt Society, 1992.

Barbot, John. *A Description of the Coasts of North and South Guinea, and of Ethiopia
Inferior, Vulgarly Angola*. Vol. 5 of *A Collection of Voyages and Travels*. Edited by
Awnsham Churchill and John Churchill. London: By Assignment for Messrs.
Churchill, 1732.

Bosman, William. *A New and Accurate Description of the Coast of Guinea, Divided into
the Gold, the Slave and the Ivory Coasts*. London: James Knapton, 1705.

Burns, Robert I., ed. *Las Siete Partidas*. Trans. Samuel Parsons Scott. 5 vols.
Philadelphia: University of Pennsylvania Press, 2001.

"Carta al rey del oidor doctor don Benito de Noboa Salgado." *Revista de los Archivos
Nacionales* (Costa Rica) 3, nos. 5–6 (1939): 227–28.

Catechism of the Council of Trent for Parish Priests, Issued by Order of Pope Pius V.
Trans. John A. McHugh and Charles J. Callan. 1923. Rockford, IL: TAN Books,
1982.

*Concilio III Provincial Mexicano celebrado en el año de 1585, confirmado en Roma por
el Papa Sixto V, y mandado observar por el gobierno español en diversas reales
órdenes*. Mexico City: Eugenio Maillefert, Editores, 1859.

*Costa Rica–Panama Arbitration: Documents Annexed to the Argument of Costa
Rica*. . . . 4 vols. Rosslyn, VA: Commonwealth, 1913.

Delbée. "Journal du voyage du Sieur Delbée, commissaire general de la marine, aux
isles, dans la coste de Guinée, par l'établissement du commerce en ces pays, en
l'année 1669 & la presente: Avec la description particuliere du royaume
d'Ardres; & de ce qui s'est passé entre les françois, & le roy de ce pays." In
*Relation de ce qui s'est passé dans les isles et Terre-ferme de l'Amerique pendant
la dernière guerre avec l'Angleterre*. . . . Edited by J. de Clodoré, 2:347–494. Paris:
G. Clouzier, 1671.

Douglass, Frederick. *Narrative of the Life of Frederick Douglass*. In *The Classic Slave
Narratives*. Edited by Henry Louis Gates, 323–436. New York: Signet, 2002.
Originally published in 1845.

Fernández, León, ed. *Colección de documentos para la historia de Costa Rica*. 10 vols.
San José: Imprenta Nacional [vols. 1–3], Paris: Imprenta Pablo Dupont [vols. 4–5],
Barcelona: Imprenta Viuda de Luis Tasso [vols. 6–10], 1881–1907.

[Haya Fernández, Diego de la.] "Informe de don Diego de la Haya Fernández sobre la provincia de Costa Rica. Marzo de 1719." In *Don Diego de la Haya Fernández*. Luz Alba Chacón de Umaña, 164–90. San José: Editorial Costa Rica, 1967.

Herrera y Tordesillas, Antonio. *Historia general de los hechos de los castellanos en las islas y tierra firme del mar océano*. 27 vols. Madrid: Real Academia de la Historia, 1934. Originally published in 1601–1615.

Janzen, John M., and Wyatt MacGaffey. *An Anthology of Kongo Religion: Primary Texts from Lower Zaïre*. Lawrence: University of Kansas Press, 1974.

Jobson, Richard. *The Discovery of the River Gambra (1623)*. Edited by David Gamble and P. E. H. Hair. London: Hakluyt Society, 1999.

Jopling, Carol F., ed. *Indios y negros en Panamá en los siglos XVI y XVII: Selecciones de los documentos del Archivo General de Indias*. Antigua, Guatemala: Centro de Investigaciones Regionales de Mesoamérica, 1994.

Justesen, Ole, ed., and James Manley, trans. *Danish Sources for the History of Ghana, 1654–1754*. Vol. 1. *1657–1735*. Copenhagen: Det Kongelige Danske Videnskabernes Selskab/Royal Danish Academy of Sciences and Letters, 2005.

Meléndez, Carlos, ed. *Reales cédulas relativas a la provincia de Costa Rica (1540–1802)*. San José, 1992.

Pérez Valle, Eduardo, ed. *Nicaragua en los cronistas de Indias: Oviedo*. Serie Cronistas 3. Managua: Fondo de Promoción Cultural, Banco de América, 1976.

Phillips, Thomas. "A Journal of a Voyage Made in the *Hannibal* of London, 1693–1694." In *A Collection of Voyages and Travels*. Edited by Awnsham Churchill and John Churchill, 6:171–239. London: By Assignment for Messrs. Churchill, 1732.

Rask, Johannes. *A Brief and Truthful Description of a Journey to and from Guinea*. Translated by Selena Axelrod-Winsnes. Accra: Sub-Saharan Publishers, 2009. Originally published in 1754 as *En kort og sanfærdig rejse-beskrivelse til og fra Guinea* in Trondheim, Norway, by Jens Christensen Winding.

Real Academia Española. *Diccionario de autoridades*. 3 vols. Madrid: Editorial Gredos, 1963. Originally published in 1726 in 6 vols. in Madrid by Imprenta de Francisco del Hierro.

"Real cédula que aprueba las ordenanzas dictadas en favor de los indios por el Dr. Benito de Noboa Salgado, oidor de la Audiencia de Guatemala y visitador de la provincia de Costa Rica.—Año de 1676." *Revista de los Archivos Nacionales* (Costa Rica) 1, nos. 3–4 (1937): 152.

Revista de los Archivos Nacionales (Costa Rica).

Ripalda, Jerónimo de. *Doctrina cristiana del P. Jerónimo de Ripalda e intento bibliográfico de la misma años 1591–1909*. Edited by Juan M. Sánchez. Madrid: Imprenta Alemana, 1909.

Rømer, Ludewig Ferdinand. *A Reliable Account of the Coast of Guinea (1760)*. Translated and edited by Selena Axelrod Winsnes. Oxford: Oxford University Press for the

British Academy, 2000. Originally published in 1760 as *Tilforladelig efterretning om kysten Guinea* in Copenhagen.

Sandoval, Alonso de. *Un tratado sobre la esclavitud.* Edited by Enriqueta Vila Vilar. Madrid: Alianza Editorial, 1987. Originally published in 1627 as *Naturaleza, policia sagrada i profana, costumbres i ritos, disciplina i catechismo evangelico de todos Etiopes* in Seville by Francisco de Lira.

Tilleman, Erick. *A Short and Simple Account of the Country Guinea and Its Nature (1697).* Translated and edited by Selena Axelrod Winsnes. Madison: African Studies Program, University of Wisconsin–Madison, 1994.

Van Dantzig, A. "English Bosman and Dutch Bosman: A Comparison of Texts." *History in Africa* 2 (1975): 185–216; 3 (1976): 91–126; 4 (1977): 247–73.

———, ed. and trans. *The Dutch and the Guinea Coast, 1674–1742: A Collection of Documents from the General State Archive at The Hague.* Accra: Ghana Academy of Arts and Sciences, 1978.

Vega Bolaños, Andrés, ed. *Colección Somoza: Documentos para la historia de Nicaragua.* 17 vols. Madrid, 1945–1957.

Secondary Sources

Acosta Saignes, Miguel. *Vida de los esclavos negros en Venezuela.* Havana: Casa de las Américas, 1978. Originally published in 1967 in Caracas by Hesperides.

Acuña León, María de los Angeles. "Endogamia y exogamia en la sociedad colonial cartaginesa." *Revista de Historia* (Costa Rica), no. 23 (1991): 107–44.

———. "Mujeres esclavas en la Costa Rica del siglo XVIII: Estrategias frente a la esclavitud." *Diálogos: Revista Electrónica de Historia* (Costa Rica) 5, nos. 1–2 (April 2004–February 2005). Universidad de Costa Rica. http://www.historia.fcs.ucr. ac.cr/articulos/esp-genero/1parte/CAP1Marielos/CAP1Marielostexto.html.

———. "Papel reproductivo y productivo de las mujeres esclavas en Costa Rica del siglo XVIII." *Revista de Historia* (Costa Rica), nos. 57–58 (2008): 135–61.

Acuña León, María de los Angeles, and Doriam Chavarría López. "Cartago colonial: Mestizaje y patrones matrimoniales 1738–1821." *Mesoamérica*, no. 31 (1996): 157–79.

Adams, David P. "Malaria, Labor, and Population Distribution in Costa Rica: A Biohistorical Perspective." *Journal of Interdisciplinary History* 27, no. 1 (1996): 75–85.

Adams, Richard N. "Internal and External Ethnicities: With Special Reference to Central America." In *Estado, democratización y desarrollo en Centroamérica y Panamá.* Edited by Manuel Rivera, Giovani Duarte, and María Dolores Marroquín, 475–99. Guatemala: Asociación Centroamericana de Sociología (ACAS), 1989.

Adediran, Biodun. *The Frontier States of Western Yorubaland, circa 1600–1889: State Formation and Political Growth in an Ethnic Frontier Zone.* Ibadan, Nigeria:

Institut Français de Recherche en Afrique/French Institute for Research in Africa, 1994.

―――. "Yoruba Ethnic Groups or a Yoruba Ethnic Group? A Review of the Problem of Ethnic Identification." *África* (Centro de Estudos Africanos, Universidade de São Paulo) 7 (1984): 57–70.

Afroz, Sultana. "The Manifestation of *Tawhid*: The Muslim Heritage of the Maroons in Jamaica." *Caribbean Quarterly* 45, no. 1 (1999): 27–40.

Aguilar Bulgarelli, Oscar R., and Irene Alfaro Aguilar. *La esclavitud negra en Costa Rica: Origen de la oligarquía económica y política nacional.* San José: Progreso Editora, 1997.

Aguirre Beltrán, Gonzalo. *La población negra de México, 1519–1810: Estudio etnohistórico.* 2nd ed. Mexico: Fondo de Cultura Económica, 1972.

Alagoa, E. J. "The Slave Trade in Niger Delta Oral Tradition and History." In *Africans in Bondage: Studies in Slavery and the Slave Trade.* Edited by Paul E. Lovejoy. Madison: African Studies Program, University of Wisconsin–Madison, 1986.

Altman, Ida. *Transatlantic Ties in the Spanish Empire: Brihuega, Spain, and Puebla, Mexico, 1560–1620.* Stanford, CA: Stanford University Press, 2000.

Alvarez Solar, María C. *La esclavitud como institución económica y social en Costa Rica, 1680–1725.* Kristiansand, Norway: Høyskoleforlaget, 1999.

Austin, Allan D. *African Muslims in Antebellum America: A Sourcebook.* New York: Garland, 1984.

―――. "Islamic Identities in Africans in North America in the Days of Slavery (1731–1865)." *Islam et Sociétés au Sud du Sahara* 7 (1993): 205–19.

Awolalu, J. Omosade. *Yoruba Beliefs and Sacrificial Rites.* London: Longman, 1979.

Balandier, Georges. *Daily Life in the Kingdom of the Kongo from the 16th to the 18th Century.* Translated by Helen Weaver. London: George Allen & Unwin, 1968. Originally published in 1965 as *La vie quotidienne au royaume de Kongo du XVIe au XVIIIe siècle* in Paris by Hachette.

Barrantes Ferrero, Mario. *Un caso de esclavitud en Costa Rica.* San José: Instituto Geográfico Nacional, 1968.

Barry, Boubacar. *Le royaume de Waalo, 1659–1859: Le Sénégal avant la conquête.* Paris: François Maspero, 1972.

―――. *Senegambia and the Atlantic Slave Trade.* Translated by Ayi Kwei Armah. Cambridge: Cambridge University Press, 1998.

Bartle, Philip. "The Universe Has Three Souls: Notes on Translating Akan Culture." *Journal of Religion in Africa* 14 (1983): 85–114.

Bascom, William. *The Yoruba of Southwestern Nigeria.* New York: Holt, Rinehart and Winston, 1969.

Bay, Edna G. "Servitude and Worldly Success in the Palace of Dahomey." In *Women and Slavery in Africa.* Edited by Claire C. Robinson and Martin A. Klein, 340–67. Madison: University of Wisconsin Press, 1984.

Beckles, Hilary McD. "Caribbean Anti-Slavery: The Self-Liberation Ethos of Enslaved Blacks." *Journal of Caribbean History* 22, nos. 1–2 (1990): 1–19.

——. *Natural Rebels: A Social History of Enslaved Black Women in Barbados*. New Brunswick, NJ: Rutgers University Press, 1989.

Bennett, Herman L. *Africans in Colonial Mexico: Absolutism, Christianity, and Afro-Creole Consciousness, 1570–1640*. Bloomington: Indiana University Press, 2003.

——. *Colonial Blackness: A History of Afro-Mexico*. Bloomington: Indiana University Press, 2009.

——. "A Research Note: Race, Slavery, and the Ambiguity of Corporate Consciousness." *Colonial Latin American Historical Review* 3, no. 2 (1994): 207–13.

Berlin, Ira. *Generations of Captivity: A History of African-American Slaves*. Cambridge, MA: Belknap Press of Harvard University Press, 2003.

——. *Many Thousands Gone: The First Two Centuries of Slavery in North America*. Cambridge, MA: Belknap Press of Harvard University Press, 1998.

Berlin, Ira and Philip D. Morgan. "Introduction: Labor and the Shaping of Slave Life in the Americas." In *Cultivation and Culture: Labor and the Shaping of Slave Life in the Americas*. Edited by Ira Berlin and Philip D. Morgan, 1–48. Charlottesville: University Press of Virginia, 1993.

Blackburn, Robin. *The Making of New World Slavery: From the Baroque to the Modern, 1492–1800*. London: Verso, 1997.

——. "Slave Exploitation and the Elementary Structures of Enslavement." In *Serfdom and Slavery: Studies in Legal Bondage*. Edited by M. L. Bush, 158–80. London: Longman, 1996.

Blanco Segura, Ricardo. *Historia eclesiástica de Costa Rica, del descubrimiento a la erección de la diócesis (1502–1850)*. San José: Editorial Universidad Estatal a Distancia (EUNED), 1983. Originally published in 1967 in San José by Editorial Costa Rica.

——. *Obispos, arzobispos y representantes de la Santa Sede en Costa Rica*. San José: EUNED, 1984.

Bockie, Simon. *Death and the Invisible Powers: The World of Kongo Belief*. Bloomington: Indiana University Press, 1993.

Bolland, O. Nigel. "Proto-Proletarians? Slaves Wages in the Americas." In *From Chattel Slaves to Wage Slaves: The Dynamics of Labour Bargaining in the Americas*. Edited by Mary Turner, 123–47. London: James Currey, 1995.

Borucki, Alex. "Shipmate Networks and Black Identities in the Marriage Files of Montevideo, 1768–1803." *Hispanic American Historical Review* 93, no. 2 (2013): 205–38.

Boulègue, Jean. *Les anciens royaumes Wolof (Sénégal): Le grand Jolof XIII–XVIe siècles*. Paris: Éditions Façades, 1987.

Bowser, Frederick P. *The African Slave in Colonial Peru, 1524–1650*. Stanford, CA: Stanford University Press, 1974.

Boyd-Bowman, Peter. "Negro Slaves in Early Colonial Mexico." *The Americas* 26 (1969): 134–53.

Broadhead, Susan Herlin. "Slave Wives, Free Sisters: Bakongo Women and Slavery c. 1700–1850." In *Women and Slavery in Africa*. Edited by Claire C. Robinson and Martin A. Klein, 160–81. Madison: University of Wisconsin Press, 1984.

Bromley, Julian, and Viktor Kozlov. "The Theory of Ethnos and Ethnic Processes in Soviet Social Sciences." *Comparative Studies in Society and History* 31, no. 3 (1989): 425–38.

Bühnen, Stephan. "Ethnic Origins of Peruvian Slaves (1548–1650): Figures for Upper Guinea." *Paideuma* 39 (1993): 57–110.

Burnard, Trevor G. "Slave Naming Patterns: Onomastics and the Taxonomy of Race in Eighteenth-Century Jamaica." *Journal of Interdisciplinary History* 31, no. 3 (2001): 325–46.

———. *Mastery, Tyranny, and Desire: Thomas Thistlewood and His Slaves in the Anglo-Jamaican World*. Chapel Hill: University of North Carolina, 2004.

Bush, Barbara. *Slave Women in Caribbean Society, 1650–1838*. Bloomington: Indiana University Press, 1990.

Cáceres, Rina. "Costa Rica, en la frontera del comercio de esclavos africanos." *Reflexiones* (Facultad de Ciencias Sociales, Universidad de Costa Rica), no. 65 (1997): 3–14.

———. "El trabajo esclavo en Costa Rica." *Revista de Historia* (Costa Rica), no. 39 (1999): 27–49.

———. *Negros, mulatos, esclavos y libertos en la Costa Rica del siglo XVII*. Mexico City: Instituto Panamericano de Geografía e Historia, 2000.

Capo, Hounkpatin. "Le gbe est une langue unique." *Africa* 53, no. 2 (1983): 47–57.

Cardoso, Fernando Henrique. *Capitalismo e escravidão no Brasil meridional: O negro na sociedade escravocrata do Rio Grande do Sul*. 2nd ed. Rio de Janeiro: Paz e Terra, 1977.

Carreira, António. *Cabo Verde: Formação e extinção de uma sociedade escravocrata, 1460–1878*. 2nd ed. N.p.: Com o patrocínio da Comissão da Comunidade Económica Europeia para o Instituto Caboverdeano do Livro, 1983.

Carroll, Patrick J. *Blacks in Colonial Veracruz: Race, Ethnicity, and Regional Development*. Austin: University of Texas Press, 1991.

Castellanos, Jorge, and Isabel Castellanos. "The Geographic, Ethnologic, and Linguistic Roots of Cuban Blacks." *Cuban Studies* 17 (1987): 95–110.

Chacón de Umaña, Luz Alba. *Don Diego de la Haya Fernández*. San José: Editorial Costa Rica, 1967.

Chambers, Douglas Brent. "Ethnicity in the Diaspora: The Slave-Trade and the Creation of African 'Nations' in the Americas." *Slavery & Abolition* 22, no. 3 (2001): 25–39.

———. "'He Is an African but Speaks Plain': Historical Creolization in Eighteenth-Century Virginia." In *The African Diaspora*. Edited by Alusine Jalloh and Stephen E. Maizlish, 100–133. College Station: Texas A&M University Press, 1996.

———. "The Significance of Igbo in the Bight of Biafra Slave-Trade: A Rejoinder to Northrup's 'Myth Igbo.'" *Slavery & Abolition* 23, no. 1 (2002): 101–20.

———. "Tracing Igbo into the African Diaspora." In *Identity in the Shadow of Slavery.* Edited by Paul E. Lovejoy, 55–71. London: Continuum, 2000.

Cope, R. Douglas. *The Limits of Racial Domination: Plebeian Society in Colonial Mexico City, 1660–1720.* Madison: University of Wisconsin Press, 1994.

Cortés Alonso, V. "Procedencia de los esclavos negros en Valencia, 1482–1516." *Revista Española de Antropología Americana* 7 (1972): 123–51.

Craton, Michael. *Searching for the Invisible Man: Slaves and Plantation Life in Jamaica.* Cambridge, MA: Harvard University Press, 1979.

Curtin, Philip D. *The Atlantic Slave Trade: A Census.* Madison: University of Wisconsin Press, 1969.

Curto, José C. "The Story of Nbena, 1817–1820: Unlawful Enslavement and the Concept of 'Original Freedom' in Angola." In *Trans-Atlantic Dimensions of Ethnicity in the African Diaspora.* Edited by Paul E. Lovejoy and David V. Trotman, 43–64. London: Continuum, 2003.

Daaku, Kwame Yeboa. *Trade and Politics on the Gold Coast, 1600–1720: A Study of African Reaction to the European Trade.* Oxford: Clarendon Press, 1970.

Dalby, David. "Distribution and Nomenclature of the Manding People and Their Language." In *Papers on the Manding.* Edited by Carleton T. Hodge, 1–13. Bloomington: Indiana University Press, 1971.

Davies, K. G. *The Royal African Company.* London: Longman, Grion & Co., 1957.

DeCorse, Christopher. "The Danes on the Gold Coast: Culture Change and the European Presence." *African Archaeological Review* 11 (1993): 149–73.

Denevan, William M., ed. *The Native Population of the Americas in 1492.* 2nd ed. Madison: University of Wisconsin Press, 1992.

Diouf, Sylviane. "Devils or Sorcerers, Muslims or Studs: Manding in the Americas." In *Trans-Atlantic Dimensions of Ethnicity in the African Diaspora.* Edited by Paul E. Lovejoy and David V. Trotman, 139–57. London: Continuum, 2003.

———. *Dreams of Africa in Alabama: The Slave Ship* Clotilda *and the Story of the Last Africans Brought to America.* Oxford: Oxford University Press, 2007.

———. *Servants of Allah: African Muslims Enslaved in the Americas.* New York: New York University Press, 1998.

Duncan, T. Bentley. *The Atlantic Islands: Madeira, the Azores, and Cabo Verde in the Seventeenth Century.* Chicago, IL: University of Chicago Press, 1972.

Dunn, Richard S. *Sugar and Slaves: The Rise of the Planter Class in the English West Indies, 1624–1713.* Chapel Hill: University of North Carolina Press, 1972.

Egblewogbe, E. Y. "Personal Names as a Parameter for the Study of Culture: The Case of the Ghanaian Ewe." In *Peuples du golfe du Bénin.* Edited by François de Medeiros, 209–19. Paris: Karthala, 1984.

Elkins, Stanley M. *Slavery: A Problem in American Institutional and Intellectual Life.* 3rd ed. Chicago, IL: University of Chicago Press, 1976.

Eltis, David. *The Rise of African Slavery in the Americas.* Cambridge: Cambridge University Press, 2000.

Eltis, David, David Richardson, Stephen D. Behrendt, and Herbert S. Klein, eds. *The Trans-Atlantic Slave Trade: A Database on CD-ROM.* Cambridge: Cambridge University Press, 1999.

Fernández, León. *Historia de Costa Rica durante la dominación española, 1502–1821.* Madrid: Tipografía de Manuel Ginés Hernández, 1889.

Ferry, Robert J. "Encomienda, African Slavery, and Agriculture in Seventeenth-Century Caracas." *Hispanic American Historical Review* 61, no. 4 (1981): 609–35.

Fields, Barbara J. "Ideology and Race in American History." In *Region, Race, and Reconstruction: Essays in Honor of C. Vann Woodward.* Edited by J. Morgan Kousser and James M. McPherson, 143–77. New York: Oxford University Press, 1982.

Floyd, Troy S. *The Anglo-Spanish Struggle for Mosquitia.* Albuquerque: University of New Mexico Press, 1967.

Fonseca, Elizabeth. *Costa Rica colonial: La tierra y el hombre.* 3rd ed. San José: Editorial Universitaria Centroamericana (EDUCA), 1986.

———. "El cultivo de la caña de azúcar en el Valle Central de Costa Rica: Epoca colonial." In *Costa Rica colonial.* Edited by Luis F. Sibaja, 79–104. San José: Ediciones Guayacán, 1989.

Fonseca Corrales, Elizabeth, Patricia Alvarenga Venutolo, and Juan Carlos Solórzano Fonseca. *Costa Rica en el siglo XVIII.* San José: Editorial de la Universidad de Costa Rica, 2001.

Franco Silva, Alfonso. *Regesto documental sobre la esclavitud sevillana (1453–1513).* Seville: Publicaciones de la Universidad de Sevilla, 1979.

Franklin, John Hope, and Loren Schweninger. *Runaway Slaves: Rebels on the Plantation.* New York: Oxford University Press, 1999.

Fuente García, Alejandro de la. "Esclavos africanos en La Habana: Zonas de procedencia y denominaciones étnicas, 1570–1699." *Revista Española de Antropología Americana* 20 (1990): 135–60.

———. "Los ingenios de azúcar en La Habana del siglo XVII (1640–1700): Estructura y mano de obra." *Revista de Historia Económica* (Spain) 9, no. 1 (1991): 35–67.

Fyfe, Christopher. *A History of Sierra Leone.* London: Oxford University Press, 1962.

Fynn, J. K. *Asante and Its Neighbors, 1700–1807.* Evanston, IL: Northwestern University Press, 1971.

García Fuentes, Lutgardo. "Licencias para la introducción de esclavos en Indias y envíos desde Sevilla en el siglo XVI." *Jahrbuch für Geschichte von Staat, Wirtschaft und Gesellschaft Lateinamerikas* 19 (1982): 1–46.

Gayibor, Nicoué Lodjou. *Le Genyi: Un royaume oublié de la côte de Guinée au temps de la traite des noirs.* Lomé, Togo: Éditions HAHO, 1990.

Genovese, Eugene D. *Roll, Jordan, Roll: The World the Slaves Made.* New York: Pantheon, 1974.

Gluckman, Stephen J. "Preliminary Investigations of a Shipwreck, Pumpata Cahuita National Park, Costa Rica." In *Maritime Archaeology: A Reader of Substantive and Theoretical Contributions.* Edited by Lawrence E. Babbits and Hans Van Tilburg, 453–67. New York: Plenum Press, 1998.

Gøbel, Erik. "Danish Trade to the West Indies and Guinea, 1671–1754." *Scandinavian Economic History Review* 33, nos. 1–3 (1985): 21–49.

Gomez, Michael A. *Exchanging Our Country Marks: The Transformation of African Identities in the Colonial and Antebellum South.* Chapel Hill: University of North Carolina Press, 1998.

———. "Muslims in Early America." *Journal of Southern History* 60, no. 4 (1994): 671–710.

Gorender, Jacob. *A escravidão reabilitada.* São Paulo: Editora Ática, 1990.

Graham, Richard. "Slave Families on a Rural Estate in Colonial Brazil." *Journal of Social History* 9, no. 3 (1976): 382–402.

Graham, Sandra Lauderdale. *Caetana Says No: Women's Stories from a Slave Society.* Cambridge: Cambridge University Press, 2002.

———. "Honor Among Slaves." In *The Faces of Honor: Sex, Shame, and Violence in Colonial Latin America.* Edited by Lyman L. Johnson and Sonya Lipsett-Rivera, 201–28. Albuquerque: University of New Mexico Press, 1998.

Granda Gutiérrez, Germán de. "Datos antroponímicos sobre negros esclavos musulmanes en Nueva Granada." *Thesaurus* (Bogotá) 27, no. 1 (1972): 89–103. http://cvc.cervantes.es/lengua/thesaurus/pdf/27/TH_27_001_089_0.pdf

———. "Testimonios documentales sobre la preservación del sistema antroponímico twi entre los esclavos negros de la Nueva Granada." *Revista Española de Lingüística* 1, no. 2 (1971): 265–74.

Greene, Sandra E. "Cultural Zones in the Era of the Slave Trade: Exploring the Yoruba Connection with Anlo-Ewe." In *Identity in the Shadow of Slavery.* Edited by Paul E. Lovejoy, 86–101. London: Continuum, 2000.

———. *Gender, Ethnicity and Social Change on the Upper Slave Coast.* Portsmouth, NH: Heinemann, 1996.

Gudeman, Stephen, and Stuart B. Schwartz. "Cleansing Original Sin: Godparenthood and the Baptism of Slaves in Eighteenth-Century Bahia." In *Kinship Ideology and Practice in Latin America.* Edited by Raymond T. Smith. Chapel Hill: University of North Carolina Press, 1984.

Gudmundson K, Lowell. "Materiales censales de finales de la colonia y principios del período republicano en Costa Rica." *Revista de Historia* (Costa Rica) 6, no. 11 (1985): 173–227.

———. "Mecanismos de movilidad social para la población de procedencia africana en Costa Rica colonial: Manumisión y mestizaje." *Revista de Historia* (Costa Rica) 2, no. 3 (1976): 131–82. http://www.revistas.una.ac.cr/index.php/historia/article/view/2150.

Gudmundson Kristjanson, Lowell Wayne. *Estratificación socio-racial y económica de Costa Rica, 1700–1850.* San José: EUNED, 1978.

Gutkind, Peter C. W. "The Canoemen of the Gold Coast (Ghana): A Survey and an Explanation in Precolonial African Labour History." *Cahiers d'Études Africaines* 29, nos. 3–4 (1989): 339–76.

Hair, P. E. H. "Black African Slaves at Valencia, 1482–1516: An Onomastic Inquiry." *History in Africa* 7 (1980): 119–31.

———. "Ethnolinguistic Continuity on the Guinea Coast." *Journal of African History* 8, no. 2 (1967): 247–68.

———. "An Ethnolinguistic Inventory of the Upper Guinea Coast before 1700." *African Language Review* 6 (1967): 32–70.

Hall, Gwendolyn Midlo. "African Ethnicities and the Meanings of 'Mina.'" In *Trans-Atlantic Dimensions of Ethnicity in the African Diaspora*. Edited by Paul E. Lovejoy and David V. Trotman, 65–81. London: Continuum, 2003.

———. *Africans in Colonial Louisiana: The Development of Afro-Creole Culture in the Eighteenth Century*. Baton Rouge: Louisiana State University Press, 1992.

Harpelle, Ronald N. *The West Indians of Costa Rica: Race, Class, and the Integration of an Ethnic Minority*. Kingston: Ian Randle Publishers, 2001.

Hastings, Adrian. "The Christianity of Pedro IV of the Kongo, 'the Pacific.'" *Journal of Religion in Africa* 28, no. 2 (1998): 145–59.

Hawthorne, Walter. "'Being Now, as It Were, One Family': Shipmate Bonding on the Slave Vessel *Emilia*, in Rio de Janeiro and Throughout the Atlantic World." *Luso-Brazilian Review* 45, no. 1 (2008): 53–77.

———. *From Africa to Brazil: Culture, Identity, and an Atlantic Slave Trade, 1600–1830*. Cambridge: Cambridge University Press, 2010.

———. "Nourishing a Stateless Society During the Slave Trade: The Rise of Balanta Paddy-Rice Production in Guinea-Bissau." *Journal of African History* 42, no. 1 (2001): 1–24.

———. *Planting Rice and Harvesting Slaves: Transformations Along the Guinea-Bissau Coast, 1400–1900*. Portsmouth, NH: Heinemann, 2003.

———. "The Production of Slaves Where There Was No State: The Guinea-Bissau Region, c. 1450–c. 1950." *Slavery & Abolition* 20 (1999): 97–124.

Helms, Mary W. "Miskito Slaving and Culture Contact: Ethnicity and Opportunity in an Expanding Population." *Journal of Anthropological Research* 39, no. 2 (1983): 179–97.

Hernæs, Per O. *Slaves, Danes, and African Coast Society: The Danish Slave Trade from West Africa and Afro-Danish Relations on the Eighteenth-Century Gold Coast*. Trondheim, Norway: Department of History, University of Trondheim, 1995.

Herrera, Robinson A. "The African Slave Trade in Early Santiago." *Urban History Workshop Review* 4 (1998): 6–12.

Herskovits, Melville J. *Dahomey: An Ancient West African Kingdom*. 2 vols. New York: J. J. Augustin, 1938.

Heuman, Gad J. "Runaway Slaves in Nineteenth-Century Barbados." *Slavery & Abolition* 6, no. 3 (1985): 95–111.

Heywood, Linda M. "The Angolan-Afro-Brazilian Cultural Connections." *Slavery & Abolition* 20, no. 1 (1999): 9–23.

———, ed. *Central Africans and Cultural Transformations in the American Diaspora.* Cambridge: Cambridge University Press, 2002.

Heywood, Linda M. and John K. Thornton. *Central Africans, Atlantic Creoles, and the Foundation of the Americas, 1585–1660.* Cambridge: Cambridge University Press, 2007.

Hilton, Anne. *The Kingdom of Kongo.* Oxford: Clarendon Press, 1985.

Hiskett, Mervyn. *The Development of Islam in West Africa.* New York: Longman, 1984.

Hoetink, H. *Caribbean Race Relations: A Study of Two Variants.* Oxford: Oxford University Press for the Institute of Race Relations, 1967.

Hofstee, Erik J. W. "The Great Divide: Aspects of the Social History of the Middle Passage in the Trans-Atlantic Slave Trade." PhD diss., Michigan State University, 2002.

Holm, John Alexander. "The Creole English of Nicaragua's Miskitu Coast: Its Sociolinguistic History and a Comparative Study of its Lexicon and Syntax." PhD thesis, University of London, 1978.

Horta, José da Silva. "Evidence for a Luso-African Identity in 'Portuguese' Accounts on 'Guinea of Cape Verde' (Sixteenth-Seventeenth Centuries)," *History in Africa* 27 (2000): 99–130.

———. "La perception du mandé et de l'identité mandingue dans les textes européens, 1453–1508." *History in Africa* 23 (1996): 75–86.

Hünefeldt, Christine. *Paying the Price of Freedom: Family and Labor Among Lima's Slaves, 1800–1854.* Translated by Alexandra Stern. Berkeley: University of California Press, 1994.

Ibarra Rojas, Eugenia. *Las sociedades cacicales de Costa Rica.* San José: Editorial de la Universidad de Costa Rica, 1990.

Indice de los protocolos de Cartago. 6 vols. San José: Tipografía Nacional, 1909–1930.

Indice de los protocolos de Heredia, 1721–1851. San José: Tipografía Nacional, 1904.

Indice de los protocolos de San José, 1721–1836. 2 vols. San José: Tipografía Nacional, 1905.

Jassan, Muhammad Abdul. "Muslims' Struggle Against Slavery and Their Efforts for Retention of Cultural Identity in the Caribbean Territories." *Hamdard Islamicus* (Pakistan) 21, no. 1 (1998): 75–84.

Johnson, Lyman L., and Sonya Lipsett-Rivera, eds. *The Faces of Honor: Sex, Shame, and Violence in Colonial Latin America.* Albuquerque: University of New Mexico Press, 1988.

Johnson, Walter. *Soul by Soul: Life Inside the Antebellum Slave Market.* Cambridge, MA: Harvard University Press, 2000.

Jones, Norrece T., Jr. *Born a Child of Freedom, Yet a Slave: Mechanisms of Control and Strategies of Resistance in Antebellum South Carolina.* Hanover, CT: Wesleyan University Press, 1990.

Kea, Ray A. "'I Am Here to Plunder on the General Road': Bandits and Banditry in the

Pre-Nineteenth Centuries." In *Banditry, Rebellion, and Social Protest in Africa.* Edited by Donald Crummey, 109–32. Portsmouth, NH: Heinemann, 1986.

———. *Settlements, Trade, and Polities on the Seventeenth-Century Gold Coast.* Baltimore, MD: Johns Hopkins University Press, 1982.

Kiple, Kenneth F. *The Caribbean Slave: A Biological History.* Cambridge: Cambridge University Press, 1984.

Klein, Herbert S. *African Slavery in Latin America and the Caribbean.* Oxford: Oxford University Press, 1986.

———. "African Women in the Atlantic Slave Trade." In *Women and Slavery in Africa.* Edited by Claire C. Robinson and Martin A. Klein, 29–38. Madison: University of Wisconsin Press, 1984.

———. *Slavery in the Americas: A Comparative Study of Virginia and Cuba.* Chicago, IL: University of Chicago Press, 1967.

Klein, Martin A. "Servitude Among the Wolof and Sereer of Senegambia." In *Slavery in Africa: Historical and Anthropological Perspectives.* Edited by Suzanne Miers and Igor Kopytoff, 335–63. Madison: University of Wisconsin Press, 1977.

Kolapo, Femi J. "The Igbo and their Neighbours During the Era of the Atlantic Slave Trade." *Slavery & Abolition* 25, no. 1 (2004): 114–33.

Kolchin, Peter. *American Slavery, 1619–1877.* New York: Hill and Wang, 1993.

Lane, Kris. "Captivity and Redemption: Aspects of Slave Life in Early Colonial Quito and Popayán." *The Americas* 57, no. 2 (2000): 225–46.

Lara, Silvia Hunold. *Campos da violência: Escravos e senhores na capitania do Rio de Janeiro 1750–1808.* Rio de Janeiro: Editora Paz e Terra, 1988.

Lavrin, Asunción. "Sexuality in Colonial Mexico: A Church Dilemma." In *Sexuality and Marriage in Colonial Latin America.* Edited by Asunción Lavrin, 47–95. Lincoln: University of Nebraska Press, 1989.

Law, Robin. "Between the Sea and the Lagoons: The Interaction of Maritime and Inland Navigation on the Pre-Colonial Slave Coast." *Cahiers d'Études Africaines* 29, no. 2/114 (1989): 209–37.

———. "Ethnicities of Enslaved Africans in the Diaspora: On the Meanings of 'Mina' (Again)." *History in Africa* 32 (2005): 247–67.

———. "Ethnicity and the Slave Trade: 'Lucumi' and 'Nago' as Ethnonyms in West Africa." *History in Africa* 24 (1997): 205–19.

———. "Ideologies of Royal Power: The Dissolution and Reconstruction of Political Authority on the 'Slave Coast,' 1680–1750." *Africa* 57, no. 3 (1987): 321–44.

———. *The Kingdom of Allada.* Leiden, Netherlands: Research School CNWS, School of Asian, African, and Amerindian Studies, 1997.

———. *The Oyo Empire, c. 1600–c. 1836: A West African Imperialism in the Era of the Atlantic Slave Trade.* Oxford: Clarendon Press, 1977.

———. "Religion, Trade and Politics on the 'Slave Coast': Roman Catholic Missions in Allada and Whydah in the Seventeenth Century." *Journal of Religion in Africa* 21 (1991): 43–77.

———. *The Slave Coast of West Africa, 1550–1759.* Oxford: Clarendon Press, 1991.

Law, Robin and Paul E. Lovejoy. "Borgu in the Atlantic Slave Trade." *African Economic History* 27 (1999): 69–92.

Lenin, V. I. *Collected Works.* 45 vols. Moscow: Foreign Languages Publishing House, 1963–1970.

Lobo Wiehoff, Tatiana. "Cimarrones." In *Negros y blancos: Todo mezclado.* Tatiana Lobo Wiehoff and Mauricio Meléndez Obando, 34–36. San José: Editorial de la Universidad de Costa Rica, 1997.

———. "José Cubero." In *Negros y blancos: Todo mezclado.* Tatiana Lobo Wiehoff and Mauricio Meléndez Obando, 47–52. San José: Editorial de la Universidad de Costa Rica, 1997.

———. "La negra marinera." In *Negros y blancos: Todo mezclado.* Tatiana Lobo Wiehoff and Mauricio Meléndez Obando, 22–24. San José: Editorial de la Universidad de Costa Rica, 1997.

———. "La travesura de don Tomás." In *Negros y blancos: Todo mezclado.* Tatiana Lobo Wiehoff and Mauricio Meléndez Obando, 38–41. San José: Editorial de la Universidad de Costa Rica, 1997.

———. "Primeros fundadores de San José." In *Negros y blancos: Todo mezclado.* Tatiana Lobo Wiehoff and Mauricio Meléndez Obando, 24–39. San José: Editorial de la Universidad de Costa Rica, 1997.

Lobo Wiehoff, Tatiana and Mauricio Meléndez Obando. *Negros y blancos: Todo mezclado.* San José: Editorial de la Universidad de Costa Rica, 1997.

Lockhart, James. *Spanish Peru, 1532–1560: A Colonial Society.* 2nd ed. Madison: University of Wisconsin Press, 1994.

Lohse, Russell. "Africans in a Colony of Creoles: The Yoruba in Colonial Costa Rica." In *The Yoruba Diaspora in the Americas.* Edited by Toyin Falola and Matt D. Childs, 130–56. Bloomington: Indiana University Press, 2005.

———. "Cacao and Slavery in Matina, Costa Rica, 1650–1750." In *Blacks and Blackness in Central America: Between Race and Place.* Edited by Lowell Gudmundson and Justin Wolfe, 57–91.

———. "*La Negrita*, Queen of the Ticos: The Black Roots of Costa Rica's Patron Saint." *The Americas* 69, no. 3 (2013): 323–55.

———. "Mexico and Central America." In *The Oxford Handbook of Slavery in the Americas.* Edited by Robert L. Paquette and Mark M. Smith, 46–67. Oxford: Oxford University Press, 2010.

———. "Slave Trade Nomenclature and African Ethnicities in the Americas: Evidence from Early Eighteenth-Century Costa Rica." *Slavery & Abolition* 23, no. 3 (2002): 73–92.

Lokken, Paul. "From Black to *Ladino*: People of African Descent, Mestizaje, and Racial Hierarchy in Rural Colonial Guatemala, 1600–1730." PhD diss., University of Florida, 2000.

———. "From the 'Kingdoms of Angola' to Santiago de Guatemala: The Portuguese Asientos and Spanish Central America, 1595–1640." *Hispanic American Historical Review* 93, no. 2 (2013): 171–203.

———. "Marriage as Slave Emancipation in Seventeenth-Century Rural Guatemala." *The Americas* 58, no. 2 (2001): 175–200.

López Leal, Carlos Roberto. "Una rebelión indígena en Talamanca: Pablo Presbere y el alzamiento general de 1709." Licenciatura thesis, Universidad de San Carlos de Guatemala, 1973.

Love, Edgar F. "Marriage Patterns of Persons of African Descent in a Colonial Mexico City Parish." *Hispanic American Historical Review* 51, no. 1 (1971): 79–91.

Lovejoy, Paul E. "The African Diaspora: Revisionist Interpretations of Ethnicity, Culture and Religion Under Slavery." *Studies in the World History of Slavery, Abolition and Emancipation* 2, no. 1 (1997). http://ejournalofpoliticalscience.org/diaspora.html.

———. "Identifying Enslaved Africans in the African Diaspora." In *Identity in the Shadow of Slavery.* Edited by Paul E. Lovejoy, 1–29. London: Continuum, 2000.

———. "Methodology Through the Ethnic Lens: The Study of Atlantic Africa." In *Sources and Methods in African History: Spoken, Written, Unearthed.* Edited by Toyin Falola and Christian Jennings, 105–17. Rochester, NY: University of Rochester Press, 2003.

———. "Slavery, the Bilad al-Sudan and the Frontiers of the African Diaspora." In *Slavery on the Frontiers of Islam.* Edited by Paul E. Lovejoy, 1–29. Princeton, NJ: Markus Wiener, 2004.

———. *Transformations in Slavery: A History of Slavery in Africa.* 2nd ed. Cambridge: Cambridge University Press, 2000.

Lovejoy, Paul E. and David Richardson. "Competing Markets for Male and Female Slaves: Prices in the Interior of West Africa, 1780–1850." *International Journal of African Historical Studies* 28, no. 2 (1995): 261–94.

Lovejoy, Paul E. and David V. Trotman. "Enslaved Africans and Their Expectations of Slave Life in the Americas: Towards a Reconsideration of Models of 'Creolisation.'" In *Questioning Creole: Creolisation Discourses in Caribbean Culture.* Edited by Verene A. Shepherd and Glen L. Richards, 62–91. Kingston: Ian Randle Publishers, 2002.

Lovejoy, Paul E. and David V. Trotman, eds. *Trans-Atlantic Dimensions of Ethnicity in the African Diaspora.* London: Continuum, 2003.

Lutz, Christopher H. *Santiago de Guatemala, 1541–1773: City, Caste, and the Colonial Experience.* Norman: University of Oklahoma Press, 1994.

MacGaffey, Wyatt. "Kongo Identity, 1483–1993." *South Atlantic Quarterly* 94, no. 4 (1995): 1025–37.

MacLeod, Murdo J. *Spanish Central America: A Socioeconomic History 1520–1720.* Berkeley: University of California Press, 1973.

MacLeod, Philip S. "On the Edge of Empire: Costa Rica in the Colonial Era (1561–1800)." PhD diss., Tulane University, 1999.

Madrigal Muñoz, Eduardo. "Los lazos sociales en la dinámica de un grupo subordinado en una sociedad colonial periférica: Los cacaoteros de Costa Rica, 1660–1740." *Mesoamérica*, no. 53 (2011): 106–32.

Maeyama, Takashi. "The Masters Versus the Slaves Under the Plantation Systems in Brazil: Some Preliminary Considerations." *Latin American Studies* (University of Tsukuba, Japan) 3 (1981): 115–41.

Malone, Ann Patton. *Sweet Chariot: Slave Family and Household Structure in Nineteenth-Century Louisiana.* Chapel Hill: University of North Carolina Press, 1992.

Mandel, Ernest. *An Introduction to Marxist Economic Theory.* New York: Pathfinder Press, 1970.

———. *Marxist Economic Theory.* Translated by Brian Pearce. London: Merlin Press, 1968.

Mann, Kristin. "Shifting Paradigms in the Study of the African Diaspora and of Atlantic History and Culture." *Slavery & Abolition* 22, no. 1 (2001): 3–21.

Manning, Patrick. "Merchants, Porters and Canoemen in the Bight of Benin: Links in the West African Trade Network." In *The Workers of African Trade.* Edited by Catherine Coquery-Vidrovitch and Paul E. Lovejoy, 51–74. Beverly Hills, CA: Sage, 1985.

Marrero, Levi. *Cuba: economía y sociedad.* 11 vols. Madrid: Editorial Playor, 1975.

Martín Casares, Aurelia. *La esclavitud en la Granada del siglo XVI: Género, raza, religión.* Granada, Spain: Editorial Universidad de Granada, 2000.

Marx, Karl. *Wage Labour and Capital* and *Value, Price and Profit.* New York: International Publishers, 1985. Originally published in 1849 and 1865.

———, and Frederick Engels. *The German Ideology.* Edited by C. J. Arthur. New York: International Publishers, 1995. Originally published in 1932.

Mattoso, Katia M. de Queirós. *To Be a Slave in Brazil, 1550–1888.* Translated by Arthur Goldhammer. New Brunswick, NJ: Rutgers University Press, 1986. Originally published in 1979 as *Être esclave au Brésil, XVIe-XIXe siècles* in Paris by Hachette.

McCusker, John J. *Money and Exchange in Europe and America, 1600–1775: A Handbook.* Chapel Hill: University of North Carolina Press, 1992.

McFeely, William S. *Frederick Douglass.* New York: W. W. Norton, 1991.

McKnight, Kathryn Joy. "'En su tierra lo aprendió': An African *Curandero*'s Defense Before the Cartagena Inquisition." *Colonial Latin American Review* 12, no. 1 (2003): 63–84.

Meillassoux, Claude. *The Anthropology of Slavery: The Womb of Iron and Gold.* Translated by Alide Dasnois. Chicago, IL: University of Chicago Press, 1991. Originally published in 1986 as *Anthropologie de l'esclavage: Le ventre de fer et d'argent* in Paris by Presses Universitaires de France.

Meléndez, Carlos. *Conquistadores y pobladores: Orígenes histórico-sociales de los costarricenses.* San José: Editorial Universidad Estatal a Distancia, 1982.

———. *Costa Rica: Tierra y poblamiento en la colonia.* San José: Editorial Costa Rica, 1977.

———. "El negro en Costa Rica durante la colonia." In *El negro en Costa Rica.* Carlos Meléndez and Quince Duncan, 11–50. San José: Editorial Costa Rica, 1972.

Meléndez Obando, Mauricio. "Los Calvo." In *Negros y blancos: Todo mezclado.* Tatiana Lobo Wiehoff and Mauricio Meléndez Obando, 137–39. San José: Editorial de la Universidad de Costa Rica, 1997.

————. "Los Madriz." In *Negros y blancos: Todo mezclado*. Tatiana Lobo Wiehoff and Mauricio Meléndez Obando, 134–36. San José: Editorial de la Universidad de Costa Rica, 1997.

————. "Los Ulloa." In *Negros y blancos: Todo mezclado*. Tatiana Lobo Wiehoff and Mauricio Meléndez Obando, 128–34. San José: Editorial de la Universidad de Costa Rica, 1997.

————. "Manumisión." In *Negros y blancos: Todo mezclado*. Tatiana Lobo Wiehoff and Mauricio Meléndez Obando, 104–10. San José: Editorial de la Universidad de Costa Rica, 1997.

Mena García, María del Carmen. *La sociedad de Panamá en el siglo XVI*. Seville: Artes Gráficas Padura, 1984.

Menard, Russell R., and Stuart B. Schwartz. "Why African Slavery? Labor Force Transitions in Brazil, Mexico, and the Carolina Lowcountry." In *Slavery in the Americas*. Edited by Wolfgang Binder, 89–114. Würzburg: Königshausen & Neumann, 1993.

Mercier, P. "The Fon of Dahomey." In *African Worlds: Studies in the Cosmological Ideas and Social Values of African Peoples*. Edited by Darryl Forde, 210–34. London: Oxford University Press, 1954.

Metcalf, Alida. *Family and Frontier in Colonial Brazil: Santana de Parnaíba, 1580–1822*. Berkeley: University of California Press, 1992.

Miers, Suzanne, and Igor Kopytoff, eds. *Slavery in Africa: Historical and Anthropological Perspectives*. Madison: University of Wisconsin Press, 1977.

Miller, Joseph C. "Central Africa During the Era of the Slave Trade, c. 1490s–1850s." In *Central Africans and Cultural Transformations in the American Diaspora*. Edited by Linda Heywood, 21–70. Cambridge: Cambridge University Press, 2002.

————. "Retention, Reinvention, and Remembering: Restoring Identities Through Enslavement in Africa and Under Slavery in Brazil." In *Enslaving Connections: Changing Cultures of Africa and Brazil During the Era of Slavery*. Edited by José Curto and Paul E. Lovejoy, 81–121. New York: Humanity Books, 2004.

————. *Way of Death: Merchant Capitalism and the Angolan Slave Trade, 1730–1830*. Madison: University of Wisconsin Press, 1988.

Mintz, Sidney W. "Was the Plantation Slave a Proletarian?" *Review* (Fernand Braudel Center) 2, no. 1 (1978): 81–98.

Mintz, Sidney W. and Richard Price. *The Birth of African-American Culture: An Anthropological Perspective*. Boston, MA: Beacon Press, 1992. Originally published in 1976 as *An Anthropological Approach to the Afro-American Past* in Philadelphia, PA, by the Institute for the Study of Human Issues.

Moitt, Bernard. *Women and Slavery in the French Antilles, 1635–1848*. Bloomington: Indiana University Press, 2001.

Monge Alfaro, Carlos. *Historia de Costa Rica*. 14th ed. San José: Librería Trejos, 1978.

Morgan, Philip D. "The Cultural Implications of the Atlantic Slave Trade: African Regional Origins, American Destinations and New World Developments." *Slavery & Abolition* 18, no. 1 (1997): 122–45.

———. *Slave Counterpoint: Black Culture in the Eighteenth-Century Chesapeake and Lowcountry*. Chapel Hill: University of North Carolina Press, 1998.

Mullin, Gerald W. *Flight and Rebellion: Slave Resistance in Eighteenth-Century Virginia*. New York: Oxford University Press, 1972.

Munford, Clarence J. *The Black Ordeal of Slavery and Slave Trading in the French West Indies, 1625–1715*. 3 vols. Lewiston, NY: Edwin Mellen Press, 1991.

Nazer, Mende. *Slave*. New York: Public Affairs, 2003.

Newson, Linda A. "The Depopulation of Nicaragua in the Sixteenth Century." *Journal of Latin American Studies* 14, no. 2 (1982): 253–86.

———. *Indian Survival in Colonial Nicaragua*. Norman: University of Oklahoma Press, 1987.

Newson, Linda A. and Susie Minchin. *From Capture to Sale: The Portuguese Slave Trade to Spanish South America in the Early Seventeenth* Century. Leiden, Netherlands: Brill, 2007.

Ngou-Mve, Nicolás. *El Africa bantú en la colonización de México (1595–1640)*. Madrid: Consejo Superior de Investigaciones Científicas, Agencia Española de Cooperación Internacional, 1994.

———. "São Tomé et la diaspora bantou vers l'Amérique hispanique." In *Cahiers des Anneaux de la Mémoire*, no. 3 (2001): 65–83.

Niane, D. T. "Mali and the Second Mandingo Expansion." In *Africa from the Twelfth to the Sixteenth Century*. Vol. 4 of *UNESCO General History of Africa*. Edited by D. T. Niane, 117–71. Berkeley: University of California Press, 1984.

Nørregård, Georg. *Danish Settlements in West Africa, 1658–1850*. Translated by Sigurd Mammen. Boston, MA: Boston University Press, 1966. Originally published in 1954 as "De danske etablissementer paa Guineakysten" in *Vore gamle tropekolonier*, edited by Johannes Brønsted, in Copenhagen.

———. "Forliset ved Nicaragua 1710" (The shipwreck off Nicaragua, 1710). In *Årbog 1948*, 67–98. Helsingør, Denmark: Handels- og Søfartsmuseet på Kronborg, 1948.

Northrup, David. "Igbo and Myth Igbo: Culture and Ethnicity in the Atlantic World, 1600–1850." *Slavery & Abolition* 21, no. 3 (2000): 1–20.

———. *Trade Without Rulers: Pre-Colonial Economic Development in South-Eastern Nigeria*. Oxford: Clarendon Press, 1978.

Nwokeji, G. Ugo. "African Conceptions of Gender and the Slave Traffic." *William & Mary Quarterly* 3rd ser., 58, no. 1 (2001): 47–68.

———. "The Biafran Frontier: Trade, Slaves, and Aro Society, c. 1750–1905." PhD diss., University of Toronto, 1999.

Offen, Karl. "Creating Mosquitia: Mapping Amerindian Spatial Practices in Eastern Central America, 1629–1779." *Journal of Historical Geography* 33 (2007): 254–82.

———. "The Miskitu Kingdom Landscape and the Emergence of a Miskitu Ethnic Identity, Northeastern Nicaragua and Honduras, 1600–1800." PhD diss., University of Texas at Austin, 1999.

————. "Race and Place in Colonial Mosquitia." In *Blacks and Blackness in Central America: Between Race and Place.* Edited by Lowell Gudmundson and Justin Wolfe, 92–129. Durham, NC: Duke University Press, 2010.

————. "The Sambo and Tawira Miskitu: The Colonial Origins and Geography of Intra-Miskitu Differentiation in Eastern Nicaragua and Honduras." *Ethnohistory* 49, no. 2 (2002): 319–72.

Olien, Michael D. "Black and Part-Black Populations in Colonial Costa Rica: Ethno-historical Resources and Problems." *Ethnohistory* 27 (1980): 13–29.

————. "The Negro in Costa Rica: The Ethnohistory of an Ethnic Minority in a Complex Society." PhD diss., University of Oregon, Eugene, 1967.

O'Toole, Rachel Sarah. *Bound Lives: Africans, Indians, and the Making of Race in Colonial Peru.* Pittsburgh, PA: University of Pittsburgh Press, 2012.

————. "From the Rivers of Guinea to the Valleys of Peru: Becoming a *Bran* Diaspora Within Spanish Slavery." *Social Text* 25, no. 3/92 (2007): 19–36.

Palmer, Colin A. "From Africa to the Americas: Ethnicity in the Early Black Communities of the Americas." *Journal of World History* (Honolulu) 6, no. 2 (1995): 223–36.

————. *Human Cargoes: The British Slave Trade to Spanish America, 1700–1739.* Urbana: University of Illinois Press, 1981.

————. *Slaves of the White God: Blacks in Mexico, 1570–1650.* Cambridge, MA: Harvard University Press, 1976.

Palmer, Paula. *"What Happen": A Folk-History of Costa Rica's Talamanca Coast.* 2nd ed. San José: Publications in English, 1993.

Parker, John. *Making the Town: Ga State and Society in Early Colonial Accra.* Portsmouth, NH: Heinemann, 2000.

Parramore, Thomas C. "Muslim Slave Aristocrats in North Carolina." *North Carolina Historical Review* 77, no. 2 (2000): 127–50.

Parreira, Adriano. *Economia e sociedade em Angola na epoca da rainha Jinga (século XVII).* Lisbon: Editorial Estampa, 1990.

Parrinder, Geoffrey. *West African Religion: A Study of the Beliefs and Pratices of Akan, Ewe, Yoruba, Ibo and Kindred Peoples.* 2nd ed. New York: Barnes & Noble, 1970.

Patterson, Orlando. *Slavery and Social Death.* Cambridge, MA: Harvard University Press, 1982.

Pavy, David. "The Provenience of Colombian Negroes." *Journal of Negro History* 52, no. 1 (1967): 35–58.

Payne Iglesias, María Elizet. "Actividades artesanales, siglo XVII (Maestros, oficiales y aprendices)." In *Costa Rica colonial.* Edited by Luis F. Sibaja, 39–60. San José: Ediciones Guayacán, 1989.

————. "Organización productiva y explotación indígena en el área central de Costa Rica, 1580–1700." Licenciatura thesis, Universidad de Costa Rica, 1988.

Pérez Brignoli, Héctor. "Deux siècles d'illégitimité au Costa Rica, 1770–1974." In *Marriage and Remarriage in Populations of the Past.* Edited by J. Dupâquier, E. Helin, P. Laslett, M. Livi-Boci, and S. Sogner, 481–93. London: Academic Press, 1981.

———. *La población de Costa Rica según el obispo Thiel.* Avances de Investigación 42. San José: Centro de Investigaciones Históricas, Universidad de Costa Rica, 1988.

Pérez Zeledón, Pedro. "Fusión de sangres." In *Gregorio José Ramírez y otros ensayos.* Pedro Pérez Zeledón, 89–94. San José: Editorial Costa Rica, 1971. Originally published in *Athenea* (San José) 2, no. 6 (1918).

Peristiany, J. G. "Introduction." In *Honour and Shame: The Values of Mediterranean Society.* Edited by J. G. Peristiany, 9–18. Chicago, IL: University of Chicago Press, 1966.

Piñero, Eugenio. "Accounting Practices in a Colonial Economy: A Case Study of Cacao Haciendas in Venezuela, 1700–1770." *Colonial Latin American Historical Review* 1, no. 1 (1992): 36–66.

Pitt-Rivers, Julian. "Honour and Social Status." In *Honour and Shame: The Values of Mediterranean Society.* Edited by J. G. Peristiany, 19–77. Chicago, IL: University of Chicago Press, 1966.

Postma, Johannes M. "The Dutch and the Asiento Slave Trade: African Slaves to the Spanish American Colonies, 1662–1715." In *De la traite à l'esclavage du Ve au XVIIIème siècle: Actes du Colloque Internationale sur la traite des noirs, 1985.* Edited by Serge Daget, 1:299–324. Nantes: Centre de Recherche sur l'Histoire du Monde Atlantique, 1988.

———. *The Dutch in the Atlantic Slave Trade, 1600–1815.* Cambridge: Cambridge University Press, 1990.

Prado, Eladio. *La orden franciscana.* San José: Editorial Costa Rica, 1983. Originally published in 1925.

Price, Richard. "Introduction: Maroons and Their Communities." In *Maroon Societies.* Edited by Richard Price, 1–30. 2nd ed. Baltimore, MD: Johns Hopkins University Press, 1979.

Proctor, Frank T., III. "Gender and the Manumission of Slaves in New Spain." *Hispanic American Historical Review* 86, no. 2 (2006): 309–36.

———. "Slavery, Identity, and Culture: An Afro-Mexican Counterpoint, 1640–1763." PhD diss., Emory University, 2003.

Quartey-Papafio, A. B. "The Use of Names Among the Gãs or Accra People of the Gold Coast." *Journal of the African Society* 13 (1913–1914): 167–82.

Quesada Camacho, Juan Rafael. *Historia de la historiografía costarricense, 1821–1940.* San José: Editorial de la Universidad de Costa Rica, 2001.

Quirós Vargas, Claudia. "Aspectos socioeconómicos de la ciudad del Espíritu Santo de Esparza y su jurisdicción (1574–1878)." Licenciatura thesis, Escuela de Historia y Geografía, Universidad de Costa Rica, 1976.

———. *La era de la encomienda.* San José: Editorial de la Universidad de Costa Rica, 1990.

Quirós Vargas, Claudia and Margarita Bolaños Arquín. "El mestizaje en el siglo XVII: Consideraciones para comprender la génesis del campesinado criollo del Valle Central." In *Costa Rica colonial.* Edited by Luis F. Sibaja, 61–78. San José: Ediciones Guayacán, 1989.

Reindorf, Carl Christian. *The History of the Gold Coast and Asante*. Basel: printed by author, 1895.

——. *The History of the Gold Coast and Asante*. 2nd ed. Accra: Ghana Universities Press, 1966.

Reis, João José, and Flavio dos Santos Gomes. "Introdução: Uma história da liberdade." In *Liberdade por um fio: Historia dos quilombos no Brasil*. Edited by João José Reis and Flavio dos Santos Gomes, 9–25. São Paulo: Companhia das Letras, 1996.

Restall, Matthew. "Black Conquistadors: Armed Africans in Early Spanish America." *The Americas* 57, no. 2 (2000): 171–205.

——. *The Black Middle: Africans, Mayas, and Spaniards in Colonial Yucatan*. Stanford, CA: Stanford University Press, 2009.

Robertson, Claire C. "Post-Proclamation Slavery in Accra: A Female Affair?" In *Women and Slavery in Africa*. Edited by Claire C. Robertson and Martin A. Klein, 220–45. Madison: University of Wisconsin Press, 1983.

Robertson, Claire C. and Martin A. Klein, eds. *Women and Slavery in Africa*. Madison: University of Wisconsin Press, 1983.

Rodney, Walter. "Jihad and Social Revolution in Futa Djalon in the Eighteenth Century." *Journal of the Historical Society of Nigeria* 4, no. 2 (1968): 269–84.

——. "Upper Guinea and the Significance of Origins of Africans Enslaved in the New World." *Journal of Negro History* 54 (1969): 327–45.

Romero Vargas, Germán. *Las estructuras sociales de Nicaragua en el siglo XVIII*. Managua: Editorial Vanguardia, 1988.

——. *Las sociedades del atlántico de Nicaragua en los siglos XVII y XVIII*. Managua: Fondo de Promoción Cultural–BANIC, 1995.

Rosés Alvarado, Carlos. "El ciclo del cacao en la economía colonial de Costa Rica, 1650–1794." *Mesoamérica* 3, no. 4 (1982): 248–78.

Rush, Dana Lynn. "Vodun Vortex: Accumulative Arts, Histories, and Religious Consciousnesses Along Coastal Benin." PhD diss., University of Iowa, 1997.

Sanneh, Lamin O. *The Jakhanke Muslim Clerics: A Religious and Historical Study of Islam in Senegambia*. Lanham, MD: University Press of America, 1989.

Saunders, A. C. de C. M. *A Social History of Black Slaves and Freemen in Portugal, 1441–1555*. Cambridge: Cambridge University Press, 1982.

Schiltz, Marc. "Yoruba Thunder Deities and Sovereignty: Ara Versus Sango." *Anthropos* 80 (1985): 67–84.

Schottman, Wendy. "Baatonu Personal Names from Birth to Death." *Africa* 70, no. 1 (2000): 79–106.

Schwartz, Stuart B. "The Manumission of Slaves in Colonial Brazil: Bahia, 1684–1745." *Hispanic American Historical Review* 54 (1974): 603–35.

——. *Slaves, Peasants, and Rebels: Reconsidering Brazilian Slavery*. Urbana: University of Illinois Press, 1992.

——. *Sugar Plantations in the Formation of Brazilian Society: Bahia, 1550–1835*. Cambridge: Cambridge University Press, 1985.

Scott, Julius Sherrard, III. "The Common Wind: Currents of Afro-American Communication in the Era of the Haitian Revolution." PhD diss., Duke University, 1986.

Searing, James F. *West African Slavery and Atlantic Commerce: The Senegal River Valley, 1700–1860.* Cambridge: Cambridge University Press, 1993.

Seed, Patricia. *To Love, Honor and Obey in Colonial Mexico: Conflicts over Marriage Choice, 1574–1821.* Stanford, CA: Stanford University Press, 1988.

Sempat Assadourian, Carlos. *El tráfico de esclavos en Córdoba 1588–1610.* Córdoba, Argentina: Universidad Nacional de Córdoba, 1965.

Sibaja, Luis, ed. *Costa Rica colonial.* San José: Ediciones Guayacán, 1989.

———. "La encomienda de tributo en el Valle Central de Costa Rica (1569–1683)." *Cuadernos Centroamericanos de Ciencias Sociales* (Universidad de Costa Rica), no. 11 (1984): 43–83.

———. "Los indígenas de Nicoya bajo el dominio español, 1522–1560." *Estudios Sociales Centroamericanos* 11, no. 32 (1982): 27–29.

Singleton, Brent. "The *Ummah* Slowly Bled: A Select Bibliography of Enslaved African Muslims in the Americas and the Caribbean." *Journal of Muslim Minority Affairs* 22, no. 2 (2002): 401–12.

Slenes, Robert W. "The Great Porpoise-Skull Strike: Central African Water Spirits and Slave Identity in Early Nineteenth-Century Rio de Janeiro." In *Central Africans and Cultural Transformations in the American Diaspora.* Edited by Linda Heywood, 183–208. Cambridge: Cambridge University Press, 2002.

———. "'*Malungu ngoma* vem!' África encoberta e descoberta no Brasil.' *Revista USP* (Brazil), no. 12 (Dec. 1991–Feb. 1992): 48–67.

———. *Na senzala uma flor: Esperanças e recordações na formação da família escrava— Brasil sudeste, século XIX.* Rio de Janeiro: Editora Nova Fronteira, 1999.

Smallwood, Stephanie E. *Saltwater Slavery: A Middle Passage from Africa to American Diaspora.* Cambridge, MA: Harvard University Press, 2007.

———. "Salt-Water Slaves: African Enslavement, Migration, and Settlement in the Anglo-Atlantic World, 1660–1700." PhD diss., Duke University, 1999.

Soares, Mariza de Carvalho. *Devotos da cor: Identidade étnica, religiosidade e escravidão no Rio de Janeiro, século XVIII.* Rio de Janeiro: Civilização Brasileira, 2000.

———. "Mina, Angola e Guiné: Nomes d'África no Rio de Janeiro setecentista." *Tempo* (Brazil) 3, no. 6 (1998): 73–93.

Solórzano Fonseca, Juan Carlos. "El comercio exterior de Costa Rica en la época colonial (1690–1760)." Licenciatura thesis, Universidad de Costa Rica, 1977.

Solórzano Fonseca, Juan Carlos and Claudia Quirós Vargas. *Costa Rica en el siglo XVI: Descubrimiento, exploración y conquista.* San José: Editorial de la Universidad de Costa Rica, 2006.

Steckel, Richard H. "Miscegenation and the American Slave Schedules." *Journal of Interdisciplinary History* 11, no. 2 (1980): 251–63.

Stein, Stanley J. *Vassouras: A Brazilian Coffee County, 1850–1890*. New York: Atheneum, 1970. Orignally published Cambridge, MA: Harvard University Press, 1957.

Stevenson, Brenda. *Life in Black and White: Family and Community in the Slave South*. New York: Oxford University Press, 1996.

Stone, Samuel Z. *La dinastía de los conquistadores*. San José: Editorial Universitaria Centroamericana [EDUCA], 1975.

Sundström, Lars. *The Exchange Economy of Pre-Colonial Africa*. New York: St. Martin's, 1974. Originally published in 1965 as *The Trade of Guinea* in Lund, Sweden, by Hakan Ohlsson.

Surgy, Albert de. *Le système religieux des évhé*. Paris: L'Harmattan, 1988.

Sweet, James H. *Recreating Africa: Culture, Kinship, and Religion in the African-Portuguese World, 1441–1770*. Chapel Hill: University of North Carolina Press, 2003.

Tadman, Michael. "The Demographic Cost of Sugar: Debates on Slave Societies and Natural Increase in the Americas." *American Historical Review* 105, no. 5 (2000): 1534–75.

Tannenbaum, Frank. *Slave and Citizen: The Negro in the Americas*. New York: Knopf, 1946.

Tardieu, Jean-Pierre. *El negro en Cusco: Los caminos de la alienación en la segunda mitad del siglo XVII*. Lima: Pontifícia Universidad Católica del Perú, 1998.

Terborg-Penn, Rosalyn. "Women and Slavery in the African Diaspora: A Cross-Cultural Approach to Historical Analysis." *Sage* 3, no. 2 (1986): 11–14.

Thiel, Bernardo A. "Monografía de la población de Costa Rica en el siglo XIX." In *Revista de Costa Rica en el Siglo XIX*. Edited by Juan Fernández Ferraz, Francisco Iglesias, Paul Biolley, and Comisión Conmemorativa de Costa Rica en el Siglo XIX, 1:1–52. San José: Tipografía Nacional, 1902.

Thornton, John K. *Africa and Africans in the Making of the Atlantic World, 1400–1680*. 2nd ed. Cambridge: Cambridge University Press, 1998.

———. "Cannibals, Witches, and Slave Traders in the Atlantic World." *William & Mary Quarterly* 60, no. 2 (2003): 273–94.

———. "Central African Names and African-American Naming Patterns." *William & Mary Quarterly* 3rd ser., 50, no. 4 (1993): 727–42.

———. "The Coromantees: An African Cultural Group in Colonial North America and the Caribbean." *Journal of Caribbean History* 32, nos. 1–2 (1998): 161–78.

———. *The Kingdom of Kongo: Civil War and Transition, 1641–1718*. Madison: University of Wisconsin Press, 1983.

———. *The Kongolese Saint Anthony: Dona Beatriz Kimpa Vita and the Antonian Movement, 1684–1706*. Cambridge: Cambridge University Press, 1998.

Tingbé-Azalou, Albert. "Rites de dation du nom initial de naissance chez les Aja-Fon du Bénin." *Anthropos* 85 (1990): 187–92.

Twinam, Ann. "Honor, Sexuality, and Illegitimacy in Colonial Spanish America." In

Sexuality and Marriage in Colonial Latin America. Edited by Asunción Lavrin, 118–55. Lincoln: University of Nebraska Press, 1989.

Vansina, Jan, and T. Obenga. "The Kongo Kingdom and Its Neighbours." In *Africa from the Sixteenth to the Eighteenth Century* Vol. 5 of *UNESCO General History of Africa*. Edited by B. A. Ogot, 546–87. Paris: UNESCO, 1992.

Vega Franco, Marisa. *El tráfico de esclavos con América (Asientos de Grillo y Lomelín, 1663–1674)*. Seville: Escuela de Estudios Hispano-Americanos de Sevilla, 1984.

Velásquez, Melida. "El comercio de esclavos en la Alcaldía Mayor de Tegucigalpa, siglos XVI al XVIII." *Mesoamérica*, no. 42 (2001): 199–222.

Verger, Pierre. *Trade Relations Between the Bight of Benin and Bahia from the 17th to the 19th Century*. Translated by Evelyn Crawford. Ibadan, Nigeria: Ibadan University Press, 1976.

Vila Vilar, Enriqueta. *Hispanoamérica y el comercio de esclavos: Los asientos portugueses*. Seville: Escuela de Estudios Hispano-Americanos de Sevilla, 1977.

Villa-Flores, Javier. "'To Lose One's Soul': Blasphemy and Slavery in New Spain, 1596–1669." *Hispanic American Historical Review* 82, no. 3 (2002): 435–68.

Vogt, John L. "The Early São Tomé-Príncipe Slave Trade with Mina, 1500–1540." *International Journal of African Historical Studies* 6, no. 3 (1973): 453–67.

Von Bülow, Tulio. "Apuntes para la historia de la medicina en Costa Rica durante la colonia." Part 3. *Revista de los Archivos Nacionales* (Costa Rica), 11–12 (1945): 458–75.

Warner-Lewis, Maureen. "Jamaica's Muslim Past: Misrepresentations." *Journal of Caribbean History* 37, no. 2 (2003): 294–316.

Wescott, Joan, and Peter Morton-Williams. "The Symbolism and Ritual Context of the Yoruba Laba Shango." *Journal of the Royal Anthropological Institute* 92 (1962): 23–37.

Westergaard, Waldemar. *The Danish West Indies Under Company Rule (1671–1754), with a Supplementary Chapter, 1755–1917*. New York: Macmillan, 1917.

Wheat, David. "The First Great Waves: African Provenance Zones for the Transatlantic Slave Trade to Cartagena de Indias, 1570–1640." *Journal of African History* 52, no. 1 (2011): 1–22.

Wiethoff, William E. *The Insolent Slave*. Columbia: University of South Carolina Press, 2000.

Wilks, Ivor. "The Rise of the Akwamu Empire, 1650–1710." *Transactions of the Historical Society of Ghana* 3, no. 2 (1957): 99–136.

Wilson, S. "Aperçu historique sur les peuples et cultures dans le golfe du Bénin: Le cas des 'mina' d'Anécho." In *Peuples du golfe du Bénin: Aja-éwé (colloque de Cotonou)*. Edited by François de Medeiros, 127–50. Paris: Karthala, 1984.

Wolf, Eric R., and Sidney W. Mintz. "Haciendas and Plantations in Middle America and the Antilles." *Social and Economic Studies* (Jamaica) 6, no. 3 (1957): 81–91.

Index

Page numbers in italic text indicate illustrations.

of child, 193; overview, 16; preference for free women as wives, 133; reunification after sale, 187; separation, 170–71, 198; separation by sale, 182, 183–85, 188, 190, 193; slave infants as gifts, 185; women's honor, 167–68

Fante speakers, 55

female slaves: confined to masters' homes, 171, 189; contacts with white men, 175; disadvantages of marriage to, 192; early period, 50; earning money for widows, 125–26; folk medicine, 50; gendered division of labor, 118; likelihood of manumission, 179; limitations of, 202; loss of children, 182, 183–85; manumission, 196–97; marriages of black and mulatta, 226t; marriages in Cartago, 225t; mother's status dictating legal status of child, 193; preference for, in African societies, 20; raising masters' children, 125; reproductive capacity, 175–76; scrutiny and interference, 189, 198, 202; sense of honor, 167–68; single mothers, 171–74, 198; skilled work, 132; weddings celebrated, 192

firearms, 22, 249n105

flight, 148–51; costs and benefits, 169; disruption from, 162–63; from Miskitus, 111, 152, 207–8, 214; overview, 16; to Panama, 52; to Talamanca Indians, 61. *See also* fugitive slaves

folk medicine, 50, 113–14

Fon peoples, 100

Franciscan friars, 84, 134, 187

Fredericus Quartus, 6–8; captives' stories, 8, 17, 35–36, 38–39; crew mutiny, 33; disease and mortality, 33; fate of captives, 33–35; Gold Coast captives, 66; route, 31–32; shipboard rebellion,

7, 30, 39; slave cargo, 26–27; slave rebellion, 30, 39; voyage to Africa, 18–19; Yoruba, 58

free black population, 11; religion, 111–12; women, 174

free community of color, 199; slave identification with, 203

freedom: doctrine of "original freedom," 209; family and community, 146. *See also* male slaves, relative autonomy of

free mulatto population, 123; artisans, 127; passing, 154; servants, 124; sugar workers, 128

free pardo militias, 154–55

free women: as marriage partners, 171, 190–97, 199; race of, 194

French Caribbean, 99

fugitive slaves, 148–56, 217t–21t; edict against hiding servants and, 160; flight from Miskitus, 111, 152, 207–8, 214. See also *cimarrón*; flight

Ga speakers, 22, 23–24, 27, 72, 100, 205

Gbe speakers, 27, 67, 72, 103, 205

Gemmir y Leonart, Juan, 212

gendered division of labor, 118; degree of oversight, 15–16; domestic service reconsidered, 125; Matina, 119; rates of manumission, 180t, 180; slave family and slave culture formation, 171

gender of slaves: by decade, 52; high proportion of females, 52; manumission, 180t, 180

gender parity: ideal cargoes, 30; slave trade, 29–30

Gold Coast, 19; Akwamu wars, 23–26; as captives, 48; captives on *Fredericus Quartus*, 66; casta names, 60, 65–67; map, 44

Gómez de Lara, Miguel, 10, 11, 12, 134

González Coronel, Blas, 129

missions, 134, 201
Morel de Santa Cruz, Pedro Agustín, 12
Mosquito Shore, 34
mulatto population, 11; Central Valley,
243n41; children, 173, 179; early slavery, 50; Honduras and Nicaragua,
243n40; mulattas as marriage partners, 194–95; U.S. slaves, 175
mulatto slaves: on cacao haciendas, 140;
conquerors' entourage, 50; flight,
162; free wives, 194; likelihood of
children's manumission, 179, 180,
181t, 182; as majorities, 205; marriages, 223t–24t, 226t; mulatta versus
black female manumission, 179; somatic norm image of mulattas, 179;
population, 51–52, 51

names/naming: African, 100; Christian
and surnames, 102; diasporic surnames, 102–3; ethnic origins, 102;
identifications with masters, 101–2;
María and Juan, 101; Mexico,
264n56; Portuguese, 101; renaming
bozal slaves, 101; slave master concerns, 101. See also casta names; slave
names
nangu peoples, 58
New Laws, 120–21
Ni Ayi (king), 25
Nicoya Península, 120
Njaay, Njaajaan, 54
North Pacific: economy, 121–23; population, 10; prevalence of illegitimacy,
173
Nuestra Señora de la Soledad y Santa
Isabel, 67, 71, 86–88, 104–5, 148–50,
157, 286n8

obedience, 95, 98
Ouidah, 27–28, 40; slave purchases at,
29–30

overseers on haciendas, enslaved, 121–
22, 123, 141, 143, 145
Oviedo y Valdés, Gonzalo Fernández
de, 49–50
Oyo people, 28, 68

Panama: center of slave trade, 76; choice
slaves to, 64; map, 77; slaves from,
80–81; trade with, 200
Panama City, 76
paternalism, discourse of, 171
patriarchy, 97
patronage ties, 203
patron-client relations, 47
pearl diving, 39, 105, 118, 123, 150
personal service, 121
Peru, choice slaves to, 64, 79–80
Pfeiff, Diedrich, 27, 31, 32, 33, 39
plantation agriculture, societies outside of, 1, 4; modes of production,
117
plantation colonies in New World, 23,
105
popo peoples, 67, 68, 73
population estimates, 10–12, 11t
Portete, 36
Portobello: Danish captains, 7, 32–33;
procedures for disembarkment, 77–
78; slave trade, 76
Portuguese slavers: Kongo defeat, 64;
shift to West Central Africa, 48; trade
routes, 76; use of term mandinga, 55
property ownership, 131–32
Providence Island (Santa Catalina), 32,
32, 33
Punta Blanca, 83
Punta Carreto, 35

race relations: patterns distinct, 4; racial
homogeneity myth, 5–6; struggle
against racial oppression, 204
rape, 96–97